ROMAN GRANARIES
AND
STORE BUILDINGS

ROMAN GRANARIES
AND
STORE BUILDINGS

GEOFFREY RICKMAN

Senior Lecturer in Ancient History
University of St Andrews

CAMBRIDGE
AT THE UNIVERSITY PRESS
1971

Published by the Syndics of the Cambridge University Press

Bentley House, 200 Euston Road, London N.W.1

American Branch: 32 East 57th Street, New York, N.Y.10022

© Cambridge University Press 1971

Library of Congress Catalogue Card Number: 76-116843

I S B N: 0 521 07724 9

Printed in Great Britain
at the University Printing House, Cambridge
(Brooke Crutchley, University Printer)

FOR ANNA

Nunc argumentum vobis demensum dabo,
non modio, neque trimodio, verum ipso horreo:
tantum ad narrandum argumentum adest benignitas.

Plautus, *Menaechmi*, lines 15 ff.

CONTENTS

CONTENTS

CONTENTS

FIGURES

The Figures are based on illustrations appearing in the works cited

FIGURES

FIGURES

PLATES

PLATES

PREFACE

The origins of this book are no doubt all too obvious. The thesis, upon which it is based, entitled 'The Design, Structure and Organisation of *Horrea* under the Roman Empire', was written in Rome and Oxford in the years 1958–62.

The attraction of the subject lay not least in that it had both archaeological and historical aspects, and that it had been curiously neglected. The only general studies were in the form of articles in the French, German and Italian classical encyclopaedias. Among these the only comprehensive attempt to deal with the whole topic—design, structure and organisation—was in the Italian article by Professor Romanelli. But this impressive piece of work was published in 1922 and without illustrations.

Since then our knowledge has been greatly increased, particularly by the excavations at Ostia just before the Second World War. The town plan now revealed derives much of its distinctive character, perhaps of its distinction, from the dispositions of the *horrea* which occupy so much of it. It is to be hoped that a full study of these buildings will appear in the brilliant *Scavi di Ostia* series. Certainly the brief descriptions and discussion of the Ostian *horrea* in Chapter I of this book in no way compensate for the lack of a detailed joint study of these buildings by an architect and archaeologist. But any work on *horrea* undertaken now must not simply take account of the Ostian evidence, but must start from a consideration of the Ostian buildings. They are the best-preserved and most readily accessible examples of one of the finest building-types in the Roman architectural repertoire.

For Rome itself we have far fewer excavated examples, but we have the unique evidence of the Severan Marble Plan of Rome. This evidence is now available in a more accurate form than ever before, thanks to the patient detective-work of a devoted group of Italian archaeologists. The result is one of the great achievements in Italian archaeology in this century. It is now possible to combine the evidence from Rome and Ostia so as to provide a vivid picture of the storage facilities of both the capital and its port.

The amount of new work undertaken in the military installations in the provinces of the Roman Empire during this century needs no advertisement, but there had been little attempt at comparative study of the evidence obtained.

Constant excavations provide endless new material. When therefore in 1967 Cambridge University Press accepted my work for publication, there was the difficult task of trying to take account of the new discoveries since 1962. This was particularly important for the study of wooden military granaries of the early first century A.D. because of Professor Schönberger's excavations at Rödgen in Germany and Professor Cunliffe's work at both Richborough and Fishbourne in Britain. I have tried to take account of all work up to the summer of 1968.

But the study of *horrea* includes more than the archaeological evidence and its problems. The historical and legal aspects of warehousing may not be neglected. Since I wrote my thesis a French book has been published, concerned directly with these legal aspects: C. Alzon, *Problèmes relatifs à la location des entrepôts en Droit romain* (Paris, 1965). M. Alzon is a student of Roman law and mainly concerned with the legal problems inseparable from the renting of warehouses, but he takes a broad view of his subject and discusses in passing many topics, including the administration, appearance and geographical distribution of *horrea*. The author is clearly a man of enthusiasm, and the book is remarkable mainly for its collection of evidence, more or less relevant to *horrea*, amassed in the enormous footnotes. The value of the work is sometimes impaired by a lack of discrimination in using the evidence collected, sometimes by a lack of knowledge, or the quotation of out-of-date sources, about the physical remains. I have tried to take account of Alzon's views, particularly on legal matters, where these seemed unusual or new, but I have often found no reason to change the opinions I had already formed.

The fact is that anyone who attempts to take in all the many aspects relevant to the study of Roman granaries and storehouses lays himself open to criticisms of inadequacy in dealing with some parts of the evidence. But the attempt to deal with the whole subject has advantages, which perhaps justify the risks.

The risks I have taken have been lessened by the generous help I have received, both while writing the thesis and preparing the book for publication.

The thesis was supervised by the late Sir Ian Richmond. At every stage he followed the work with the keenest interest, and subjected it to sharp and stimulating criticism. His death in 1965 was both a severe personal loss and a devastating blow to the study of the archaeology of the Roman Empire.

It is a pleasure to acknowledge a debt to the Craven Committee for election to the Henry Francis Pelham Studentship in 1958 and to The Queen's College, Oxford, for election to a Junior Research Fellowship in 1959. The first made possible the work on the Ostian *horrea* by taking me to Rome for a year; the second allowed me to continue my research in distinguished congenial company for three years.

In Rome and Ostia I have to thank particularly Mr J. B. Ward-Perkins and Professor Pietrogrande. Dr and Mrs M. H. Ballance and the late Miss Marion Blake also gave encouragement and advice on architectural matters.

The examiners of the thesis, Professor S. Frere and Mr R. Meiggs, made valuable criticisms, and Professor Frere has directed my attention to new work since 1962.

On legal matters Mr J. Crook in Cambridge, and Professor A. M. Honoré and Mr J. K. B. Nicholas in Oxford, helped at various stages to save me from several errors in the chapter on *Locatio–Conductio*.

Others who have helped in various ways include Dr H. W. Catling, Professor G. E. F. Chilver, Mr M. Frederiksen, Mr E. W. Gray, Professor J. R. Harris, Professor R. M. Harrison, Dr F. G. B. Millar and Mr P. J. Parsons.

Professor Gordon Williams in St Andrews read the Introduction to the book to my profit.

My greatest debt in this respect is, however, to Professor Jocelyn Toynbee, who urged me to publish my work, and who read the whole text prior to publication and tried to bring it nearer to her own impeccable standards of accuracy and lucidity.

Mrs P. Clarke of the Ashmolean Museum, Oxford, undertook the burdensome task of drawing most of the plans, which were paid for by the Research Fund of St Andrews University.

I am most grateful to the staff of the Cambridge University Press for their meticulous concern over the lay-out and the accuracy of the book. Mistakes would be more numerous and the text less readable without their help. The responsibility for the blemishes which remain is mine.

Much of what I have written is based upon the work of others, excavators and scholars, whose writings I have ransacked and sometimes ungratefully criticised. To all of them I owe a great debt, which I wish to acknowledge now. If the need to correct what I, in my turn, have said in this book stimulates new interest in *horrea* and the many problems connected with them I shall be satisfied.

My wife typed the manuscript of the thesis several times and then retyped the book. More important she retained her confidence in the work at times when I had lost mine. The book is in consequence dedicated to her. G. E. R.

St Andrews, September 1970

ABBREVIATIONS

*AA*⁴	*Archaeologia Aeliana*, 4th Series
ACl	*Archeologia Classica*
AE	*L'Année Épigraphique*
AJ	*Archaeological Journal*
AJA	*American Journal of Archaeology*
Ann.Eg.	*Annales du Service des Antiquités de l'Égypte*
Ann.Inst.	*Annali dell'Instituto di Corrispondenza Archeologica*
AntCl	*L'Antiquité Classique*
Arch.Cambr.	*Archaeologia Cambrensis*
ArchPF	*Archiv für Papyrusforschung und verwandte Gebiete*
BCH	*Bulletin de Correspondance Hellénique*
BCom	*Bullettino della Commissione Archeologica Comunale di Roma*
BInstFrAOr	*Bulletin de l'Institut Français d'Archéologie Orientale*
BonnJb	*Bonner Jahrbücher*
Bull.Inst.	*Bullettino dell'Instituto di Corrispondenza Archeologica*
CIL	*Corpus Inscriptionum Latinarum*
CPL	Robert Cavenaile, *Corpus Papyrorum Latinarum*
CRAI	*Comptes Rendus de l'Académie des Inscriptions et Belles-Lettres*
*CW*²	*Transactions of the Cumberland and Westmorland Antiquarian and Archaeological Society*, 2nd Series
Diz.Epig.	*Dizionario Epigrafico di Antichità Romane di de Ruggiero*
D–S	Daremberg et Saglio, *Dictionnaire des Antiquités*
EE	*Ephemeris Epigraphica*
IG	*Inscriptiones Graecae*
IGLS	*Inscriptions Grecques et Latines de la Syrie*
IGRR	*Inscriptiones Graecae ad res Romanas pertinentes*
ILS	*Inscriptiones Latinae Selectae*
Jahresbericht Pro Vindon.	*Jahresbericht (Gesellschaft Pro Vindonissa)*
JEgA	*Journal of Egyptian Archaeology*
JHS	*Journal of Hellenic Studies*
JJurP	*Journal of Juristic Papyrology*
JRS	*Journal of Roman Studies*

ABBREVIATIONS

MAAR	*Memoirs of the American Academy at Rome*
MDInstKairo	*Mitteilungen des Deutschen Archäologischen Instituts. Abteilung Kairo*
Mélanges	*Mélanges d'Archéologie et d'Histoire de l'École Française de Rome*
MonAnt	*Monumenti Antichi Pubblicati per Cura della Reale Accademia dei Lincei*
NSc	*Notizie degli Scavi di Antichità*
OJh	*Jahreshefte des Österreichischen Archäologischen Instituts in Wien*
ORL	*Der Obergermanisch-Raetische Limes des Römerreiches*
PBSR	*Papers of the British School at Rome*
PSAL	*Proceedings of the Society of Antiquaries of London*
PSAS	*Proceedings of the Society of Antiquaries of Scotland*
PSI	*Papyri Greci e Latini (Pubbl. della Società Italiana)*
RA	*Revue Archéologique*
RAfr	*Revue Africaine*
RAL	*Rendiconti della Classe di Scienze Morali, Storiche e Filologiche dell'Accademia dei Lincei*
RE	Pauly–Wissowa, *Real-Encyclopädie der Classischen Altertumswissenschaft*
REA	*Revue des Études Anciennes*
REG	*Revue des Études Grecques*
RendPontAcc	*Rendiconti. Atti della Pontificia Accademia Romana di Archeologia*
RIntDroitsAnt	*Revue Internationale des Droits de l'Antiquité*
RM	*Mitteilungen des Deutschen Archäologischen Instituts, Römische Abteilung*
RStLig	*Rivista di Studi Liguri*
SDHI	*Studia et Documenta Historiae et Iuris*
TAPA	*Transactions of the American Philological Association*
TrierZ	*Trierer Zeitschrift*
ZSavignyStift	*Zeitschrift der Savigny-Stiftung für Rechtsgeschichte, Romanistische Abteilung*

ABBREVIATIONS

SPECIAL ABBREVIATIONS

Frank, *ESAR* Tenney Frank, *An Economic Survey of Ancient Rome*, 5 vols. (Baltimore, 1933–40)

Lugli, *Tecnica* G. Lugli, *La tecnica edilizia romana*, 2 vols. (Rome, 1957)

Meiggs R. Meiggs, *Roman Ostia* (Oxford, 1960)

Pianta Marm. G. Carettoni, A. Colini, L. Cozza, G. Gatti, *La pianta marmorea di Roma antica*, 2 vols. (Rome, 1955)

Romanelli *Dizionario epigrafico di antichità romane* (de Ruggiero), s.v. *horrea*

Rostovtseff, *SEHRE* M. Rostovtseff, *The Social and Economic History of the Roman Empire* (2nd ed., by P. M. Fraser), 2 vols. (Oxford, 1957)

Scavi *Scavi di Ostia* I– (Rome, 1953)

INTRODUCTION

Tertullian, writing in the second century A.D. and warning his Christian flock against the dangers of heresy, used a homely metaphor of which the Church has remained fond. The chaff of little faith, he warned, would be blown away and only the good grain be gathered up into the storehouses of the Lord.[1] This simple metaphor still works for us, and it worked for Tertullian because the Latin word he used for storehouses, *horrea*, was part of the everyday life of the Roman world in which he lived. It was used constantly and in widely different contexts. It occurred in simple rural transactions, military orders, sophisticated commercial dealings and even, in transferred or metaphorical uses, in the conceits of literary authors.[2] The word *horrea* simply designated buildings where anything could be stored.

I

A major problem both for Rome itself and for her armies was the proper organisation of a food supply. Adequate storage facilities for foodstuffs were clearly one of the keys to the solution of this problem. The most important food in the ancient world was corn, and buildings devoted to the storage of corn have to meet certain demands. In general they must be well placed to serve their particular purpose, easy of access, with adequate space for loading and unloading, and completely secure. Such general considerations helped to dictate the siting of strong granaries, whether in legionary fortresses and auxiliary forts along the frontiers, or in Ostia and Rome. But the actual plan and structure of such granaries was more influenced by the special difficulties imposed by a granary's function. Grain must be kept dry when in store. The safe limit of moisture in stored grain is usually between 10 and 15% depending upon the type of grain, the climate, and the length of storage. Grain must also be kept cool, if possible below 60 °F, and free from vermin, which tend to breed if the grain overheats. If grain is stored

---

[1] Tertullian, *De Praescr. Haeret.* 3. 9.
[2] *Thes. Ling. Lat.*, s.v. *horreum*. The Latin word *horrea* is, of course, a neuter plural, but when, as often throughout this book, it is used to refer to a single building or a single building complex, I have treated it as a singular concept.

loose or in bins, the walls of a grain store must be capable of supporting considerable lateral thrust. The lateral pressure of grain is about two-thirds of the vertical pressure. So, for example, the walls of a container holding 30 tons of grain must be able to resist a pressure of 20 tons.

These problems, of course, bedevil the storage of grain in any age, but they became enormous for Rome as a result of her growth in size and power in the third and second centuries B.C. The Republican stages of the Roman attempt to deal with storage problems are to some extent lost, because the material remains of most of the warehouses we have found belong to the Imperial period, but there are some clues.

In Roman military installations under the Empire, the granary was always a long, narrow, rectangular building, strongly constructed, with buttresses if built in stone, and with raised floors, under which a freely flowing current of air was created by means of ventilators set in the walls.[1] These buildings are so common that they were amongst the first military buildings whose function was clearly identified and they occur in a more or less standard pattern (although with local variations) all over the Roman Empire. The building type seems to have been fixed early for, if we can trust Schulten's excavations at Numantia, there are clear Republican examples in the camp built by Scipio Aemilianus in 134 B.C. while besieging Numantia. It may be that the Romans themselves were drawing on a building type current in the Hellenistic world and even much earlier in the East, because five arsenals of similar proportions with raised floors and ventilators dated 283–261 B.C. have been excavated on the acropolis at Pergamon, and twelve granaries, remarkably similar to the Pergamene examples but dated about 2000 B.C., have been discovered at Harappā on the Indus. There was no doubt development in the various structural devices used in these buildings. For example, it may have been the case that only wooden floors were originally raised, a common tradition anyway in the damp climate of north Europe, and that the building of raised floors composed of tiles or slabs of stone was a later and more sophisticated development. Certainly the methods of supporting the floors by dwarf-walls or small piers changed from time to time. At all times these buildings were most carefully constructed. Wooden granaries dealt with the weight of the grain by means of ties and trusses within the building. Stone granaries had walls of great thickness (3–4 feet thick)

[1] See Chapter VII.

and large buttresses from 2½ to 3 feet square bracing the long sides of the buildings at intervals of 7–15 feet. Whatever materials were used in the walls, the roofs were always constructed of slates or tiles and often had a wide overhang at the eaves to shelter the grain as much as possible.

These granaries inside forts and fortresses were always carefully positioned. In auxiliary forts they were near if not flanking the head-quarters building itself, but often had their entrance opening on to a quiet square where loading and unloading would cause the least in-convenience. In the legionary fortresses, they were positioned near the gates, and particularly near those gates that might be connected with some form of water transport. The cartage of bulky goods was always tedious and expensive in the ancient world, and the Romans used water transport wherever they could. The problem may have been particu-larly difficult in Britain, where most of the corn-growing districts were south of the Trent–Severn line, and the main military installations were from the end of the first century A.D. well to the north and west. As many supplies as possible must have been shipped to places like South Shields and *Horrea Classis* on the Tay, and cleared from there as far as possible by river.

The military supply system even in the early Principate was still largely one of purchase, *frumentum emptum*, with payment by the troops for their food, backed up by *ad hoc* plundering and some requisi-tions. Gradually, however, there did evolve a specific tax-in-kind, the *annona militaris*, devoted to feeding the troops, organised by the state at the expense of the provincials.[1] It was known from the *Codex Theo-dosianus* that a great network of collecting depots, quite distinct from the granaries within the forts, grew up in connection with this tax. Now we have two actual examples of this kind of storehouse of the late Empire, one found at Trier, a key centre in the Empire for the organisation along the Rhine, and the other at Veldidena near Innsbruck on the main route from Italy through the Brenner Pass to the Danube. Each consists of two huge halls separated by a courtyard but bound into one architectural unit by curtain walls. The only difference is that at Veldidena the whole unit was fortified with square projecting towers. Other examples of this type of late Roman warehouse will surely be found in the future.

It has also become increasingly clear in recent years that in legionary

[1] See Chapter VIII.

1-2

fortresses at least there was in addition to the granaries yet another type of storage building, perhaps serving the purpose of a general baggage store. These *horrea*, of which the best and most recent example was discovered at Vindonissa in Switzerland, consist of a great open central courtyard, around which were constructed four ranges of rooms opening on to an arcade.

These buildings are particularly interesting because they are exactly comparable with the largest civil *horrea* in Ostia and Rome itself.[1]

What the origin and development of this type of building was we do not know, although a tentative derivation from a building tradition prevalent in the ancient Near East is suggested later.[2] The main difficulty is that Ostia, our best source of information about this type of building under the Empire, has its Republican levels more or less completely covered by later buildings. It is doubtful anyway whether it would fill in the gap in our knowledge, since it was Puteoli, more or less unexcavated, that was important as the port of Rome in the late Republic and even in the early Empire, before the Emperors Claudius and Trajan improved the river port of Ostia so that it could cope with the bulk of Rome's imports.

It is certain that Rome itself does not provide us with an answer to when these courtyard *horrea* began to be built or what their derivation was. From literary sources[3] it seems that the major development of Rome's river port and its attendant warehouses did not take place until the early second century B.C. Earlier the old Forum Boarium and Forum Holitorium in the centre of Rome seem to have coped with the main flow of food imports which had probably come down the Tiber from the Italian hills. But in the early second century B.C. the Aventine district further south below the Pons Sublicius, the first city bridge, and away from the centre of Rome's political life, was systematically developed to cope with the landing, storage and distribution of the massive imports up the Tiber from the sea. At first all that seems to have been done was the paving of a stretch of the river bank with steps down to the river itself, and the building of a great portico measuring some 1,500 feet by 300 feet. This, the great Porticus Aemilia, remained a feature of the district down to the late Empire, but it belongs essentially to the Greek tradition of the commercial *stoa*. Even the name,

---

[1] See Chapter I and Chapter II.   [2] See Chapter IV.
[3] Livy 35. 10. 12 (193 B.C.) and 41. 27. 8 (174 B.C.).

Emporium, which was early attached to this district, suggests Greek influence. The *horrea* which were built in such great numbers that this whole thirteenth region of Rome finally had the name *horrea* or *orrea* attached to it,[1] must have been built later in the second and first centuries B.C.

The largest *horrea* in Ostia and Rome were very large indeed. In Rome the *Horrea Galbana* covered some 225,000 square feet, and more than 140 rooms were available for storage on the ground floor alone. The remains at Ostia show that they were carefully constructed of the finest materials of the day, large tufa blocks or concrete faced with brick and tufa, and that great attention was paid to devices for raising the floors on dwarf walls, draining the courtyards, and, in some of the buildings, locking not only the doors to individual rooms but also the doors to staircases between the different floors of the building.

The *horrea* which provided such massive storage capacity in these areas seem not only to have been built by great Roman families, for example the Sulpicii, the Lollii, but perhaps to have been owned by them originally.[2] Whether or not that is true, there can be no doubt that *horrea* or parts of *horrea* in Rome were available for hire, either to merchants storing their goods temporarily or to private citizens storing their valuables. As a result of this the organisation of civil *horrea* has a fascinating complexity. On the one hand the state was vitally concerned with any organisation that involved the storage of grain. In fact the state exercised an increasing amount of interference exemplified in the great stream of detailed orders preserved in the *Codex Theodosianus*. On the other hand the renting of storage facilities to private individuals involved more general questions in Roman law about contracts, liability and protection of all the individuals involved.[3]

It must be admitted that much of the evidence, material, epigraphic and legal, for the study of civil *horrea* has particular reference to Ostia and Rome. It may, therefore, be as well to indicate now the background to this evidence and the special problems that had to be faced there.

[1] See Appendix 5.   [2] See Chapter V.
[3] See Chapter VI.

2

Originally not only Rome, but Ostia as well, were river ports.[1] The river Tiber, despite some seasonal variation in level, did not dry up or lower its water level disastrously in the summer months.[2] Although its current was swift and it brought down large deposits of silt, it was navigable, certainly between Ostia and Rome, for ships of a certain size. What was the largest size of ships that could get from Ostia to Rome has always been something of a problem. Until recently it has been widely believed that ships of only 78 tons capacity were the largest that could manage the journey.[3] It seems more likely now that ships carrying up to 200 tons could in theory get as far as Rome, a suggestion which is reinforced by the fact that in the nineteenth century when the Tiber was still used regularly for navigation, ships of 190 tons could get even 100 miles upstream.[4]

Whether all those ships, which *could* make the journey, would wish to, is another matter. It was not easy for ancient merchant ships to go upstream against the current on a winding course, where they might be unable to make much use of the wind with their square-rigged sails. For most merchantmen—of whatever size—the only way of getting upstream was to be towed. Philostratus reveals that the trip up the Tiber by boat to Rome took three days,[5] while the journey by road, either the Via Ostiensis or the Via Portuensis, took only 2½–3 hours.

In addition to this, recent work done on the tonnage of ancient merchant shipping suggests that even 200 tons would be well below the average of big sea-going merchantmen, particularly those involved in the corn trade.[6] Although the smallest capacity encouraged by the Emperor Claudius for the corn trade was a mere 10,000 *modii* (about 70–80 tons),[7] it is clear that by the end of the second century A.D. the standard size of ship used for the transport of grain had to have a

---

[1] For the whole question of commerce in the Mediterranean see J. Rougé, *Recherches sur l'organisation du commerce maritime en Méditerranée sous l'empire romain* (Paris, 1966).
[2] J. Le Gall, *Le Tibre, fleuve de Rome, dans l'antiquité* (Paris, 1953).
[3] For example, Meiggs, p. 51.
[4] H. T. Wallinga, 'Nautika I: The units of capacity for ancient ships', *Mnemosyne* XVII (1964), 1–40; L. Casson, 'Harbour and river boats of ancient Rome', *JRS* LV (1965), 31–9. On the difficult question of tonnage in general, see Rougé, *Recherches*, p. 66.
[5] Philostratus, *Vit. Apoll. Tyan.* VII. 16. Cf. Le Gall, *Le Tibre*, p. 257.
[6] L. Casson, 'The size of ancient merchant ships', *Studi in onore di Calderini e Paribeni* I (1956), 231. [7] Suet. *Claud.* 18; Gaius, *Inst.* I. 32c.

capacity of at least 50,000 *modii* (between 340 and 400 tons).[1] The great Alexandrian corn freighter described in detail by Lucian in his *Navigium* has been computed to have had a carrying capacity of between 1,200 and 1,300 tons.[2]

Originally the very biggest of these ships could not contemplate docking in Rome nor run the hazards of unloading at the mouth of the Tiber. They went therefore to Puteoli and from there the corn was sent in smaller vessels up the coast to the Tiber mouth. Other ships too big to make the journey to Rome would either dock at Ostia or more likely unload at the river mouth into lighters. Most of the goods that were unloaded in this way were in transit for Rome and therefore the warehousing facilities at Ostia were bound to provide accommodation only until the goods could be cleared away upstream. This basic fact about Ostia was not changed by the later developments and should not be forgotten in assessing the evidence from Ostia.

Despite, apparently, the plans of Caesar for a proper harbour at Ostia, Augustus and Tiberius seem to have devoted themselves only to improving the existing facilities, including warehousing at the old river port of Ostia. It was Claudius, and later Trajan, who created the proper harbours just to the north of the river mouth at Ostia. Claudius' great circular basin of about 200 acres and Trajan's smaller hexagonal basin of about 80 acres together made up an outer and inner harbour, and offered proper protection for big sea-going ships as they unloaded.[3]

These new arrangements meant ultimately that the Alexandrian and African corn fleets, and no doubt other big ships, no longer went to Puteoli, but to the Ostia harbours. In the end this helped to create a new centre, Portus, that was to be independent of Ostia itself, but this was certainly not the immediate result. In both the Claudian and Trajanic–Hadrianic periods the warehousing facilities at Ostia itself were much increased. But the rhythm of the city and its life was to some extent changed by the existence of the new harbours—not least in the diminishing importance of the sea-going lighters prepared to unload ships at the river mouth, and the vastly increased importance of tugs which seem to have met the ships at the harbour mouth, assigned berths to them and if necessary helped to pull them into position.[4]

[1] Scaevola, *Digest* L. 5. 3.
[2] L. Casson, 'The Isis and her voyage', *TAPA* LXXXI (1950), 51–6.
[3] See Chapter III.   [4] L. Casson, *JRS* LV (1965), 34–5.

As the ships arrived at the harbours there must have been a mass of paper-work involved: the checking of ships' papers, the inspection of cargo and payment of harbour dues. There may even, in the case of ships carrying corn, have been the checking of the quality of the cargoes against the *digmata*,[1] the samples often sent in small sealed pots or leather wallets with such ships to prevent fraud during the course of the journey.

The cargoes were laboriously unloaded by countless porters, the *saccarii*, who ran along the gang planks laid from the prows of the ships to the quayside and humped either bundles, or sacks of produce, or *amphorae* of wine and oil on their backs. The *saccarii* took their goods either straight to the storerooms earmarked for them or loaded them on carts for more distant warehouses, where in turn they would be unloaded again by porters. In no example known to me was it possible for carts to enter the courtyards of the Ostian warehouses. Everything, even the staircases partly, but only partly, constructed in the form of ramps, was designed for *men* who carried the loads. Given the fact that many of the Ostian warehouses would act largely as stores for goods in transit, the goods may have been left in the containers in which they arrived. Certainly the warehouses were often positioned near the river or the sea, with their entrances conveniently situated for goods from that direction.

The goods for Rome were reloaded into a special form of lighter, the *navis codicaria*, which, among all the different types of craft making their way to Rome, was both the most common and specially suited to this job. The mast in these ships was set well forward and was used perhaps for a fore-and-aft sprit sail to allow it to catch what wind there might be and certainly for attaching a tow rope. These ships were most often dragged up the Tiber by teams of men, although animals, such as oxen, may also have been used. There were towpaths on either side of the Tiber and although we are ill-informed about them, they must have been carefully maintained and protected from floods. Procopius[2] reveals that in the sixth century A.D. the towpath from Ostia to Rome along the left bank of the Tiber had already disappeared, although that on the right bank from Portus to Rome was still regularly used.

[1] *Cod. Theod.* XIV. 4. 9 (A.D. 417); see Chapter V.
[2] Procopius, *De Bell. Goth.* v. 26. 9.

8

As the *naves codicariae*, barges and smaller merchantmen neared the city wharves, there must again have been some sort of attempt at organisation. The masters of many ships no doubt knew to which warehouses they had to deliver their cargoes and consequently went to the appropriate quays. Others with goods of a specialised kind, such as marble blocks, seem to have gone to the particular wharf which dealt with their material. The Via Marmorata just below the Aventine preserved in its name the memory of just such a specialist area, where in fact many abandoned flawed marble blocks were found in excavations. We know of specialist warehouses, too, such as the *Horrea Piperataria*, *Horrea Chartaria* and *Horrea Candelaria*.[1]

Long stretches of the river bank in the Aventine area and on the opposite side of the Tiber were carefully walled, particularly in the Trajanic and Hadrianic periods, in a way not to be equalled until the modern embankments. There were plentiful mooring points made from great travertine blocks, sometimes shaped in animal heads set into the concrete brick-faced embankments. In many places there were ramps and steps leading down to the river, either from the quays or directly from the warehouses themselves.

To these wharves and the great buildings along the river banks came the traders of the capital and even ordinary townsfolk to buy directly from the ships or the warehouses the goods they wanted.[2] In the case of grain there can have been little haggling, the government being keen to keep the price low and level even if that meant a state subsidy to the merchants. But in the case of goods such as wine landed in bulk near Monte Testaccio, there would have been brisk business and auctions of cargoes in whole or in part, involving no doubt some convivial sampling of the quality. The docks were thus a magnet for many different kinds of people including quite ordinary inhabitants of Rome, in a way totally unlike the commercial docks of the modern world.

The size and complexity of the problems concerning storage and organisation of commerce that faced Rome were not helped by the fact that the sea was more or less closed to regular merchant traffic from November to March.[3] It is true that merchantmen caught at the end of the sailing season in mid-Mediterranean and wintering in a friendly

[1] See Chapter II.
[2] H. J. Loane, *Industry and Commerce of the City of Rome, 50 B.C.–200 A.D.* (Baltimore, 1938).
[3] Vegetius IV. 39.

harbour might be tempted to make a run in a spell of fine weather,[1] but this does not alter the fact that most ships reached the ports of Rome in the summer.

The Egyptian grain, for example, seems to have been collected in Egypt by the central administration in the period from March till May. It was gathered first into the village storehouses, then assembled at the harbours on the canals and the Nile itself, and finally systematically cleared down the Nile to Alexandria.[2] The Alexandrian corn fleet, often sailing as one group, ran laboriously against the prevailing northerly winds in a journey that might take up to two months from Alexandria to Rome.[3] Seneca told of the excitement and sense of relief when the lookouts spotted the first ships of the Alexandrian fleet making for Puteoli in his day[4]—with reason, for Egypt sent Rome 20 million *modii*, nearly 150,000 tons of corn, in the mid-first century A.D. The arrival might be a relief but the docking, unloading and administrative arrangements had to be able to take the sudden strain. The barging of the goods upstream could be spread out over the winter months, if need be, but the sea-going ships had to be freed as quickly as possible so as to make other journeys and that might not always be easy. In a famous letter of late second century A.D.[5] from a man who had sailed with the Alexandrian corn fleet, we know that he arrived on 30 June, but did not unload until 12 July. He himself went up to Rome on 19 July and even on 2 August no member of the fleet had been allowed to leave for the return journey.

Egyptian grain was, of course, only a small part of the problem. Africa, outside Egypt, sent twice as much grain as Egypt to Rome and there were corn imports from Sicily, Gaul, Spain and places like the Thracian Chersonese. In addition there were massive imports of wine and oil, building materials, fabrics and luxury items, adding up, I suspect, to perhaps one million tons of goods passing through the docks of Rome each year.[6]

To cope with such a volume of goods the labour force must have been gigantic. If the 70 million *modii* of corn from Sicily, Egypt and

[1] Not always safely; compare the experience of St Paul being brought, on an Alexandrian freighter, to Rome in A.D. 62 (Acts 27).
[2] See Appendix 2.
[3] L. Casson, *TAPA* LXXXI (1950), 43.   [4] Seneca, *Ep.* 77.
[5] Hunt and Edgar, *Select Papyri* (Loeb), I, no. 113.
[6] Loane, *Industry and Commerce of the City of Rome.*

Africa alone is divided into sackloads able to be carried by a man, we must think of about 10½ million sacks, which have to be moved from ship to warehouse to ship at Ostia, and then unloaded again at Rome. It would need 1,400 merchant ships to bring 70 million *modii* of corn to Rome, if the *average* capacity of a corn ship was 50,000 *modii*, as the *Digest* might seem to suggest. If the average capacity of the river craft used to transport goods upstream to Rome was about 68 tons, then the 70 million *modii* alone would provide 8,000 boat loads. Given the fact that it took some three days to be towed upstream to Rome, it is clear that even with the winter months being used for barging goods up the Tiber, a massive number of river craft would have to be available. This supposition is clearly borne out by the passage in Tacitus' *Annals*[1] which reports the loss of 200 ships, almost certainly *naves codicariae*, in the Claudian harbour at about the same time as a hundred ships full of corn were burned by a chance fire at the docks in Rome itself. Besides the large numbers of porters, sailors, and towpath men implied by these figures, there were also men like *saburrarii*, the men who carried off the sand used for ballast, the *urinatores*, who seem to have salvaged merchandise that had fallen overboard or from ships that had sunk, and *mensores* everywhere.

3

In both military and civil life, therefore, the storage of goods set the Romans problems in architecture, law and administration, all the more complicated because of the extent of Rome's power and the size of the Imperial city itself. The architectural and structural problems led to the use of the finest available building materials and specific structural devices, such as ventilators, raised floors, slit windows and buttresses to deal with the particular problems raised. The building types adopted in military and civil life were not the same, but each was so well constructed and so apt for its purpose that they have both featured amongst the best preserved and most easily identifiable buildings constructed by the Romans. They may well have had an influence on later architectural themes not always recognised. The administrative problems were perhaps never so completely solved, or at least our evidence does not permit us to say that a fully successful solution was achieved. The tendency in both military and civil administration as the Empire evolved

[1] Tac. *Ann.* XV. 18. 3 (A.D. 62).

was for a constant growth in direct state interference and bureaucracy, which still did not achieve its aim of simple efficiency, but the struggle to try to make the system work is fascinating to watch.

It is often very difficult to build up from our literary, legal and epigraphic sources a realistic picture of how things actually worked in the ancient world. This study of Roman granaries and storehouses, with its stress on *Realien*, will, I hope, shed a little light on some aspects of Roman commerce and the Roman military system.

CIVIL *HORREA*:
DESIGN AND STRUCTURE

I

OSTIA

The proper identification of buildings of uncertain purpose as *horrea* must depend upon a comparison with those buildings which are known to have been *horrea*. For such a comparison to be possible and effective, we must have detailed descriptions of the buildings which are to be the paradigms. The greatest concentration of Imperial *horrea* known at present and open to inspection is at Ostia. Since these buildings have never been published as a whole, the first task is to describe them as accurately as possible.

The *horrea* will be described in numerical order (with one exception), according to the Italian numbering of regions and *insulae*. Thus the first to be described will be the so-called *Piccolo Mercato* (Reg. I. Is. VIII. 1) situated in the north-west part of the town, and the last the *Horrea di Hortensius* (Reg. V. Is. XII. 1) situated in the south-east part near the *Porta Romana* (Fig. 1).

The references to information already published concerning the *horrea* are mainly to four works:

(*a*) G. Calza, G. Becatti, I. Gismondi, *Scavi di Ostia*, I, *Topografia generale* (1953), with complete plan of Ostia at the back;

(*b*) G. Lugli, *La tecnica edilizia romana*, 2 volumes (1957);

(*c*) M. Blake, *Ancient Roman Construction in Italy to Augustus* (1947), and the succeeding volume, *Roman Construction in Italy from Tiberius through the Flavians* (1959);[1]

(*d*) R. Meiggs, *Roman Ostia* (1960). This is not so much an archaeological description as a brilliant social and economic survey.

The Latin nomenclature used in describing the wall facings and floors will have the meanings suggested by Lugli,[2] but what is meant will generally be indicated in English as well.

---

[1] A third volume was in preparation on Roman construction in the second century A.D. Miss Blake kindly allowed me to read the relevant sections when I was in Rome, before she died.

[2] Lugli, *Tecnica* I, p. 48.

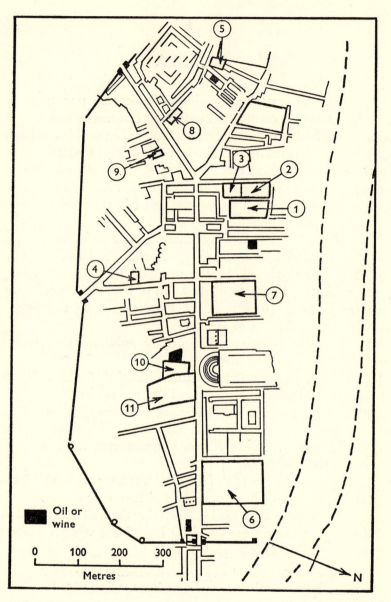

Fig. 1 Ostia, distribution of *horrea*. (1) *Piccolo Mercato*; (2) *Horrea* (Reg. I. Is. VIII. 2); (3) *Horrea Epagathiana et Epaphroditiana*; (4) *Horrea* (Reg. I. Is. XIII. 1); (5) *Horrea* (Reg. III. Is. XVII. 1); (6) *Horrea Antoniniani*; (7) *Grandi Horrea*; (8) *Horrea* (Reg. III. Is. II. 6); (9) *Horrea* (Reg. IV. Is. V. 12); (10) *Horrea dell'Artemide*; (11) *Horrea di Hortensius.*

16

1   Ostia, *Piccolo Mercato*, general view of interior looking
south-east towards the Capitolium

2   Ostia, *Piccolo Mercato*, view south along western portico

3   Ostia, *Piccolo Mercato*, ramp staircase in north-west corner of courtyard

4   Ostia, *Piccolo Mercato*, east wall of *horrea* restored with brick facing

5   Ostia, *Piccolo Mercato*, main entrance to the north, seen from inside

6 Ostia, *Piccolo Mercato*, two splayed windows in back wall of western room

7 Ostia, *Piccolo Mercato, opus spicatum*
flooring of central court

8 Ostia, *Horrea* (Reg. I. Is. VIII. 2), entrance
corridor looking north

9   Ostia, *Horrea* (Reg. I. Is. VIII. 2), most northerly room on east side of courtyard, incorporating pre-existing tufa wall; note slighted headers on left side of Plate

10   Ostia, *Horrea* (Reg. I. Is. VIII. 2), travertine threshold to room with raised floor with air vents cut in the threshold itself

11   Ostia, *Horrea Epagathiana et Epaphroditiana*, general view of front façade, looking south-east

12   Ostia, *Horrea Epagathiana et Epaphroditiana*, restored main entrance

13 Ostia, *Horrea Epagathiana et Epaphroditiana*, restored cross-vaulted portico around central courtyard

14 Ostia, *Horrea Epagathiana et Epaphroditiana*, central courtyard

15   Ostia, *Horrea Epagathiana et Epaphroditiana*, ornamental
niches in central courtyard

16   Ostia, *Horrea* (Reg. I. Is. XIII. 1), general view of interior

17 Ostia, *Grandi Horrea*, general view of interior, looking south

18 Ostia, *Grandi Horrea*, room on west side showing side walls of *horrea*
built of large tufa blocks

19   Ostia, *Grandi Horrea*, traces of north-eastern pre-Severan staircase

20   Ostia, *Grandi Horrea*, Severan (left) and Commodan (right) brickwork

21 Ostia, *Grandi Horrea*, sleeper walls for support of raised room floor

22 Ostia, *Grandi Horrea*, south-east staircase and entrances to rooms with raised floors

23   Ostia, *Grandi Horrea*, support for raised floor and room threshold

24   Ostia, *Grandi Horrea*, south end of main entrance corridor, and staircase

25   Ostia, *Grandi Horrea*, raised threshold in northern room

26   Ostia, *Grandi Horrea*, brick-faced infilling in eastern portico,
seen from the west

27 Ostia, *Horrea* (Reg. III. Is. II. 6), general view of exterior

28 Ostia, *Horrea* (Reg. III. Is. II. 6), small internal court with ornamental niche

29 Ostia, *Horrea* (Reg. III. Is. II. 6), room entrances,
east side of north corridor

30 Ostia, *Horrea* (Reg. III. Is. II. 6), side wall of room in tufa
rubble-work (left), back wall in reticulate

31 Ostia, *Horrea* (Reg. IV. Is. V. 12), main entrance, seen from interior

32 Ostia, *Horrea* (Reg. iv. Is. v. 12), north-west corner of central corridor, and room entrance

33 Ostia, *Horrea dell' Artemide,* general view from the north

34 Ostia, *Horrea dell' Artemide*, late restoration of room walls in block and brick

35   Ostia, *Horrea di Hortensius* general view from the north-west

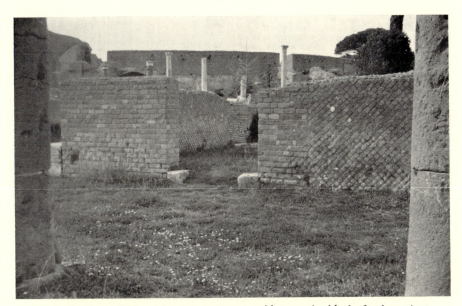

36 Ostia *Horrea di Hortensius*, room entrance, with travertine blocks for door pivots

37 Ostia, *Horrea di Hortensius*, relieving arch in side walls of southern rooms

38 Rome, *Horrea Agrippiana*, general view looking east along north portico

39 Rome, *Horrea Agrippiana*, general view looking east across central courtyard, showing the line of the *Clivus Victoriae* and the Palatine Hill in the background

40 Rome, *Horrea Agrippiana*, view north along east portico towards the Temple of Divus Augustus

41 Rome, *Horrea Agrippiana*, central courtyard filled with late brick structures

SALVT·GENIVM·HORREOR
GRIPPIANORVM·NECOTIANTIB
L·A·R·I·V·S· HERMES
C·VARIVS· POLYCARPVS
C·PACONIVS·CHRYSANTHVS
IMMVNES· S· P· D· D

42 Rome, *Horrea Agrippiana*, dedicatory inscription in central courtyard

44 Rome, *Horrea Agrippiana*, room on north side

43 Rome, *Horrea Agrippiana*, gutter around central courtyard

45 Rome, *Horrea Agrippiana*, travertine capitals

46 Rome, *Horrea Galbana*, general view of excavations, 1955

47 Rome, *Horrea Galbana*, reticulate facing of wall of *horrea* revealed in 1955 excavations

48 Rome, *horrea* revealed in the *Castra Praetoria*, 1966

49 Rome, *horrea* in *Castra Praetoria*, wall facing in *opus mixtum*

50 Myra, *horrea*, general view

51 Myra, *horrea*, busts of Hadrian and Sabina (?) over central doorway

52 Corbridge, *horrea* general view looking south

1 PICCOLO MERCATO (Reg. I. Is. VIII. 1)

General

This building forms part of the complex near the Tiber and to the north of the Capitolium and Forum, which was completely remodelled in the time of Hadrian (Fig. 1). With the reconstruction of the *Cardo Maximus* as a broad street flanked by shops, it seems that the area to the west was earmarked for *horrea*[1] of which the so-called *Piccolo Mercato* was to our knowledge the biggest. The western limit of the building was determined by the masonry wall of a Julio-Claudian building, the southern by the wall of the ancient *castrum* at Ostia.[2]

It is clearly separated on all sides from the buildings that surround it— on the east by a wide alley (the so-called *Via Tecta*)[3] from the shops on the *Cardo Maximus*; on the west by a narrow division from the *Horrea* Reg. I. Is. VIII. 2, and the *Horrea Epagathiana*; while on the north its front arcade faces on to the Via dei Misuratori del Grano. Only to the south does it actually make contact with another building, although even there it does not share a common wall.

Apart from an oblique façade (north-west–south-east) parallel with the roadway to the north which follows the line of an earlier orientation, it has a rectangular plan consisting of a central courtyard with a portico of brick piers on to which open ranges of long, narrow rooms on the three sides east, south and west (Fig. 2 and Pls. 1, 2).

The style of building is *opus mixtum*, that is, large panels of reticulate work framed with bonding courses of brickwork and with brickwork at doorways[4] (Pl. 3). This alone would have suggested a Trajanic-Hadrianic date; and the brick stamps, examined by Bloch, indicate a date about A.D. 120.[5] The northern section of the east wall of the *horrea* was, however, restored in Severan times in brickwork only (Pl. 4).

The building is in good preservation, apart from the rooms on the east side. The rooms on the south side and one or two at the south end of the east side have been restored by the Soprintendenza to house various objects, inscriptions, etc., found in the excavations. Most of the rooms on the west side are only partially excavated.

[1] *Scavi* I, p. 131.
[2] Part of the Julio-Claudian building is incorporated in the east wall of *Horrea* (Reg. I. Is. VIII. 2). [3] *Scavi* I, Tav. XLI. 4. [4] *Scavi* I, Tav. LIII. 2. Lugli, *Tecnica* II, Tav. CLI. 3.
[5] *Scavi* I, pp. 216–17.

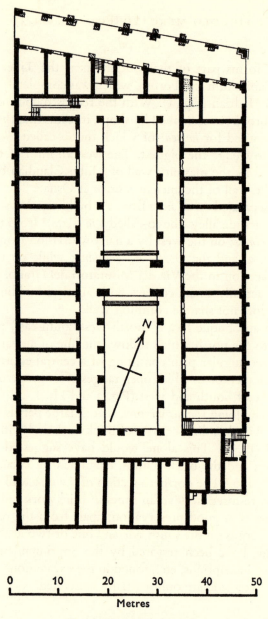

0   10   20   30   40   50

Metres

Fig. 2   Ostia, *Piccolo Mercato*

18

Description

The main entrance to the *horrea* lies on its north side (Pl. 5). The whole north side is fronted by a wide arcade of slender piers of fine-grained red bricks, which were so slender that they had to be reinforced immediately. The entrance corridor is trapezoidal in plan as a result of the difference between the 'oblique' façade of the shop fronts and the four-square orientation of the *horrea* proper. It is flanked by shop doorways, three on either side, and two staircases, one immediately to the west, the other one shop away to the east. Whatever were the arrangements at the main outer threshold, it is quite clear that the threshold to the *horrea* proper (3·25 metres wide) was of the usual type, that is, threshold with marginal check and with two pivot holes for doors, which opened outwards. The springing of the fine brick arch of the entrance way can still be seen.

Surrounding the central arcaded courtyard are, on the west side eleven rooms, on the east ten rooms, and on the south seven rooms of which the most easterly is only half the depth of the others. The dimensions of the rooms to the east and west are more or less exactly similar, 11·85 × 5·30 metres, but the rooms to the south are considerably deeper, 13·20 × 5·10 metres. The entrances to the rooms on the other hand have a consistent measurement, 2·30–2·40 metres; the thresholds with marginal check, two pivot holes and a central bolt hole are set flush with the floor level of the arcade and the floor of the room behind. The front walls of the rooms are faced entirely with brick and the side walls with *opus mixtum* (Pl. 2), great panels of fine reticulate in tufa divided and framed by bands of brickwork (generally six courses) and brick quoining. The back walls of the rooms again are faced with *opus mixtum* on the whole, but there are exceptions, viz. a stretch of the south wall is in tufa and appears to be a part of the defensive wall of the early Republican *Castrum* of Ostia,[1] while the north part of the east wall was entirely rebuilt in brick in the Severan period.

For the characteristics of *opus mixtum* at Ostia at this period of its greatest perfection, see *Scavi* I, pp. 201–2. In general the great panels of reticulate measure 1·18, 1·33 or 1·48 metres in height and are composed of carefully cut cubes in tufa (6·5 × 6·5–7 × 7 centimetres) set with great precision at 45° with thin mortar joints of 1–1·2 centimetres. The bricks

---

[1] *Scavi* I, p. 67.

are either broken tiles or half *bessales*; even a building such as the *Piccolo Mercato* which has *bessales* in its inner walls may well have a façade of broken tiles. In general the bricks are of very fine-grained texture and of medium thickness (3·2–4 centimetres). They are some 23–6 centimetres in length, separated by mortar joints 1·3–1·8 centimetres (height of ten courses, 50 centimetres); the bricks in the piers forming the portico are set with even finer mortar joints, *circa* 1 centimetre (height of ten courses, 45 centimetres).[1]

The Severan brickwork of the restoration of the east wall differs significantly; considerably more reddish in colour, the bricks are of inferior quality and smaller size, particularly in thickness (2·8–3 centimetres), and the mortar joints have become wider (2 centimetres or more) (height of ten courses, 54 centimetres).

The rooms were very lofty (*circa* 7 metres), with massive barrel vaults made of concrete (whose aggregate consists of small pieces of tufa) supported on walls 60 centimetres thick. They were entered through tall doorways above whose segmental archways were superimposed square windows (Pl. 1). (Some of the doorways, particularly on the south side, were apparently reduced in size at a late period by being partly walled up,[2] but nothing of this filling is visible now.) A slightly projecting string course of bricks marks the spring of the vault on the side walls. The rooms were apparently given further light and ventilation by two splayed slit windows set above the springing of the vault in the back wall; the lower parts of two of these have been preserved in the back wall of one room on the west side (Pl. 6). By analogy with completely preserved windows of this type in *Horrea* (Reg. I. Is. VIII. 2), *Horrea* (Reg. III. Is. II. 6), etc., we may infer that the windows were topped not by an arch but by a flat lintel.

The rooms open on to an arcade 3·65 metres wide, floored with *opus*

---

[1] See Blake, *Roman Construction from Tiberius*, p. 164, for the history of the use of triangular bricks, made mainly from *bessales* (19·7 centimetres), and the use of tiles. Miss Blake, in her projected book on Roman construction from the time of Trajan, divided the bricks used in the *Piccolo Mercato* (and *Cardo Maximus*) into three grades: (*a*) very fine-grained red bricks made from tiles, perhaps exclusively from roof tiles, used in all piers and some façades; (*b*) lighter red bricks, also from tiles, used in most other secondary walls; (*c*) speckled yellow triangles in less important parts, particularly in the north-east part of the building. An example of a red façade interlocked with yellow facing occurs east of the main entrance.

[2] J. Carcopino, 'Ostiensia—II. Le quartier des docks', *Mélanges* XXX (1910), 421, n. 2 and fig. 10.

spicatum, that is, herring-bone bricks, in the same way as is the whole central area[1] (Pl. 7). The arcade consists of twenty-eight brick piers, set on blocks of travertine, surrounding a central courtyard. These piers, evenly spaced, although rather closer to each other on the north and south sides, have the same measurements, 1·05 metres (north–south) × 1·20 metres (east–west), except for the two pairs of central piers, one on the east and the other on the west side. The space between these piers is left free on each side, but all other intervals on these sides are blocked by an infilling wall of tufa reticulate, which is so thin (35 centimetres wide) that it can never have been more than a balustrade: it is not bonded with the piers and may well be later than the original construction, whether this implies a different moment of construction or a specifically later date.

The four central piers are considerably larger (1·05 × 2·34 metres) and of remarkable construction (Pl. 1). Those on the east side are each all of one build at the base, while those on the west side comprise two abutting piers of equal size from the bottom upwards. The outer members on each side, which project into the court, were linked at the same height by segmental arches turned in *bipedales*, parallel with the arcade, the eastern one alone being now preserved. The height from the *opus spicatum* flooring to the soffit of the arch is only 2·30 metres. There is no doubt that a passage way ran *across* the court from arch to arch since two tufa gutters (internal width 40 centimetres, depth 13 centimetres) border the space in question, and this in turn implies that the space was covered by a gabled roof. The problem is to discover at what level this was constructed.

The comparatively low height of the segmental arches, 2·30 metres, is only satisfactorily explained if we think of it in terms of gaining the necessary height for the springing, on either side, of a further great arch across the centre of the courtyard. This would have supported a passage way at the level of the first floor.

It must be admitted that no trace of such a great archway has been preserved. It is a fact, however, that in order to span the gap of approximately 8 metres across the court at this point by a round arch with the purpose of supporting a passage way at a height of 7 metres plus, it would be necessary to have the springing of the arch about 3 metres above ground level.

---

[1] Carcopino, 'Ostiensia', Pl. xiii.

The suggestion that the space is too wide to have been spanned by a concrete arch and that we must think of a wooden structure is not compelling. Large concrete barrel vaults were used extensively in this building and all the expert opinion consulted was unanimous in rejecting the idea that the Romans would have found any difficulty in this task.

An explanation of the difference in the construction of the east and west piers may be found if it is supposed that the spanning of the centre of the court was a change in plan during the construction of the building, after the erection of the west arcade, but before the central piers on the east side were built. But this is pure supposition.

Two staircases, one at the north-west, the other at the south-east corner of the courtyard, prove that the building was at least two-storeyed. These staircases, approached from within the building, have the usual form of two opposed flights separated by a landing, but, to facilitate the carrying of goods for storage in the upper rooms, after the bottom five or six travertine steps they take the form of ramps of easy gradient paved with herring-bone bricks. (Pl. 3.)

There is an alternative minor entrance to the building in the south-east corner just behind the Capitolium. It is framed with pilasters in brickwork and was surmounted by an ornamental pediment in brick-work decorated with dentil mouldings. Of modest size, 2·47 metres in width, it led into the eastern extension of the south arcade near the south-east staircase. A self-contained unit immediately to the east of this entrance may have been the door-keeper's station.

The fourth room from the west end of the south side has a small doorway, later blocked, in its back wall which leads into a complex of rooms and staircase to the south. It does not seem clear whether they are to be regarded as part of the *horrea* or not, although the doorway is clearly contemporary with the main building. Perhaps they may be connected with the administration of the *horrea*.

Set into one of the façade walls between the rooms on the west side is a tile slab with a coiled snake carved on it.[1]

[1] See Appendix 4 (especially p. 313).

Summing up

The so-called *Piccolo Mercato* must be *horrea* rather than a *macellum*.[1]
Its position, its plan, the depth of its rooms, the restricted number of its
entrances and the buttressing of its long side walls all suggest an important building for *storage* purposes. It was massively constructed and
served its purpose relatively unaltered at least until beyond the Severan
period. What was stored in it is not very easy to decide. Its size and
position would suggest public ownership and the corn supply, but there
is no direct evidence and it lacks the distinguishing feature of raised
floors, at least those of a permanent nature noticeable in *Horrea* (Reg. I.
Is. VIII. 2), the *Grandi Horrea*, and the *Horrea Antoniniani*. Whatever was
stored in it, the ramp staircases show that the upper floor was also used
for storage purposes. This is important because it supports a passage, as
restored by Mommsen, in *Codex Theodosianus* (XV. I. 12) and finally
proves wrong Lanciani's division of *horrea* into lower rooms for
storage and upper rooms for administration.[2] Perhaps we should seek
the administrative offices above the shops along the front of the *horrea*
or in the rooms attached to the south side.

It must be emphasised that all the thresholds of rooms *within* the
horrea have a raised marginal check and pivot holes for doors. This
emphasis is necessary because Paschetto[3] stated that the *horrea* in this
area have grooved thresholds for holding upright shutters. This type of
threshold is particularly associated with shops and Paschetto in fact gives
an accurate description of the thresholds of the shops along the *Cardo
Maximus* and the shops along the *front* of the *Piccolo Mercato* on the
Via dei Misuratori del Grano; the error lies in supposing these to be
horrea.

The design of the building seems to reflect the desire of the Hadrianic
planners for a four-square orientation and systematic lay-out, while
still respecting the earlier orientation of the Via dei Misuratori; the
differences of orientation are masked by the irregularly shaped shops.

It is interesting to compare the size of the central courtyard with that
of the Julio-Claudian *Horrea di Hortensius*. The desire for a roomy

[1] A. Boëthius, *The Golden House of Nero* (Michigan, 1960), p. 134, persists in regarding
it as a 'market-place'.
[2] R. Lanciani, 'Ricerche topografiche sulla città di Porto', *Ann. Inst.* XL (1868), 178 ff.
[3] L. Paschetto, *Ostia, colonia romana; storia e monumenti* (Rome, 1912), pp. 317 ff.

courtyard allowing freedom of movement is now balanced by a need for saving space; this may be a result of the particular conditions in Ostia.[1]

2 HORREA (Reg. 1. Is. VIII. 2)

General

This building occupies the north-east part of Reg. 1. Is. VIII and is bounded to the east by the so-called *Piccolo Mercato*, to the south by the *Horrea Epagathiana et Epaphroditiana*, to the west by the Via degli Horrea Epagathiana and to the north by the Via del Piccolo Mercato (Fig. 1). In short, it formed part of that area close to the Tiber, developed under Hadrian, particularly used for accommodating *horrea*.

Its northern front towards the Tiber was excavated by Vaglieri but the remainder of the building was covered deep by the enormous dumps of earth from the *Piccolo Mercato*.[2] In 1938 these dumps were cleared completely in the northern half of the building but only cleared down to a level sufficient to recover the general plan in the southern half.

It is separated by a long narrow gap (approximately 1·20 metres wide with a gutter laid in it) from the *Piccolo Mercato* to the east, and although it actually abuts on to the *Horrea Epagathiana* to the south, it does not share a common wall with it. (Rain water from the roofs of the two buildings may have been drained eastwards to fall into the gutter along the side of the *Piccolo Mercato*.) It is surrounded on the north and west sides by shops; the main entrance on the north side is flanked by two shops to the east and three smaller ones to the west, while a row of shops runs down the whole west side (Fig. 3).

The plan of the whole is a long rectangle, consisting of a very narrow central courtyard surrounded by an arcade, made up of brick piers with the intervals filled by reticulate work, around which are ranged on the three sides, east, south and west, the usual rows of long narrow rooms.

The style of facing is *opus mixtum* (Pl. 8) as in the *Piccolo Mercato*, but with a greater use of broken tiles.[3] The Hadrianic date, A.D. 119–20, for the building, suggested by its style, is confirmed by Bloch's study of the

---

[1] A model of an Italian restoration of the building exists in the Museo della Via Ostiense in Rome. A photograph of it is reproduced in *Palladio* I (1937), 223.

[2] De Vaglieri, 'Monumenti repubblicani di Ostia', *BCom* XXXIX (1911), 228; Carcopino, 'Ostiensia', p. 397; G. Becatti, 'Horrea Epagathiana et Epaphroditiana', *NSc* XVIII (1940), 32 and plan.

[3] *Scavi* I, p. 201.

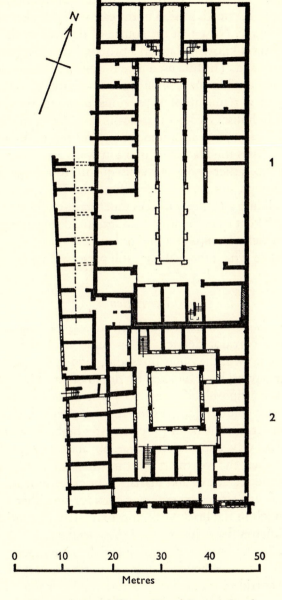

0   10   20   30   40   50

Metres

Fig. 3   Ostia, (1) *Horrea* (Reg. I. Is. VIII. 2) and
(2) *Horrea Epagathiana et Epaphroditiana*

brick stamps.[1] However, there is a stretch of tufa *opus quadratum* incorporated in the north section of the east wall (Pl. 9), that is, towards the *Piccolo Mercato*. Now that the course of the wall of the Republican *castrum* of Ostia is known, Vaglieri's proposal that this formed part of it is no longer valid. The tufa used here is more yellowish and finer than the Fidene tufa used in the *castrum* wall. There can be little doubt that this walling is a remnant of a previous building on the site, very possibly a warehouse. At least it is possible to detect in three different places the presence of header stones marking the position of division walls. In two cases the Hadrianic division walls are in almost the same positions as the earlier walls and consequently the headers have been slighted, although not beyond identification. The contractor for the Hadrianic building seemingly used as much as he could of the stone wall and moreover kept its orientation throughout, disregarding the Via dei Misuratori which was also at a higher level.

The height to which the walls are still preserved varies considerably.

Description

The building is entered from the north through a long and relatively wide entrance corridor defined by an outer and an inner threshold (Pl. 8). Of these two, the outer threshold, 2·70 metres wide, shows no signs of ever having been blocked by doors of any kind; it consists ot simple flat travertine blocks with no pivot holes or bolt hole. Two decorative brick columns (40 centimetres in diameter, built of yellowish bricks), on tall travertine bases 36 centimetres high, frame the entrance, not, in the usual way, affixed to the *antae*, but actually inside the entrance resting on either end of the travertine threshold. Presumably they supported some architrave and perhaps a brick pediment.

About half way along the entrance corridor on either side there are vertical channels in the brickwork approximately 23 centimetres wide and 25 centimetres deep. Just beyond these to the south appears a clear division line in the brickwork showing that the entrance walls of the *horrea* proper were not bonded with the northern part of the walls in the entrance corridor. Immediately before the inner threshold, in either side wall, two splayed slit windows are visible at a height of approximately 1·80 metres from the ground. These windows, built in brick and

---

[1] *Scavi* I, p. 217. Cf. H. Bloch, 'I bolli laterizi', *BCom* LXV (1937), 87–97.

presenting the appearance of narrow slits on to the entrance corridor, gave light to the two staircase wells situated to the right and left of the entrance corridor. These staircases were accessible only from within the *horrea* (or, in the case of the western one, accessible also from a small postern door in the west side of the *horrea*). The splayed slit windows typical in the outer walls of *horrea* are particularly interesting here in that they confirm that the outer threshold never had doors and that therefore anyone could gain access as far as the inner threshold.

The inner threshold is again of travertine but has a marginal check, pivot holes and central bolt hole indicating doors which opened outwards. This is perhaps accounted for by the fact that doors opening inwards would restrict still further the already constricted space for circulation along the internal arcades. There is no evidence as to how the doors were locked.

This inner entrance gives access to the *horrea* proper and leads straight into the arcade surrounding the inner courtyard. The flooring of both the entrance and the east side of the arcade is made up of fragments of marble and travertine in concrete. The west side of the arcade is at a slightly higher level (about 50 centimetres), and is reached by means of two brick steps the width of the arcade, immediately inside the *horrea* to the west. This side is floored entirely with bipedal tiles. The central courtyard itself is floored with *opus spicatum*, that is, herring-bone brick, with a row of *bipedales* (60 × 60 centimetres) laid round the entire court forming a margin 80 centimetres wide beyond the brick piers.

The small oblong brick piers which surround the central courtyard are linked one with another by a wall approximately 46 centimetres wide faced with tufa reticulate which seems to be contemporary in that it is well bonded with the piers (in contrast with the infilling walls in the *Piccolo Mercato*). Perhaps its function was to protect the rooms opening on to the arcade from sun and rain, to both of which dangers they would have been exposed from the beginning because of the narrowness of the arcade (3·50 metres wide). However, they must have had large openings left in them at a higher level in order to provide sufficient light and ventilation. Regular openings exist through this linking wall, one in the wall near the entrance, one in the centre of each long side and perhaps one at the south end.

The rooms opening on to the arcade, certainly in the northern completely excavated part, have approximately similar dimensions, *circa* 4·80 × 7·80 metres; the doorways, too, remain standard, around 1·70 metres in width.

The most interesting feature of the rooms, however, is the raised flooring and air vents at the entrances to the rooms (Pl. 10). The raising of floors in *horrea* is a common feature,[1] and achieved either by a system of low piers (as in hypocausts) or of dwarf walls with lateral vents to allow a free flow of air; a sensible method to safeguard the goods stored from damp and overheating. In the surprisingly few examples of raised floors in the *horrea* at Ostia, a system of dwarf walls is used, each 30 centimetres wide and 30 centimetres from the other, running back from the mouth of the room parallel with the side walls. The flooring is generally of bipedal tiles (60 × 60 centimetres) laid from the middle of one dwarf wall over the air tunnel to the middle of the next, three or four layers of tiles with mortar between building up the floor. This flooring normally stops short of the doorway to allow room for the travertine threshold supported on brick piers.

There are two points of interest concerning the raised floors in *Horrea* (Reg. I. Is. VIII. 2). First, so far as one can judge from the three small brick piers supporting the thresholds at the entrances to the rooms, the raising of the floors was not contemporary with the Hadrianic building. The brick piers supporting either end of the threshold, although set flush against the entrance walls to the rooms, are not bonded with them; they are composed of distinctly different bricks, yellow instead of pink or red, of mixed thicknesses (2·2–3 centimetres), and unevenly set with wider mortar joints (approximately 2·5 centimetres). This is not conclusive for the later dating of the floor structure of the rooms, since it may represent later tampering only with the mouths of the rooms (perhaps in connection with changes of threshold), but given the fact that the only other two examples of such raised floors yet known in *horrea* in Ostia[2] are both dated to the period of Commodus, *circa* A.D. 180, we may suspect perhaps that a similar date, later in the second century, is possible in this case too. Secondly, at some date after the raising of the floors (if that represents indeed a separate period of construction), the spaces between the brick piers supporting the thresholds were blocked by small pieces of tufa set in

[1] See Appendix I.
[2] *Grandi Horrea* (Reg. II. Is. IX. 7); see Calza, 'Gli *horrea* tra il Tevere e il decumano', *NSc* (1921), 360 ff. Cf. Appendix I. *Horrea Antoniniani* (Reg. II. Is. II. 7); see *Scavi* I, pp. 143 and 204.

mortar and capped by a course or two of brickwork. At this time presumably the vents through the travertine threshold itself were cut to compensate for the blocking of the air vents between the piers. The date and purpose of these changes are obscure. Explanations connected with the flooding of the Tiber are weakened by the fact that the changes took place in rooms on both sides of the court in disregard of the already higher level of the western rooms and corridor.

The style of building shows much the same characteristics as the Hadrianic *opus mixtum* of the *Piccolo Mercato*, with which it is closely contemporary; insets of reticulate were used, however, in the front walls of the rooms as well, and there is a greater use of broken tiles.

The stretch of tufa walling (Pl. 9) on the east side of the *horrea* extends only from the staircase recess along the back of the first room and part of the second on that side. Seven or eight courses of large tufa blocks are visible at some points, the blocks measuring some 60 centimetres in height and approximately 1·40 metres in length. This tufa wall is capped by eight courses of brickwork and then the usual reticulate panels of *opus mixtum*, and when it ends there is first a brick panel and then the reticulate work. The thickness of the walls in general is between 53 and 54 centimetres.

Large areas of stucco are to be found, some with red paint still adhering.

The existence of at least one more storey is indicated by the two staircases to the west and east of the northern entrance already mentioned, and one in the southern part of the building.

An oven was built at a later date in one of the western side rooms.

Summing up

The building as a whole derives its interest mainly from the compactness of its plan, from the system of raised floors in its rooms, and from the incorporation of some tufa walling of an earlier building. If we can accept a date for the raised floors later than that for the building as a whole, we have the odd fact that there are only three *horrea* in Ostia with permanently raised floors and that all three are dated towards the end of the second century A.D. If we accept the tufa wall incorporated in the Hadrianic building as part of an earlier warehouse, we have an indication that, although the planning of this area near the Tiber changed under Hadrian, the purpose served by the buildings was the same.

Another feature of great interest is that whereas the later filling-in of the colonnades or porticoes of *horrea* is quite common (see *Grandi Horrea*, and possibly *Piccolo Mercato*), in this building one has a clear example of a contemporary infilling.

Miss Blake in her projected book on 'Roman construction from the time of Trajan' suggested that, although this building was constructed at the same time as the *Piccolo Mercato* and with the same kind of bricks, it was the work of a different contractor who used his bricks with less finesse.

3 HORREA EPAGATHIANA ET EPAPHRODITIANA
(Reg. I. Is. VIII. 3)

General

Situated on the Via degli Horrea Epagathiana to the west of the Capitol, the building is bounded on the east by the *Piccolo Mercato*, on the north by the *Horrea* (Reg. I. Is. VIII. 2), and on the south by the Casette Repubblicane (Fig. 1).

When it was found it was in a ruinous condition. It was carefully restored in connection with the projected Esposizione Universale in 1942 and now stands complete up to the first floor.[1]

It is clearly dated to about A.D. 145–50 not only by its materials and building style (it is faced entirely with bricks) but also by the style of the mosaic in its central courtyard and by dated brick stamps.[2]

Its plan (Fig. 3) consists of a small square central courtyard, surrounded by a brick-piered arcade on to which face rooms of differing shape and size on all four sides. Two staircases lead to the first floor where there is a similar arrangement of rooms facing on to an arcade and staircases leading to yet another floor not restored.

It is the only building in Ostia clearly designated as *HORREA* by an inscription on a marble slab on the architrave of the main entrance, giving its name (*CIL* XIV. Suppl. 4709).

The building has been published in an excellent article by Becatti,[3] who gives not only plans of the ground and first floors, but also sectional drawings.

---

[1] *Scavi* I, Tav. X. 3 and XI. 2.   [2] *Scavi* I, p. 217.
[3] Becatti, *Horrea Epagathiana et Epaphroditiana*, 32 ff.

Description

The building is entered from the west through a long entrance corridor which is flanked to the north by two small entrances, one with stairs leading to an upper storey, the other opening into a room under these stairs, and to the south by four larger entrances to four shops (Pl. 11).

This asymmetrical façade is in fact clearly delimited and given a certain organic unity by some simple decorative motifs. Delimitation to the north takes the form of a projecting pilaster of brickwork with a base moulded on the south and west sides which acts as a sort of terminal *anta*. The stretches of walling between the doorways to the south of the main entrance are decorated with much shallower pilasters which rise to a simple cornice at the level of a mezzanine floor. Below this cornice over each shop doorway is a shallow relieving arch in brickwork, and above it another well-rounded relieving arch framing a square window; to the north over the two smaller entrances is only one large shallow arch, and one well-rounded relieving arch framing two square windows. All these doorways had lintels of wood originally. Above the level of the mezzanine floor is another deeper cornice from which sprang the 'balcony' (restored at the southern end of the building) which was perhaps a decorative feature rather than actually to be used.

The main entrance to the *horrea* is marked out by a more imposing arrangement[1] (Pl. 12); the doorway is not squared but has a rounded brick archway framed by two attached columns of brickwork, unfluted, with Attic bases on a high plinth and with simplified Corinthian capitals (double row of leaves). These support a smooth architrave, bounded at top and bottom by cornices, the upper with ionic dentils, on which was fixed the marble slab with the inscription, found in pieces in the excavation but now reconstructed. The whole was surmounted by a pediment of which the brick cornice is carried upon small consoles linked by tiny arches.

The four shops to the right of the main entrance have no intercommunicating doorways, but the first communicates by a doorway in its north side with the main entrance to the *horrea*, and the last by a doorway in its back wall with a long southern room of the *horrea*. Another doorway opens off the main entrance corridor on the other (northern) side, leading under the staircase and then through another

[1] Cf. Lugli, *Tecnica* II, Tav. CLXXV. 3.

doorway into a small concealed area formed by the space between the west wall of the *horrea*, the back wall of the shops on the street and the south wall of *Horrea* (Reg. I. Is. VIII. 2).

The main entrance corridor has two travertine thresholds *in situ*. The first at the actual mouth is very ruined, but enough remains to indicate a travertine threshold with marginal check and two large pivot holes (14 centimetres in diameter) at either end for doors opening inwards. About 1·35 metres above the pivot hole on the northern side, set into the brick wall, is a travertine block with a squared hole in it (10 × 13 centimetres)—clearly to hold one end of a large wooden bar. Unfortunately the corresponding block in the opposite wall is missing. The second threshold occurs slightly more than halfway along the corridor and is aligned with the west retaining wall of the *horrea* itself (Fig. 4). The whole doorway here is better preserved and of massive construction. Not only the threshold, but also the door jambs and a flat arch are of travertine. This second threshold is similar in type to the outer one—with marginal check, bolt holes and depressions for pivot holes (for doors opening inwards), but in this case the pivot holes are preserved in the architrave as well (15 centimetres wide and 10 centimetres deep), and the system for barring the doors is completely preserved in the travertine door jambs. It can be directly compared with the system found in the postern door of *Horrea* (Reg. III. Is. II. 6),[1] except that here it is on a larger scale. It is clear that the doorway was barred on both inside and outside. Basically the system consists of a simple squared hole in one door jamb opposite a more complex squared hole in the opposite door jamb, approximately 1½ metres from the ground. The second squared hole is more complex in that it generally has a groove running to it (in this case from the side) and a further smaller slot within it running deeper into the doorpost. Apparently the bar, having been lodged in the one hole, is slid along the groove into the opposite hole and there secured by sliding a bolt home into the smaller slot and securing it, probably by a padlock. In order to be effective, the bar on the outside must have dropped into a series of L-shaped metal brackets attached to the door. It is interesting to note that whereas it is on the southern side that the inner bar was locked into position, the outer bar was locked on the northern side.

This system of barring the doors was used not only at the main

[1] See p. 55.

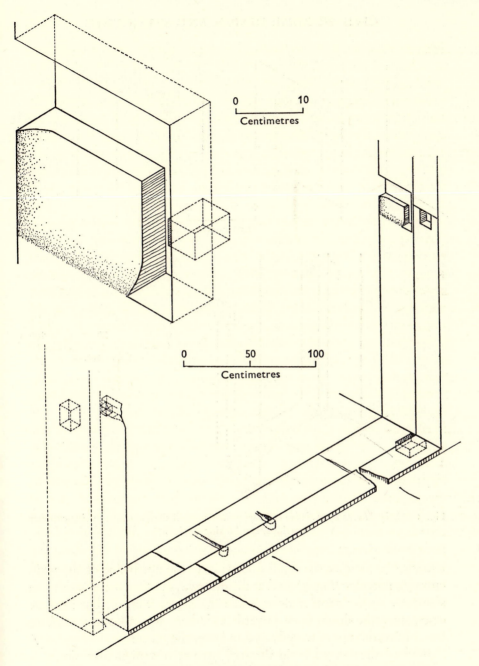

0   10
Centimetres

0   50   100
Centimetres

Fig. 4   Ostia, *Horrea Epagathiana et Epaphroditiana,* inner main entrance
and locking devices

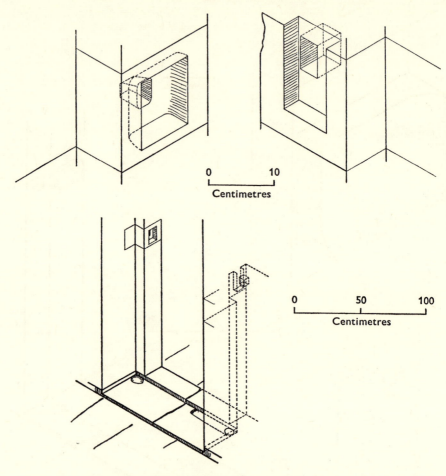

Fig. 5   Ostia, *Horrea Epagathiana et Epaphroditiana*, small doorway, north side entrance
corridor, and locking devices

entrance but also at the small doorway on the north side of the main
entrance corridor (Fig. 5), and at the doorways to the rooms and to the
staircases on the ground floor inside the *horrea* (Fig. 6), but in these
cases, since the doors open inwards and there was no other access to
the rooms, the doors were barred only on the outside.

Beyond the second main threshold are two semicircular niches in
reticulate—white alternated with red—with the apses composed of
white limestone and grey-black pumice in concentric rings. The niches

34

are framed by pilasters of brick resting on a cornice ornamented with a meander pattern, and the whole is crowned by a pediment. These niches are similar to two more niches in the main quadrangle of the building (Pl. 15). They must have held small statues of the tutelary deities of the establishment, perhaps Aphrodite and Agathe Tyche.

The main corridor (with restored cross-vaulting) leads straight into the central court with its brick piers, double at the corners, forming three equal arcades on each of the three sides north, west and south

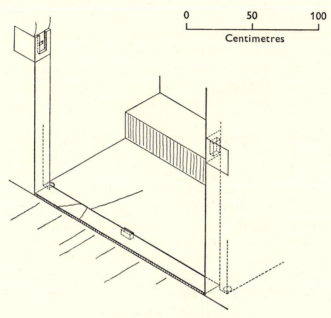

Fig. 6   Ostia, *Horrea Epagathiana et Epaphroditiana,*
staircase doorway and locking devices

(Pl. 13), while on the east side, two side arches frame a wide doorway with segmental arch, leading into a room whose depth includes the width of the eastern portico (Pl. 14). In order not to interrupt circulation, however, this large room has two side entrances opening on to the portico. This large room is roofed with two cross-vaults, one larger and one smaller corresponding to the width of the portico. Its purpose is not clear, but perhaps it served as an office.

In the stretches of wall on either side of the main doorway to this large room are apsidal niches similar to those in the entrance corridor (Pl. 15).

The brick piers of the north and east side and that of the south-west corner were found preserved up to the spring of the arch; the others had all lost their upper parts and have been restored. Only the vaulting of the east side and part of the north side is original; the others are restored from ancient material.

The arcades have thresholds of *bipedales* and tufa blocks more or less preserved, and are raised above the level of the central courtyard.

The courtyard itself is decorated in the middle by a black and white mosaic with meander patterns, a swastika, a tiger and a panther on it.[1]

Almost in the centre of the mosaic is a cover for the collection of rain water, while the water from the roofs was taken at the four corners of the courtyard through terracotta pipes built into the walling, and a drain under the floor of the cortile conveyed it into the sewer in the road.

The rooms opening on to the porticoes were roofed with cross-vaulting, and patches of white stucco are preserved. They are arranged fairly evenly, but differ markedly in size.

Two staircases with two flights each lead to the first floor at the north-west and south-west corners of the portico.

On the south side the building is extended by a long rectangular room, which could be entered from one of the shops on the street. It is divided by a corridor, a continuation of the eastern portico, from a similar smaller room on the same axis to the east, aligned with the other rooms facing on to the eastern portico. The larger of these two rooms is roofed with a barrel vault for some two-thirds of its length, and cross-vaulted only in that section corresponding to the row of rooms on the west side of the portico. The division corridor and the smaller eastern room have cross-vaulting.

The southern wall of these rooms rests for much of its length on four courses of Fidene tufa blocks, coarse-grained with many black lumps in them (60 centimetres in height and 40 centimetres–1·50 metres in length). This is part of the original wall of the *Castrum* of Ostia traced by Calza.[2] This wall is pierced by a doorway at the end of the division

---

[1] For a description and discussion of this mosaic, see Becatti, '*Horrea Epagathiana et Epaphroditiana*', pp. 41 ff.

[2] G. Calza, 'Ostia—Scavo presso l'edificio delle Pistrine', *NSc* (1914), 246–7; (1923), 178. Cf. *Scavi* I, Tav. XVI. I.

corridor which leads into the Via delle Casette Repubblicane, but which was blocked at a late date by *opus listatum* (bricks and small tufa blocks mixed). The flooring of these southern rooms is lower than the others in the building, and near the tufa wall runs a drain covered by a lid.

The restored upper storey[1] repeats the same scheme of rooms facing on to a portico, which looks down into the courtyard below. However, the principal room on the eastern side does not absorb the whole width of the portico; it simply juts forward rather more than the rest. The arcades are regular, and the flooring of the portico was *opus spicatum*. The section corresponding to the great southern room below is here completely divided off, and was later separated into a series of little rooms, which were connected with the floor above by a staircase.

The careful brickwork with bipedal courses[2] suggests a date in the reign of Antoninus Pius, and this is confirmed by examples of the brick stamp, 1057 (A.D. 137), on *bipedales in situ* in the south-west staircase.

Summing up

It is generally agreed[3] that this *horrea* is of a type rather distinct from anything else yet found in Ostia; it is comparable neither with the great storehouses, nor with the small corridor type. On the other hand it is the one building clearly labelled '*horrea*' in Ostia, and its elaborate locking devices, not only at the main entrance but also at the entrances to the rooms and at the bottom of the staircases, make it clear that it stored something of value. Schaal suggests that it was the quarters of an export–import firm run by the two freedmen Epagathus and Epaphroditus, and quotes as an earlier example of the same sort of building used for the same sort of purpose the *Magasin des Colonnes* on the harbour front at Delos.[4] Becatti says more generally that it must have been a private storehouse for expensive goods, and had a character between an oriental bazaar and 'nostri grandi case-magazzini di articoli vari'.

Its moderate size and elaborate locking precautions would suggest on the other hand the sort of 'safe deposit' storehouses where one might

---

[1] Becatti, 'Horrea Epagathiana et Epaphroditiana', fig. 12, plan Tav. II.

[2] Cf. *Scavi* I, p. 203.

[3] Becatti, '*Horrea Epagathiana et Epaphroditiana*', p. 48; H. Schaal, *Ostia* (Bremen, 1957), p. 64; Meiggs, p. 277.

[4] A. Jardé, 'Le Magasin des Colonnes de Délos', *BCH* XXIX (1905), pp. 21 ff.

hire storage space for goods, known from the *Digest*.[1] Meiggs also inclines towards this suggestion.

These are the possibilities; lack of evidence prevents a closer definition of its function.

4 HORREA (Reg. I. Is. XIII. 1)

General

The building is situated on the west side of the Semita dei Cippi, a road running south from the *Decumanus Maximus* towards the *Porta Laurentina* (Fig. 1).

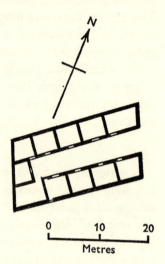

The plan consists of a central corridor with five rooms on each side and one room at the end facing towards the entrance (Fig. 7). Because, however, the building is set at an angle to the road, the outline of the whole is not a rectangle but rather a parallelogram; but this shape is not followed internally and consequently the shapes and dimensions of the corner rooms vary considerably.

Although it abuts on to the Terme del Foro to the north and east, it does not share a common wall.

Fig. 7   Ostia, *Horrea* (Reg. I. Is. XIII. 1)

It is faced with *opus mixtum*, that is, tufa reticulate panels framed by bands and quoins of brickwork. The excellence of its building[2] and the complete mastery of the style suggests a Hadrianic date, although Miss Blake in her projected book considered it possibly late Trajanic.

It is well preserved internally, often to a considerable height (12–15 feet).

Description

The entrance visible now is almost completely ruined and difficult to imagine; but the plan in *Scavi* I shows an entrance way the same width as the internal corridor (4·30 metres) flanked by two square piers.

---

[1] *Digest* I. 15. 3. 2, cf. Chapter VI.
[2] *Scavi* I, p. 134. Cf. Lugli, *Tecnica* II, Tav. CLI. 4.

The central corridor was floored with *opus spicatum* into which was set at least one travertine block with a hole of 10 centimetres diameter, presumably for drainage purposes, thereby suggesting that the corridor was unroofed.

The rooms had entrances 1·40–1·50 metres wide with travertine thresholds with marginal check and pivot holes set flush in the ground (Pl. 16). Overhead the doorways must have been roofed with wooden lintels, now restored in cement by the Soprintendenza. There were apparently no windows *immediately* above the doorways and no wooden blocks set half way up the door jambs on either side of the entrance as in *Horrea* (Reg. III. Is. II. 6).

In one room the back wall is sufficiently well preserved to show the lower half of one splayed slit window typical of *horrea* in Ostia. A comparison with completely preserved examples leads to the conclusion that the window was topped by a flat lintel and not an arch.

The panels of reticulate beautifully set with fine mortar joints, particularly in the front façades of the rooms, are framed with brickwork composed of broken tiles (3·5–4 centimetres thick, 22–7 centimetres in length, of pinkish colour; height of ten courses, 49 centimetres) dovetailed into the reticulate work with six-course insets (Pl. 16). The extremely high standard of these façades is not maintained inside the rooms where, although the work is good, the mortar joints are thicker and the whole was covered with stucco, patches of which remain. It is also noticeable that whereas the façades have bands of six courses of brickwork, the back walls of the rooms have generally bands only of five courses, and the side walls of only three courses. There seems also to be no strong bond between the side walls of rooms and the back wall.

There was originally a side entrance to the building to the south which led into a room on the south side; and opposite this entrance was another from the room into the central corridor. Both these were blocked and faced on the outer side with brickwork, while the sides facing into the room were faced with reticulate.

Summing up

This building shows perhaps the finest example of brick and reticulate work in Ostia. There are no indications of how it was roofed or of the existence of any upper storey. Clearly the building is not to be compared with the great State warehouses but rather with buildings such as Reg. IV. Is. V. 12 and Reg. III. Is. XVII. 1.

5 HORREA (Reg. III. Is. XVII. 1)

Situated at the north-western end of the Via degli Aurighi, this building can be considered in close connection with the building Reg. I. Is. XIII. 1, which it resembles closely in plan, building style and date (Fig. 1).

Its plan is basically that of two rows of rooms ranged on either side of a central corridor which runs north–south. The rooms vary in size, becoming larger to the north because of the trapezoidal shape of the area occupied by the building (Fig. 8).

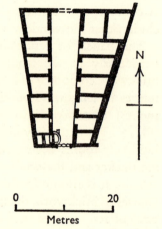

The walls are faced with panels of reticulate work divided by brick bands and in quoins in the usual *opus mixtum* of Hadrianic date. (Bricks pinkish, 3·5–4 centimetres thick; 16–22 centimetres long; height of ten courses, 52·5 centimetres.)

The remains of the original entrance show that the doorway was framed by two brick pilasters. The room just to the

Fig. 8   Ostia, *Horrea* (Reg. III. Is. XVII. 1)

left inside the main entrance later had a tiny bath suite built into it with mosaic floors.

Opposite the main entrance at the north end of the corridor another entrance was made later, whose threshold is preserved. It has marginal check, bolt hole and two rectangular depressions, seemingly to hold metal casings for the door pivots at each end of the threshold.

One or two thresholds are preserved in the room entrances (1·40 metres wide) and they have a marginal check.

Summing up

Miss Blake suggested to me privately that both these buildings, Reg. I. Is. XIII. I and Reg. III. Is. XVII. I, were not storehouses but bazaars. It is true that both buildings are rather small for storehouses and very finely constructed; but they bear no resemblance to the one undoubted bazaar in Ostia, the so-called *Caseggiato del Larario* (Reg. I. Is. IX. 3).[1] Not only are their ground plans quite different, but also they have none of the particular features of that bazaar; they do not have shop thresholds with grooves for holding upright shutters, and there are no traces of mezzanine floors or the little staircases leading to them. Pending further evidence it seems better to regard them as small, perhaps privately owned, storehouses.

6 HORREA ANTONINIANI (Reg. II. Is. II. 7)

This building is only partially excavated and even that part, the south-east corner, is now rather overgrown and difficult of access. It is part of a large building, with a central rectangular courtyard surrounded by a portico, situated a short way from the *Porta Romana* on the north side of the *Decumanus Maximus*, a situation comparable with that of the *Grandi Horrea* (Fig. 1). It has its front façade to the north towards the Tiber, and besides the rooms opening on to the inner court, there are two rows of rooms opening outwards on the east and west sides on to two streets running towards the Tiber. On the south side the building is closed by a long wall reinforced by buttresses, to the south of which, after an intervening space, is the line of shops (Hadrianic in date) which flank the *Decumanus Maximus*.

The date ascribed to the building by the excavators is late Antonine, probably Commodan, although no brick stamps are reported to confirm this.[2] The internal walls are faced with halved *bessales* approximately 21 centimetres long,[3] while the front walls are faced with broken tiles (3–3·5 centimetres thick, colour red, height of ten courses, 48 centimetres).

The only parts really accessible now are the rooms on the eastern

[1] G. Calza, 'Le origini Latine dell'abitazione moderna II', *Architettura e arti decorative* I, No. 2 (1923), 54 ff.
[2] *Scavi* I, p. 143.   [3] *Scavi* I, p. 204.

side (Fig. 9). These rooms are massively constructed with walls some 90 centimetres thick, and they all have raised floors. The *suspensurae* are of the type usual in Ostia, and consist of dwarf walls running from the back of the room towards the mouth, supporting a floor made up of layers of *bipedales* laid across the gaps. The dwarf walls as revealed by one ruined entrance do not seem to come right to the mouth of the

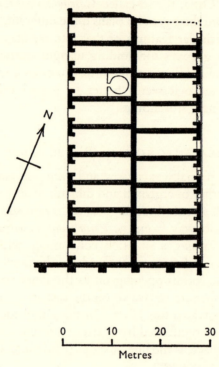

0   10   20   30
Metres

Fig. 9   Ostia, *Horrea Antoniniani*

room but stop short, leaving space for an independent system supporting the threshold itself. The thresholds with marginal check and pivot holes are unusual in type in that they project slightly out of the rooms. The most odd feature about the room entrances is, however, that at present there are no ventilation spaces under the thresholds to allow the air to circulate at all under the floor. A similar lack of vents under the thresholds is a characteristic of the *horrea* at Djemila in North Africa.[1]

[1] Y. Allais, 'Les greniers publics de Djemila', *RAfr* (1933), p. 259. Cf. Chapter III (p. 142).

Although only partially excavated, this building, so far as it is known, is particularly interesting because its position, size, date and raised floors make it a parallel to the Commodan form of the *Grandi Horrea*. Its size and position suggest a State-owned storehouse, and its raised floors suggest the storage of corn or similar perishable foodstuff. Meiggs[1] has suggested that this *horrea* shows a plan more developed than the plans of the earlier *horrea* in Ostia and that it betrays the influence of the back-to-back ranges of storerooms built around Trajan's harbour. This is possible, but since we do not possess the full plan, the similarity may be partly illusory. The building still seems to have a central courtyard.

7 GRANDI HORREA (Reg. II. Is. IX. 7)

General

The largest, perhaps the most interesting and certainly the most complicated building of its kind yet excavated at Ostia, this structure has attracted a certain amount of attention in print. *Scavi di Ostia* I, although nowhere treating it fully, nevertheless touches on its plan and construction several times, and has some fine photographs of wall facings.[2] F. Wilson, in his two articles on the social and economic history of Ostia, has some important passing references to it,[3] while Marion Blake gives an admirably short description of the earliest phases of its constructional history.[4] The fundamental study of the building, however, remains that of Calza[5] in 1921, published shortly after the excavation which laid the building completely open. Although it has been proved wrong at least in one important chronological point (the date of the added rooms on the east and south sides), it remains a monumental piece of work upon which any later study must be based.

The building as a whole lies between the Theatre complex to the east and the *Capitolium* to the west, in an area just north of the *Decumanus Maximus*, and extends northwards towards the Tiber (Fig. 1). As the remains stand at present, the building (of some 7,200 square metres) (Fig. 10) consists of three ranges of rooms on the east, west and

[1] Meiggs, p. 280.   [2] *Scavi* I, p. 118 general.
[3] F. Wilson, 'Studies in the social and economic history of Ostia, I', *PBSR* XIII (1935), 51, n. 4; XIV, p. 157.
[4] Blake, *Roman Construction from Tiberius*, p. 65.
[5] Calza, 'Gli *horrea* tra il Tevere e il decumano', pp. 360 ff.

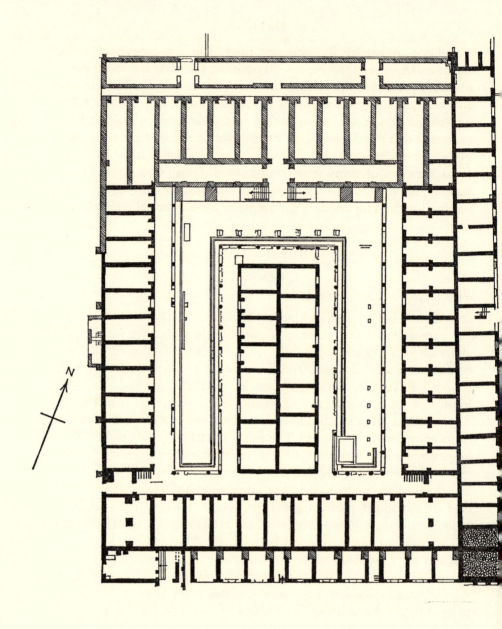

0   10   20   30   40   50
|————————————————————————————————————|
                Metres

Fig. 10   Ostia, *Grandi Horrea*

44

south sides (eleven rooms each) facing inwards on to what usually would be an open rectangular courtyard. In this case the inner courtyard has been given the form of a U with its base towards the north by the construction of a central block of rooms, fifteen in all, ranged eight one side and seven the other, backing on to a common wall, placed near the south side (Pl. 17). The porticoes fronting the side rooms and central rooms, and the tufa gutter parallel to them, echo this U-shape. In the south-east and south-west corners of the courtyard are two staircases. The whole northern section of the building is at a higher level than the remainder (some 50 centimetres higher than the level of the inner rooms) and consists of two staircases, a corridor running east–west, and twelve long rooms, six on either side of a central passage, facing north on to a narrow corridor; to the north of this again lie three long rooms with an east–west axis, with two entrances to the *horrea* as a whole dividing them from one another. Added to the east side of the building are nineteen rooms, and a staircase centrally placed, which face east on to the Via dei Grandi Horrea; attached to the south side are eleven rooms, and three staircases facing south, on to an enclosed area.

That this building as it stands is the product of a long and complicated structural history is clear not only from the differences of level, but also from the materials used. The bounding walls on the east and west sides of the building are of large tufa blocks; the raised northern section is built of brickwork; the division walls of the rooms around the courtyard are of a distinctly different type of brickwork, and the walls of the central block, although it is difficult to see since they were razed almost to threshold level, are composed of bricks different yet again.

For the unravelling of the main outline of the history of the building and particularly of its earliest phase, which depends on a careful study of foundations, we owe a debt to Calza.

Description

Phase I.[1] Calza's study of the extant remains and foundations enables the original plan to be recovered (Fig. 11). In basic shape and size it was the same as that which we see today. The building was bounded to the east and west by the tufa walls still visible (Pl. 18). To the south it was bounded by a brick-faced concrete wall with small buttresses 2·10 metres

[1] Calza, 'Gli *horrea* tra il Tevere e il decumano', pp. 360 ff., fig. 10.

apart; only the western end of the present south wall is original. To the north the building ended where it does today, but with an open pillared portico, square tufa drums resting on travertine bases (1·18 × 0·59 metres), entered from the east and west as well as from the north. The northern

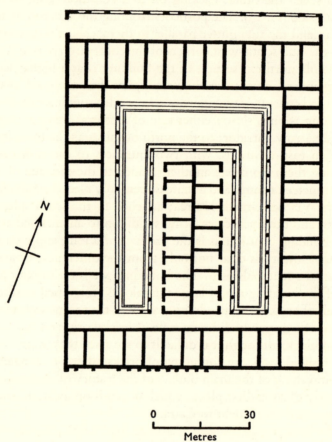

0   30

Metres

Fig. 11   Ostia, *Grandi Horrea*, phase 1

range of rooms faced on to this portico. The internal arrangements were basically the same as we see them today, although none of the brick-work still visible is original. The U-shape of the central courtyard was the same, except that the base of the U to the north was broader in that the northern portico had not yet been absorbed into the corridor and staircase arrangements of the northern section.

The floors of the rooms were not raised, but composed of *opus signinum* (crushed sherds) 20 centimetres thick.[1]

The building would appear to have been one-storeyed, since no trace of staircases for the first phase has been discovered.

The rain water was taken from the tufa gutters by means of two drains which ran down the centre of the two side courts, united at their base and became one single conduit 45 centimetres wide which went to the Tiber.

The tufa walls are composed of rusticated blocks of Anio tufa which vary in height from 53 to 66 centimetres but which have a constant width of 59 centimetres.[2] They were tied together by swallow-tail clamps, and the position of the division walls of the inner rooms is marked by headers.[3] That the inner division walls were composed of brick or reticulate work and not tufa blocks is suggested by the different foundation levels and by the fact that no clamp holes are found on the headers other than those necessary to tie them into the tufa wall. This use of tufa was presumably for greater strength, and as a precaution against fire; the southern wall of brick must have been thought sufficiently protected by the space between it and the buildings to the south on the *Decumanus*. Reddish yellow triangular bricks (17·5–18 × 4·5 centimetres) were used in the rear wall, while slightly larger bricks of the same kind (22·2 × 4·2–4·5 centimetres) were used in the central block of rooms.[4] The internal tufa porticoes were composed of columns (60 centimetres wide at bottom, 53 centimetres wide at top) with Doric capitals in travertine.[5]

The date of this original building must be somewhere in the middle of the first century A.D. because of the materials used and because we know that the first addition to it, namely the building of the rooms on the east and south sides, took place under Nero or soon after.[6] It has plausibly been suggested that Claudius was responsible for the building.

That the rooms added on the east and south sides (Fig. 12) are contemporary with one another was proved by an examination of their

[1] *Ibid.* p. 371.   [2] *Scavi* I, p. 197 and fig. 44; Tav. XLIV. 3.
[3] Calza, 'Gli *horrea* tra il Tevere e il decumano', fig. 8.
[4] Blake, *Roman Construction from Tiberius*, p. 65.
[5] Calza, 'Gli *horrea* tra il Tevere e il decumano', fig. 9.
[6] H. Bloch, *Scavi* I, p. 221; brick stamp, *CIL* XV (1) 666, was wrongly dated to the end of the first century by Calza.

portico foundations and gutters,[1] but they differ markedly in construction. On the east side the front walls to the rooms are built again of tufa blocks, although not rusticated, and on the north end and the south of the whole row, tufa is also used, buttressed outside by four spur walls. The division walls of the rooms are in brickwork of a fine type: speckled yellow triangles (20·8 × 4·2–4·5 centimetres).[2] Travertine corbels supported a mezzanine floor and the rooms were at a later date floored with selce blocks (as was the portico on to which they faced). The thresholds were approximately 1½ metres wide with marginal check, pivot holes and bolt hole, and the tufa blocks at the doorway were recessed. There was a staircase with a double ramp leading to the upper floor in the centre of this row, the lower ramp being 60 centimetres narrower than the upper to create more room on the ground floor.

The rooms added to the south side, however, were quite different;[3] they were built entirely of brickwork but with different types of bricks. Spur walls were built southward at every other pilaster of the rear wall to create the rooms and staircases. These partition walls were mostly faced with yellow and reddish yellow triangles with an admixture of broken tiles, while the actual front walls of the rooms were faced entirely with broken roof tiles (red and 3·6–4 centimetres thick). The two types of brickwork are dovetailed together in places.[4]

The staircases are of travertine 1·20 metres wide (rise 28 centimetres, tread 31 centimetres) and double corbels to support mezzanines were found in the rooms.

The thresholds to the rooms are odd in that the threshold block is much wider than the actual opening for the doors, and the discrepancy is filled by a thin wall at either side only 30 centimetres wide.[5] Calza says that this shows a *later* narrowing of the doorways, but for this to be true we should have to imagine that the rooms previously had had no doors at all, since there is only one set of pivot holes and bolt hole in each case, namely that for the narrow doorway.

These rooms to the south were built on the remains of some pre-existing rooms, and Calza has suggested that the trapezoidal area in

---

[1] Calza, 'Gli *horrea* tra il Tevere e il decumano', p. 375.
[2] *Scavi* I, Tav. XLIV. 4 (tufa blocks); Tav. L. 3 (brickwork).
[3] *Scavi* I, Tav. LI. 2.
[4] Blake, *Roman Construction from Tiberius*, Plate 20, fig. 3.
[5] Calza, 'Gli *horrea* tra il Tevere e il decumano', fig. 11.

which these southern rooms were built was always intimately connected with the *horrea* and perhaps housed the administration.

Phase 2.[1] After this building activity about the middle of the first century A.D., there are no signs of any major changes until the middle

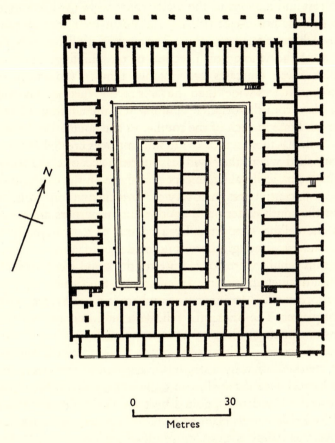

Fig. 12   Ostia, *Grandi Horrea*, phase 2

of the second century A.D. It seems clear that then all the internal rooms of the building except the central block, that is, only the rows on the south, east and west sides facing inwards, and the row on the north side facing outward, were completely rebuilt, but to more or less the same

[1] *Ibid.* fig. 7. Cf. *Scavi* I, fig. 33.

plan (Fig. 12). They were destroyed right to the level of the foundations, which were then raised 30 centimetres in height by the construction of new foundations on top, on which the brick division walls visible today on the south, east and west sides were based. The rebuilding of the north side at this time has left no trace except for the back walls of a room to the east and a room to the west which were used to support two staircases in the north-east (Pl. 19) and north-west corners of the courtyard, which continued to be used even after the later (Severan) reconstruction of the whole north section of the building. The walls which support these staircases are notably thinner (60 centimetres instead of 90 centimetres wide) than the later reconstruction. The main difference in plan from the original building was the addition of these two staircases and one in each of the south-east and south-west corners of the courtyard. All these staircases are not in places created for them but simply attached where they will least impede access to the rooms. All the rooms are basically alike, except that those on the east side had buttresses (68 × 59 centimetres) half way along their division walls, and the rooms in the south-eastern and south-western corners are double rooms with the ceiling supported by a central pier. Presumably all rooms were vaulted, although there is no evidence for this.

The walls thus rebuilt were 60 centimetres thick and faced with fine brickwork of a distinct character, particularly on the façades[1] (Pl. 20): the work is more careless on inner walls where it was covered with a thick layer of plaster. The bricks are yellowish pink in colour, slightly porous, 3–3·5 centimetres thick, 15–25 centimetres long (height of ten courses, 52 centimetres), divided into bands by bipedal courses 1·45 metres apart, marked often by a stripe of red paint. In fact these often prove not to be real *bipedales* at all, and sometimes entered only a short way into the wall. The date suggested by these general characteristics is supported by brick stamps claimed to have been found by Calza of the time of Marcus Aurelius and Commodus.[2]

With this reconstruction of a whole building almost to its original plan but at a slightly higher level and with an extra storey may be connected the introduction in all the rooms of the system of *suspensurae*, that is, raised floors.[3] Running from the back of the rooms to the mouths, a series of low dwarf walls, approximately 30 centimetres wide with

[1] *Scavi* I, pp. 204–5 and Tav. LIV. 2 and 4.
[2] Calza, 'Gli *horrea* tra il Tevere e il decumano', p. 381.   [3] *Ibid.* p. 378.

30 centimetres gaps between them, were built in order to allow a free circulation of air under a floor composed of bipedal bricks laid from the centre of one dwarf wall to the centre of the next, and then built up in layers and covered with crushed sherds (Pl. 21). Sometimes it seems that the dwarf walls themselves were allowed to come right to the mouth of the room as the supports for the travertine threshold; normally two such dwarf walls would appear in the entrance forming a system of two central supports and three ventilation gaps, with the threshold supported at either end by two thin ledges of brickwork (Pl. 22). However, there are not a few examples where the dwarf walls stop short of the entrance, and after a transverse gap a quite independent support system for the threshold is constructed, consisting of a wide central pier, two ventilation gaps and two wide brick supports at either side (Pl. 23). This latter is the type of *suspensurae* used in the *Horrea Antoniniani*, also of Commodan date.

On the south and west sides particularly, buttresses have been added at the entrances to the rooms, 42 centimetres wide and stretching back into the room some 60 centimetres. Often these are not of one build with the entrance wall, but they appear to be contemporary (Pl. 18).

Phase 3.[1] The most dramatic change to occur next was the raising and total rebuilding of the northern section from the portico on the northern façade to the internal portico, an area some 30 metres wide. The whole area was raised 50 centimetres above the level of the internal rooms; the walls were built much thicker, 90 centimetres wide, and the final northern stretch of the tufa wall on the west was encased in brickwork, increasing its thickness from 60 centimetres to 110 centimetres. The front portico was encased in walling, and inside the building the northern portico of the central courtyard was incorporated, making a corridor with three large windows, to east and west of the main entrance corridor, facing south into the courtyard. The two rooms at the east end and two at the west end of the new northern row, however, were extra long in that they incorporated in themselves what had been the internal north portico.

As has been pointed out, the Commodan staircases in this northern section were left in position for a time: their position is easily distinguishable on the plan because of the comparative thinness of their

---

[1] *Scavi* I, fig. 34 and pp. 205–6.

support walls. However, it was not long before two new staircases were built to the south of this corridor (Pl. 24), thus encroaching even further into the central courtyard and causing the blocking of the windows facing south. These staircases were apparently in the form of ramps except for the first eight steps.

To the north of the new range of rooms, the wide corridor on to which they faced was reduced considerably by the construction of three long transverse rooms, flanking the two northern entrances, which blocked the ancient east side entrance and narrowed that on the west side.

The brickwork in the main reconstruction of this northern part has mixed colour bricks of no great width (2·5–3 centimetres), evenly laid, but with fairly wide mortar joints (height of ten courses, 50 centimetres) (Pl. 20, left side). It has been attributed to the Severan period; the addition of the staircases was slightly later. The northern rooms all have raised floors. A travertine threshold carved like those in *Horrea* (Reg. I. Is. VIII. 2) has been preserved (Pl. 25, cf. Pl. 10).

A small square niche is preserved in the front wall of one of these northern rooms; it is framed by small pilasters in brickwork and probably held the statue of some tutelary deity.

It is also clear that the closing of the intercolumniations of the portico on the east, south and west sides of the inner court with brickwork also occurred at this period, since a brick stamp of Severus was found by Calza.[1] Presumably large windows were left in the tops of these infilling walls to give light, and narrow entrances were certainly left at regular intervals (Pl. 26).[2]

The chronology of the other late changes in the building is by no means as clear. Certain it is that the intercolumniations of the portico *outside* the building on the east, and the inner portico around the central block of rooms, were filled with reticulate work: in the case of the outer portico, the work was good, and small rectangular tufa blocks were also used at the corners, while in the inner portico the work was rougher. Uncertain, however, are the dates and the purpose. Perhaps connected with the slighting of the porticoes is the series of small brick piers which were built at regular intervals in the courtyard itself, presumably to create yet more covered space. Calza would

[1] Calza, 'Gli *horrea* tra il Tevere e il decumano', p. 379.
[2] These are well preserved on the east side, see *ibid.* fig. 1.

suppose the closing of the outer portico to be about the middle of the second century A.D., while the inner, in view of the inferior work of the filling, was not closed until the end of the second and beginning of the third century A.D.[1]

It is also clear that the great brick buttresses added to the southern rear wall of the building, which replaced the original smaller buttresses, are contemporary with the Severan raising of the north part. However, it is not so obvious when the water tank was added in the courtyard, nor when precisely the central block of rooms was completely destroyed to threshold level and the whole level of the courtyard was raised; but Calza would place this last in the extraordinarily complicated history of this building.[2]

Summing up

Its size, complexity and solidity, and not least its position, all indicate that the *Grandi Horrea* was a publicly owned storehouse, and the presence of *suspensurae*, at least from the middle of the second century, would indicate that perishable foodstuff, probably corn, was stored in it. The materials of which it was built show the early imperial preoccupation with tufa walling, particularly for storehouses, and the solidity of its construction, whatever its type or period, shows a concern for a strong building able to bear internal stresses. Its plan, predominantly of the usual open courtyard surrounded by ranges of rooms, has the added refinements of a northern range facing straight toward the river and a central block to utilise space otherwise wasted. Its history bears witness to the increasing economic expansion in Ostia in the mid-first century A.D. and attests a constant preoccupation with storage problems through the second century down to Severus, whose interest in the corn supply is mentioned in literary sources,[3] and beyond.[4]

But the building, quite apart from the problems of the stages of its history, poses many more general questions. Why was the northern part so drastically rebuilt and raised when it had already been rebuilt recently? Is this connected with a general raising of level to the north to

[1] *Ibid.* pp. 381–2.   [2] *Ibid.* p. 380.

[3] SHA *Severus*, §8: Rei frumentariae, quam minimam reppererat, ita consuluit ut excedens vita septem annorum canonem populo Romano relinqueret.

[4] A group of post-Constantinian coins was found underneath a fallen wall in the north part of the building, see Calza, 'Gli *horrea* tra il Tevere e il decumano', p. 382.

cope with the rise in the level of the bed of the Tiber? How is one to explain the dearth of entrances into the *horrea*? Presumably there was a wide entrance in the original building, but certainly the latest phase of building makes entry very difficult—and certainly impossible for carts. What was the purpose of closing the colonnades? To create extra room? Is there any connection between this fact and the *intercolumnia* for hire, mentioned in the inscriptions (see *CIL* VI. 33860 and others)? Can one draw any significant conclusion from the fact that the original building had floors of *opus signinum* and that it was not until the second century that *suspensurae* were installed, or is it just chance or a change in the purpose of the building?

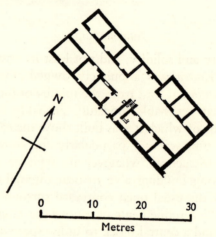

Fig. 13   Ostia, *Horrea* (Reg. III. Is. II. 6)

8 HORREA (Reg. III. Is. II. 6)

General

This building is situated in the western part of Ostia some distance from the Tiber, with its entrance facing south-westwards on to the Via degli Aurighi, an important road running north-west from the western continuation of the *Decumanus Maximus* (Fig. 1).

Essentially its plan consists of two rows of rooms of irregular size ranged on either side of a narrow corridor whose long axis is parallel with the road outside (Fig. 13). It seems clear that the irregular shape of the building is the result of the need to fit it in among the pre-existing buildings around it. Despite the fact that it makes contact with other buildings on three sides, it does not share a common wall with any of them.

The building is firmly dated by a brick stamp to the Trajanic period.[1] Apart from the brick ornamental entrance, the walling is predominantly in tufa reticulate, with quoining in small tufa blocks at doorways and corners. Patches of later brickwork, and *opus listatum*, indicate that the building had a long history.

Most of the walls are in good preservation and stand about 12–15 feet in height.

Description

The building is entered from the Via degli Aurighi through a moderately fine brick entrance (Pl. 27). The doorway itself, 1·90 metres wide, has a travertine threshold with marginal check and recessed door jambs suggesting pivoted doors shutting from the inside; it is framed by two brick columns supporting an ornamental pediment all in brickwork. Immediately to the right of this imposing entrance there is a narrow low postern doorway leading in under the staircase. This doorway, only 70 centimetres wide and 1·60 metres high with a travertine threshold, is constructed, on the side nearest the main entrance, of the same fine brickwork as the latter, while on the other side it is of small tufa blocks: the shallow arch crowning the door is of long tufa bricks.[2] The particular interest of this doorway lies in the system for barring the entrance preserved in the travertine blocks set in the door jambs on either side at a height of approximately 90 centimetres—1 metre from the level of the threshold (Fig. 14). Although here it is on a smaller scale, it is exactly similar to the system employed in the *Horrea Epagathiana*. It consists of a simple oblong hole cut in one block, opposite a hole in the other block, which is similar, except that it has a groove in the brickwork above leading to it and a smaller, deeper hole within the first. It would seem that they were meant for a bar which could be lodged first in the plain hole and then dropped into the grooved one. To prevent the bar being lifted out of position there must have been some locking system at the end of the bar whereby a bolt could be shot into

---

[1] *Scavi* I, p. 222. Cf. Tav. L. 1 and 2; Lugli, *Tecnica*, Tav. CLI. 2.

[2] Similar tufa bricks are used in the relieving arches in south rooms of *Horrea di Hortensius* (Pl. 37).

the second smaller hole and secured, probably by a padlock. Moreover, in order to be effective this outside bar must have dropped into some L-shaped metal brackets attached to the door itself. It seems that this system of barring the doors was applied not only on the outside; in this particular case, on the south side approximately 8–9 centimetres in from the inner edge of the kerb of the threshold and at its lowest point some 85 centimetres above the ground level, there is a long slot cut

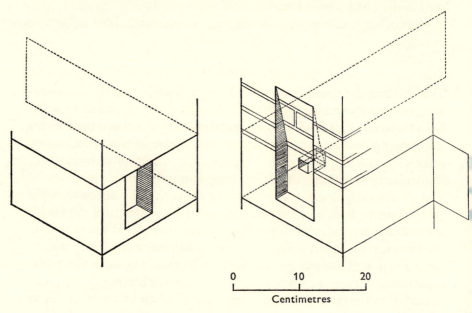

Fig. 14   Ostia, *Horrea* (Reg. III. Is. II. 6), small postern door,
locking devices

into the tufa block quoining (10 centimetres wide and 8 centimetres deep at the bottom, some 39 centimetres high including the shallow grooving). Similar slots in the brickwork occur inside the main entrance (where, on the other hand, the travertine blocks have no slots cut in them). It is noticeable that where both inside and outside barring slots are preserved, the side for actually locking the bar into position alternates.

The main entrance and its corridor, defined by a second threshold further in, lead straight to the heart of the building: a small court paved with *opus spicatum* (Pl. 28). Opposite the corridor is a recessed stretch of walling with a semicircular niche in it 1·60 metres from the ground, the base composed of two travertine console brackets, 1·20 metres apart, linked by moulded brickwork; the top of the niche is not preserved.[1] To left and right open out two corridors of different width, each flanked by three rooms on each side, although they too differ in size one from another.

However, all the room entrances have the same dimensions and pattern (Pl. 29): 1 metre wide at their narrowest, they are all built with recessed door jambs in small oblong tufa blocks, and small rectangular windows immediately above the doorways.

The side walls to the rooms are composed of a curious type of what can only be called tufa 'rubble work' (Pl. 30). This consists of odd-shaped lumps of tufa set anyhow in mortar, but presenting a relatively flat surface. These walls, however, are clearly contemporary with the reticulate structure in general (e.g. room to left of entrance corridor: faced with reticulate on public side, with tufa rubble work on the other).

A particularly intriguing feature which occurs on the back wall in the corners of some of the rooms (in at least five) is a small L-shaped slot (Pl. 30); generally 70 centimetres–1 metre above the ground, it extends some 40–5 centimetres from the side wall with a width of 10 centimetres—at this point it turns a right angle and extends vertically up the back wall with a slightly reduced width of 8–9 centimetres for some 26–8 centimetres. Its significance is not known to me.

The rooms, particularly those backing on to the Via degli Aurighi, have in their back wall a splayed slit window set high up. These windows are built of small tufa blocks but often are defined at top and bottom by a single large brick. There are also examples of small square windows set even higher in the side walls of some of the rooms on the north-eastern side, thus forming inter-room windows.

Opposite the staircase which led to an upper floor, immediately next to the recess with the niche and flush against the front wall of a room, is a square pillar composed of long tufa blocks (Pl. 28).

Structurally the building is interesting because of its combination of wall facings. The brickwork of the main entrance façade is composed of fine-grained pink bricks 3–3·5 centimetres thick and 18–22 centi-

[1] This niche probably held a small statue of a tutelary deity, cf. similar niches in *Horrea Epagathiana et Epaphroditiana,* and *Grandi Horrea.*

metres long, regularly laid with thin mortar joints (height of ten courses is 40 centimetres). The brickwork on the inner side of the main entrance, however, is laid with much thicker mortar joints (height of ten courses is 51 centimetres).

The reticulate work used as a facing in the majority of the walls is composed of tufa cubes, 9 centimetres in diameter, evenly set to form the fish-net pattern. A band of brickwork is visible at the bottom of the façade wall on the Via degli Aurighi and another above mezzanine level; the area between is entirely reticulate work. The small tufa blocks used for quoining are of a standard size.

The side walls of the rooms, however, some 45 centimetres thick, are composed of the rubble-work mentioned above.

No thresholds are preserved in any of the room doorways.

There is no indication as to how it was roofed.

Summing up

Its small size and irregular plan make it unlikely that it was a State storehouse. Its size and the locking devices preserved at the postern door (and presumably typical of the room doorways as well, although this is conjecture, since the original blocks have disappeared) bring it into line with the *Horrea Epagathiana et Epaphroditiana* rather than with the *Piccolo Mercato* or *Grandi Horrea*. It may have been a storehouse for private purposes, or for more costly goods, or perhaps a small example of the 'safe-deposit' *horrea*, in view of its locking devices.

It is a good example of the care that must be taken when discussing the dates of building styles; if the only guide had been the style of construction, a much earlier date would have suggested itself than the Trajanic one made certain by the level and the brick stamp.

9 HORREA (Reg. IV. Is. V. 12)

General

This building is situated to the south of the continuation of the *Decumanus Maximus* beyond the Forum. As it stands at present it is curiously inaccessible, being approached only from the south (Fig. 1). To the north it is cut off from the *Decumanus Maximus* by the Terme delle Sei Colonne; to the west it is bounded by the Schola del Traiano and to the east by the Cortile del Dionisio, although there is a doorway in the back wall of the middle room on the eastern side of the *horrea* leading into this cortile. Even on the south side its entrance is not on a roadway but forms the end of a kind of *cul-de-sac*, which presumably debouched into a road as yet unexcavated.

This inaccessibility must be the result of later planning and building in the area, since the *horrea* is dated by its almost exclusively reticulate construction to a period very early in the first century A.D.[1]

The building is very small and consists of six rooms, three on either side of a wide central corridor, with a blank wall at the end of the corridor facing the entrance (Fig. 15).

The southernmost room on the east side was later converted into a Mithraeum, the Mitreo delle Sette Porte.[2]

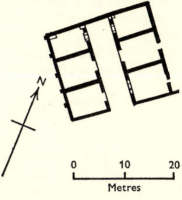

0	10	20

Metres

Fig. 15   Ostia, *Horrea*
(Reg. IV. Is. V. 12)

Description

The building is entered now from the south through an imposing brick archway, which seems to belong to the complex of buildings (of Hadrianic date) just *outside* the *horrea* to the south rather than to the *horrea* itself (Pl. 31). Certainly this brick archway was simply built against the older walls of our building and is of quite different character and materials.

The entrance way leads straight into a wide central corridor 4·80 metres approximately wide, on to which open three rooms on each side. The rooms, with entrances 2·34 metres wide, are faced with tufa reticulate work with quoining in small tufa blocks (7·5–8 centimetres high, 22–5 centimetres long and 8–10 centimetres deep) at the doorways, and sometimes in the corners of the rooms. The façades of the front division walls between the rooms have panels of brickwork in the centre dovetailed with the tufa-block work in three-course insets,

[1] *Scavi* II, p. 93, but cf. Blake, *Roman Construction from Tiberius*, p. 66.
[2] *Scavi* II, Tav. XIX ff.; dated *circa* A.D. 160–70.

but all these façades show signs of much reorganisation, and Miss Blake suggests that probably none of it is original.

At the northern end of the *horrea*, built flush against the northern retaining wall of the building, are three great buttresses composed of oblong travertine blocks (Pl. 32). The biggest is in the north-west corner of the north-west room, and is composed of blocks with dimensions (three layers are preserved) 74 centimetres wide, 68 centimetres high and 1·20 metres long, although they tend to become smaller higher up. The other two buttresses are composed of slightly

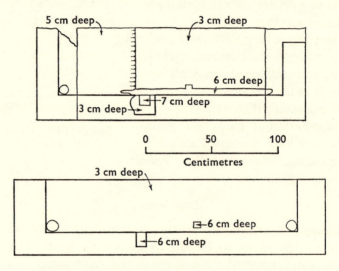

Fig. 16   Ostia, *Horrea* (Reg. IV. Is. V. 12), thresholds

shorter blocks and are placed at the junction between the north wal and the front walls of the two most northerly rooms. It seems clear that whatever their precise date and purpose, these travertine piers were built at a date later than the west and north walls of the *horrea*, whose reticulate facing passes behind them, but earlier than the front walls of the rooms into which they have been incorporated, and which we have seen reason to believe above were much reorganised at a later date.

There was possibly a small back door to the building at the north-west end of the central corridor, where some tufa quoining is preserved 80 centimetres from the front wall of the north-west room (Pl. 32).

Certainly its use must have ended with the construction of the Trajanic Terme delle Sei Colonne.

There was certainly a side entrance to the building on the east in the back wall of the central room, 1·20 metres wide and with the usual quoining in small tufa blocks.

Four thresholds are preserved in the building (one in the room opposite the Mitreo delle Sette Porte not marked on the plan in *Scavi* I). Three of them are all of the same type, with marginal check, two pivot holes, a small central bolt hole in the usual position and another larger one in the kerb itself. One, however, in the north-west room, although originally of this type, was converted at a later time into a type commonly found in shops, that is, a long groove was cut along the front of the threshold for holding upright plank shutters, and a shallow wide depression was cut at one end of the threshold for sliding these into position (Fig. 16).

The walls are about 60 centimetres thick, and there is no evidence for the roofing arrangements.

Summing up

Its size and simplicity of layout would suggest a small, privately owned storage place of some merchant, and this would be borne out by its location well away from the public land near the river bank.

Its interest lies in that it seems typical of the smaller, privately owned storehouses with rooms ranged on either side of a corridor. Its converted threshold is of particular interest in that it is the only threshold of this type in *horrea* in Ostia. This conversion and the transformation of one of the rooms into a mithraeum *circa* A.D. 160–70 would suggest that it ceased to be a storeplace during the second century of the Empire.

10 HORREA DELL'ARTEMIDE (Reg. V. Is. XI. 8)

General

Situated on the south side of the *Decumanus* opposite the Theatre and immediately west of the *Horrea di Hortensius*, the building is trapezoidal in shape in that its eastern wall accommodates itself to the line of the *Horrea di Hortensius* (Fig. 1).

It was built over the remains of earlier buildings including a house whose tufa peristyle is laid bare in the south-eastern corner of the courtyard, and thus the level of its inner court is higher than that of the earlier *Horrea di Hortensius*.

Its plan (Fig. 17) consists of the usual ranges of rooms on the three sides east, west and south, facing on to a central court, basically a

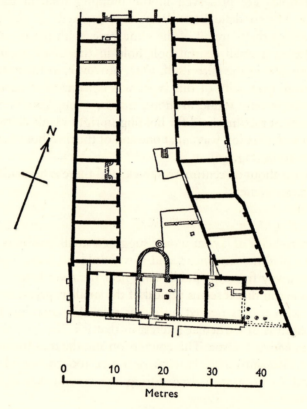

Fig. 17   Ostia, *Horrea dell'Artemide*

rectangle pulled out of shape at the south-east corner (Pl. 33). There is no portico.

The building is known to be of Trajanic date because of brick stamps found bedded in the structure,[1] but its large reticulate panels and sparing use of bricks make it look rather earlier.

[1] H. Bloch, *Suppl.* No. 252 (*Harvard Studies in Classical Philology* LVI–LVII (1947), 1–128). See *Scavi* I, p. 199.

It clearly had a long history and there are many traces of later work notably in the apsidal feature on the south side and in the closing and patching of rooms at the north-west corner in Severan times and later (Pl. 34).

The building received its present name from a statue found in the central courtyard.

Description

The building is entered from the *Decumanus* through an entrance corridor flanked by shops. The level of this corridor and the shops and their portico, all later work, is very much higher (1 metre?) than that of the *Decumanus*, which accounts for the fact that even though the inner courtyard must be at the level of, if not higher than, the *Decumanus*, it is necessary to step down into the *horrea* from the entrance corridor.

The north wall of the *horrea* itself is divided from the back walls of the shops by a space later partitioned off. The main threshold, 2·50 metres wide, is framed by the remains of two brick pilasters. The threshold has a marginal check and a number of pivot holes for doors opening inwards. To the east of this main doorway is another narrower opening approximately 1·20 metres wide, with, instead of a proper threshold, a smooth marble sill with two pivot holes in it.

The rooms ranged on the three sides vary in size, but have a fairly constant doorway width of 1·75 metres. I could find no thresholds preserved, but across the mouth of each room is a stretch of ruined brickwork, the width of the door jambs.

It was possible to enter the narrow alley between this building and the *Horrea di Hortensius* either from the space between the north wall of the *horrea* and the shops on the *Decumanus*, or by a doorway in the back wall of a room half way along the east side.

Generally, the construction of the rooms consists of walls of reticulate based on brickwork, with brickwork used at doorways and dovetailed into the reticulate in five-course insets. But there are variations. For example, in some of the north rooms on the east side brick panels with five-course insets are set half way along the division walls of the rooms, much in the manner of those in the *Horrea di Hortensius*, and in some of the south rooms on the east side a brick buttress (60 centimetres wide) is set half way along the back walls, projecting 60 centimetres into the rooms.

The bricks, half *bessales*,[1] are 26–8 centimetres in length, 3·5–4 centimetres thick (height of ten courses, 56 centimetres) and pinkish yellow in colour.

It is no longer possible to see how either the rooms or the central court were paved.

There are no traces of staircases: therefore it was presumably only of one storey.

There is no evidence as to how the building was roofed.

Summing up

The main interest of this building lies in the fact that in plan it seems to be half way between a courtyard storehouse and a corridor storehouse. Its size and storage capacity rate it almost alongside the *Hortensius* and the *Piccolo Mercato*, if not the *Grandi Horrea*, but it differs from all these in that it has no portico and the rooms open straight on to the central court.

It is one of the few *horrea* placed south of the *Decumanus Maximus* and is not very well situated for direct communication with the Tiber.

II HORREA DI HORTENSIUS (Reg. V. Is. XII. I)

General

The building is situated south of the *Decumanus Maximus*, approximately 300 metres from the *Porta Romana*, that is, almost opposite the Theatre–Foro delle Corporazioni complex (Fig. 1).

It consists of a large rectangular courtyard surrounded on all four sides by ranges of long narrow rooms (Fig. 18): the whole set back from the *Decumanus* and divided from it by a colonnade and complex of shops flanking the street itself.[2]

The shape of the internal courtyard is a perfect rectangle, but because it is set at a slight angle to the line of the *Decumanus*, the depth of the rooms on the north side of the cortile varies, becoming progressively shallower towards the east. A further anomaly in general shape is that the east and west containing walls of the *horrea* run parallel with the axis of the internal courtyard in the north part of the building, but at a

[1] See *Scavi* I, p. 208.　　　　　[2] *Scavi* I, Tav. XL. 2.

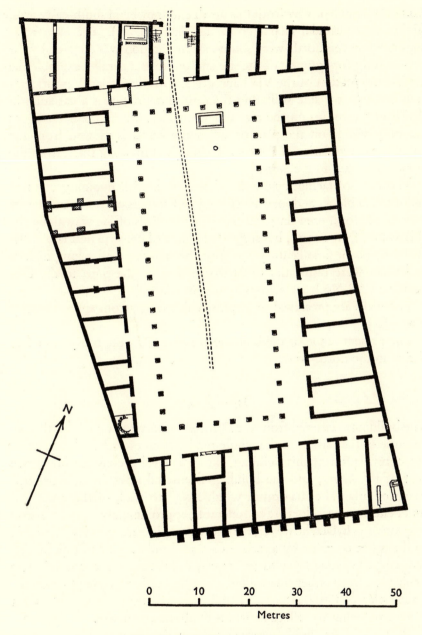

| 0 | 10 | 20 | 30 | 40 | 50 |

Metres

Fig. 18 Ostia, *Horrea di Hortensius*

point less than half way from this north end they bend south-eastwards, giving a trapezoidal character to the plan (Pl. 35). The excavators suggest[1] that this north-west–south-east orientation was dictated by the pre-existing topography of the site and quote as a parallel example the similar orientation of the Via Laurentina. This dissimilarity in orientation between the side walls and the central court causes a variation in depth in the rooms on the east and west sides, but all these variations are only visible on the plan or when the *horrea* is viewed from the theatre, the regularity of the central courtyard masking them from the person standing in the *horrea*.

The style of facing, *opus reticulatum* in tufa with quoining of small oblong tufa blocks at doorways (Pl. 36) and corners of rooms and a very little brickwork, used simply in panels two-thirds of the way along the side walls of the rooms, has suggested a date of construction late in the first half of the first century A.D. But the building had a long history and there were restorations of parts of it from the third to the fifth century A.D.[2] No brick stamps are recorded.

The walls are preserved to heights which range from approximately 3 to 6 feet.

The present name of the building is taken from the mosaic in a late shrine in the north-west corner of the courtyard.

Description

The building is entered from the *Decumanus Maximus* on the north side. Because of the raising of the whole road system of Ostia subsequent to the construction of this building, the road level is considerably above that of the *horrea*, and the building is entered now down four steps made of tufa. The maximum widths, wall to wall, of the outer and inner entrance corridors are considerable, approximately 12 and 9 metres respectively. In fact, however, the effective widths are severely restricted: in the outer corridor by a series of squared pillars built of tufa blocks, reducing the passage way to 3·7 metres, and in the inner corridor by the projection from either side wall of a feature marked as a staircase on the Italian plan of Ostia, although I could see no clear evidence as to what it was, reducing the effective width to about 4·5 metres.

There is no threshold preserved in the main entrance. The dominant

[1] *Scavi* I, p. 118.　　　　　　　　　　　[2] *Scavi* I, p. 153.

internal feature of the *horrea* is the long rectangular (62 × 25 metres approximately) colonnade surrounding the central courtyard, which was open to the sky and has a long drain running down the middle of it. The columns are made of drums of tufa with finely carved Doric capitals, except for the angle columns which are entirely of travertine.

The width of the colonnade is, with minor variations, just over 5 metres, except at the north-west corner where the construction in the late third and early fourth century of the small shrine of Hortensius reduced the passage to 1·65 metres. There is no evidence as to the flooring of the colonnade still visible: possibly, as in the case of all other *horrea* where evidence is preserved, some form of *opus spicatum* was used. The north and south 'wings' of the colonnade extend beyond the immediate limits of the courtyard and thus give access to the rooms which range along the whole north and south sides. In the east wall of the building, accessible from the east extension of the south colonnade, was a small door, 1 metre approximately wide, which was later filled in.

The rooms vary, as has been indicated, in their dimensions, although in general the rooms along the south side are considerably deeper than those on any other side. (Representative measurements of a room on the south side—5·30 × 14·75 metres: compare room on north side flanking entrance corridor—5·22 × 9·10 metres: but of course the tilted plan of the *horrea* makes definitive statements about room dimensions difficult, e.g. north end of west side—5·5 × 13·90 metres: whereas south end of west side—9·52 × 4·52 metres at shallowest depth.)

The entrances of the rooms, however, show more consistency in their measurements, as one would expect. In general, the width of the doorways is 1·70–1·80 metres. The rooms are faced with good quality *opus reticulatum*, the small tufa cubes measuring 7 centimetres across the diameter, but at the corners of the rooms and at the doorways sections of small rectangular tufa blocks (20–30 × 8–8·5 × 8–11 centimetres) are used, dovetailed into the reticulate in three-course insets. This quoining extends over the whole face of the front wall of a room at certain points where two sections of such quoining would overlap or render the size of the reticulate panel so small as to be not worth the bother, for example, the west front wall of the room immediately east of the entrance corridor, and the east front wall of the north-easternmost room of the *horrea*[1] (Pl. 36). In the doorways, and set close against the

---

[1] *Scavi* I, Tav. XLIX. 4.

jambs of tufa blocks, are two travertine blocks, each with one pivot hole cut in the top towards the front. Between these two travertine blocks are often visible remains of brickwork which filled in the gap and formed the threshold. This is an example of the sparing use of travertine in the early Empire when it was employed only at points of stress. As in later *horrea* in Ostia, the room entrances were closed by means of doors hung on pivots.

The long side walls of the rooms are reinforced by a panel of brick-work set about half way along, interlocked with the *opus reticulatum* by five-course insets.[1] The bricks, half *bessales*,[2] are yellowish pink in colour, 3–4 centimetres thick, 20–1 centimetres in length and are tailed deeply into the wall. On the south side only there is a relieving arch in each of the long side walls of the rooms, which springs from ground level immediately to the south of the central brick panel (Pl. 37). These small relieving arches composed of bricks on the side nearest the brick panel are in the main constructed of tufa blocks *circa* 9 × 22·5 centimetres and presuppose some drain which runs under all these southern rooms.

Except for the brick panels in the side walls of the rooms, there is no other brickwork which dates from the original construction. There are, however, stretches of brick wall in the north-east retaining wall of the *horrea* and in the south wall and several rooms at the north end of the west side. These all represent later reconstruction, sometimes in *opus reticulatum* divided into panels by brick bonding courses, as in the south wall, sometimes in brickwork only, as in the four rooms on the west side, reconstructed under Severus.

In certain rooms on the south and west sides brick buttresses were later introduced to support some of the walls.

The most unusual room is a small, shallow one on the south side which has been created by cutting off part of the usual long southern room. It is marked out not only by its shape but by its wide threshold composed of travertine blocks with holes cut in them, which suggest they held perhaps a metal screen set in them. A shrine? Whatever it was, the threshold was very little used: it is in good condition, with sharp and unworn edges.

The only evidence now visible for the flooring of the rooms is in a restored room in the north-eastern corner where an *opus spicatum* floor is suggested. But on the whole the most likely flooring at this date

---

[1] *Scavi* I, fig. 43, Tav. XLIX. 3.   [2] *Scavi* I, p. 196.

would be the beaten *opus signinum* floors discovered by Calza in the early levels of the *Grandi Horrea*. Certainly there seems no evidence for the existence of *suspensurae* allowing the circulation óf air beneath the floors—at least not in brick or stone.[1]

There is no evidence as to how the building was roofed. The walls are thick enough to support concrete vaults (52 centimetres front walls, 60 centimetres side walls). At such an early date, however, and in so large a building perhaps one should posit a timber system of beams and king posts for the roof rather than the concrete vaults of later *horrea*.

Summing up

The *Horrea di Hortensius* is one of the few large *horrea* which lie south of the *Decumanus Maximus*, but it is well positioned, with its entrance placed on the north side and has direct communication with the Tiber by means of the road running along the east side of the Theatre–Foro delle Corporazioni complex.

As a whole the building is clearly demarcated from the buildings on either side of it—particularly on the west side from the later (Trajanic) *Horrea dell'Artemide*. A clear division some 2 metres wide runs between the two buildings.

The size of its court gives it an elegance of proportion slightly unusual and represents a time at Ostia, which was not to be repeated, when such buildings might be allowed to spread. Later under Hadrian even the larger *horrea*, such as the *Piccolo Mercato*, show much greater concern with saving space.

However this may be, the *Horrea di Hortensius* was not demolished and rebuilt entirely, but continued in its original form right down to late antiquity.

Its size and obvious importance would suggest perhaps public ownership and connection with the corn supply, but there is no evidence for this.

Its early date is reflected also in its style of building and its use of materials, particularly in its sparing use of travertine for thresholds.

---

[1] Meiggs, p. 280, includes *Horrea di Hortensius* among those storehouses with permanently raised floors, but I could find no evidence for them, and Dr Squarciapino, via Dr M. Ballance, confirmed that none were found in the excavation of the building.

MISCELLANEOUS HORREA

In addition to the *horrea* already described individually, there are in Ostia others which for various reasons may be dealt with more summarily. The main reason in most cases is either that they are not fully excavated or that little remains of their structure. There are three buildings, however, which can be dealt with here because I do not believe that they were strictly *horrea*, although they bear that label on the plan of Ostia.

The first is the so-called *Horrea dei Mensores* (Reg. I. Is. XIX. 4) built under Trajan on the north side of the Via della Foce. The south-east corner of the whole ensemble was cut off from the remainder and provided space for the Aula and Temple of the *mensores*. The remainder of the building was grouped about an oblong central court. A single group of rooms flanked the court on the east and a double group on the west. This double group was originally divided down the centre by a continuous wall so that one series of rooms opened into the court to the east, the other on to an alley to the west, paved with *opus spicatum*, which surrounded the group on three sides and separated the perimetral walls from the so-called *horrea* proper. The perimetral wall on the Via della Foce had a foundation of one or two courses of reused (?) tufa blocks and was pierced by two entrances, one leading to the main courtyard, the other into the alleyway. A wide ramp in the south-east corner gave access to an upper storey. The shape and grouping of the rooms on both sides of the court were most unusual. Rooms of ordinary dimensions were alternated with chambers of enormous width (some 12 metres) whose roofs had to be supported by central piers.

The building was constructed either of brick alone or of brick with insets of reticulate work. The bricks were light reddish brown, 3·5–4 centimetres thick and of fine-grained texture. *Bipedales* were used at the base of walls, but no bonding courses or relieving arches were visible.

Although it is clear, both from its plan and its position near the river, that this building had a commercial purpose, it seems to me more likely that it was used as a corn measuring centre rather than as *horrea* proper. The comparative spaciousness and openness of the plan suggest that manoeuvrability rather than storage capacity was aimed at.

Immediately to the west of the *Horrea dei Mensores*, with only a small bath suite interposed between them, was another building constructed slightly later, A.D. 125-6, although called the *Horrea Traiani* (Reg. I. Is. XX. I). The name was given because the building bore a superficial resemblance to Trajan's Market in Rome and from the presence of a few Trajanic brick stamps.

The building is composed of three units: (*a*) four shops opening on to the Via della Foce and orientated with it rather than with the rest of the building; (*b*) five halls modified in course of construction and even more drastically later; (*c*) a long barrel-vaulted hall on to which opened rooms from either side. The most interesting feature is the barrel-vaulted hall. Wide doorways with flat arches of upright *bipedales* under great relieving arches open off it. The pilasters framing them have moulded tile string courses at the level where capitals would have been. The bricks of the façades are fine-grained, reddish brown and vary in thickness from 3 to 3·5 centimetres. There are bonding courses of *bipedales* and in the arches every fifth or sixth tile is whole, to act as a bonding member. Fallen vaulting shows smallish tufa *caementa* closely laid. Two wide staircases led to an upper storey, above the barrel-vaulted hall which was paved with coarse black and white mosaic. The ground floor rooms are ventilated and lighted by splayed windows, one in the back wall of each room. The whole building is now surrounded by barbed wire and more or less inaccessible. The plan and the general quality of the building make it unlikely that it was simply *horrea*. The barrel-vaulted hall may well have been a market hall which could be entered straight from the Tiber wharves.

Outside the *Porta Marina* in south-west Ostia another building, designated as *Horrea* (Reg. IV. Is. VIII. 5), was constructed in the Hadrianic period. It is situated to the south and west of the Foro di Porta Marina and the Temple of the Bona Dea and consists of a range of long spacious rooms aligned behind an arcade of brick piers along the Via di Cartilio Poplicola. Traces of a black and white mosaic pavement with geometric patterns are still visible in the portico. It is difficult to see why the building was regarded as *horrea*. It shows none of the characteristics of other *horrea* in Ostia. Moreover, ranges of long spacious rooms along the streets of Ostia are quite common. The rooms in this building are no more suited to *horrea* than, for example, those of the so-called 'Caseggiato della fontana con lucerna' just inside the *Porta Marina*.

Apart from these three buildings, in my view, identified falsely as *horrea*, there are four more buildings at Ostia which were quite clearly *horrea*, but of which so little remains that they may be described in brief.

Horrea (Reg. v. Is. i. 2) was constructed towards the middle of the first century A.D. on the east side of the Semita dei Cippi just inside the *Porta Laurentina*. This street was of great importance in Ostia in that it led directly north to the *Decumanus Maximus* opposite the Via dei Molini which led again to the Tiber bank. The building was quite large (some 59 × 45 metres) and consisted of a series of small rooms (7 × 4 metres) opening on to an internal courtyard. The retaining wall on the Semita dei Cippi was constructed in squared tufa blocks now completely robbed except at the corner. The other walls of the building are of concrete faced with tufa reticulate. The quoining at the doorways is carried out *not* in small tufa blocks, as in the *Horrea di Hortensius*, but in neat dovetailing of bricks made from broken tiles. This brickwork, at least on the façade towards the central court, is extremely elegant: the bricks are hard and fine-grained, made from reddish tiles, *circa* 3·5 centimetres thick (height of ten courses, 37·5 centimetres) and set with extremely fine and even mortar joints made possible by anathyrosis. The face of the door jamb inside the room has similar bricks less carefully laid. The two types of brickwork are dovetailed together in the jamb with three-course insets. The façade bricks are dovetailed with the reticulate work in five-course insets. The building is only partially excavated, but it is clear that considerable renovation and remodelling was carried out in the fourth century A.D.

Immediately to the north of the *Piccolo Mercato* and built at the same period is a building which was probably *horrea* (Reg. i. Is. vii. 2). Only the shops flanking the roads have been fully excavated and we have no knowledge of its internal arrangements. A relief plaque (representing a corn *modius* and measuring rod) over the doorway indicates the building's commercial character.

East of the *Horrea di Hortensius* another large *horrea* was erected in the early Hadrianic period (A.D. 120–5), a date confirmed by brick stamps. The building consisted of a large rectangular courtyard surrounded by rows of rooms, although the internal arrangements are not well known. The *horrea* proper is set back from the *Decumanus Maximus*, just as the *Horrea di Hortensius* and *Horrea dell'Artemide* are set back, in order to accommodate six shops and their back quarters which flanked the main street. The entrance to the *horrea* is set mid-way between the six shops and the entrance corridor is very narrow (some 2 metres wide). The north retaining wall of the *horrea* is thicker than usual (approximately 1 metre thick) and is buttressed on the outside. A flight of stairs opens off the entrance corridor before the entrance to the *horrea* proper, and whether it led to rooms above the shops or to an upper floor of the *horrea* is uncertain. The west wall of the *horrea* is separated from the *Horrea di Hortensius* by a narrow space with occasional buttressing between the two walls. The long east wall of the *horrea* abutting on to the Via del Sabazeo is broken by only two doorways. This wall is faced with tufa reticulate panels framed by wide bands of brickwork. The partition walls of the internal rooms were faced with a rough *incertum* of tufa pieces. The only partition walls completely unearthed are those containing the so-called Sabazeo, and they show quoining in small tufa blocks at the door jambs.

Even more fragmentary is our knowledge of a great building which was almost certainly *horrea*, situated at the western edge of the excavations. Its great eastern wall and parts of its southern wall, both reinforced by heavy buttresses, are visible behind the *Serapeum* in Region III. It was an enormous building extending from the Via della Foce to the Cardo degli Aurighi. The east wall of the building and its great buttresses are faced entirely with brickwork, probably Severan in date. The partition walls seem to belong to an earlier period and are faced with *opus mixtum* (reticulate and a little brickwork), but even these walls show signs of much reorganisation.

Although these miscellaneous *horrea* do not add significantly to our knowledge of structural detail, they help to reinforce the overall impression already gained. Further, they help to recall that there were many more *horrea* in Ostia than have yet been excavated. This fact must make the drawing of general conclusions concerning the *horrea* at Ostia a matter of delicate judgement.

DOLIA DEFOSSA

One final group of buildings in Ostia, quite unlike the *horrea* so far described, remains to be discussed.

The buildings concerned each consist simply of a walled area, in which a number of great earthenware jars were embedded in the ground almost up to their necks.

We know from the elder Pliny[1] that it was customary in temperate climates to store wine in such sunken jars. The jars were called *dolia*. *Dolia*, of course, need not be embedded in the ground and could be used for storage of almost anything, liquids such as wine and oil, solids

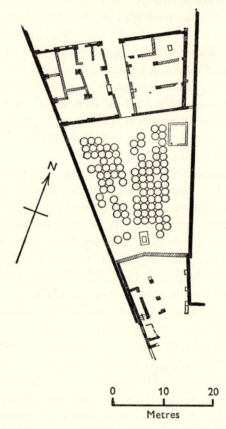

Fig. 19   Ostia, Magazzino Annonario, with *dolia defossa*

such as grain, fruit, ham and even Diogenes himself.[2] When the jars were sunk into the ground, various terms were used to designate this. We hear of *dolia demissa*, or *defixa* or *depressa*,[3] but the most common usage, particularly in the legal passages in the *Digest*, was *dolia defossa*.[4]

[1] Pliny, *NH* 14. 133, 134.   [2] *Thes. Ling. Lat.*, s.v. *dolium*.
[3] Columella 12. 18. 6; *Digest* 32. 93. 4 (Scaevola); *Digest* 33. 6. 3. 1.
[4] *Digest* 7. 1. 15. 6 (Ulpian); 18. 1. 76 (Paulus).

The lawyers' interest in these sunken jars was concerned particularly with sale; for example, whether the embedded jars automatically were sold with the building concerned and what was the legal position in respect to jars that leaked.

In Ostia four concentrations of these *dolia defossa* have so far been discovered: the so-called Magazzino dei dolii[1] (Reg. III. Is. XIV. 3), which was next to the house of Annius, an oil merchant; the so-called Caseggiato dei dolii (Reg. I. Is. IV. 5), located immediately below the Museum at Ostia; the so-called Magazzino annonario (Reg. V. Is. XI. 5) (Fig. 19), with over one-hundred sunken jars, located south of the *Decumanus Maximus* beside the *Horrea dell'Artemide*; and finally, a building excavated in the late eighteenth century on the Tiber bank near the *Horrea dei Mensores*.[2]

So far as we can judge from the facings of the walls of these deposits, they were all created in the Hadrianic period when so many of Ostia's commercial activities were stimulated and so much of Ostia was replanned and rebuilt. The numbers of jars in these buildings naturally varied. The building near the Tiber had at least twenty-two jars, the Caseggiato some thirty-five jars, while the Magazzino annonario had over one-hundred.

Some of the jars near the Museum had been mended in antiquity with lead strips, and in many cases the capacity of the jar was incised, after firing, on the lip of the vessel.[3] The capacity of the jars near the Tiber varied between 23 and 45 *amphorae*, the average size being 33 *amphorae*. In the area below the Museum the jars were slightly larger still, ranging from a minimum of $28\frac{1}{2}$ *amphorae* to a maximum of 47 *amphorae*, with the average size about 40 *amphorae* (40 *amphorae* is equivalent to 230 gallons). If each *dolium* held about 200 gallons, the Caseggiato had a total capacity of 8,500 gallons and the Magazzino annonario a capacity of more than 20,000 gallons.

Almost certainly it was wine or oil, and not grain, that was stored in these Ostian *dolia defossa*, and given the position of at least three of the deposits, well away from the Tiber, it is likely that they were for storing wine or oil for Ostian consumption rather than wine or oil for

[1] R. Calza, E. Nash, *Ostia* (Florence, 1960), Pl. 107.
[2] J. Carcopino, 'Ostiensia—I. Glanures épigraphiques', *Mélanges*, XXIX (1909), 359 and Pls. XX, XXI.
[3] G. Gatti, 'Ostia—Rinvenimento di dolii frumentarii', *NSc* (1903), p. 201.

Rome. Goods for Rome would more likely remain in their own containers ready for reshipment up the Tiber.[1] In Rome itself *cellae vinariae*[2] might very often have been provided with such *dolia defossa* of their own.

Dolia defossa must in fact have been very common in many farmsteads and *villae rusticae*, as at Boscoreale, near Pompeii.[3] The interest of the Ostian examples is that they show how in an area where the majority of the inhabitants lived in *insulae*, without their own storage space, storage for liquids tended to be concentrated at specific points and that the storage capacity available could be quite considerable.

HORREA AT OSTIA: GENERAL CONCLUSIONS

Position

The eastern section of the *Decumanus Maximus* ran for its whole length parallel to the ancient course of the River Tiber, and it is a significant fact that most of the important *horrea* in Ostia so far excavated lie to the north of it.[4] This is not surprising. The section to the north of the *Decumanus Maximus* must always have been the most convenient for the landing and storage of goods, and its public importance was recognised early, as the Caninius' *cippi* show.[5] The only notable exceptions to this rule are the two Julio-Claudian buildings, *Horrea di Hortensius* (Reg. v. Is. xii. 1) and *Horrea* (Reg. v. Is. 1. 2) at the south end of the Semita dei Cippi, and the Trajanic *Horrea dell'Artemide* (Reg. v. Is. xi. 8), although they are each situated on or near a direct route to the Tiber. The Claudian *Grandi Horrea* (Reg. ii. Is. ix. 7), the whole group of *horrea* developed by Hadrian north of the Forum and the Commodan *Horrea Antoniniani* (Reg. ii. Is. ii. 7) are all situated north of the *Decumanus Maximus*. For the same reason almost all the important *horrea* have their façades and entrances on the north side for speed and ease of receiving and sending goods. There are exceptions, of course, but these are for the most part small storehouses of few rooms with a 'corridor' plan. Ostia itself was essentially a river port, and the position and orientation of the *horrea* reflect that fact.

[1] Meiggs, p. 275. [2] *CIL* vi. 8826.
[3] A. Mau (trans. F. Kelsey), *Pompeii* (New York, 1899), p. 358, and Plan iv. But at Boscoreale wine was produced, not simply stored.
[4] For distribution of *horrea* in Ostia, see Fig. 1.
[5] Cf. Meiggs, p. 32. C. Caninius, c.f. pr(aetor) urb(anus) de sen(atus) sent(entia) poplic(um) ioudic(avit).

Design

Rigorous division into types is often misleading.[1] The avowed aim of this is greater clarity and systematisation: the result is often a strait-jacket in which nothing sits comfortably. So far as the *horrea* at Ostia are concerned, it seems advisable to make only a general division between two main types: (*a*) the quadrangle type; (*b*) the corridor type.

Examples of the quadrangle type are the *Horrea di Hortensius* (Reg. v. Is. xii. 1) (Fig. 18), *Grandi Horrea* (Reg. ii. Is. ix. 7) (Fig. 10), *Horrea dell'Artemide* (Reg. v. Is. xi. 8) (Fig. 17), *Piccolo Mercato* (Reg. i. Is. viii. 1) (Fig. 2), *Horrea* (Reg. i. Is. viii. 2) and the *Horrea Epagathiana et Epaphroditiana* (Reg. i. Is. viii. 3) (Fig. 3).

Examples of the corridor type are *Horrea* (Reg. iii. Is. ii. 6) (Fig. 13), *Horrea* (Reg. i. Is. xiii. 1) (Fig. 7), *Horrea* (Reg. iii. Is. xvii. 1) (Fig. 8) and *Horrea* (Reg. iv. Is. v. 12) (Fig. 15).

Within each type there is variety. The shape and dimensions of the quadrangle may vary. The small courtyard of the *Horrea Epagathiana* is like that of a house, something which could not be said, for example, about the courtyard of the *Horrea di Hortensius*. Moreover, around the quadrangle there may or may not be a portico. The *Horrea dell'Artemide* is without a portico. Even if there is a portico, it may be composed either of columns or of brick-faced piers. In Rome, although not so far in Ostia, the quadrangle type could be doubled or even tripled, that is, two or even three courtyards flanking each other, divided by double lines of rooms placed back to back. The nearest approach to this in Ostia is in the *Grandi Horrea* where a central block of rooms back to back in the original Claudian building *almost* divided the courtyard into two.

Within the corridor type the length and width of the central corridor on to which the rooms open on either side may vary. There may or may not be a room opening on to the corridor at the end opposite the entrance. Moreover, even though it is generally the case that these *horrea* are entered at one end of the central corridor, in the case of the *Horrea* (Reg. iii. Is. ii. 6) the entrance is in one of the long sides of the

[1] R. Staccioli, 'I criptoportici forensi di Aosta e di Arles', *RAL* ix (1954), 647, n. 1, divides the Ostian *horrea* into four types. This is too complicated and there is in Ostia no building of his type (*c*) with double court, which is known so far only in Rome.

building and the central corridor extends parallel with the road and not at right angles to it.

It seems more sensible to regard such differences as variations within a type rather than types in themselves.

It does not seem possible to confine one type to one period. Examples of each type exist side by side at any given period. Moreover, it does not seem possible to trace any evolution or development in either type, so far as ground plan is concerned. The variations in plan seem generally to be dictated by the purpose the building served and by the exigencies of space available. Meiggs[1] claims that some development took place in that the ground plan of the *horrea* around Trajan's harbour (long ranges of store-rooms placed back to back) was adopted when the Commodan *Horrea Antoniniani* in Ostia itself was built. But the plan of these Commodan *horrea* is not well known, and it may be that the similarity to the Portus plan is an illusion. There still seems to have been some sort of central quadrangle.

There was, however, one development, probably the result of particular conditions in Ostia. The quadrangle type, without necessarily becoming smaller, becomes more compact in plan and less wasteful of possible storage space. The huge central court of the Julio-Claudian *Horrea di Hortensius* was not to be repeated. Later, even large *horrea* such as the Hadrianic *Piccolo Mercato* have restricted courtyards. This, how-ever, was probably not so much dictated by improved *horrea* design as by the growing need to conserve space in Ostia, to build up rather than out.

One of the most constant features of *horrea* planning in Ostia is the emphasis laid upon keeping each warehouse distinct from the sur-rounding buildings. This is particularly noticeable in the case of the *Horrea di Hortensius*, which is separated from the buildings on both sides by an interval some 2 metres wide (Pl. 35). The same is true of the *Piccolo Mercato* separated from the *Horrea* (Reg. I. Is. VIII. 2) and the *Horrea Epagathiana* by a narrow division, and from the shops on the *Cardo Maximus* by a wide alley (the so-called Via Tecta). Moreover, even in the case of the smaller corridor *horrea*, even though they may make physical contact with the buildings which surround them, they never share a common wall with them. The main reason for this clear division was the danger of fire. In the late Empire the emperors were much concerned with the encroachment of private building upon *horrea* everywhere, and in A.D. 398 the Praetorian Prefect[2] was ordered to tear

---

[1] Meiggs, p. 280.   [2] *Cod. Theod.* XV. I. 38.

down all private buildings adjoined to State storehouses so as to leave
them free on all sides 'as they were built from the beginning'.

Buttressing is used in the Ostian *horrea* but not extensively. The plan
of the warehouses, whether of the 'quadrangle' or of the 'corridor'
type, was such that the support for the weight of goods stored was
derived from a counterbalance system. Only certain external walls at
the end of a row of rooms were buttressed from the beginning, for
example in the *Grandi Horrea* and the *Horrea di Hortensius*. Buttresses
were, however, an important feature of the long side walls of the
Piccolo Mercato. It is also the case that the walls in *horrea* were of unusual
thickness, never less than 60 centimetres thick, and often 90 centimetres or
1 metre thick. Such buttresses as there are in these buildings have often
been introduced at a later date to give extra support to a weakened wall.

A striking feature of all plans of *horrea* in Ostia is the economy of
entrances. It is true that even the modest *Horrea* (Reg. III. Is. II. 6) has its
postern door leading in under the stairs, cf. *Horrea* (Reg. I. Is. VIII. 2),
in addition to the main entrance, but often these two are the only means
of access. The *Grandi Horrea*, in particular, after the Severan reconstruction of the northern part, has remarkably few entrances for a
building of its size, and they are remarkably narrow (approximately
1½ metres). In a sense this is what one would expect: the need for small,
easily-barred entrances would be of primary importance in a building
used for storage purposes. But this fact, together with other significant
points such as the difference in levels between different parts of one
warehouse (as in the *Grandi Horrea*) or between the warehouse and the
road (as in the *Horrea di Hortensius*), the comparative narrowness of
some of the porticoes and the constant flooring of the porticoes with
opus spicatum, makes it unlikely that there was ever a 'free circulation of
carts and the unloading of merchandise under shelter'.[1] We are to think
more in terms of *porters—saccarii*.

Every detail of the Ostian evidence is important because the buildings
at Ostia are the 'living' embodiment of what is known for Rome itself
only from the Marble Plan made under Septimius Severus. The
arrangements of the *horrea* depicted on that plan receive confirmation
and illustration from the design and structure of the Ostian *horrea*.[2]

[1] R. Lanciani, *Ancient Rome in the Light of Recent Discoveries* (London, 1888), p. 250,
referring to the *Horrea Galbana* in Rome.
[2] See further Chapter II (p. 108).

Structure

There is no indication at Ostia that any one material or style of building was regarded as specially suitable for the construction of *horrea*. In general they were built of concrete and faced with tufa reticulate, a mixture of reticulate and bricks, or bricks alone—whichever was fashionable at the time of construction. There is some evidence that walling in *opus quadratum*, great tufa blocks held together by iron clamps, was regarded even in the first century A.D. as being particularly suitable for *horrea*. The *Grandi Horrea* had its two main side walls constructed in tufa blocks under Claudius (Pl. 18), when the style had gone out of fashion generally, as did *Horrea* (Reg. v. Is. 1. 2). Moreover, a patch of tufa walling incorporated in the east wall of *Horrea* (Reg. 1. Is. VIII. 2) (Pl. 9) almost certainly belonged to an earlier warehouse before the building of the Hadrianic *horrea* on the site. In Rome itself, in his building operations for the Golden House, Nero pulled down among other buildings *horrea* described as being built of stone,[1] and the Augustan *Horrea Agrippiana* was originally almost completely built of large tufa blocks[2] (Pl. 38). In the *Grandi Horrea* and the *Horrea* (Reg. v. Is. 1. 2) the tufa blocks were used only in the important perimetral walls, not in the division walls of the rooms, and were thus a deliberate retention, considered suitable for the outer walls of important storehouses which must be protected from fire and theft. It seems, however, that this device was soon considered inessential and it was not used in the Trajanic and Hadrianic *horrea*, which are constructed entirely in faced concrete.

A similar development is noticeable in the materials used for the porticoes of the quadrangle *horrea*. The Julio-Claudian *Horrea di Hortensius* has a portico of columns, made of drums of tufa with finely carved Doric capitals, except for the angle columns which are entirely of travertine (Pl. 35). In the Claudian *Grandi Horrea* a continuous plinth of tufa blocks supports the columns made of tufa drums, which had Doric capitals carved in travertine, at least at the angles of the court (Pl. 17). The Hadrianic *Piccolo Mercato* (Pl. 1) and *Horrea* (Reg. 1. Is. VIII. 2) and the Antonine *Horrea Epagathiana* (Pl. 13) all have arcades supported by brick-faced concrete piers. After the middle of the first century A.D., therefore, tufa and travertine colonnades were not used

---

[1] Suet. *Nero*, 38. 1. [2] See Chapter II (p. 94).

and brick-faced concrete arcades became normal practice. The change in materials and in structural form from columns to piers did not involve any loss of elegance or impressiveness.

Certain structural details peculiar to *horrea* deserve attention.

Where windows occur inside the buildings, for example, above the doorways to the rooms or in the walls between the rooms, they are simply squared openings (Pls. 1 and 29). The windows, however, in the outer walls are taller, narrower and splayed so as to present the narrowest possible opening to the outside world (Pl. 8). They vary in both height and size, but seem to occur in pairs more often than singly, placed high in the back walls of the rooms (Pl. 6). Most often the top and bottom of the window is made of one flat stone or tile, although it is possible for them to be splayed at top and bottom as well as at the sides. Their shape is clearly dictated by the purpose of the buildings and the need for security. They cannot have admitted much light and their main purpose must have been ventilation. Light was admitted through the doorway and the squared window normally set above it.

The thresholds preserved in the *horrea* at Ostia are all of one main type. They are cut in travertine with a raised marginal check against which two doors hung on pivots (for which the holes are cut at either end of the threshold) were closed and secured in position by a square bolt dropped into a slot in the middle of the threshold (Fig. 16). The only exceptions to this are the small threshold blocks in the *Horrea di Hortensius*, which supported only the pivots of the doors (Pl. 36), and one reworked threshold in *Horrea* (Reg. IV. Is. V. 12), which had originally been of the type with marginal check. This needs emphasising because Paschetto and Romanelli[1] claimed that the method of closing rooms in *horrea* at Ostia was the same as that in Roman shops, that is, by means of a series of upright boards held by grooves in the threshold and architrave. This is an error. Paschetto based his conclusion on evidence taken from the rows of rooms on either side of the *Cardo Maximus*, north of the Forum, which are shops and not part of any *horrea*. There are minor variations in the size and position of pivot and bolt holes, depending on the size and importance of the doorway concerned. In the main entrance to the *Horrea Epagathiana* the pivot holes (15 centimetres wide and 10 centimetres deep) are preserved in the

---

[1] L. Paschetto, *Ostia, colonia romana; storia e monumenti* (Rome, 1912), pp. 317 ff. Cf. Romanelli, p. 974.

architrave, as well as in the threshold. In *Horrea* (Reg. III. Is. XVII. 1), instead of round pivot holes, there are rectangular depressions for whole renewable pivot casings.

The system of *suspensurae* employed for raising the floors of the rooms in three of the *horrea* has been described in some detail in each case. A general discussion of the question is given in an appendix.[1]

The remains of staircases have been found in several *horrea*, indicating the existence of an upper storey. The Julio-Claudian *Horrea di Hortensius* and Claudian *Grandi Horrea* apparently had no staircases. It is clear, however, that the later Hadrianic *Piccolo Mercato* (Pl. 3) and *Horrea* (Reg. I. Is. VIII. 2), and the *Horrea Epagathiana* were designed with staircases. Moreover, the *Grandi Horrea* after its reconstruction under Commodus had staircases (Pls. 19 and 24). Nor was it only the great quadrangle *horrea* that had staircases to upper storeys, as the *Horrea* (Reg. III. Is. II. 6) shows. In general, they were built near the main entrance of the building. Where they have been sufficiently preserved it can be seen that after the first half dozen travertine steps, they were constructed as ramps paved with *opus spicatum*, herring-bone bricks, for the easier transportation of goods to the upper floor. There is a fine example in the *Piccolo Mercato*.

Special locking devices in the door jambs of rooms and the main entrances have been preserved only in two of the smaller and presumably private warehouses: *Horrea Epagathiana* (Figs. 4–6) and *Horrea* (Reg. III. Is. II. 6) (Fig. 14). It would be unwise to assume that they were a feature of every *horrea* in Ostia. The system of barring the doors has been described in detail in the description of the *horrea* concerned. Obviously the purpose was to ensure the greater security of the goods stored. This becomes even clearer when it is realised that this was the system for barring the gates of Rome itself. Procopius[2] gives an exact description of the system when giving an account of the opening of the *Porta Asinaria* to Totila in A.D. 546 and traces have been found at the other gates of Rome. Moreover, the gateways of military forts were similarly barred. On Hadrian's Wall in Britain[3] such bar holes exist at

---

[1] See Appendix 1.

[2] Procopius, *De Bello Gothico* III. 20. Cf. I. A. Richmond, *The City Wall of Imperial Rome* (Oxford, 1930), p. 40.

[3] I. A. Richmond and F. A. Child, 'Gateways of forts on Hadrian's Wall', *AA*[4] XX (1942), 140; milecastle 37, cf. *AA*[4] XI (1934), Pl. XVI. 2 and p. 108; milecastle 42, cf. *AA*[4] XIII (1936), 270.

Housesteads, Chesters and Birdoswald, showing that two bars were provided behind the lower half of the doors. Similar devices have been found at milecastle 42 (south gate) and milecastle 37 (north gate) where the runway for moving the bar was not vertical but horizontal, as at the main entrance of the *Horrea Epagathiana*.

The arrangements for roofing the *horrea* are not well known. The great masses of fallen concrete vaulting in the *Piccolo Mercato* (Pl. 1) make it clear that its rooms were covered by large barrel vaults, and the Antonine *Horrea Epagathiana* also were roofed in concrete cross-vaulting, now largely restored (Pl. 13). It may be, however, that the Claudian *Grandi Horrea* and the *Horrea di Hortensius* had room-ceilings of wood, although the walls are thick enough to have supported concrete vaults. In general the roofs must have been gabled. At all events there are gutters set in the *Grandi Horrea* court following the line of the internal portico, and drainage arrangements in the courts of the *Horrea di Hortensius* and the *Piccolo Mercato*, in addition to the gutter set between the *Piccolo Mercato* and the *Horrea* (Reg. I. Is. VIII. 2). The gutters, when they follow the portico, are so set that we must suppose an overhang by the eaves of about 1 metre.

The most curious structural feature of the *horrea* in Ostia is the filling in at a later date of the intercolumniations or the spaces between the brick piers (used instead of columns) around the central courtyard. This took place certainly in the *Grandi Horrea* where some of the inter-columniations were filled in the Severan period with brick-faced concrete walls of a width equal to the column diameters (Pl. 26). Narrow entrances were left at a restricted number of points. Other intercolumniations around the central block of rooms were filled by walls faced with rough tufa reticulate of uncertain date. The spaces between the brick piers of the arcades in the *Piccolo Mercato* and *Horrea* (Reg. I. Is. VIII. 2) were filled by walls, faced with tufa reticulate, 35 centimetres wide in the *Piccolo Mercato* and 46 centimetres wide in the other building. In the *Horrea* (Reg. I. Is. VIII. 2) these infilling walls are well bonded with the piers and would seem to be contemporary with them, but in the *Piccolo Mercato* they were not bonded with the piers and may well be later than the original construction.

The purpose of this infilling is not clear. In the only case where the infilling seems to be contemporary with the original construction of the building, *Horrea* (Reg. I. Is. VIII. 2), it is likely that its purpose was to compensate for the narrowness of the portico and give added protection from sun and rain. What was the purpose of the later infilling in the other two examples is not clear. It was perhaps to create greater covered space and storage room: there was certainly a late attempt in the *Grandi Horrea* to use even one of the courts to provide extra storage space. There are, however, no traces of small transverse walls to cut up the new space into manageable portions and the blocking of the porticoes with stored goods would have been intolerable. Another possibility is that they were to ensure greater security by restricting the access to the corridor and thus to the rooms. This would be a more attractive suggestion if there were any indication that the ways through the infilling wall were locked, but there is none.

Historical Note

It is a fact that all the *horrea* discussed were erected during the Empire. *Horrea* must have been built during the Republic, but since the town plan as we have it is largely the result of the rebuilding in the Empire, and particularly in the Hadrianic period, it is not surprising that all the *horrea* date from the first century A.D., if not later. Part of an earlier warehouse built of tufa blocks was incorporated in *Horrea* (Reg. I. Is. VIII. 2) (Pl. 9), but whether that dated from the Republican period is doubtful. Perhaps the only Republican warehouse discovered in Ostia is that revealed in a deep level excavation between the Casa del Serapide and the building Reg. III. Is. XVII. 1. Only parts of some walling are revealed, faced with irregular reticulate work and with door jambs constructed of small tufa blocks. The plan of the building is not known.

The date of the construction of the *horrea* at Ostia bears some relation to the dates of the work on improving Rome's harbours. Claudius, who first created a proper harbour at Ostia, was probably responsible for the *Grandi Horrea*, the biggest *horrea* in Ostia at that time. Similarly the great spate of *horrea* building late under Trajan and under Hadrian was probably not unconnected with the new inner harbour created by Trajan.[1]

The great mass of storehouses constructed around the harbours at Portus did not therefore render the storage capacity of Ostia unnecessary. On the contrary they stimulated further building activity at

[1] Meiggs, p. 280.

Ostia. This was true throughout the Antonine period and even of the reign of Septimius Severus. The capacious *Horrea Antoniniani* were constructed under Commodus and the *Grandi Horrea* were completely rebuilt with an upper storey at the same period.

There are signs of constant interest in the structure of the *horrea*, and small repairs and extra buttresses show that they continued in use in the third and fourth centuries A.D. But it is a fact that this interest in the late Empire took the form of rebuilding and restoring existing buildings rather than of building new *horrea*.

Storage of grain

At least three of the great *horrea* in Ostia had permanent raised floors, designed to protect grain from damp and overheating.[1] How was that grain stored? The answer is unfortunately even now not certain.

The principal ways of storing grain in any age are three: in sacks, in bins, or loose in heaps on the floor.[2]

It is generally assumed that in military *horrea* designed as long hangars, grain was stored in bins arranged laterally on either side of a central gangway.[3]

If a similar system of bins had been adopted in the rooms of the Ostian *horrea*, we should expect to see some trace of the system. Although the bins themselves might have been made of wood, holes for fixing them might be expected in the walls of the rooms. There are none. Moreover, on reflection it is clear that the system of bins is suitable only to large open barns or hangars, and that the room divisions themselves in the Ostian *horrea* serve a purpose similar to that of bins, namely the division of storage space into manageable portions.

We are thus left with these alternatives: storage in sacks or in loose heaps. For storage in loose heaps, the floors of the building must be absolutely damp-proof and the walls strong enough to withstand the pressure of the grain on them. There must be no possibility of surface water finding its way into the building, and the grain must be properly dried and cooled before being put in store, since it would be very

---

[1] Cf. Appendix I.

[2] J. Holt and J. S. Nix, *Farmer and Stockbreeder* (9 May 1961), p. 103; cf. J. S. Nix, Report No. 44, 'Drying and Storing Grain', issued by The School of Agriculture, Cambridge (1956).

[3] I. A. Richmond, 'The Agricolan Fort at Fendoch', *PSAS* LXXIII (1938–9), 129 ff.

difficult to deal with a local hot spot somewhere in the middle of the heap. For storage in sacks, the only special features of the building are that it should be dry and that it should not be necessary to negotiate too many steps in getting the sacks into position. The main drawback is that a great deal of labour is needed.

Both methods demand that there shall be not too much light in the building and as much protection as possible against vermin and insects. The insects cause damage by eating the endosperm (or germ) and by causing heating, but if the grain is kept very cool (below 60 °F) the most noxious insects such as the saw-toothed grain beetle have no chance of breeding.

It is difficult to decide which method the Romans adopted at Ostia, but there are certain considerations which suggest that storage in sacks may have been more common.

It is certain that the transporting of the grain from ship to shore was done, not by carts, but by individual porters carrying sacks. This is shown not only by the large number of inscriptions recording *saccarii*, but also by pictures showing such porters at work.[1] Moreover, it was certainly impossible for carts to enter the *horrea* at Ostia and unload inside the building. The entrances are too few and too small, the porticoes not wide enough nor suitably paved, and the levels within the *horrea* too varied. Moreover, the arrangement of the staircases in the form of sloping ramps approached by travertine steps in the *Piccolo Mercato* and the *Grandi Horrea* show that they were designed to aid *men* carrying heavy loads. If this was true, and if it was also true that most of the grain would be stored at Ostia only until it could be reshipped up the Tiber in barges, then it would seem sensible to suppose that the grain was stored in the sacks in which it had been carried from the ships and in which it would have to be carried back. The main disadvantage of such a storage system, that it demanded an immense amount of labour, would not have been important at a time when cheap slave labour was plentiful.

[1] For *saccarii* see J. P. Waltzing, *Étude historique sur les corporations professionnelles chez les Romains* (Louvain), II, 59 ff.; picture of *Isis Giminiana* being loaded by *saccarii*, Meiggs, p. 294 and fig. 25 e.

II

ROME

INTRODUCTION

There are two main sources of evidence for the design of the *horrea* in Rome itself, first actual excavations of *horrea* and second, the plans of *horrea* preserved on the Marble Plan of Rome made in the reign of Septimius Severus between A.D. 203 and 211. For the structure of the *horrea*, of course, excavation is the only possibility.

So far as excavation is concerned, it must be admitted that the resulting knowledge is not as precise as might have been hoped. The only great *horrea*, which have been excavated and left open for public inspection, are the *Horrea Agrippiana*; and even there only part of one courtyard was excavated. In every other case the excavations have been filled in or built over and no proper publication of the results has been made. Thus in 1880 and 1910 large areas of the Testaccio district were laid out with new houses and a mass of *horrea* walls and foundations were revealed as a result.[1] No systematic publication was made and only in 1934 did G. Gatti[2] make an heroic attempt to sort out the scrappy references to the earlier excavations. Similarly the Domitianic *Horrea Piperataria* were excavated below the nave of the Basilica of Maxentius in the 1920s and early 1930s, but our knowledge of the results, apart from a very short report by Maria Barosso,[3] is due in large measure to the fortuitous fact that A. Minoprio, an architect at the British School at Rome at that time, was carrying out a study of the Basilica of Constantine and incorporated the excavations in his plan and description.[4]

The ancient Marble Plan of Rome is a fascinating document and deserves a few words of introduction, for it has had an extraordinary history. It was cut on great slabs of marble during the reign of

---

[1] S. B. Platner and T. Ashby, *A Topographical Dictionary of Ancient Rome* (London, 1929), p. 261, s.v. *Horrea Galbae*.

[2] G. Gatti, '"Saepta Iulia" e "Porticus Aemilia"', *BCom* LXII (1934), 123 ff.

[3] M. Barosso, 'Le costruzioni sottostanti la Basilica Massenziana e la Velia', *Atti del V Congresso nazionale di studi romani* II (1940), pp. 58–62.

[4] A. Minoprio, 'A restoration of the Basilica of Constantine, Rome', *PBSR* XII (1932), 23–4.

Septimius Severus, and mounted on a wall of a room opening off the Forum Pacis. When complete it was nearly 60 feet wide and over 40 feet high, and composed of 151 rectangular slabs. During excavations in 1562 near the wall, some 92 fragments of it came to light and aroused great interest. Fortunately, drawings were made at the time which are now in the Vatican Library. The fragments themselves, which comprised only about a tenth of the whole plan, became the possessions of the Farnese family until finally in 1741, after quite a number of pieces had been lost over the years, they came into the public ownership of the city authorities. This helps to explain the fact that, although there was an obsessive interest in medieval Rome as to the layout and appearance of ancient Rome, no use was made of the fragments until Piranesi used them for his plan of the Campus Martius in 1756.[1] The result oddly enough was not increased accuracy but a fantasy, although, admittedly, one of extraordinary beauty. The standard scholarly edition of the fragments was until recently that by Heinrich Jordan, issued in 1874.[2] This, although impressive in its day, has now been superseded by a new study by the Italian scholars Carettoni, Colini, Cozza and Gatti, with the help of many others.[3] This new study, *La Pianta Marmorea di Roma Antica*, includes the latest fragments to be discovered, gives for the first time a complete photographic record of the fragments and discusses such problems as the date of the plan and its position, the scale, the position of the fragments preserved, the technique of the engravers and the conventional signs used in the plan. It is therefore the fundamental instrument for the study of the plan and has made really possible for the first time the study of the individual types of building represented.

Fortunately, the wall to which the plan was clamped survives as the south wall of the church of SS. Cosmas and Damian. The new edition has established by painstaking research on the blocks themselves and the dowel holes in the wall the arrangement of many of the surviving fragments and their place in the plan as a whole. This has been parti-

[1] A. P. Frutaz, *Le Piante di Roma* (Rome, 1962), II, Tav. 71 ff.
[2] H. Jordan, *Forma Urbis Romae Regionum XIIII* (Berlin, 1874).
[3] G. Carettoni, A. Colini, L. Cozza, G. Gatti, *La Pianta Marmorea di Roma Antica*, 2 vols. (Text and Plates) published in a limited edition of 400 copies (Rome, 1955); reprinted 1961. All the fragment numbers given in the text are taken from the numbering of the new Italian edition. A concordance with the old numbering of Jordan is given in vol. I, p. 241.

cularly fruitful for the so-called *Emporium* district of Rome below the Aventine Hill and for the opposite bank of the Tiber outside the modern Porta Portese. These areas, vital for Rome's river port, were poorly known previously. The area by the Porta Portese became again in the medieval period the river port of Rome, the *porto di ripa grande*, and in consequence the ancient buildings were covered with later structures. But on the other side of the river, near the Aventine Hill, there were no medieval structures, only the vineyards which covered so much of Rome in the middle ages, with the crumbling remains of ancient structures scattered among them. The whole area was built over again only in the late nineteenth and early twentieth centuries, but tragically no proper records or publications were made of the Roman buildings discovered. What we have lost can be seen in Lanciani's tantalising references[1] to being present at the discovery of storerooms, some containing elephants' tusks, others lentils and amphorae.

In this situation the evidence from the Marble Plan takes on an added importance.

HORREA AGRIPPIANA

As the only firmly identified *horrea* in Rome whose remains it is still possible to visit, this building has attracted a certain attention in print. The study of it has been bedevilled by the identification made by Lanciani in 1885 of two fragments published separately as numbers 37 and 86 in Jordan's *Forma Urbis Romae*.[2] He suggested that the building with three diminishing trapezoidal courts was between the *Clivus Victoriae* and the *Vicus Tuscus* and was a representation of the *Horrea Agrippiana* known to have been in Region VIII from the *Curiosum* and *Notitia*.[3] Excavations were carried out by Boni in 1911–12 in the area beneath the Palatine bounded on the north by the so-called Temple of Augustus and S. Maria Antiqua, on the west by the Via di San Teodoro (above the ancient *Vicus Tuscus*), on the south by the church of San Teodoro and on the east by the *Clivus Victoriae*. In 1911 an article by Schneider-Graziosi[4] appeared with a plan of the excavations and a short

[1] R. Lanciani, *Ancient Rome* (London, 1888), p. 250.
[2] R. Lanciani, 'Di un frammento della pianta marmorea Severiana rappresentante il clivo della Vittoria ed il vico Tusco', *BCom* XIII (1885), 157–60. Cf. *Pianta Marm.* frag. 42.   [3] See Appendix 6.
[4] G. Schneider-Graziosi, 'La identificazione topografica delle *Horrea Germaniciana et Agrippiana* dell'ottava regione Augustea', *BCom* XXXIX (1911), 158.

description. He supported the topographical identification made by Lanciani, but introduced a further complication by claiming that the correct name of the building was *Horrea Germaniciana et Agrippiana*, the form used in the *Notitia*. In the 1912 excavations a statue base was found in a *sacellum* in the centre of the courtyard with a dedication [*Pro*] *salut(e) Genium horreorum Agrippianorum*. This was striking confirmation that the building was rightly identified: as for the name, Schneider-Graziosi[1] admitted only that until the end of the second century and the beginning of the third century A.D. (the date of the inscription) it was known by one name—thereafter *Germaniciana* was added, before the mention of it in the *Notitia*.

In 1921 Bartoli[2] published what still remains the fundamental description with plan and photographs of the excavations. He fixed the date of the original building and tried to trace its history. He rejected the double name for the building quite rightly, but retained the identification of the two fragments of the Marble Plan with the site excavated.

Lugli in 1941[3] admitted certain problems about identifying the fragments as the *Horrea Agrippiana* and pointed out a certain lack of correlation between that plan and the remains discovered wherever further tests could be made.

In 1954 Berucci[4] avoided the problem of the Marble Plan fragments and made the first systematic attempt to reconstruct in detail the architectural orders and decoration of the building.

Finally in the new study of the Marble Plan, the Italians have firmly rejected the identification of the fragments (No. 42 in their series) with the *Horrea Agrippiana*.[5]

It is difficult to see why the identification was not rejected from the moment the excavations were started. The fragment of the Marble Plan shows a trapezoidal court bounded on two sides by rooms which

[1] G. Schneider-Graziosi, 'Genius Horreorum Agrippianorum', *BCom* XLII (1914), 25 ff.

[2] A. Bartoli, 'Gli *Horrea Agrippiana* e la *diaconia* di San Teodoro', *MonAnt* XXVII (1921), col. 373. Until this treatment the name problem had become so confused that Ch. Hülsen, *Forum und Palatin* (Munich, 1926), p. 51, even wrote, 'In einem dieser Höfer ist eine Marmorbasis gefunden welche den Namen des Gebäudes, *Horrea Germaniciana*, nennt.'

[3] G. Lugli, 'Aedes Caesarum in Palatio et templum Divi Augusti', *BCom* LXIX (1941), 56-7.

[4] M. Berucci, 'L'architettura degli *Horrea Agrippiana*', *Palladio*, n.s. IV (1954), 145 ff.

[5] *Pianta Marm.* p. 78.

opened outwards. This in no way corresponds to what was found (Fig. 20). The rectangular or square courtyard excavated was bounded on at least three sides by rooms opening inwards. In the Marble Plan the courtyard was surrounded by columns, in the excavations the courtyard was surrounded by pilasters fronted with half columns. We can only suppose that the fact that Lanciani had proved to be so

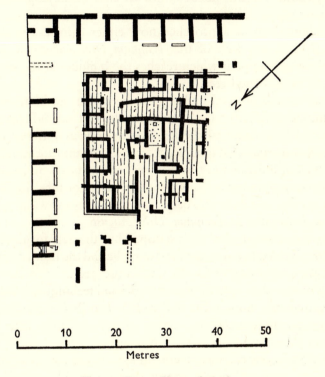

Fig. 20   Rome, *Horrea Agrippiana*

brilliantly right in guessing *where* the *Horrea Agrippiana* was to be found had made scholars wary of disregarding the other half of his guess. Whatever the reason, there is no longer any need to see in these Marble Plan fragments a representation of the *Horrea Agrippiana* and not even of *horrea* at all. The proper study of the design and structure of *Horrea Agrippiana* depends solely upon the excavations.

The area exposed by excavation is the north-eastern section of an open courtyard surrounded on at least three sides by rows of rooms opening on to an arcade around it[1] (Pls. 38 and 39). The whole north side and a considerable length of the east side is completely exposed, but the south end of the courtyard still lies buried in the great ramp of earth supporting the way up to the Palatine north of the church of San Teodoro. On the west side only two division walls of the most northerly rooms and the side of a third are clear of the slope supporting the modern Via di San Teodoro.

The building can be approached now either from the Forum itself along a path to the west of the *Templum Divi Augusti* or from the *Clivus Victoriae* by a path which reaches the building at the south-west corner of the excavated area.

The date of the original building of the *horrea* can be fixed within certain limits. Behind the third room on the east side adhering to the Palatine rock and rising to the level of the *Clivus Victoriae* is a wall 4 feet thick constructed of tufa pieces set in abundant mortar faced with *opus incertum* of Sullan date: this wall was cut vertically in building the *horrea*. It is clear that the *horrea* was built entirely of tufa blocks originally, but on the north side the back wall to the rooms was replaced by the brick wall of the *Templum Divi Augusti* (Pl. 40) certainly of Domitianic date fixed by a brick stamp. Thus the date for the building of the *horrea* is fixed between the late Republic and the time of Domitian. Bartoli[2] plausibly tried to fix the date more precisely to the time of Augustus by pointing to its type of material and technique, comparing it with the Augustan shops in the *Basilica Julia* and *Basilica Aemilia*. It thus seems possible to connect the name of the building with that of Augustus's friend and aide, Marcus Agrippa.

Certain late constructions were added to the original building. Between the rear wall of the rooms of the east side and the *Clivus Victoriae* in a space hollowed out in the hillside are a number of structures superimposed in three storeys which rise to the level of the *Clivus Victoriae* (Pl. 39). They include a barrel-vaulted gallery, staircases and rows of rooms; the whole ensemble was accessible through a doorway at the back of the third room on the east side. This area may well have been used for some purpose, perhaps administrative, in connection with the *horrea* from the beginning, but as they stand they

[1] Cf. E. Nash, *Pictorial Dictionary of Ancient Rome* (London, 1961, 1962), pp. 475 ff.
[2] Bartoli, 'Gli *Horrea Agrippiana*', col. 384-8.

are entirely built of concrete faced with bricks of a type comparable with that of Severan structures on the Palatine.

The whole of the central courtyard is filled with later buildings (Pl. 41). The earliest of these seems to be the *sacellum* in the centre. Rectangular in plan and enclosed on three sides by walls faced with brickwork, it had a front portico of two columns *in antis*. The flooring of the *sacellum* is a mosaic, green on white, in the centre of which is a triton's head with two dolphins. At the back of the *sacellum* is the base dedicated to the *genius* of the *horrea*[1] (Pl. 42) which supported a statue now lost. Originally this *sacellum* was composed simply of four piers of brick faced with marble, one at each corner: at a later date the sides and back were closed by a continuous brick wall into which were incorporated the two corner piers. The brickwork of the piers is judged to be Severan, a date which the mosaic supports. The infilling of the sides is later in date. The inner sides were plastered and painted and divided at half their height by a projecting string course.

The other buildings filling the central court are of a much later date. In front of the *sacellum* is a small fountain, rectangular with one rounded end, built of tufa blocks and bricks. The other structures are rooms of small proportions, built haphazardly. Some are of tufa blocks and a few brick courses, some of shapeless pieces of tufa, others of peperino and travertine. The main interest of these poor and very late structures is that they indicate that the *horrea* was in use for a very long period. Moreover, since the buttresses of these late buildings were placed to correspond with the pillars of the original portico, we have some proof that the pillars were still *in situ* when these very late buildings were constructed.

Originally the central courtyard was entirely free from buildings; it was an open courtyard paved with travertine flagstones and edged by a travertine gutter 23 centimetres wide and 7 centimetres deep (Pl. 43).

This courtyard was surrounded by an arcade certainly on the three sides excavated. In the south-east corner of the excavation the bases of two travertine piers, fronted by half columns of the Tuscan order,

[1] The full correct version of the inscription on this base is given by L. Wickert in 'Nota epigraphica', *RM* XL (1925), 213–14 and 'Nachtrag zu *RM* XL, 213ff', XLI (1926), 229. All earlier versions, even that given by Bartoli, are either wrong or incomplete. Wickert also established that the *immunes* of the inscription were *immunes* of the *collegium* and did not owe their *immunitas* to participation in the corn trade, as previous commentators had suggested.

which formed part of the arcade, were found *in situ*. They had originally been covered with stucco. With the half columns facing into the courtyard they overlap the *slabs* in which the gutters are cut, although they are short of the gutter itself by 30 centimetres. They are so spaced that two intercolumniations of the arcade correspond to the width of each room behind. The arcade was floored with *opus spicatum*— herring-bone brick.

The rooms opened on to the arcade and were constructed for the most part in large tufa blocks, 62 centimetres wide, 60 centimetres high and with lengths which vary from less than a metre to one and a half metres (Pl. 44). The walls of the rooms were built without mortar between the blocks and are still preserved in places to a considerable height (7–10 courses of blocks). The fifth and seventh courses are always composed of wider blocks (approximately 80 centimetres) and therefore provide two small ledges along each side wall of the rooms. From the two ledges at the level of the seventh course sprang the barrel vaults which covered the rooms. This is proved not only by the remains of cement still adhering to these ledges but also by the position of the scars left in the brickwork of the northern wall of the *horrea* (Pl. 40). The purpose of the two ledges at the fifth course level is not so clear. They may well have been used to support some kind of mezzanine floor; large beam holes are to be seen at a point just above the fifth course ledge.[1]

Originally *all* the walls of the buildings were constructed of tufa blocks, but when the *Templum Divi Augusti* was built under Domitian, the north wall was replaced by brick-faced concrete based on blocks of travertine. On the east side certain repairs have been made in the walls.

A large number of thresholds have been preserved, but only two are of the type found in all the *horrea* at Ostia, that is, a travertine threshold with marginal check, central bolt hole and pivot holes for doors opening inwards. In all other cases the entrances to the rooms were closed by means of upright wooden shutters, fitted into grooves in the threshold and presumably the architrave (Fig. 21). In some examples a

[1] The arrangement of the holes would suggest that a beam was fitted from one side wall to the other into two square holes cut immediately above the projecting fifth course of tufa blocks at a point approximately a metre from the back of the room. This in its turn supported two beams which ran out into the room from the back wall. Consequently the slots for the beams in the back wall are placed slightly higher than those in the side walls.

wide depression is cut to permit the introduction of the upright planks, which were then moved along the groove parallel with the front of the threshold (cf. Fig. 16). More often immediately behind the shallow groove (approximately 2 centimetres deep), which runs the whole length of the threshold, are cut at intervals shorter, deeper slots (approximately 7 centimetres deep). The method of closing the room entrance in these cases would seem to be as follows: each upright shutter was placed with one end in this deeper slot, its other end was fitted into the groove in the architrave, the whole plank was thus lifted into the groove in the threshold and then moved along it into position. Most of the

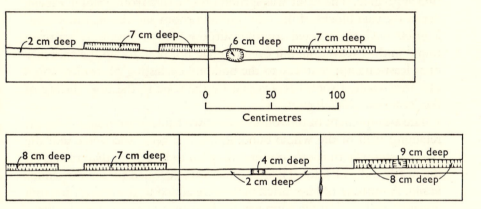

Fig. 21 Rome, *Horrea Agrippiana*, thresholds

thresholds show signs of severe wear. The difference between the type of threshold found here and that found in the *horrea* at Ostia seems significant. The shuttering of entrances was particularly common in Roman shops and may indicate here that a large number of the rooms on the ground floor of the *Horrea Agrippiana* were used for retail purposes.

The arrangement of the rooms in the north-east and north-west corners of the excavated area has not been made clear in Bartoli's plan (Fig. 20).[1] In the north-east corner he recognised the existence of only one tufa wall whose stones are now completely robbed; but I suspect there were two such walls, as the scars left in the brick facing of the *Templum Divi Augusti* show (Pl. 40). One of them, aligned with the

[1] Bartoli, 'Gli *Horrea Agrippiana*', Tav. I.

room entrances on the east side, framed the doorway to the first room on the east side; the other formed the east wall of one of the rooms on the north side. The space between these two walls formed *not* a room but, as its flooring of herring-bone bricks shows, an extension of the arcade on the east side. This extension provided access to the corner room. In the north-west corner there seems to have been a similar extension of the north arcade, although certainty is not possible.

At the north-west corner of the building was found a small staircase, now partly restored by the Soprintendenza. The steps, the bottom two at least being of travertine, were supported on a vault of concrete with tufa aggregate. The vault was sprung on one side from a sloping ledge cut in the tufa blocks of the side wall of a room and on the other from a brick wall constructed for the purpose. This is the only staircase found in the excavation, but even if it had not been found the existence of at least one upper storey to the building consisting of similar ranges of barrel-vaulted rooms is revealed by the scars in the brick facing of the *Templum Divi Augusti*.

The arrangement of the rooms on the west side is not clear. The west retaining wall of the whole building has not been discovered and the two most northern rooms on this side seem to be deeper than rooms on the north and east sides. Their entrances are revealed by the thresholds *in situ*. A number of later brick piers were added to the ends of the tufa division walls and in the entrances to the rooms in order to make them narrower.

So far as the possibility of reconstructing the architectural features of the building is concerned, Berucci has made a gallant attempt.[1] Besides the two travertine bases of the arcade found *in situ*, many other architectural fragments were found. Berucci lists them: three travertine blocks forming parts of column shafts, four with Corinthian capitals (Pl. 45), two with Tuscan bases, five with the impost of arches. There were also many tufa fragments, some so much weathered and worn as to be almost shapeless. Berucci concerns himself primarily with the travertine fragments and tries to show that, apart from the two bases *in situ* and a fragment of the cornice, all the travertine fragments belong to the order of the upper storey. He attempts a complete reconstruction of that order. Although the attempt is careful and considered, the details must naturally be regarded with suspicion. Above all there seems to be

---

[1] Berucci, 'L'architettura degli *Horrea Agrippiana*', pp. 145 ff.

no obvious explanation of the serious problem of what appears to have been the *indiscriminate* use of tufa and travertine in the building's architectural orders. There seems to have been no rational division of materials according to their position and purpose in the building.

Whatever may be the truth with regard to the details of the architectural arrangement, there can be no doubt that this building of commercial character lived up to the monumental area in which it was placed.

Any attempt to define more closely the commercial character of these *horrea* must depend upon the inscriptions studied elsewhere.[1] Suffice it to say here that a warehouse purely for storage would be oddly placed next to the Forum and below the Palatine: we are perhaps to think of retail, and this is a suggestion which is supported by the threshold type found *in situ* and the inscriptions. Neither inscriptions nor thresholds alone are decisive, but together they suggest strongly that the *horrea* had a purpose that was at least partly that of retailing goods.

HORREA GALBANA

The attempt to discover upon what evidence the few plans and meagre pieces of structural information concerning the *Horrea Galbana* are based is a depressing business. It is true that the main shape and outline of the *Horrea* are clear, but as soon as one demands detail and evidence there is nothing but confusion.

The *Horrea Galbana*[2] are known from the *Curiosum* and *Notitia* to have been in Region XIII beneath the Aventine Hill. Since the whole Testaccio area was dug over in the 1880s and again just after 1910 when new blocks of houses were built and new drains laid, it might have been expected that a detailed plan and much structural evidence would have emerged. But this is not the case; the fact is that the *Horrea Galbana*, and indeed the whole *Emporium* area, have never been properly studied and the excavations have never been systematically published. Our knowledge of the ground plan of the *horrea* is based entirely upon (*a*) the reconstruction by Lanciani on Tav. XL of his *Forma Urbis Romae*,[3] which incorporated some information from the excavations of his day;

---

[1] See Chapter V (p. 174).

[2] Platner–Ashby, *A Topographical Dictionary*, p. 261, s.v. *Horrea Galbae*.

[3] On this plan Lanciani tried to include all the evidence of excavations in his own day.

(*b*) Frags. 24*a* and *c* of the Severan Marble Plan which were reidentified as a representation of the *Horrea Galbana* by G. Gatti in 1934[1] (Fig. 22); (*c*) the plan Tav. II drawn by Gatti to illustrate his article in 1934, which was apparently an attempt to combine the two. As will be shown later, these plans, while having an overall similarity, do not agree in detail. Our knowledge of structural details is even worse, in that it seems to be limited to certain stray remarks made by Gatti in his article and to a few photographs of walling revealed by excavation in 1955[2] (Pl. 46).

Such are the bare facts, but this is not the impression given by Platner–Ashby or Romanelli[3] in their discussion of the *horrea*. A stream of references is given to excavations in the 1880s and post-1910. These, however, always prove to be a half-page (or less) précis of isolated excavations which revealed a piece of walling or a column base or two. In the 1880 reports the situation of the finds is given in only the vaguest way—'in the Testaccio area'; while in the later reports, where more exact locations are given, the finds belong to areas to the north or west of the *Horrea Galbana* as positioned by Lanciani and Gatti.

The basic instrument for the study of the design and structure of the *Horrea Galbana* is the article by Gatti: his reidentification of the Marble Plan fragments has been almost universally accepted,[4] he made the first attempt to sort out the earlier excavation reports and fix their location exactly, and he claimed to have consulted all the plans made by Lanciani in the 1880s of what was found in the Testaccio area, which have been preserved by the Institute of Archaeology in Rome. This, however, does not mean that we are forced to agree with Gatti in detail.

What was the ground plan of the *Horrea Galbana*? Before we can answer that question we have to assess the relative value of our evidence. On sheet 40 of Lanciani's *Forma Urbis Romae* he incorporated the evidence from excavations in his own day, indicated in heavy black ink. This is invaluable, for in general it justifies his reconstruction and

---

[1] Gatti, '"Saepta Iulia" e "Porticus Aemilia"', p. 123. The building had previously been thought to be the Barracks of the *Vigiles*. This identification was accepted by P. K. Baillie-Reynolds, *The Vigiles of Imperial Rome* (London, 1926), Pl. ii (p. 46), and is perpetuated by Meiggs, p. 305.

[2] Gatti, '"Saepta Iulia" e "Porticus Aemilia"', p. 143. Lugli, *Tecnica*, p. 508 and Tav. CXLI. 2. Nash, *Pictorial Dictionary*, pp. 483, 484 (1955 excavations).

[3] Romanelli, p. 984. [4] *Pianta Marm.* p. 81, n. 3.

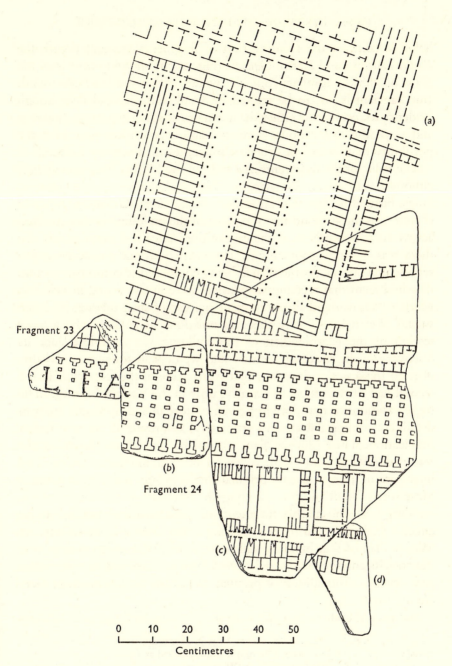

Fragment 23

Fragment 24

(a)

(b)

(c)

(d)

0   10   20   30   40   50
Centimetres

Fig. 22 Rome, *Horrea Galbana*, *Porticus Aemilia*,
Severan Marble Plan fragments 23 and 24

99

helps to confirm the identification of fragments 24*a* and *c* with the *Porticus Aemilia* and *Horrea Galbana* (Fig. 22) by showing how well the plans on those fragments coincide overall with what has been found. But Lanciani is not to be trusted in detail, since he had not enough evidence to reconstruct either the north or the south end of the building and since the excavations were so fragmentary there is always the possibility that he misconstrued or misrepresented what was found.

The value of the fragments 24*a* and *c* of the Marble Plan as evidence, although very great, has two possible weaknesses of quite different kinds. First, although identification with the *Horrea Galbana* is virtually certain, it is slightly odd that the name of the building was not inserted across the courtyards, as in the case of the *Horrea Lolliana* (Fig. 23), for there was certainly room for it. The portico around the courtyard is represented on the Marble Plan as being composed of columns, whereas it would seem that rectangular pilasters were in fact found *in situ*. The Marble Plan can and does represent the use of such pilasters and one would like to know why this was not done here. Secondly, a large section of the Marble Plan of this building has been lost since its discovery in the sixteenth century and we depend for our knowledge of it on the series of drawings that were made of the fragments in the second half of the sixteenth century, now in the Vatican Library.[1] The representations of that drawing given by Jordan and by Gatti[2] differ in details concerning entrances. Fortunately, as a result of the new Italian publication of the Marble Plan, we can be sure of the details of the Vatican drawing,[3] but we are of course left with the further problem of how careful a copy of the original *that* drawing was. We can exert some sort of control by comparing the drawing of the corner of the building with the marble fragment still preserved and, perhaps more effectively, by comparing the drawing of the *Horrea Lolliana* with the Marble Plan of that building still preserved.[4] From such a comparison the copyist emerges with credit; certain details are slightly misplaced, and a certain rationalising of peculiar details has taken place, but there are no crude errors.

We may therefore proceed with some confidence towards a recon-

[1] *Pianta Marm.* p. 81. Nash, *Pictorial Dictionary*, p. 482, seems to be a photograph of a *modern* copy of this lost piece, although it is not labelled as a copy.

[2] Jordan, *Forma Urbis Romae Regionum XIIII*, frag. 36*c*. Gatti, '"Saepta Iulia" e "Porticus Aemilia"', p. 148, fig. 7.

[3] *Pianta Marm.* Tav. IV and XXIV.   [4] *Pianta Marm.* Tav. IV and XXV.

struction of the ground plan of the *horrea*, bearing in mind the exca-
vational details of Lanciani's plan. This apparently is what Gatti also
did in order to produce the large plan, Tav. II, which accompanies his
article and it is this plan which is repeated in the handbooks on Roman
topography by Lugli.[1]

With a part of his reconstruction we must agree. The westernmost
range of rooms is depicted by Lanciani as a double row of rooms placed
back to back. Gatti preferred to follow the Marble Plan which depicts
a single row of rooms opening inwards only on to the courtyard. For
the south and north ends of the building for which Lanciani supplied a
hypothetical blank wall or left completely uncertain, Gatti sensibly
followed the rows of rooms depicted on the Marble Plan, but for no
apparent reason changed their number and their disposition. Similar
liberties have been taken with the entrances. This is quite unjustifiable;
if the Marble Plan is deemed to be worth following at all, and I think
it must be, it must be followed completely. Only when the results of
actual excavation contradict the Marble Plan is there a case for rejecting
its details, and even then, considering the fitful nature of these excavations and the period at which they were carried out, the case for changing
a detail of the Marble Plan must be very carefully weighed.

The Marble Plan, therefore, as represented by the fragment surviving
and the Vatican drawing, must be regarded as the best source that we
have for the plan of this *horrea* and must be supplemented, for details
such as the drainage system in the courtyards, by Lanciani's plan. Our
main effort thus must be given to *understanding* the Marble Plan.

As represented on the Marble Plan (Fig. 22), the building measures
approximately 167 metres by 146 metres,[2] and is divided into three
great rectangular colonnaded courtyards 28 metres by 118 metres, on
to which face rows of rooms on all four sides. The whole building is
represented as slightly tilted, with no angle forming a perfect right
angle. Although Lanciani depicted his building as perfectly rectangular,
there is evidence in the drawing of excavations done in the 1890s of a
distortion similar to that rendered on the Marble Plan.[3]

[1] For example, G. Lugli, *I monumenti antichi di Roma e suburbio* (Rome, 1938), III,
p. 599, fig. 111.
[2] All measurements of buildings represented on the Marble Plan are calculated on the
scale fixed by the Italians, 1:240 (*Pianta Marm.* p. 207) and must be regarded as very
approximate.
[3] Gatti, '"Saepta Iulia" e "Porticus Aemilia"', p. 147.

The plan of the east court has not been wholly preserved, but it appears to be significantly different from the others. If the Vatican drawing is correct, the colonnade was extended further north than in either of the other courts; there can have been little or no room for a row of inward-facing rooms closing the north end of this court. Furthermore, down the centre of the open court are drawn two parallel lines: enclosing these two continuous lines are two broken lines. What are these meant to represent? Two long walls, parallel, and flanked by two broken walls or a series of pilasters? We know from excavations that two long walls were built down the centre of this court.[1] What sort of building was involved is a difficult matter: presumably a shed down the centre of the courtyard or perhaps two sheds back to back and separated by a passage way. Possibly this was the result of a later need to save more space, and we may compare with it the series of brick pilasters found in the courtyard of the *Grandi Horrea* in Ostia:[2] these flank the court in the same way as do the pilasters of broken walls represented on the Marble Plan, and were probably used to support a roof over the courtyard. In the *Grandi Horrea* the width to be spanned by the roof was not great, and thus there would have been no need for central support.

The fact that a part of the plan of the easternmost court is missing renders any calculation of the number of rooms available for storage difficult. Between 130 and 140 rooms are clearly marked on the Plan as we have it, and we may be sure that there were more than that on the ground floor alone. The rooms vary in size. The largest measure some 13 metres by 5 metres and are grouped in two great rows back to back in the central part of the building. The rooms forming the east and west flanks of the building are rather smaller, approximately 11 metres by 5 metres, while those flanking the north end of the court are still smaller, some 6 metres by 5 metres, although they vary in size and therefore in number from court to court.

The main entrances to at least two of the courts were on the north side, towards the river, and about 5 metres wide. In each case the rooms on either side of the entrance were used to house staircases to the upper floor. Whether these four staircases were in the form of ramps, as in the *Piccolo Mercato* at Ostia,[3] is of course not known, but certainly

---

[1] R. Lanciani, *Forma Urbis Romae* (Milan, 1893–1901), Tav. XL.
[2] See Chapter I (p. 52). [3] See Chapter I (p. 22).

not improbable. Presumably the east court was also entered from this
north side. So far as we know there was only one other subsidiary
entrance, 3–4 metres wide, at the south-west corner of the west court.
This gave access to the west extension of the south arcade of that court.
This position is similar to that of the subsidiary entrance to the *Grandi
Horrea* in Ostia.[1]

Whether there were other minor entrances is not very clear. Gatti in
his plan indicates two at the south end of the central court (although not,
curiously enough, the subsidiary entrance just discussed). There seems
to be no evidence for such entrances, certainly not in the positions
indicated by Gatti.

We may conceivably have a hint of minor entrances in the cutting of
a line across the retaining wall of the *horrea*. This happens at three
points: first at the north extension of the east arcade of the west court,
secondly at the south end of the west arcade of the central court, and
thirdly at the south end of the west arcade of the east court. It is
impossible to assert with conviction that these cuts do represent small
postern doors, but the positions would not be inappropriate for such
posterns.

There are certain minor problems in understanding the version of the
horrea on the Marble Plan. Two rooms at least, on the north-west and
south-east corners of the west court, appear to have no means of
entrance and it is difficult to understand the room to the south of the
north-west corner.

It is stated by Lugli[2] that the east court had raised floors: 'sotto il
pavimento un intercapedine a cavi continui, come si vede in Ostia e in
Porto'.

We know from the excavations made in Lanciani's day that the open
courts were drained by means of a gutter which enclosed the courtyard
on all four sides, in a way similar to the drainage arrangement in the
Grandi Horrea at Ostia and the *Horrea Agrippiana* in Rome.

The structural features of the building are not at all well known to us.
Almost all the walls which were found in the random excavations were
in concrete faced with *opus reticulatum*; whether that meant *opus
incertum*, *opus quasi-reticulatum* or *opus reticulatum* proper was not really
known to Gatti.

In an excavation in 1955 a small section of the *Horrea Galbana* was

[1] See Fig. 10.　　　　　　　　　　[2] Lugli, *I monumenti antichi*, III, p. 608.

uncovered and the walls were found to be faced with a slightly irregular *opus reticulatum* (Pl. 47) dated by Lugli to a period 50 B.C.–A.D. 50.[1] In view of the complete lack of brick panels and the slightly irregular quality of the work, the earliest part of that period would be the most likely date of construction. A building which had as long a period of continuous use as this *horrea* should show signs of repair work, and there is evidence for such work at least under the Flavians and Hadrian.[2]

Despite the limitations of our evidence concerning the *Horrea Galbana*, the plan, so far as it is now known, fully justifies the premier place which these warehouses held. For sheer size and storage capacity we have nothing to compare with them: they dwarf even the largest of the Ostian *horrea*. Their plan is a perfect example of the courtyard-type *horrea* arranged in a triple group with two common walls. The whole ensemble was so designed as to give the maximum ease of sorting, manipulating and depositing goods, while also ensuring the maximum security for them once stored by limiting severely the number of entrances from the world outside.

HORREA PIPERATARIA

The study of the *Horrea Piperataria* has been bedevilled by a mis-identification in the early part of this century. In 1899 the *Sacra Via* in front of the Basilica of Constantine was excavated to pre-Neronian levels. On the north side rooms were found placed back to back in rows which continued under the Basilica of Constantine. The publication of these excavations and the article by Hülsen two years later[3] mistakenly identified this complex of rooms as the *Horrea Piperataria* known to have been built by Domitian here.[4] This view was corrected by Miss Van Deman in 1923 in her work on the Neronian *Sacra Via*.[5] She showed conclusively that the Neronian *Sacra Via* was a straight road

---

[1] Lugli, *Tecnica*, p. 508 and Tav. CXLI. 2. Nash, *Pictorial Dictionary*, pp. 483, 484.
[2] Lugli, *I monumenti antichi*, III, p. 607.
[3] R. Lanciani, 'Le escavazioni del Foro, II: I magazzini delle droghe orientali', *BCom* XXVIII (1900), 8–13; Ch. Hülsen, 'Ausgrabungen auf dem Forum Romanum', *RM* XVII (1902), 95.
[4] Chronographus ad A.D. 354 (T. Mommsen, *Chronica Minora* (1892–8), I, p. 146).
[5] E. Van Deman, 'The Neronian *Sacra Via*', *AJA* XXVII (1923), 400. Cf. 'The *Sacra Via* of Nero', *MAAR* V (1925), 115 ff.

flanked on either side by two great porticoes. The curving *Sacra Via* revealed by the 1899 excavation was the pre-Neronian road and therefore the buildings in association with it were also pre-Neronian. A distinction had to be drawn between the rooms which were laid bare at the Augustan level to the south of the Basilica (and which are still visible) and those remains under the nave of the Basilica itself at a higher level.

Excavations in the nave of the Basilica itself revealed that the *Horrea Piperataria* had been created by Domitian within the Neronian portico to the north of the *Sacra Via* and that a serious remodelling of that portico had been necessary. Unfortunately, no complete publication in detail of those excavations was ever made, and they are now no longer open for inspection. We are dependent upon a very short report by Maria Barosso[1] in 1940, with some sketches and sections reproduced in a minute form. The best plan and description of what was found in the early 1930s we owe to the chance that A. Minoprio, an architect at the British School at Rome, was carrying out a study of the Basilica above at that time. He incorporated in his plan the walls revealed by excavation in the nave, and added an archaeological appendix to his article.[2]

Nero's work had created a massive, hypostyle, completely roofed portico which mounted the slope of the Velia on three great steps or platforms. These different levels were masked by a front arcade on to the *Sacra Via* which rose with a steady slope.[3] Domitian preserved these different levels: two could be seen clearly in the excavations in the nave and fragments of the *opus spicatum* flooring of the third or easternmost level were to be seen in the eastern bay of the Basilica's nave. This arrangement favoured the dividing up of the building into groups with open courts. This would serve two purposes, giving light and saving the expense of the roofing of the large area to which Nero had committed himself. The excavations showed a group of rooms arranged around an open court floored with *opus spicatum* and provided with a central water tank. This involved an extensive remodelling of Nero's work. But Domitian's work was also modified in the second century, for the

[1] Barosso, 'Le costruzioni sottostanti la Basilica Massenziana e la Velia', pp. 58–62.

[2] Minoprio, *PBSR*, XII (1932), 23–4.

[3] Boëthius, *The Golden House of Nero*, p. 110, n. 25, says that Van Deman's reconstruction of the porticoes along the *Via Sacra* has been shown 'by later research' to be unfounded. I have been unable to discover what this later research is.

courtyard received new piers and door jambs, with new small water tanks built against them.

The extent of these *horrea* may have been considerable, and the area occupied by them was probably much the same as that occupied by the Basilica. The second-century wall of the *horrea* was used as a foundation for the west wall of the Basilica. Similarly in the easternmost part of the Basilica traces of the highest level of the *horrea* have been found. As for the north limit of the *horrea*, that may be given to us by part of the Marble Plan which represents the *Forum Pacis* and which includes a row of rooms which must have formed part of the *Horrea Piperataria*.[1] The superimposing of that fragment on the plan of the Basilica shows that the rooms would be of an appropriate size and orientation for the *horrea*.

Beyond this meagre outline we cannot go, but even so the details revealed are interesting enough. The whole structure was in concrete faced with brickwork of a predominantly Domitianic date.[2] The courts seem to have been modest in size for *horrea* and the same is the case with the rooms. We may suspect that the purpose was not solely storage of exotic drugs and peppers,[3] but also the convenient retailing of them in one place where adequate control would be exercised.

The most unusual feature seems to be the number of water tanks and troughs revealed in only one court. These may have been made necessary by the nature of the goods. The work in a pepper warehouse would be intolerable without some dampening of the atmosphere.

We should notice also at this point that the *Horrea Piperataria* were created out of a *porticus*. In this case serious modification of the *porticus* was involved, but there are examples where by the construction of walls between the pillars a *porticus* could be developed into *horrea*-type storerooms. We need only think of the so-called *Porticus Margaritaria* on the opposite side of the *Via Sacra*, the *Porticus Aemilia* between the *Horrea Galbana* and the Tiber, and the *porticus* whose remains lie under the shops on the west side of the *Via Lata* (the modern Via del Corso).[4] The *porticus* played a prominent part in the history of commercial architecture at Rome, as we shall see.

[1] G. Lugli, *Roma antica, il centro monumentale* (Rome, 1946), p. 272.

[2] Lugli, *Tecnica* I, p. 600; Blake, *Roman Construction from Tiberius*, p. 114.

[3] Dio, LXXII. 24 (ed. Boissevain). Cf. Chapter V (p. 170).

[4] E. Sjöqvist, 'Gli avanzi antichi sotto la chiesa di S. Maria in Via Lata', *Opuscula Arch.* IV (1946), 48–95.

HORREA SEIANA

The identification of the material remains of other *horrea* whose names are known to us is almost impossible. The most promising attempt is that made for the *Horrea Seiana*. Lanciani tried to identify their position in the Testaccio area by the place of discovery of an inscription referring to them, and plotted on sheet XL of his plan the odd walls which had been traced in that area. Remains of odd walls faced in both reticulate and brick have been ascribed to these *horrea*, but it is impossible from the slight reports either to deduce a proper plan for the buildings or to say how much belonged to the original building period.[1]

EXCAVATIONS

There are, however, *horrea* whose names and administration are not known to us from epigraphic or literary evidence, but which have been revealed by excavation. Beneath the subterranean church of San Clemente a structure has been partly excavated which was certainly *horrea* erected probably before the fire of A.D. 64.[2] The external walls of Anio tufa with a travertine coping enclose a space approximately 45 × 35 metres. These walls are of blocks 60 centimetres high, rusticated on the outside and laid with thin mortar joints. The partition walls, forming at least eight rooms along the sides and four smaller rooms towards the west arranged around a central open court, are of concrete faced with reticulate reinforced by bands of triangular bricks with brick quoins. The tufa work is not to be dated with accuracy, but the type of facing on the partition walls, although early, seems not to be Augustan. The bricks are 3–4 centimetres thick with mortar joints 1–1·5 centimetres. The wall ends are enlarged to form pilasters to carry the arches over the doorways for barrel vaults of concrete. Windows beneath these arches give light and air to the rooms. There are no windows in the external walls and no entrances to the structure have yet been found. Similarly it is not known whether there was a second storey or not, but there would be room for a staircase in the unexcavated part. The rooms have no means of communication and the room

[1] Platner–Ashby, *A Topographical Dictionary*, p. 263; Blake, *Roman Construction from Tiberius*, pp. 15–16 for references.
[2] Blake, *op. cit.* p. 29 and references. Nash, *Pictorial Dictionary*, p. 353.

entrances are not quite 2 metres wide, with travertine thresholds *in situ*. Its type of construction and position not far from the *Domus Aurea* site, in what was essentially a monumental part of the city, make it comparable to the *Horrea Agrippiana* rather than to the great warehouses near the Tiber.

In 1966 an excavation within the *Castra Praetoria* uncovered a range of rooms which were almost certainly part of a storehouse[1] (Pl. 48). The rooms, of which at least eight were exposed, were 10·63 metres deep and 4·72 metres wide and would have been about 5·20 metres in height. In fact only the springing of the concrete barrel vaults that covered the rooms was preserved at some points. The rooms, strongly constructed in concrete, faced with tufa reticulate panels divided by bands of brickwork (Pl. 49), opened on to a corridor 1·80 metres wide. One threshold, less than 2 metres wide, was preserved *in situ* and was of the normal type, with marginal check and pivot holes for a door opening inwards. The precise date and significance of this building will no doubt be made clear when it is published.

As a result of systematising the river port on the Tiber, Trajan and Hadrian constructed or repaired warehouses to the south of the *Porticus Aemilia* on the banks of the Tiber itself.[2] The remains recovered are very scattered and we have little idea of their plan. But it does seem clear that the bank was lined by rows of rooms opening towards the river. The walls were generally of concrete faced in a variety of ways, but the *opus mixtum* of Trajan and Hadrian was very prominent and reveals how much the warehouses of this area owed to those emperors. Fortunately the placing of such buildings on the river bank is partly revealed to us by the Marble Plan fragments.

SEVERAN MARBLE PLAN

On the Marble Plan are representations of all kinds of buildings whose names and designations are not known. Bearing in mind that Ostia shared the architectural styles and planning that held good in the capital itself, it is clear that it should be possible to identify *horrea* simply

---

[1] I owe my knowledge of this building to the kindness of Mr J. B. Ward-Perkins, and Signora Lissi Carona of the Soprintendenza Roma Prima who carried out the excavation.

[2] G. Cressedi, 'Sterri al Lungotevere Testaccio', *NSc* x (1956), 19–52. Le Gall, *Le Tibre*, pp. 200 ff. Nash, *Pictorial Dictionary*, pp. 380 ff.

by their ground plan. On the other hand, we may also have some idea of what they looked like and the details of their structure from what is known about the mass of *horrea* already excavated at Ostia.

In one case at least we have no problem about identification. A large building on fragment 25 is labelled *HORREA LOLLIANA*[1] (Fig. 23). This plan is of great importance because it is the only *labelled* plan of

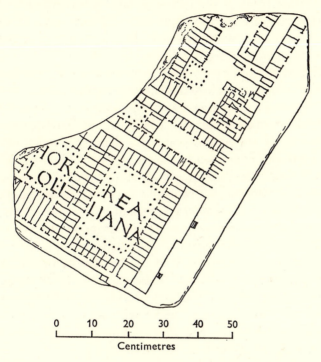

0   10   20   30   40   50

Centimetres

Fig. 23   Rome, *Horrea Lolliana*, Severan Marble Plan fragment 25

horrea in Rome that has been preserved. The building represented consisted of two large open colonnaded courts on all four sides of which open ranges of rooms. Even though the plan is not complete for the left-hand court, because of the break in the stone, we can be sure that the building had only two courts in view of the spacing of the letters in the name of the building. The two courts were not of equal size. The left-hand court was considerably smaller and squarish in shape,

[1] *Pianta Marm.* p. 83 and Tav. xxv.

24 × 29 metres approximately, while the other court was larger and more obviously rectangular, 34 × 50 metres approximately. The rooms opening on to the colonnade of the smaller court were of varying shape and size. The rooms at the bottom of the fragment were very long, 21 metres, and had an entrance at each end, one on to the colonnade, the other on to a narrow alley (3 metres wide) at the side of the building. In the room at the left-hand edge of our fragment is represented a staircase leading to an upper storey. The rooms on the opposite side of the court were wider (10 metres as opposed to 5 metres) and of only half the depth, being divided by a transverse wall. The rooms opening on to the other two sides were more uniform in shape and regular (5 × 12 metres). At least one entrance to this court, some 3 metres wide, is preserved on our fragment at the bottom right-hand corner of it. It opened into a long corridor which led past room entrances into the courtyard. (It was at this point also that a passage way 5 metres wide led from this courtyard to the larger one.) At the entrance itself was a small room with doorways both on to the alley outside and into the entrance corridor, which probably acted as a doorkeeper's lodge; this room formed one of a series of small rooms on this side of the *horrea* opening on to the alley outside. The larger court was surrounded by rooms of more regular disposition and shape, 11 × 4 metres, although there were variations (the rooms at the bottom of the fragment are only half the normal depth). The most curious anomaly seems to be that four rooms at the bottom left-hand corner of the court and two at the top of the same side seem to be without means of access. This larger court had four main entrances, 3–4 metres wide, symmetrically placed, leading into the four corners of the court. A large corner room at the bottom right entrance, with a doorway simply on to the alley outside, seems to have served as a custodian's lodge (compare the similar position of such a room guarding the south entrance to the *Piccolo Mercato* in Ostia). Immediately to the right of this court an empty quay is depicted with two sets of steps leading down to the river. It is a curious fact that none of the rooms on the side which backs on to the river have entrances towards the river, and that the main entrances to the building as a whole are all on to the two roads which lead away from the river on either side of the building. Presumably the intention was to avoid great congestion which a single entrance straight on to the quay might encourage.

That the *Horrea Lolliana* was a large and important warehouse might have been deduced solely from the inscriptions concerning it and the fact that it became part of the imperial property.[1] The plan amply confirms that importance. Although it was dwarfed by the enormous *Horrea Galbana*, it is bigger than the other buildings along the Tiber

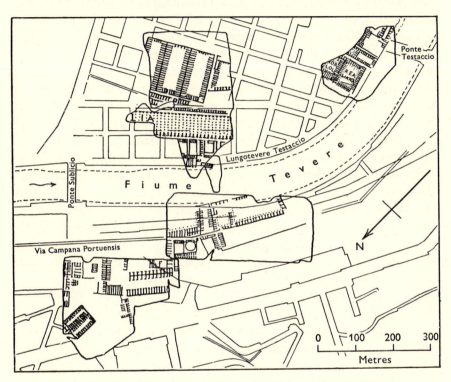

Fig. 24   Rome, Regions XIII and XIV, location of fragments of Marble Plan

bank represented on fragment 25 and fragment 24. Over eighty rooms available for storage are represented on our fragment, which does not give the complete plan. Moreover, it had a prominent position actually on the Tiber bank. Because of this fact and from a careful study of the means of fixing the Marble Plan on to its wall, the Italians have fixed the location of the *Horrea Lolliana* to the south-west of the *Horrea Galbana* (Fig. 24). The exact position of the building shown on

[1] See Chapter V (p. 164).

fragment 25 is now fixed just to the south of the Via Giovanni Battista Bodoni along the Tiber bank as far as the Ponte Testaccio.[1] This was a premier position in Rome's commercial quarter.

Just above the *Horrea Lolliana* on fragment 25 and separated from it by a road running away from the river is another smaller building which was probably *horrea* (Fig. 23). Again it consisted of two courtyards, one colonnaded, the other not. Part of the left-hand colonnaded courtyard is missing. What remains is a narrow rectangular court 11 × 14 metres surrounded on the three sides that remain by rooms of regular shape, 6 × 6 metres, although the rooms at the end are deeper (9 metres). The courtyard without colonnade, 16 × 47 metres, has no means of communication with its neighbour, although it is all part of the same building. It is surrounded on three sides by ranges of rooms averaging 5 × 6 metres. The fourth side has simply the blank back wall of the rooms of the first courtyard. Opposite this blank wall the rooms which open inwards are depicted without any back wall towards the river. There seems to be an entrance to this court about half way along the side facing towards the *Horrea Lolliana*, but this may be a postern leading in under a staircase—the plan is not clear at this point. Immediately to the south of this building, again across an intervening street, lay what seems to be a small bath house of a type similar to the Stabian baths at Pompeii.[2] To the south of this bath house again lay a series of rooms opening on to the river bank.

The problem of trying to identify possible *horrea* on the Marble Plan has in general been made easier by the new Italian study. In the Indice Tipologico,[3] R. A. Staccioli has tried to classify the plans into types such as *domus*, *templa*, *horti*, and so on. His attempted identification of *horrea* deserves particular attention because his own work in the past has been associated with them, and a study of those on the Marble Plan has been long promised by him.[4]

Fragment 3[5] shows part of a building with a central colonnaded court

[1] *Pianta Marm.* p. 83.   [2] Mau (trans. Kelsey), *Pompeii*, pp. 186 ff.

[3] *Pianta Marm.* p. 255.

[4] Staccioli, *RAL*, IX (1954), 645–57. Cf. 'Le "taberne" a Roma attraverso la "*forma urbis*"', *RAL*, XIV (1959), 56, n. 2. A preliminary study of the *horrea* on the Marble Plan has now appeared, R. A. Staccioli, 'Tipi di *horrea* nella documentazione della *Forma Urbis*', *Hommages à Albert Grenier* (Collection Latomus, LVIII) (1962), 1430 ff., but a final study is still promised.

[5] *Pianta Marm.* Tav. XV. Cf. Platner–Ashby, *A Topographical Dictionary*, p. 502.

surrounded on at least the three sides preserved by rows of rooms opening inwards. The whole building has a slightly tilted plan. The central open court was some 15 metres wide and at least 20 metres long. The rooms measure 5 × 6 metres. The building was flanked by a road labelled SUMMI CH[ORAGI]—almost certainly the *Vicus Summi Choragi*. If this is true, then the building which certainly looks like *horrea* was in Region III, where was situated the *Summum Choragium* from which the street took its name. This building, in which the machinery and apparatus for the public games in the amphitheatre were stored, is known from the discovery of a large number of inscriptions to have been situated on the south side of the Via Labicana between the Colosseum and S. Clemente. It was thus near not only the Amphitheatrum Flavium, but also the *Ludus Magnus* and *Ludus Matutinus*. The *Choragium* was an important building administered by imperial freedmen and slaves. Whether on this fragment we have part of the plan of one of its courtyards is of course not known, but it is likely that the *horrea* here represented, because of their very position, were used for the storing of theatrical machinery and equipment.

On fragment 24, in addition to the *Horrea Galbana* and the huge *Porticus Aemilia*, are represented a series of smaller buildings which must have been between the *Porticus* and the river (Fig. 22). Although these buildings must have had some commercial purpose, they are not precisely courtyard *horrea*. Basically they consist of large, empty, irregularly shaped central courtyards surrounded by rooms facing *outward*. There seems to have been little or no communication between these rooms and the courtyards. It may be that the rooms were used by private dealers or by port officials, while the central area was used for the safe dumping and sorting of goods before moving them to their proper storehouses. Between these buildings and the river is depicted another row of rooms placed back to back, the entrances of the rooms on one side opening towards the river, just as in the excavations along the Tiber bank.

Fragment 27[1] is suggested by Staccioli to contain some plans of *horrea*. This fragment depicts both sides of the river at a point which has been supposed to be just below the Ponte Palatino. Although it is certain that the river is depicted in the centre of this fragment and one might suppose the buildings on either bank to be commercial in

[1] *Pianta Marm.* Tav. XXVI.

character, there are no clear plans of courtyard *horrea* here. The area on both sides of the river gives little evidence of any systematic planning and there is simply a tangled mass of walled areas and rows of *tabernae*. Only the steps and ramps down to the river show planning. Probably the buildings here represented were used for storage, but one cannot assume that on the evidence of their ground plans: some could as easily represent *insulae* and shop facilities. There is no evidence here for the grouping of rooms to guarantee a maximum of convenience and a minimum of risk to the goods stored.

Fragment 28[1] is much more satisfactory for our purpose. Again a section of the river bank is represented at a point where the river bends (Fig. 25). As a result of the joining of several fragments, it is clear that the area represented is the bank of the Trastevere just opposite the site of the *Porticus Aemilia* and *Horrea Galbana* (Fig. 24). The great road, at points some 10 metres wide, which runs parallel with the river across the centre of our fragments, is identified with the Via Portuense. We have therefore a plan of the buildings on the Tiber in the heart of the commercial area, although on the bank opposite to that on which the better known *Horrea Galbana* stood. There can be no doubt at all that all the main buildings represented between the Via Portuense and the Tiber were *horrea*, some of them very large indeed. The first building on the left of the fragment has a rather odd plan. It is basically a central courtyard with a colonnade surrounded by rooms opening inwards, but the shape is not rectangular (the rooms furthest from the river are not parallel with it) and on the river side is inserted a small rectangular building 30 × 60 metres approximately. This has no internal walls but only an internal colonnade on three sides (not on the river side). Entrances to it are marked in all four sides and two staircases are marked leading up from the river entrance. It seems clear that there were no quays along the river bank on this stretch, and that each building had its own way down to the river (compare the steps leading up from the river into the *horrea* immediately to the right of this building). In this case, in view of the size and importance of the building, the entrance from the river was unusually elaborate. On passing through the river gate the porters could turn either to the right or to the left in order to go up the two flights of steps which led to a colonnade which must have been at the higher level of the *horrea* itself. From there they could

---

[1] *Pianta Marm.* Tav. XXVII and p. 87.

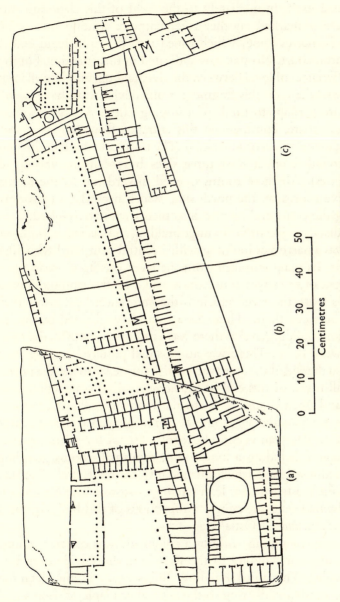

(c)

(b)

Centimetres

(a)

50

40

30

20

10

0

Fig. 25 Rome, *Horrea* Region xiv, Severan Marble Plan fragment 28

debouch either into the colonnades of the main court or into the open central area itself. Immediately to the right of this elaborate entrance way, there is marked another river entrance leading into a narrow corridor (3 metres wide) which issued into the right-hand end of the main central court. No stairs are indicated in this corridor, but in view of the differences of level between the river and the buildings flanking it, attested elsewhere on this fragment, some device must have been used, and we are perhaps to think of a sloping ramp. A large room, some 11 metres square, commanded this entrance from the river and was perhaps a guard room of some kind. The main courtyard of the building was surrounded on at least three sides by rooms of varying depth (7–20 metres). All these rooms opened inwards on to the courtyard, except five rooms on the north side, which backed on to rooms surrounding the court and opened into their own narrow yard.

Immediately adjacent to this huge building and sharing a common wall with it was a narrower building with a central courtyard which had no colonnade. Its main entrance from the river was up a broad (5 metres wide) flight of steps which may have had a central landing. The actual doorways from the river and into the *horrea* were narrower than the staircase between them. These *horrea* may have formed one unit with the previous building in that there was a minor doorway in the common wall between them. There was also a small postern opposite the river entrance at the end of the courtyard which opened into the Via Portuense. One small room of this end of the *horrea* had no connection with the interior and opened simply on to the roadway; all the other rooms, 9 × 7 metres on an average, some 21 or more, opened straight on to the inner court. The plan is entirely regular except for some structures at the north end including a long room, two small rooms guarding the postern and a staircase which intrude into the courtyard. The staircase indicates the existence of at least one upper storey. The planning without a colonnade and the general proportions of this building recall the *Horrea dell'Artemide* at Ostia[1] (Fig. 17).

This narrow building without a colonnade was certainly connected with the adjacent building to the west by a short wide corridor (4–5 metres wide). This third building differs again in the details of its planning, although adhering to the general principle of rooms opening on to an inner court. In the first place it must have depended upon the

---

[1] See Chapter I (p. 61).

116

river entrances of the buildings to its left and probably to its right as well. For, apart from one very small and narrow entrance from the river in the south-east corner of the building, the river side was closed by a series of rooms opening inwards. Away from the river the building is composed of three main elements. First there is a colonnade on to which the river side rooms opened and which acted probably as a thoroughfare between the buildings to right and left. Secondly, there is a small courtyard, some 15 metres square, surrounded by a colonnade which was double on the north side. This courtyard was flanked on the east by two huge rooms (7 × 17 metres) whose main entrances were not on to this courtyard, but on to the colonnaded thoroughfare to the south. What the disposition of the rooms on the west side was is not certain. Thirdly, to the north of this small courtyard opened a larger court (30 metres square) with a colonnade on to which rooms (4 × 9 metres) opened on two sides only, the east and the north. There was possibly a minor postern entrance on to the Via Portuense at the north-east corner of the building and probably a staircase at the south-east corner flanking the very small river entrance—although this staircase is not cut with much conviction.

The fourth building commanding the river bank on this fragment was vast. It consisted of a huge central courtyard, 50 × 140 metres (bigger, that is, than the individual courts of the *Horrea Galbana*), of a trapezoidal shape, the long axis being parallel with the river. This courtyard had a colonnade on three sides, but on the fourth, the river side, instead of columns there were substantial pilasters. The plan of the river side of these *horrea* is not fully preserved; thus although no river entrance is depicted for this building, there may well have been one. A small postern entrance existed at the north-east corner of the building on the Via Portuense. The arrangement of the rooms in these *horrea* is very regular, the only anomaly being the introduction of a small room into the west extension of the north corridor. More than forty rooms are planned, and we do not know the complete number. Two staircases, one at either end of the north row of rooms, gave access to the upper storeys. A small entrance to the *horrea* led in under one of them (compare the postern entrance under the stairs in *Horrea* (Reg. III. Is. II. 6) at Ostia)[1] (Fig. 13).

This account exhausts the *horrea* constructed along the river bank

[1] See Chapter I (p. 54).

itself in this fragment. Across a road to the west of the fourth building lay a series of smaller non-commercial structures. Across the Via Portuense to the north, however, lay more commercial buildings. It is suggested that the enormous empty walled space depicted at the bottom of fragment 28 may represent the *Horti Caesaris* known to have occupied the slopes of the Janiculum and Monteverde. Flanking these gardens and opening on to the Via Portuense was a row of shops. To the east of these is a building consisting of a narrow central corridor flanked on both sides by long narrow rooms (5 × 10 metres) which opened on to it. It was entered from the Via Portuense and had a minor entrance at the opposite end of the corridor. The rooms flanking the entrance were divided so that they were only half as deep as the others. There were only fourteen main rooms. In one of these was a small staircase immediately inside the room entrance. Whether we are dealing with *horrea* here is difficult to assert with confidence, but the ground plan is very reminiscent of *Horrea* (Reg. I. Is. XIII. I) at Ostia (Fig. 7).

It has been discovered that fragments 33 and 34 of the Marble Plan (Fig. 26) fit on to the bottom left-hand corner of fragment 28[1] (Fig. 24). We have therefore the ground plan of buildings in the Trastevere area to the north-east of the buildings we have been discussing. The buildings on fragments 33 and 34, however, lie away from the river. That a large number of storehouses are depicted here can hardly be doubted, but there is only one building which shows the typical courtyard *horrea* ground plan: the building with two courtyards on fragment 33 b. This building is orientated quite differently from those nearer the river. The long axis of its courtyards is orientated almost exactly north–south. Both the courtyards are without colonnade of any kind, and are only approximately 11 metres wide, although about 50 metres long. Rooms open on to the central courts on three sides in each case, 16 rooms on each long side, three only at the ends. The dimension of the rooms varies slightly, the central rooms of the building as a whole which share a common back wall being rather deeper, 9 metres instead of 7 metres. At a point about half way along this central block the common back wall is missing, thus providing a through corridor between the two courts. The entrances to each court were at the north end on either side of a large centrally placed chamber which blocked the end of the court and which had its own entrance on to the street: a room suitable for

[1] *Pianta Marm.* Tav. xxx and pp. 93 ff.

118

the guard personnel of the *horrea*. The unusual orientation of the *horrea* was masked from the street to the north by a row of shops of diminishing size (compare the similar situation with regard to the *Piccolo Mercato* at Ostia[1] (Fig. 2)).

Immediately to the south of this building, on fragment 33, is a suite of baths of a modest type and then what appears to be living quarters for the workers of this area. The provision of bathing facilities is

Fragment 33   Fragment 34

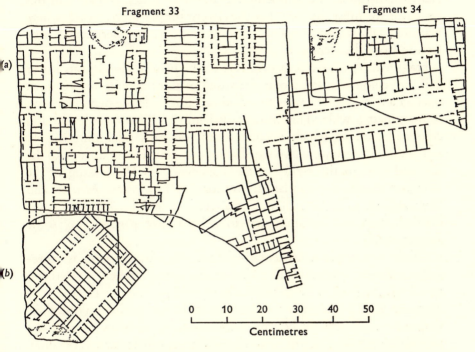

Fig. 26   Rome, *Horrea* Region XIV, Severan Marble Plan fragments 33 and 34

interesting, and recalls the similar small suite of baths to the south of the *Horrea Lolliana* on the opposite bank of the Tiber. To the east of the living quarters are great blocks of storerooms arranged back to back. They seem not to have been organised on the courtyard plan, but to have streets between them. In almost every case these storerooms opened on to arcades composed of pilasters.

Fragment 44 apparently gives us the ground plan of the *Horrea*

[1] See Chapter I (p. 17).

Candelaria.[1] I say 'apparently' because although the building is clearly labelled H[OR]REA CANDELARIA there is almost no structure to the building at all. It consisted simply of an open area, 105 metres across, quite free from structure of any kind, surrounded on at least three sides (the fourth side is not on the fragment) by a wall. Presumably the inscribed line represents a wall. In the wall at the top and the wall at the left are two entrances, one of which was some 10 metres wide. Why the *Horrea Candelaria* was represented in this way is not known. On this evidence we must suppose that they were simply a great yard where wax and tallow candles were dumped without any permanent protection from the elements.

Fragment 92 clearly preserves part of the plan of *horrea* in its lower half.[2] A colonnade ran along the front of the building and on to it opened a row of shops which flanked on either side the main entrance, some 5 metres wide. This entrance led into an open court without a colonnade, on to which opened rooms on each side. Immediately inside the entrance were two small staircases, which went up, one to the left and one to the right, to the upper storey. This placing of the staircases recalls the similar dispositions in the *Piccolo Mercato* and *Horrea* (Reg. I. Is. VIII. 2) in Ostia[3] (Figs. 2 and 3). The *horrea* was divided from the building next to it by a clear passage way some 5 metres wide.

Of the other fragments tentatively identified by Staccioli as representing *horrea*, little need be said. For example, fragment 123[4] is too small and the plan too general to admit precision. Fragment 163[5] may represent *horrea*, although a covered market hall is also a possibility. Fragment 165 more likely represents *insulae*.[6] Fragments 184 and 185 probably represent *horrea*, but the plans remaining are very small indeed.[7] In general the basic complaint against the identifications are that they are just possible, but then so are others. What about fragment 111 or fragment 285?[8] The most convincing and illuminating identifications seem to be: fragment 421, small *horrea* with a central corridor, like *Horrea* (Reg. I. Is. XIII. 1) in Ostia; fragment 543, a court-

---

[1] *Pianta Marm.* Tav. XXXIII.   [2] *Pianta Marm.* Tav. XXXVI.
[3] See Chapter I (p. 27).   [4] *Pianta Marm.* Tav. XXXVII.
[5] *Pianta Marm.* Tav. XXXIX.
[6] *Ibid.*   [7] *Pianta Marm.* Tav. XL.
[8] *Pianta Marm.* Tav. XXXVII and Tav. XLIV.

yard building at the bottom left-hand corner of the fragment with an arcade of massive pilasters and a staircase to an upper storey; fragment 548, a similar building of more than one courtyard with a less massive pilaster arcade and a staircase similarly placed in the first room to the right of the entrance; fragment 563, *horrea* with central corridor.[1]

CONCLUSION

So far as ground plans are concerned, the overall similarity with the Ostian types is proven again and again. Just as the domestic architecture of Ostia reflected the changes in style and fashion in Rome itself, so the *horrea* at Ostia seem to have been constructed to the same pattern as those in the capital. Predominantly the *horrea* of Rome seem to have been of the courtyard type. Because we have no clue in the Marble Plan as to the date of the original construction of the buildings, we do not know whether there was a tendency, as at Ostia, for the courtyards to shrink in size and perhaps to be disposed of altogether. There are on the Marble Plan storehouses consisting of deep rooms placed back to back of a type very similar to those at the Trajanic harbour at Portus, but on the whole these are not so dominant in the commercial area of Rome as we might expect. The answer may be that the commercial quarters beyond the Aventine and on the opposite bank of the Tiber were developed throughout the latter part of the Republic and thus the ground plans of the buildings in these areas belong to that period. There was little opportunity in the Empire for developing a more or less virgin site as at Portus, and what construction there was in the Testaccio area was probably concerned with repairing existing buildings. Thus it is that the walls of the *Porticus Aemilia*[2] down to the present day are of *opus incertum* of Republican date. Similarly the walls of the *Horrea Galbana* were faced with *opus reticulatum* of a late Republican date. It is interesting to note that the small bath suites in the commercial areas, for example near the *Horrea Lolliana*, were of a type similar to the 'Stabian Baths' which were built at Pompeii in the last century of the Republic.

[1] *Pianta Marm.* Tav. XLIX (421); Tav. LIII (543 and 548); Tav. LIV (563).
[2] M. Blake, *Ancient Roman Construction in Italy to Augustus* (Washington, 1947), p. 249. The exact date is disputed. Gatti, '"Saepta Iulia" e "Porticus Aemilia"', pp. 135–49, believes that the structure dates from the original building in 193 B.C. or the restoration recorded in 174 B.C. Blake prefers an unrecorded restoration about the time of Sulla.

At Ostia, because of the tremendous development of the site under the Empire, it is difficult to find traces of any Republican *horrea*, and the plans and materials used were all dictated by architectural fashions of the Empire. In Rome, at least in the Testaccio area, which began to be developed as early as 195 B.C. specifically as the *Emporium* of Rome, precisely the reverse may be true—Republican plans and building styles lasted throughout the Empire.

III

ITALY (OUTSIDE ROME AND OSTIA) AND THE PROVINCES

PORTUS

The difficulties of writing about Portus in the present state of our knowledge are well known.[1] Until recently even the outline of the Claudian harbour was not known with precision, and although more was known about the shape and dispositions of the inner Trajanic basin, the site, in the possession of the Torlonia family since 1856, has never been systematically excavated as a whole; and it has not even been open for inspection since the 1930s.

So far as the Claudian harbour is concerned, the recent work on Fiumicino airport has settled some of the problems about which there has been ingenious speculation for centuries.[2] Claudius enclosed an enormous, roughly circular area, almost a third of a square mile (about 200 acres) within two arms over half a mile apart at their maximum point. The right arm ran more or less along the land. It was about 1,800 feet long, never less than 35 feet wide, it was faced with concrete and backed by a spit of land, the Monte Giulio, which carried a road servicing the mole. Test excavations at about mid-point revealed warehouse buildings opening on to a quay 9–15 feet wide, paved with tufa, and stepped. The left arm consisted of two parts; the first was an artificially created spit of land which ran out from the coast parallel to the right arm; from this spit there ran at right angles, at least in the late Empire, a great masonry breakwater. It was about 2,300 feet long and left one entrance to the harbour over 600 feet wide facing north-west, away from the prevailing south-westerly winds. The construction of this great breakwater is slightly puzzling. For about 980 feet from the spit of land it was about 8 feet wide and composed of magnificent oblong travertine blocks carefully fastened to each other by iron cramps. For the remaining distance the travertine blocks were smothered by great masses of concrete, measuring at least 15 feet in

---

[1] Meiggs, p. 149.
[2] O. Testaguzza, 'The Port of Rome', *Archaeology* XVII (1964), 173–9.

width and gradually swelling out to the great mass of concrete 60 feet wide and 300 feet long, which seems to have supported the lighthouse. Thus the question whether the harbour had two entrances, one on either side of the lighthouse, as Suetonius and Dio both claimed, or only one, as Pliny asserted, is still not definitively settled. It may be that the left-hand entrance was sealed to prevent rough water or silt in the harbour.

Despite the excavations and the picture of the Claudian harbour on a Neronian coin which shows at least on the left mole long colonnades and a temple, no restoration of the harbour buildings and installations is possible even now. We can get some idea of what such a harbour might have looked like only from the recent Italian excavations of Lepcis Magna in Tripolitania[1] (Fig. 28). It is true that the harbour at Lepcis Magna is only 24½ acres, that is, about a ninth of the size of the Claudian harbour and only a third of the size of Trajan's inner harbour at Fiumicino. But it is interesting in showing the temple, the warehouses, stepped quays and mooring arrangements for ships. Even in such a small harbour there was room, according to the Italian calculations, for 155 berths. Moreover, it indicates clearly, what one may suspect from the remnants of the fine portico of Claudius at the Ostian harbour, that we need fear no shoddy commercial architecture in these harbour installations.

A new, smaller hexagonal basin, of about 81 acres, was excavated by Trajan in the land previously crossed by canals linking the Claudian harbour to the Tiber (Fig. 27). Trajan's harbour is poorly known, but some scraps of knowledge have been gathered over the years. Each of the quays had a length of about 1,100 feet and a constant width of 18 feet. There was a report that the quays were made up of a series of broad shallow steps, although that has not been confirmed. The sides of the basin itself were carefully constructed in brick-faced concrete. Set deeply into recesses in the quay sides were the travertine corbels, by which the ships, prow forward, made fast to the land. Each corbel was a plain block of stone 3 feet 8 inches high, and 2 feet 4 inches wide, pierced transversely by a large hole, 1 foot 4 inches in diameter, to take

---

[1] E. Caffarelli, G. Caputo, *The Buried City: Excavations at Leptis Magna* (London, 1966); see Chapter III (p. 132); cf. also M. R. de la Blanchère, *Terracine* (Paris, 1884), p. 120. At Terracina seventy-six vaulted rooms lay behind the portico on the mole itself, each room 19–20 feet wide and 23 feet deep, separated by walls 2–3 feet thick, closed alternately by grilles and doors.

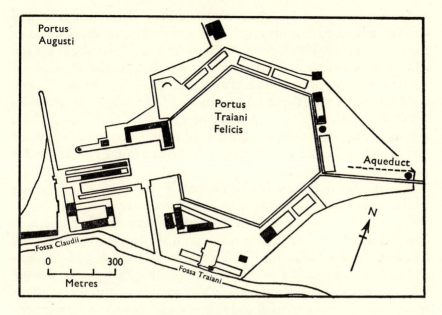

Fig. 27   Trajan's Harbour

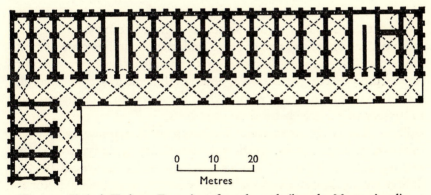

Fig. 27a   Trajan's Harbour, East wing of warehouse built under Marcus Aurelius

the ships' cables. Surrounding the basin was a colonnade on some of whose columns at least numbers were incised, perhaps referring to the ships' berths below. Beyond the colonnade was built a vastly increased acreage of warehouse facilities, the precise details of which are not known to us even now.

The foundation of modern knowledge about the buildings around the Trajanic harbour is the article by Lanciani in 1868 and his plan of the same period.[1] These incorporated all he could learn about the site and the results of excavations in his own day. In 1925 Calza[2] published the results of a small excavation at the south-west corner of the Trajanic basin which revealed the end of one of the blocks of storehouses depicted by Lanciani. In 1935 Lugli and Filibeck published *Il Porto di Roma imperiale e l'agro Portuense*, a description of what buildings still remained visible on the site. This book was published in a limited edition and is not available in Britain.

Basically we may be sure that Lanciani's plan is right in depicting the hexagonal basin surrounded on all its sides by rows of storehouses. He planned these storehouses as two ranges of rooms placed back to back on a common wall, one range with its doorways towards the harbour, the other away from it. This shape was confirmed by Calza's excavation in 1925. The rooms of the building he excavated were 5 × 16 metres and had doorways 2–2·50 metres. But the 1925 excavation revealed the interesting detail that the doorways opened on to a gallery some 5 metres wide which ran around the building. This gallery was completely enclosed by a wall and presumably lighted by windows high in it. The entrances to the gallery from the outside were few and were only about 1·75 metres wide. The existence of such a gallery around the storehouses makes more understandable this type of storehouse plan. One of the prime needs in the design of *horrea* was the absolute security of the goods stored, and it is difficult to see on Lanciani's plan how that need could be met when the rows of rooms placed back to back opened immediately into the streets.

How many rows there were of this type of storehouse on each side of the basin is not certain. Lanciani depicts double and even triple rows. According to the plan of Calza's 1925 excavation it would be very difficult to squeeze in the double row which Lanciani planned for the south-east side even if we suppose that the Constantinian wall joined the second row and resulted in the closing of all the doorways opening to the east.

[1] R. Lanciani, 'Ricerche topografiche sulla città di Porto', *Ann. Inst.* XL (1868), 144 ff. and particularly 178 ff. Plan in *Monumenti Inediti pubbl. dall'Instituto di Corrisp. Arch.* vol. VIII, Tav. XLVIIII (wrongly labelled as Tav. LXVIIII).

[2] G. Calza, 'Ricognizioni topografiche nel Porto di Traiano', *NSc* (1925), 58 ff.

Lugli and Filibeck give the following information about the store-houses of this back-to-back type.

On the north-west side of the basin[1] they were constructed of very fine *opus mixtum* and the roofing arrangements were in concrete cross-vaulting. Some of the upper rooms with the same type of construction were also preserved. Fragments of great bases were found and Corinthian capitals of white marble. There were traces of restoration of the Antonine period in the earlier walls. Originally the outer doorways of the northernmost row opened on to the wharf of the Claudian harbour, but all these entrances were blocked by the building of the Constantinian wall round the city.

On the north side of the basin[2] there seems to have been only one row some 18 metres wide from the Constantinian wall to the quayside (as opposed to two depicted by Lanciani). A series of transverse walls some 9 metres apart were joined in the middle by a longitudinal wall which formed the backbone of the building. This longitudinal wall had doorways in it between the rooms. At the east end of the whole building were pilasters some 2·30 metres in width and 0·14 metres in projection. The walls were built of very fine *opus mixtum* (reticulate *tesserae* 9 × 9 centimetres; brick 3·2 centimetres wide and yellow-brown in colour; the *caementa* of tufa pieces and tiles).

On the north-east side of the basin[3] Lugli and Filibeck record that what little was visible was in every way similar to the preceding side except that in the centre were found traces of a round temple. Because this seemed to be a temple to Bacchus with a cult figure, the suggestion is that the storehouses on this side were *horrea vinaria*.

On the south-east side[4] was the row of storehouses of which Calza excavated the south end in 1925. The fact that he records that the rooms were faced with brickwork alone and not with *opus mixtum* would indicate that this building, or at least the end excavated, had been rebuilt at a date later than the other Trajanic and Hadrianic buildings of this type. This will be important when we consider the flooring arrangements.

On the south side of the basin[5] Lugli suggested that there was a storehouse of the back-to-back type at the eastern end, but that further west

[1] G. Lugli, G. Filibeck, *Il Porto di Roma* (Rome, 1935), p. 100.
[2] *Ibid.* p. 101.   [3] *Ibid.* p. 101. But cf. Meiggs, p. 282.
[4] Lugli, Filibeck, *op. cit.* p. 102.   [5] *Ibid.* p. 104.

was a building in the form of a great triangle with its base parallel to the side of the basin. In Lugli's schematic plan this building is represented as having two internal courtyards.

In the area south of the *Darsena* it seems clear that Lanciani's plan is not to be trusted even for the general outline of buildings. Along the north bank of the *Fossa Traiani*[1] in this area stretched a range of rooms placed back to back. The walls were preserved to a height of some 7–8 metres and were constructed of *opus mixtum*. The original walls of the building were covered with new walls of fine red brickwork said by Lugli to be Severan in date. Even later restorations by Constantine were undertaken at various points to fortify the building.

To the north of the *Darsena* itself on the spur of land between it and the entrance from the Claudian into the Trajanic harbour were rows of storehouses divided by a central corridor.[2] The rooms were some 4·5 metres wide but later alterations reduced this width and restricted the central corridor.

So much then for the standard type of storehouse built around this harbour. There were of course other examples of this type, for instance along the canal between the *Darsena* and *Fossa Traiani* where the ruins were too fragmentary to justify a description. But besides this standard type there are three other buildings used for storage which deserve particular mention. First, at the east corner of the basin is an isolated building[3] at the point where the main road after entering the town reached the harbour itself. Its plan is not known in detail, but it seems to be different from that of the ordinary type. Certainly it was built later than the installation of the Port as a whole, since its structure was faced with reddish brown bricks of slender thickness with wide mortar joints. Whether it can be dated to Severus's reign with confidence is doubtful: most brick-faced structures in Portus tend to be attributed to that Emperor.

Along the sea front to the south-west of the *Darsena* there had been since the time of Claudius a great portico.[4] Lugli states that it was under Septimius Severus that this portico was converted into a great storehouse with rooms placed back to back by the building of long brick-faced walls. The rooms were vaulted and a staircase led to an upper storey.

The most imposing storehouse of them all was situated just to the

[1] *Ibid.* p. 112.　　[2] *Ibid.* p. 119.　　[3] *Ibid.* p. 104.　　[4] *Ibid.* p. 116.

north of the entrance into the Trajanic harbour. Lugli called it the 'grandi magazzini di Settimio Severo',[1] but the finding of brick stamps since then has fixed the building rather earlier, to the first ten years of the reign of Marcus Aurelius.[2] The building was erected all at one period and has survived substantially as it was built. It consisted of three ranges of rooms of unequal length, grouped around an open cortile. The north range was about 186 metres long, the east range 108 metres and the west some 65 metres long. The south side of the courtyard was open on to the sea-way between the two harbours. A corridor 5·40 metres wide surrounded the cortile on the three sides in front of the ranges of rooms which opened on to it. This corridor was covered with cross-vaulting and was lighted by doors and windows into the courtyard. Although the rooms only opened on to the corridor and courtyard which faced towards the *Darsena*, there was an entranceway in the middle of the north side which led to the wharfs around the Claudian harbour. The rooms varied in size, those on the east side being the deepest, 17 × 5 metres. All the rooms had wide arched entrances. A travertine threshold was recorded in 1925, 2·35 × 0·60 metres, with two pivot holes 2·05 metres apart.[3] This is exactly similar to the thresholds of *horrea* in Ostia itself. On the east side the rooms have two pilasters on each side wall from which spring the four ribs dividing the cross-vaulting at a height of 3·10 metres from the floor. On the north and west sides the rooms have only one such pilaster on each side wall. In the rear wall of each room were two tall splayed windows, presenting to the exterior narrow slits between the buttresses along the sides. These buttresses were arranged at regular intervals half the width of each room so that they corresponded either to the division walls of the rooms or to their axis. The windows on the north side were blocked at a later date by the building of new walls inside and outside the original wall. Calza in 1925 revealed that the flooring was of 'cocciopesto' (*opus signinum*) 10 centimetres thick (Fig. 27 a).[4]

Two ramp stairways in the east range and two in the north range led to an upper storey. The fact that the staircases are in the form of ramps makes it clear that Lanciani's guess[5] that the upper parts were living

[1] *Ibid.* p. 83.
[2] H. Bloch, *I bolli laterizi e la storia edilizia romana* (Rome, 1938), p. 280.
[3] G. Calza, *NSc* (1925), 68, Letter G.   [4] *Ibid.* p. 68, Letter G.
[5] R. Lanciani, 'Ricerche topografiche sulla città di Porto', *Ann. Inst.* XL (1868), 179.

quarters for the staff is wrong, and as in the *Piccolo Mercato* in Ostia we have upper storeys devoted to storage purposes.

The whole building was finely constructed and faced with brickwork, the *caementa* consisting of fragments of tufa together with pieces of sherd, selce and marble. A reconstruction drawing of this building is given in Lugli's book[1] and can be regarded as a fairly accurate impression of its appearance. It would be right to doubt the artist's assumption that the external buttresses were joined at the top by arches thus making rather graceful blind arcades, in view of the rarity of positive evidence for this type of structure. It is perhaps more likely that the buttresses were taken straight up to the roof.

What conclusions of general interest can be drawn from the Portus *horrea*? Great caution is needed in trying to formulate these because of the restricted nature of the evidence. However, it is a fact that what evidence there is for the raising of *horrea* floors by *suspensurae* does not disagree with the Ostian evidence. There is only unimpeachable evidence for it in Calza's excavation in 1925, and he was convinced that the floor had been raised at a later date than the original planning and construction of the building. The facing of the walls with bricks points, I think, to a similar conclusion, namely that we do not have the building as it was originally constructed. The foundations, which were of the first period and presumably contemporary with the port, had been cut off at a certain level. Above them the walls were faced with brickwork alone. This would suggest that they were later than the pure *opus mixtum* facing of the other *horrea* of this type and were re-erected some time during or after the reign of Antoninus Pius. When precisely this took place we cannot be sure, because no description of the brickwork or dated brick stamp was given. In view of the fact, however, that the *Grandi Horrea* in Ostia did not have *suspensurae* until its rebuilding under Commodus[2] and that the only *horrea* which had them from the start was the *Horrea Antoniniani* of Commodan date, we may suspect that it was not until early in the second half of the second century A.D. that the fully developed form of *suspensurae*, a floor of *bipedales* raised on dwarf walls, was used. At least the Portus evidence so far does not contradict that. Any attempt to fix the date of the *suspensurae* at Portus by pointing out that the great warehouse now known to have been

---

[1] Lugli, Filibeck, *Il Porto di Roma*, fig. 51.
[2] See Chapter I (p. 50) and Appendix 1.

built by Marcus Aurelius had flooring of *cocciopesto* 10 centimetres thick (just like the *original* floors of the *Grandi Horrea* in Ostia) and that therefore *suspensurae* were not introduced until after Marcus Aurelius must founder on the fact that we do not know whether that great building was used for grain storage. If it could be proved that it was so used, this fact would of course be suggestive.

With regard to general conclusions about the ground plans of the *horrea* at Portus, even greater caution is needed. Meiggs[1] sees in the back-to-back ranges and restricted open areas a development which he claims was to be reflected in the *Horrea Antoniniani* at Ostia. He also suggests that it probably superseded the earlier type of courtyard *horrea*. This may be true and it is certainly the case that the size of courtyards in Ostia tends to diminish. But it is worth making the point that there is little new in the shape of the Portus *horrea*. Storerooms back to back were a feature of the *Grandi Horrea* from the Claudian period and the plan of the Portus *horrea* was just that of the central ranges of rooms in the *Horrea Galbana*, which appear to have been constructed in the late Republic. All that has changed is that the courtyard has been abandoned, and this is more likely to be due to the exigencies of space and the limitations which a harbour shape imposed on the buildings which surround it. It may be remarked that where there was sufficient space for a courtyard even as late as Marcus Aurelius the Romans used one. It is also fair to point out that we do not possess the whole plan of the *Horrea Antoniniani* at Ostia and that its present apparent similarity with Portus examples may be reduced with more knowledge.

So far as other details of structure and planning are concerned, as Calza remarked, there is little difference from the *horrea* known at Ostia. In the ranges placed back to back the splayed windows are not needed, and similarly buttresses are used only at the extreme ends of each block—the weight of goods stored normally being counterbalanced by that in the rooms to either side and at the rear. However, in the courtyard *horrea* of Marcus Aurelius the usual splayed windows and buttresses are needed and are present. The pilasters along the side walls of the rooms in this building were not a regular feature of the earlier *horrea*. They are to be explained in association with the use of cross-vaulting in the roofing of the rooms: a style which had been used

[1] Meiggs, p. 280.

in the *Horrea Epagathiana et Epaphroditiana* under Antoninus Pius.[1] In the Marcus Aurelius warehouse at Portus, the great depth of the storage rooms necessitated the division of the cross-vaulting into two or three sections.

No matter how inadequate the detailed evidence from Portus may be, it is of the greatest importance simply because it is the only port in Italy about which we have any real knowledge of the harbour installation. The importance of Puteoli in the late Republic and early Empire is well known, but so far no excavation has disclosed evidence for its warehouses and their distribution around the harbour.[2] Recently there was a reference in an Italian newspaper[3] to the discovery there of five connected storerooms for grain, but no details are discoverable.

The only other possible source for the disposition and appearance of *horrea* at Puteoli might be the 'antique picture found on the Esquiline'.[4] The latest attempt to identify its location has favoured Puteoli. On it is depicted a building labelled *HORREA*. Unfortunately the location of the picture has been constantly open to question. It has even been regarded as a view of the Testaccio area by Durm.[5] Moreover, it is by no means clear to which building the word *horrea* refers, whether to the whole ensemble with the courtyard or simply to the four long hangars to which the word is appended. It seems more likely to refer to the latter but there is no means of deciding, and its possible use as evidence is of negligible importance.

LEPCIS MAGNA

The only other port in the Roman Empire which has been studied in detail recently is the Severan harbour of Lepcis Magna in Tripolitania[6] (Fig. 28).

[1] Becatti, 'Horrea Epagathiana et Epaphroditiana', p. 45, fig. 10.

[2] C. Dubois, *Pouzzoles Antique* (Paris, 1907), p. 355 and 359, reported some ranges of vaulted rooms built in concrete faced with reticulate and bands of bricks which were probably part of some *horrea*, but they were not in the immediate vicinity of the harbour.

[3] *Il Tempo*, 18 February 1961. No further reports seem to have been issued in, for example, *Notizie degli Scavi*.

[4] Ch. Hülsen, 'Di una pittura antica ritrovata sull'Esquilino nel 1668', *RM* XI (1896), 213 ff. Cf. Ch. Picard, 'Pouzzoles et le paysage portuaire', *Latomus* XVIII (1959), 23 ff.

[5] J. Durm, *Die Baukunst der Römer* (Stuttgart, 1905), p. 637.

[6] R. Bartoccini, *Il porto romano di Leptis Magna* (Rome, 1960).

The pre-Severan port and its installations was essentially a river port such as Ostia must have been prior to Claudius. The warehouses of that port probably lined the west and south sides of the hollow in the coast line and the sides of the river as it entered the sea.[1] In creating the Severan harbour some small islands just off the coast were joined to it by massive concrete moles so as to form a completely enclosed basin with a narrow mouth. It is about the warehouses on these two new

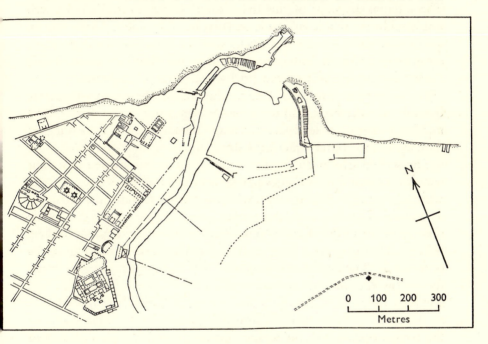

Fig. 28   Lepcis Magna

moles of the north and the east side of the basin that we know most, although it is certain that similar storehouses existed on the west side too.

The storehouses on the north side of the harbour are divided into two groups.[2] The first at the west end of the north side consists of a building some 100 metres long and approximately 12 metres deep. The building as a whole is more or less rectangular, although the north-west corner has a very acute angle. It was placed on the mole parallel to the line of

[1] *Ibid.* pp. 9–12.   [2] *Ibid.* pp. 57 ff.

wharfs of the harbour which were at a lower level. In all there were three levels: the first and lowest at approximately sea level; the second intermediate level reached from the lowest by a flight of steps at one end; the third and highest level at which the warehouses were placed was reached by a continuous flight of six steps which ran along the front of the warehouses. The colonnade in front of the entrances to the warehouse was placed in such a way that the steps also were protected by it. The internal divisions of this first group of storehouses are not well known, but the whole ensemble was divided at least into three sections. The walls, some 1·90 metres thick, were constructed in stone rubble set in concrete faced with small limestone blocks set in mortar. There were horizontal bands of tile brickwork, three courses thick, set at 1·30–1·50 metres from each other. The wall at the south end of the building and the back wall towards the open sea were reinforced by a massive facing of at least five receding courses of bossed masonry set flush against the outer wall of the storehouse.

The second group on the north side may be subdivided into four sections separated by passages paved with selce blocks some 3 metres wide linking the harbour quays with the wharfs towards the open sea. The first three of these sections consist simply of one room each, while the fourth is a range of ten rooms. The dimensions and shapes of these rooms vary because the whole ensemble is accommodated to the shape of the mole. The depths of the rooms become progressively greater the further east they are. The structure of the walls, some 1·15 metres thick, is exactly the same as that of the first group, and there is a similar heavy reinforcement of the walls towards the open sea. All the doorways of the rooms open south on to the colonnade which shelters the steps leading up to them from the harbour.

On the east side[1] the row of storerooms stretching out on the mole are more regular in size and disposition, although not completely so (Fig. 29). Eighteen rooms have been uncovered, but the room at the south end which is larger—with three entrances and divided internally into nave and aisles by six pilasters—may be a common room for the personnel rather than a storeroom proper. Because of the upward slope of the mole towards the north, the more southerly rooms have to be reached by flights of steps which lead to their doorways, the number of steps diminishing towards the north and being unnecessary at a point

[1] *Ibid.* pp. 120 ff.

about half way along the group. The rooms all opened west on to the harbour and their entrances were protected by a colonnade with Doric capitals. The back wall of the rooms towards the sea was as on the north side, heavily reinforced by stone blocks some 3 metres thick at the bottom. The structure of the walls was similar to those on the north mole in that the usual stone rubble in concrete was faced with small blocks set in mortar. But instead of the banding with brickwork, a system of long wooden beams was used, which have now rotted away except for one carbonised example. These beams were not only set

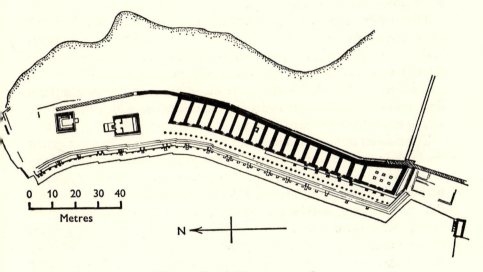

Fig. 29   Lepcis Magna, east mole

horizontally in the facing of the wall, where a brickwork band would have been, but also set transversely into the thickness of the wall at intervals, immediately above and below the horizontal beams. This substitution of wood for brickwork puzzled the excavators and they suggest, in view of the scarcity of wood in the area, that it was dictated by the need to save time in construction. The only parallel for such a type of construction they can quote is the mention by Durm[1] of its use

[1] J. Durm, *Die Baukunst der Griechen* (Leipzig, 1910), p. 36, Abb. 18. It is, however, clear that this 'lacing' of walls with wooden beams was a common structural feature in eastern building. Cf. H. Frankfort, *The Art and Architecture of the Ancient Orient* (Harmondsworth, 1954), pp. 145, 169 and fig. 81.

in Cretan and Mycenean building, and that it has often been used in Arab buildings in past centuries.

The thresholds of all twenty doorways, 1·36 metres wide, are still in position. The thresholds are each cut from one piece of stone and measure 2·10 × 1·10 metres with raised marginal check and pivot holes for doors opening inwards. The door jambs were again of one piece of stone some 2·35 metres high and fitted on to the marginal side checks. The whole doorway was finished off by the fitting of an element exactly similar to the threshold with marginal check and pivot hole on to the top of the two door jambs.

The width of the rooms varies from 5 to 5·60 metres with the exception of the two end rooms at the north, which are 6·60 metres wide. One of the middle rooms still preserves inside it the lower stone steps of a staircase which must have been continued in wood.

It is certain that on this east mole the storehouses had two storeys, since elements of an upper order for the colonnade which fronted the whole ensemble have been found.

The interest of these buildings at Lepcis Magna for us to some extent lies in their ground plans, since they are a guide to the possible dispositions of buildings in the Claudian harbour at Ostia. For in the Claudian harbour the same problems will have had to be faced, and the difficulties of arranging storehouses on a narrow mole and adapting their plan to its anomalies will have been the same. But the main interest must be in the structure of the Lepcis building. The combination of the western use of concrete with the eastern use of blocks and ashlar masonry and above all the use of timber bonding courses demand attention.

It may be further worthwhile to point out the elaborate care with which the problems of the varying levels and slopes of the harbour topography were solved, and the architectural elegance and sophistication of the colonnades which fronted such utilitarian buildings. As the architectural fragments of the *Horrea Agrippiana* in Rome have already hinted, storehouses in monumental zones did not lack impressive decoration and planning.

CONSTANZA

A building of similar elegance has recently been discovered at Constanza (Tomi) just south of the Danube mouth.[1] Built against a cliff and facing the ancient harbour, the building comprised three terraces. The first at the top of the cliff was at the level of the modern town; some 6 metres lower down a second terrace was formed by a great mosaic pavement, about 20 metres wide, which was itself supported by a range of brick-vaulted rooms, and about 9 metres high. The entrances to these rooms opened on to the third and lowest terrace, about 5 metres above sea level, and 30 metres from the actual quayside. It seems that the mosaic terrace was unroofed and that the lowest vaulted rooms, 5 metres wide and 10 metres deep, with entrances 2 metres wide, were used for storage of goods at the harbour. The date of the building is uncertain, perhaps third century A.D., more likely Constantinian.

Constanza had of course had a long history as a Greek colony before the Roman expansion of Moesia in A.D. 45 absorbed it. It owed its long history and its prosperity to its position on trade routes through the Dobrudja. The new discovery stresses the continuation of its prosperity in times of uncertainty for the Romans and shows again what skill and flair were shown in the siting and building of commercial structures at Roman ports.

MYRA AND PATARA

Although the storehouses at Lepcis and Constanza cannot be taken as typical so far as the ground plan is concerned, since that is so obviously dictated by the shape and size of the moles on the one hand and the position against a cliff on the other, it nevertheless remains a fact that the only other *horrea* we know in the North African area and the two known on the coast of Asia Minor consist similarly of a range of rooms all of whose entrances open in one side of the building. The two *horrea* in Asia Minor[2] form a pair in that they were erected at the same period, A.D. 128, by the same Emperor, Hadrian, at neighbouring places and with much the same ground plan. Both buildings were clearly labelled

[1] V. Caranache, 'L'édifice à mosaïque découvert devant le port de Tomis', *Studii Clasice* III (1961), 227.

[2] *Reisen im Südwestlichen Kleinasien* I, O. Benndorf and G. Niemann (Vienna, 1884), p. 116 (*Horrea* at Patara); II, E. Petersen and F. von Luschan (Vienna, 1889), p. 41 (*Horrea* at Myra).

and dated by an inscription across the front of the building. At Patara the *horrea* was situated to the west of the harbour. The building (Fig. 30) consisted of a huge oblong, 70 metres in length from north to south, and with a width of 27 metres. Seven transverse division walls divided the whole length into eight rooms of equal size. The building is still preserved to a considerable height, although it has lost its vaulting and roof. The material used throughout was cut stone. The outer walls were 1 metre thick, while the inner division walls were only some 80 centimetres thick. The eight rooms were covered by barrel vaults which were strengthened by archivolts resting on pilasters projecting from the division walls at the half way point. The height of the rooms to the top of the vaulting was about 10 metres. The doorways to the eight rooms were placed in the long east side and were 2 metres wide. There were

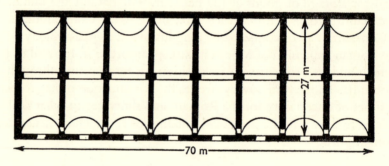

Fig. 30   Patara, sketch-plan of *horrea*

also smaller doorways only 1·13 metres wide connecting the rooms with one another, placed close to this east front of the building. The east front gives the impression that the building was two-storeyed, for above the doorways, at a point 8·3 metres from the ground, were great windows 2·3 metres in height. However, there is no evidence inside the building for a division into two storeys. The façade was constructed in well-worked hewn stones and had no ornamentation apart from two raised mouldings, one above the windows and one above the doors. The latter, however, had two consoles which jutted out of it, two over each doorway.

The other Asiatic *horrea* was placed on the southern hills of the valley between Myra and Andriake. The ground plan and general appearance (Pl. 50) have an overall similarity to the *horrea* at Patara, although there are differences of detail (Fig. 31). The *horrea* at Myra is only 65 metres in length, but six of the eight rooms have the greater depth of 32 metres as opposed to only 27 metres at Patara. The other two rooms at the end of the range have less depth, *circa* 27 metres, and thereby spoil the rectangular shape of the whole building. A further difference is that this *horrea* had projecting at the two ends of the row of entrances two small rooms with arched doorways, which opened towards each other across the façade of the building. They were probably custodians' rooms. The appearance of being two-storeyed was avoided here by the

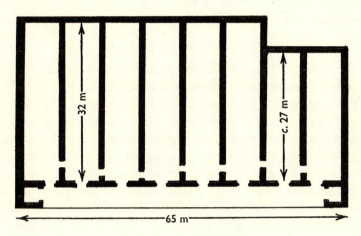

Fig. 31   Myra, sketch-plan of *horrea*

reduction of the distance between the windows and the doors. Moreover, in this case there were two smaller windows divided by an ornamental pilaster placed above each doorway. There were projecting moulded bands and consoles similar to those at Patara, and the whole façade was crowned by a flattened pediment. Besides the inscription recording the nature of the building and its date, there were two later inscriptions embedded in its walls. Over the middle doorway of the *horrea* were placed busts of Hadrian and Sabina (?) (Pl. 51). A broad pavement ran in front of the entrances to the storerooms between the two projecting custodians' rooms. The whole building was constructed, as at Patara, in dressed stones, but here the masonry was rusticated.

Despite the differences, both buildings are very similar in plan and construction. The lack of buttresses is to be explained by the thickness (1 metre) of the walls and their construction in ashlar masonry. The enormous depth of the rooms is a characteristic of both buildings and it is to be noted again in the *horrea* at Djemila in North Africa (Fig. 32). The existence of *horrea* of such size and pretensions in Asia Minor must, I think, be connected with the imperial *annona*. In this connection it may not be out of place to remark that it was at Myra that the centurion escorting St Paul to Rome found an Alexandrian freighter bound for Italy,[1] and it seems that the ports of southern Asia Minor formed a regular part of the coasting voyage to Rome for the freighters from Alexandria.

DJEMILA, NORTH AFRICA

That the *horrea* at Djemila (Cuicul)[2] in Algeria was also erected in connection with the imperial *annona* is almost certain. It is true that the inscription recording the foundation of the *horrea* in A.D. 199 records that *resp(ublica) Cuiculitanorum horrea a solo extruxit*, but the governor of the province dedicated it to Septimius Severus and the imperial family, and other inscriptions recording its officials seem to refer to them as *horrea sacra*, that is, imperial buildings. Furthermore, a series of stone measures have been found set up by the governor of the province, not by a municipal magistrate.[3] It seems very probable that they were used for measuring goods owed to the *annona* by those liable for taxes in kind, part of which would have been given back to the imperial officials, civil and military, of the district and a part transhipped to Italy as part of the African corn.

The foundation inscription was discovered in 1910, but it was not until 1926 that the actual remains of the *horrea* were revealed (Fig. 32). The building was not so large as the *horrea* at Myra and Patara: its frontage was only 22·65 metres long and none of its rooms exceeded 25 metres in length. However, it was sizeable enough to be a striking addition to the town plan and its ruins covered about 500 square metres. Essentially the ground plan is similar to the plans of the *horrea* at Myra and Patara in that the building is made up of a series of long rooms all

[1] Acts of the Apostles, 27. 1–28. 13.
[2] Y. Allais, 'Les greniers publics de Djemila', *RAfr* (1933), p. 259.
[3] *AE* (1911), no. 106. Cf. E. Albertini, 'Une inscription de Djemila', *CRAI* (1924), p. 253; and 'Table de mesures de Djemila', *CRAI* (1920), p. 315.

of which have their entrances on the same side. Nonetheless, a great distortion of this simple plan was necessitated by the previous topography of the site and the surrounding buildings. The first two rooms at the north end of the building are perfectly regular rectangles 21·60 × 3 metres, and are orientated east–west. Because the two most

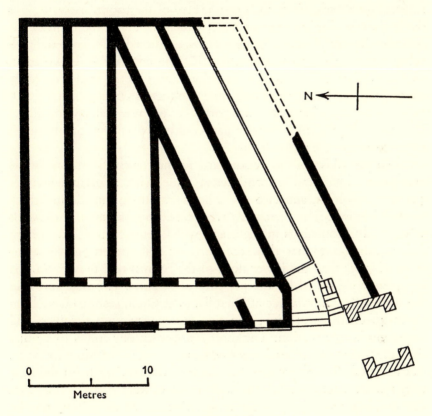

Fig. 32   Djemila, *horrea*

southerly rooms had to be accommodated to the existing topography of the site, they were given a slanting south-west–north-east orientation. The result of this is that these two rooms are longer than the rest (25 metres) and their slant cuts across the length of the two middle rooms, progressively reducing it and giving to one of them a triangular shape only some 10 metres deep.

The walls are, in general, still preserved to a height of about 2 metres and are some 60–5 centimetres thick, constructed in small pieces of stone set in mortar framed by large vertical blocks of stone 1–1·50 metres apart. This type of construction was widespread in Roman Africa. The corners of the walls are made of fine ashlar blocks. A certain amount of brick was used in the most southerly room and to support the thresholds to each room. Five of the rooms had entrances on to the corridor 3·10 metres wide, which ran along the front of the building. The sixth room at the south was entered only from the fifth room immediately to the north of it. The corridor had two main entrances from the street, one large one (2·35 metres wide) centrally placed, and one much narrower one (1·10 metres wide) which led into a part of the corridor which was partly cut off by a wall and could act as a room from which a custodian could keep an eye on the main entrance and all the room doorways.

The thresholds to the rooms are formed each from one stone 1·50 metres long and 60 centimetres wide with a marginal check 4 centimetres high, and two pivot holes for supporting doors which opened inwards. The thresholds were raised up on small brick walls which had no openings in them and which set the threshold so high (70 centimetres higher than the corridor and sometimes 80 centimetres higher than the lower floor of the rooms) that they cannot be completely explained by the presence of *suspensurae*, raised floors, in the rooms. The *suspensurae* at Djemila, as at Ostia, seem to have been about 40 centimetres high, and the discrepancy with the threshold height needs explanation. The most satisfactory one seems to be that since the whole site slopes down towards the east, very serious measures had to be taken to prevent the flooding of the granary from the road to the west. There may also be something in Miss Allais's suggestion that the height was dictated for the convenience of workmen carrying sacks on their backs. *Suspensurae* were discovered in only the four northern rooms. As at Ostia, the upper floors were made up of *bipedales* covered with concrete, in this case 12 centimetres thick. But at Djemila they were carried by a series of small piers each composed of nine bricks measuring 20 centimetres per side. In the two southern rooms there were no *suspensurae*, only floors composed of packed pebbles. The flooring of the corridor was in concrete. A small room with a flagged entranceway, which had arrangements in the door jambs for locking it by means of a wooden bar, is situated at the south-west corner of the building. Although it had no means of communication with the *horrea*, Miss Allais considered it to be an office for clerks in charge of the arrival of goods and the distribution of foodstuffs. This seems to me unlikely, and in view of its position immediately inside the city gate it is more likely to have been a guardhouse for that gate.

The plan and structure of these *horrea* at Djemila are of the greatest interest because they are the only provincial *horrea* of a civil type which we know to have had raised floors. Furthermore, the date for the building adds to our knowledge about those raised floors. Miss Allais concluded from a superficial examination of the first-century literary authorities on *horrea* that *suspensurae* were a sophisticated arrangement which became widespread in the second century A.D. All the evidence which has accrued since then concerning *suspensurae* in the form we know at Ostia and Djemila supports that view.[1] The plan, once the eccentricities imposed by the site are removed, is remarkably similar to the plans of the Myra and Patara examples, although it is on a smaller scale. It may well be that in looking for civil *horrea* of the second and third centuries A.D. in the provinces we should look, not for the court-yard or corridor types known from Ostia and Rome, nor for the back-to-back ranges known from Portus, but rather for the single range of narrow rooms of great depth all opening on to a front corridor or veranda surveyed by a control room.

Partly because of the dearth of remains of *horrea* in the provinces of the Roman Empire, and partly because there has been no detailed study of the *horrea* that do exist, the identification of buildings of uncertain purpose as *horrea* has been easy. Some of these need careful scrutiny.

In 1957 the French archaeologist Charles-Picard,[2] in publishing the excavations at Mactar in North Africa, has attempted to identify two small buildings, 'l'édifice quadrilobe' and 'l'édifice châtelain', as *horrea*. This identification has won the powerful support of Ward-Perkins. The identification seems to me unlikely. The main characteristic of both buildings is that they have two or more apsidal chambers placed opposite each other to form a 'clover-leaf' ground plan. The most curious feature about them is that they each have a series of stone

[1] Cf. Appendix 1.
[2] G. Charles-Picard, 'Civitas Mactaritana', *Karthago* VIII (1957), 136 ff. Cf. *AJA* LXIV (1960), 213 (review by Ward-Perkins).

troughs set in these apsidal shapes. Charles-Picard has collected a series of other buildings from North Africa, none with this same ground plan, but with the common characteristic of possessing these troughs. The identifications suggested for these buildings individually or together have been many and varied, ranging from stables to refectories. It seems quite clear that these buildings, at least in this form, are very late, probably fourth century A.D. Whatever the precise purpose of the troughs, I suspect that some of the buildings that contained them had been converted from some previous purpose. This seems virtually certain in the case of 'l'édifice quadrilobe' which had a mosaic floor raised on *suspensurae*. Charles-Picard makes great play with this fact and points out that *horrea* often had such raised floors. It may be remarked straightway that one of the objections which Charles-Picard uses against its identification as a stable, that stables do not usually have mosaic floors, applies equally to the identification as *horrea*. Moreover when we see that 'l'édifice quadrilobe' was at the east end of an ensemble of buildings which were a suite of baths and that it had been heated by a furnace set in the south apse, we must feel that Charles-Picard's dismissal of its use as part of the bath suite is too cavalier. It may be that when the troughs were introduced it was no longer used as part of the bath suite, but that must have been its original use and that was the reason for the *suspensurae*. Therefore Charles-Picard should not use the presence of *suspensurae* to support the identification: their presence is fortuitous. With that point dismissed, Charles-Picard's identification of the buildings at Mactar as *horrea*, or rather as 'la salle de réception d'un horreum', whatever that means, becomes like all the other attempts, a mere guess. These buildings converted from previous uses may have been used for storing supplies in kind in the late Empire, but they in no way resemble the ground plans of proper *horrea* known to us.

CRYPTOPORTICOES

French archaeologists have also been involved in a flourishing controversy about the cryptoporticoes discovered at Aosta, Arles, Reims, Bavai and Narbonne. Nearly 100 years ago Promis recognised in the great subterranean cryptoporticus with three sides at Aosta a large *horreum*. The identification went unchallenged. Romanelli refused to commit himself on the validity of it. Durm thought it might have been used for water conservation.[1] So the position rested until Benoit in 1952, without any real discussion of the problem, assumed the *horrea* identification as proved, and added to the list of such *horrea* the French cryptoporticoes.[2] This provoked a strong reaction from the Italian Staccioli,[3] who carefully assessed Promis's reasons for identifying the Aosta building as *horrea* and gave a very brief summary of the established *horrea* at Ostia and elsewhere. He rejected the identification completely. Benoit and Grenier have consistently defended the identification and Staccioli has as consistently denied it,[4] introducing more and more parallels from the east to show that the cryptoporticoes served as promenades and places of refuge from rain and heat.

In my view there can be no doubt that Staccioli is right in rejecting these buildings as *horrea*. The objections may be summarised as follows:

(1) The fact that the areas, in which some of these cryptoporticoes have been found, have been called for centuries 'Viel Mazel' (Narbonne) or 'Marché des Romains' (Aosta) is no proof concerning the identity of the subterranean constructions. If it did prove anything, it would suggest that a *macellum* was situated somewhere in the district.

(2) The plans of these cryptoporticoes in no way resemble any of the ground plans of *horrea* built above ground that are known to us. Even the underground structures at Narbonne do not compare well with *horrea* at Ostia, despite claims to the contrary. The rooms which flank the underground galleries are only 1·90 metres wide and 2·20 metres deep—minute for storerooms of any kind.

(3) The fact that certain literary authorities of the first century A.D. recommend storage below ground is no support for the identification.

---

[1] C. Promis, 'Le antichità di Aosta', *Mem. della R. Acad. d. Scienze di Torino,* Sez. II, XXI (1862). Romanelli, p. 972. Durm, *Die Baukunst der Römer*, pp. 355–6.

[2] F. Benoit, 'Le sanctuaire d'Auguste et les cryptoportiques d'Arles', *RA* XXXIX (1952), 31 ff.

[3] Staccioli, *RAL* IX (1954), 645 ff.

[4] F. Benoit, 'Observations sur les cryptoportiques d'Arles', *RStLig* XXIII (1957), 107 ff. A. Grenier, *Manuel d'archéologie gallo-romaine* III (Paris, 1958), pp. 305 ff. R. A. Staccioli, 'Gli edifici sotterranei di Bavai', *ACl* VI (1954), 284 ff.; 'Gli edifici sotterranei dell'agora di Smirne e ancora sui criptoportici forensi', *Latomus* XVI (1957), 275 ff.; 'Ancora sui criptoportici', *AntCl* XXVII (1958), 390 ff. Cf. also J. Rougé, *Recherches sur l'organisation du commerce maritime en Méditerranée sous l'empire romain* (Paris, 1966), p. 167, who rejects the identification, and C. Alzon, *Problèmes relatifs à la location des entrepôts en Droit romain* (Paris, 1965), p. 325, who accepts the identification.

Columella, Varro, Cato and the other authors are concerned with the storing of grain in proper silos sunk into the ground.

(4) Often the decoration of these cryptoporticoes is of a richness of materials, marbles and mosaics, that does not suggest *horrea*.

(5) The lack of convenience for storage inherent in the plan of these cryptoporticoes has to be reckoned with. The excessive development of length, difficulty of access and communication for men with heavy loads, the difficulty of depositing, sorting and removing goods are all impressive. In some examples the lack of internal divisions would militate against use as a store, but this is not a formidable objection, and it is clear from bar holes in the central rows of piers at Arles that temporary wooden divisions could be erected.

The latest and fullest statement of the French case was given by Grenier (too late to be discussed in Staccioli's latest article), who relied heavily on two points. First, there is the fact that the subterranean galleries show signs of elaborate protection against damp. At Arles the flooring was of three layers of oak coated with resin and the walls were covered by an impermeable stucco. Secondly, there is a passage in Vitruvius[1] which 'proves' that cryptoporticoes were used as 'magasins de réserve'.

Neither of these arguments is conclusive. If we were not inclined to think that the elimination of dampness from substructures was desirable anyway, whatever their use, even if only for walking in, the passage from Vitruvius would remind us of it. The deduction from the Vitruvius passage that the cryptoporticoes were 'magasins de réserve' is not entirely justified. The French version of the passage given by Grenier is rather free. In Latin the point is that such porticoes around gardens are extremely pleasant to walk in, and they have the further recommendation that in time of *war* they can, at a pinch, be used for storing that most necessary item, wood. At such times of war, the *ambulationes* could be opened and a ration of wood given to each person. This explains why not only theatres, but also temples, have such porticoes.

To deduce from such a passage that the cryptoporticoes at Arles and Aosta were simply *horrea* is to go beyond the evidence.

Whether the cryptoporticoes can always be regarded as part of the

---

[1] Vitruvius, v. 9. 5–9; but see especially §9: ita duas res egregias hypaethroae ambulationes praestant, unami n pace salubritatis, alteram in bello salutis.

Forum complex in each place is, however, rather doubtful. In some cases they seem to enclose a temple area, in others a Forum, in others perhaps a market area. In all cases they would serve the obvious and necessary function of substructures for the great porticoes which must have surrounded these areas, and of levelling and confining sites of an irregular nature.

The fact therefore remains that we have so far surprisingly few extant remains of *horrea* in Italy or the provinces. More will be found, certainly, in the future. For we have inscriptions recording *horrea* at places which have yet revealed no remains. Perhaps, however, we should also bear in mind the possibility that the construction of massive *horrea* was most often brought about by State interference and the needs of the imperial *annona*. For that purpose several towns may have shared one set of *horrea* and the ordinary needs of a town may not have been met by such a building. The so-called *horrea* at Pompeii,[1] for example, seems to have consisted simply of a long room divided into two halves which flanked the Forum near the Temple of Jupiter. This may have been more a reception and distributing centre than the actual storeplace, which was entered through a narrow passage to the south. This storeplace was simply an irregularly shaped, but completely enclosed, area, roughly divided into sections and with a few small rooms on its south side. The whole ensemble is simple in the extreme, and shows none of the features we have come to expect from *horrea* associated with the imperial *annona*. What was true of Pompeii may also have been true of other places.

[1] Mau (trans. Kelsey), *Pompeii*, pp. 62, 91–3. The rooms are referred to by Mau as 'market buildings', but they are labelled *horrea* in the excavations.

IV

THE ARCHITECTURAL
TRADITION

The basic feature common to the ground plans of civil *horrea* in Rome, Ostia, and the provinces was the row of deep narrow rooms. In Rome and Ostia the most typical plan involved the arranging of these rows around a central rectangular or square courtyard (for example, Figs. 2, 3, 17, 18, 22 and 23). At Portus and sometimes in Rome the courtyard was abandoned and the rows of rooms were arranged simply back to back (Figs. 26 and 27). In the provinces, at least in Asia Minor and Africa, the *horrea* ground plan consisted of only one row of rooms all opening on the same side but all of very great depth (Figs. 30, 31 and 32).

Whence did Rome derive this use of rows of deep narrow rooms and these dispositions of them for storage buildings? At what period were they introduced into the Roman architectural repertoire?

It is difficult to answer either question with precision, but the attempt is, I think, worthwhile.

But, first, it might be asked why it was not possible for the Romans to have evolved their own architectural type for storage. The Italian scholar R. Staccioli has suggested[1] that the simple corridor type of storehouse was the original from which the more elaborate courtyard *horrea* were developed and draws support for this idea from the fact that the two earliest known *horrea* in Ostia (Reg. III. Is. I. 7 and Reg. IV. Is. V. 12) are of this type. I find this difficult to believe. The two Ostian *horrea* cited by Staccioli belong to the first decades of the first century A.D. and are therefore neither very early examples nor necessarily very typical examples. The great courtyarded *Horrea Galbana* in Rome belonged to a period earlier than that: certainly the first century B.C., if not the end of the second century B.C. Given the fact that bulk storage had been a problem faced by every important power in the Mediterranean before Rome's rise, it seems sensible to investigate how that problem had been dealt with in the past and whether the Roman

---

[1] R. Staccioli, 'Tipi di *horrea*', *Hommages à Albert Grenier* III (1962), pp. 1438-9.

practice differed significantly, or could have been influenced by an older tradition.

It is natural to turn to Greece first when looking for the roots of a Roman architectural type, but it was not from classical Greece that Rome derived the plans of *horrea*. Greece had a contribution to make to Roman utilitarian building, but it was in the form of the *porticus*. The commercial structure *par excellence* for the Greeks was the *stoa*, a long colonnaded building which could be adapted for a multitude of uses and was so suitable for flanking the sides of an *agora* or a harbour.[1]

It was to this essentially Greek tradition, even though it was carried out with new Roman means and flair, that the earliest development of the commercial quarters of Rome below the Aventine belonged. We learn from Livy[2] that in their development as the *Emporium* of Rome the first important building operations were the construction of the great *Porticus Aemilia* in 193 B.C. and its reconstruction twenty years later. The whole area was made up of landing wharfs, open areas and the great porticoes. No *horrea* are mentioned. The *porticus* never lost its early importance in the commercial history of Rome. The *Porticus Aemilia* even under the Empire was still one of the great storage and sorting depots of Rome; the *Porticus Minucia* became the great store and distributing centre for the *frumentationes*, while the Sacra Via itself was flanked under Nero by two great porticoes, one of which was to be developed by Domitian into the *Horrea Piperataria*, while the other became the so-called *Porticus Margaritaria*.[3]

No *horrea* are stated to have been erected in Rome until the famous legislation of Gaius Gracchus, which was supposedly the occasion for

---

[1] R. Wycherley, *How the Greeks built cities* (London, 1949), pp. 110 ff. and 117. Cf. Pausanias I. 1. 3 (J. G. Frazer's Commentary, II, pp. 24 ff.): the μακρὰ στοὰ ἀλφιτόπωλις built by Pericles at the Peiraeus, known from the scholiast on Aristophanes, *Acharnians* 548 to have been ὅπου καὶ ὁ σῖτος ἀπέκειτο τῆς πόλεως.

[2] Livy 35. 10. 12: aedilitas insignis eo anno fuit M. Aemilii Lepidi et L. Aemilii Pauli... porticum unam extra portam Trigeminam (fecerunt) emporio ad Tiberim adiecto. Livy 41. 27. 8 (174 B.C.): (Q. Fulvius Flaccus, A. Postumius Albinus censores) extra portam Trigeminam emporium lapide straverunt stipitibusque saepserunt; et porticum Aemiliam reficiendam curarunt, gradibusque adscensum ab Tiberi in emporium fecerunt.

[3] *Porticus Aemilia*, see Blake, *Ancient Roman Construction to Augustus*, p. 249. W. L. MacDonald, *The Architecture of the Roman Empire* (London, 1965), pp. 5 ff. *Porticus Minucia*, see Platner–Ashby, *Topographical Dictionary*, p. 424. *Piperataria* and *Margaritaria*, see Platner–Ashby, *op. cit.* p. 423.

the erection of the *Horrea Sempronia*.[1] Their site and plan are equally unknown. We have no firm evidence for the existence and ground plan of *horrea* in Rome until the *Horrea Galbana* (*Sulpicia*), which in the form revealed by excavation probably date from the first century B.C.[2]

Boëthius[3] has suggested that the plan of the courtyard *horrea* of Rome was derived from the 'porticoed Hellenistic Khan (caravanserai) and commercial market places like the one of Dura Europos'. The suggestion is not argued in detail, but even in outline it seems to me to be very unsatisfactory. The majority of Khans still existing in the Middle East, whose ground plans are known, are, like those at Umm el-Walîd and Han ez-Zebîb, either of late Roman date or even of the Saracenic or Byzantine periods.[4] I can find no unimpeachable example of a Hellenistic Khan. Moreover, even if such examples do exist, the more precise parallels to such Khans in the Greek and Roman world would be the hostels and rest-houses at such places as Kassope in Epeiros.[5] Similarly the market place at Dura is not like the Roman *horrea*: it is open on one side and its rooms are small and shallow, used simply for shopping facilities.[6] If it bears any relation to a Roman building it is to a simple *forum* or *macellum*.

The basic weakness of Boëthius' attempt to trace the architectural type is that it takes no account of the main purpose of *horrea*, that is, storage. It seems better to investigate the storage facilities of the pre-Roman East. In doing this one must avoid looking specifically for *granaries* for two reasons: first, *horrea* in Rome and Ostia at least were not necessarily used only for storing grain; and secondly, the granaries of the eastern end of the Mediterranean, because of the dryness of the climate, were almost always in the form of simple grain storage pits

---

[1] Festus, p. 290. Cf. Plut. *C. Gracchus*, 6. 2.

[2] Lugli, *Tecnica*, p. 508 and Tav. CXLI. 2.

[3] Boëthius, *The Golden House of Nero*, p. 79.

[4] R. Brünnow and A. von Domaszewski, *Die Provincia Arabia* II (Strassburg, 1904–9), pp. 78 and 89.

[5] J. M. Cook, 'Archaeology in Greece, 1952', *JHS* LXXIII (1953), 120.

[6] M. Rostovtseff, F. E. Brown, C. B. Welles, *Excavations at Dura Europos, Ninth Season* (New Haven, 1944), I, *passim*. The only building whose plan resembles that of Roman *horrea* (Block L4 labelled caravanserai) appears to be Roman in date; see M. Rostovtseff, *Dura Europos and its Art* (Oxford, 1938), p. 53, 'a market on the main street' added in the Roman period; cf. its absence on *Excavations, Ninth Season*, I, fig. 12, 'Hellenistic city plan'.

sunk into the ground.[1] The search therefore must be for 'magazines', not 'granaries', and not in small towns, but in the great palaces and temple ensembles of the Middle East, where the great landlords, royal or priestly, who had vast incomes, might be expected to build on a monumental scale to house their possessions.

It is clear at once that in this context of palaces and temples there is a pre-Greek and Middle Eastern tradition of deep narrow storage rooms. The use of such storage rooms is well known in Minoan Crete, at Knossos, where the basement level of the western part of the palace was largely occupied by such rooms, although of a very narrow type. Their use was also characteristic of the Palace of Phaestos in southern Crete where they were arranged symmetrically on either side of a broad corridor.[2]

Whereas with the fall of the Minoan civilisation their use seems not to have been prolonged by the Greeks, in the Middle East the tradition was continued and developed.

Storage rooms are an important feature of the palace of Mari on the borders of Syria, *circa* 1900 B.C.[3] In the Hittite capital at Boghazkeuy,[4] *circa* 1400–1200 B.C., deep narrow storerooms were arranged on all four sides of the court which had a temple at its centre. The arrangement is irregular and the rooms vary in depth. Some 700 years later in Babylon, after its reconstruction by Nebuchadnezzar, the great Temple of Marduk, Etemenanki, stood more or less centrally in its precinct, but the two great magazines of the temple flanked the main entrance to the precinct[5] (Fig. 33). Each of the magazines consisted of a central court 61 × 54 metres, on to which opened on all four sides ranges of regular long narrow rooms. Their dimensions were 2·80–4·42 metres wide, and 14·75–17·10 metres in depth. The doorways on to the court were approximately 1·40 metres in width. The whole ensemble was regularly planned and the outer walls had buttresses at regular intervals.

---

[1] For example, granaries at Olynthus, D. M. Robinson, *Excavations at Olynthus*, Part XII (Baltimore, 1946), pp. 297 ff.

[2] J. Pendlebury, *The Palace of Minos* (London, 1954), fig. 2; L. Pernier, *Il palazzo minoico di Festos* II (Rome, 1951), pp. 77 ff.

[3] A. Parrot, *Mission archéologique de Mari* II (Paris, 1958), plan.

[4] Frankfort, *The Art and Architecture of the Ancient Orient*, p. 119 and fig. 47.

[5] F. Wetzel and F. H. Weissbach, *Das Hauptheiligtum des Marduk in Babylon* (Leipzig, 1938), pp. 19 ff. and Taf. 1, 2 and 8.

In Egypt the same tradition is apparent, although there a greater regularity in the planning is shown much earlier. At Tell-El-Amarna in the city of Akhenaten *circa* 1350 B.C., rows of storage rooms are one of the most striking features of the plan of the central city.[1] There are variations in size and in grouping. Some of the ranges have rooms with a depth of 30 metres, others have rooms less than 10 metres deep. Sometimes the rooms are arranged in simple rows, at others, two rows open on to a broad central corridor.

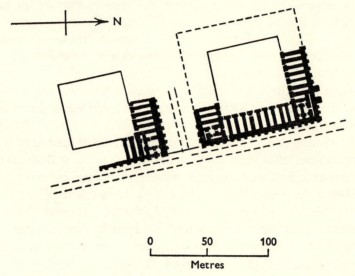

0   50   100

Metres

Fig. 33   Babylon, magazines of the Temple of Marduk, Etemenanki

Two important examples of the use of such storerooms within the precincts of temples are given by the plan of the Ramesseum (*circa* 1300 B.C.) and the temple of Medinet Habu (*circa* 1100 B.C.), both at Thebes.[2] The storerooms dominate both ground plans and are most often arranged so that the rooms open on to broad central corridors.

We lack later examples of such storerooms in Egypt, since the few temples of the Ptolemaic period which have survived do not include

---

[1] J. Pendlebury, *The City of Akhenaten* (London, 1951), III, Pls. 12, 13, 16, 18 and 21.

[2] W. S. Smith, *The Art and Architecture of Ancient Egypt* (Harmondsworth, 1958), p. 218 and p. 219, figs. 71 and 72, conveniently placed together. See further, J. E. Quibell, *The Ramesseum* (London, 1898), Pl. 1; and U. Hölscher, *The Excavation of Medinet Habu* (Chicago, 1934), I, Pl. 2.

more than the temple building itself within the precinct. The need for grouping the storerooms around the temple within a heavily fortified area would seem to have disappeared.

However, we need not doubt that the tradition survived. When Herod built his great fortress on the rock at Masada probably between 37 and 31 B.C., one of his first concerns was the provision of storage facilities.[1] As excavated, these consisted of two great rows of storerooms separated by a passage 6·5 metres wide (Fig. 34). The north row consisted of five rooms (20–1 × 3·5–4 metres); the south had eleven rooms (28·8 × 4–4·5 metres). They were built of stone plastered over and were roofed by a system of beams, reeds and plaster. Altogether some 2,416 square metres of space was available for storage.

There was therefore in the Middle East an architectural tradition for the building of magazines, the main essential being the construction of rows of narrow parallel rooms. How far did this tradition influence Roman practice? I see little reason to doubt that at least the provincial *horrea* at Myra and Patara in Asia Minor (Figs. 30 and 31), built under Hadrian, and at Djemila (Fig. 32) in North Africa, built under Septimius Severus, were the direct descendants of that tradition. The grouping of some six to ten rooms in a row all opening in the same direction is exactly the same. Moreover, the dimensions of the rooms compare well with those at Masada. This is particularly true of the depth of the rooms: 27 metres at Patara, 32 and 27 metres at Myra, and *circa* 25 metres at Djemila, which seem extraordinary when compared with examples at Rome and Ostia (13 metres at most). Given their location, it is not surprising that such imperial *horrea* should derive their ground plan from a Middle Eastern tradition.

Can we claim a similar derivation for the *horrea* in Rome and Italy? Caution is needed, for the necessary links both chronological and geographical are missing.[2] To establish a proper connection we need at least one example of the Middle Eastern magazine in the period 500–100 B.C. Moreover, ideally, we need an example of such a magazine

---

[1] Y. Yadin, *Masada* (London, 1966), pp. 87 ff. M. Avi-Yonah, *Masada, Survey and Excavations, 1955–1956* (Reprint of *Israel Exploration Journal*, vol. 7, No. 1) (1957), pp. 21 ff. and fig. 10. Cf. Josephus, *Bell. Jud.* VII. 296. The comparison suggested by the Jewish expedition with the arsenals at Pergamon seems to be based upon a complete misunderstanding of those buildings, which were more like the Roman military *horrea*, see Chapter VII (p. 252).

[2] Cf. the cautious remarks by MacDonald, *The Architecture of the Roman Empire*, p. 90, n. 34.

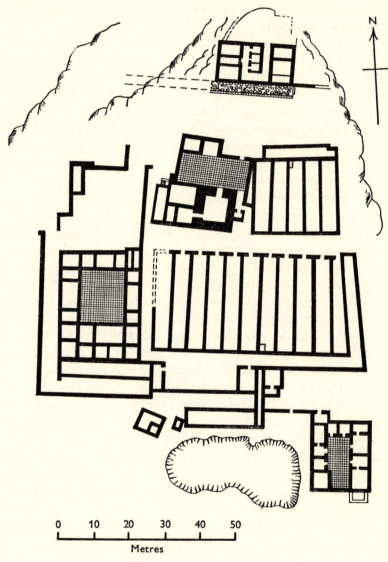

0   10   20   30   40   50

Metres

Fig. 34   Masada, magazines

at a *point* where the Romans would naturally come across it in their expansion within the period 200–100 B.C. We may suspect that excavations around the ancient harbour at Rhodes might provide answers to both needs. It is certain that the excavations on Delos,[1] the other main entrepôt port of the Hellenistic Aegean, have not. The warehouses there which line the wharfs were small courtyard stores which had been developed seemingly from the ordinary courtyard house of the islands. They are comparable only with the smaller private Roman *horrea* such as the *Horrea Epagathiana et Epaphroditiana* at Ostia (Fig. 3). Rhodes, however, was the great entrepôt port for corn and ordinary commercial goods (as opposed to the slaves and perfumes of Delos), and we might hope for the discovery of greater warehouses there.

Even though caution is needed, it is clear that by 600–500 B.C. the magazines at Babylon (Fig. 33), for example, were being planned in a way not unlike that of the later *horrea* in Rome and that the proportions of the individual rooms were changing, the length was being reduced and the width slightly increased.

Tentatively, therefore, I would suggest the following sequence in the introduction of types of commercial building into Rome. First, the adoption of the *porticus* at a period when Rome's contacts with Greece were being greatly increased *circa* 200 B.C. Secondly, and probably much later, the introduction of the courtyard *horrea* plan as the result of Rome's further expansion towards the East and the South which occurred during the second century B.C. (If it was from Sicily that Rome derived the *horrea* plan, then the introduction into the Roman repertoire may have been earlier, since that island had come into her control as early as the end of the third century.) Whether it was from Hellenistic Rhodes, Hellenistic Syracuse, or Hellenistic Carthage, before its destruction in 146 B.C., that Rome derived it, I do not know, but it seems possible that whatever the point of contact, the tradition was essentially Eastern.

How long did the *horrea* of the Roman world survive? This is a question impossible to answer except in the case of the city of Rome itself, but one which is not without importance. Boëthius[2] has suggested that the popularity of the porticoed courtyard in medieval and Renaissance architecture may be due, not so much to its use in Roman palaces, as to its

---

[1] Jardé, *BCH*, xxix (1905), 21 ff. Cf. Schaal, *Ostia*, p. 64.
[2] Boëthius, *The Golden House of Nero*, p. 134.

employment regularly in more utilitarian buildings such as *horrea*, and that the survival of such buildings into the medieval period is worth study.

It seems clear that at Ostia, although no new *horrea* were built in the late Empire, the existing ones were kept in good repair in the third and fourth centuries A.D., as patches of late construction in some of their walls show. After that period Ostia itself was a decaying city.[1] In each of the invasions by Goths, Huns or Vandals it was an obviously easy prey without real defensive walls. The city was inhabited for 400 years more, but its function as the harbour of Rome had gone, and by the twelfth century only a handful of people survived. The buildings, however, remained: when Richard Cœur de Lion landed at the Tiber mouth, he found 'immense ruins of ancient walls', some of which are likely to have belonged to *horrea*.

Ostia's decline was hastened by the silting of the river mouth and the ever growing importance of Portus. While Ostia's *horrea* were redundant, Rome still depended on the warehouses of Portus.[2] Despite its capture by Alaric in 408, the harbour revived and its buildings continued to be used. Its importance, however, was finally to be destroyed by the same silting which ruined Ostia. Meiggs has suggested that the sand had probably won by the eighth century.

In Rome itself, however, the story is rather different and the *horrea* of the capital can be shown to have enjoyed a considerably longer life and continued use. The clearest proof of this is given by the *Horrea Agrippiana* (Fig. 20).[3] Not only were the usual third- and fourth-century repairs to the rooms found in these *horrea*, but the whole central court paved with travertine blocks was completely filled by mean brick structures of an even later period. They were arranged in such a way (corresponding to the original arcade surrounding the court) as to suggest that the original building was still in use. In short, these *horrea*, even in a period after the collapse of the Roman Empire, were in use and even supplemented.

It would be natural to attribute the responsibility for such constructive work, in a period of chaos and dissolution, to the church in Rome, and there is evidence that this was the case. Gregory of Tours[4] mentions that in A.D. 590

---

[1] Meiggs, pp. 97 ff.   [2] Meiggs, pp. 169 ff.
[3] Bartoli, 'Gli *Horrea Agrippiana*', 391 ff.
[4] Gregory of Tours, *Historia Francorum*, Bk. x. 1.

diaconus noster ab urbe Roma sanctorum cum pigneribus veniens, sic retulit, quod anno superiore, mense nono tanta inundatione Tiberis fluvius Romam urbem obtexerit ut aedes antiquae diruerentur, horrea etiam ecclesiae subversa sint, in quibus nonnulla milia modiorum tritici periere.

The *Liber Pontificalis*[1] reveals that a little later in A.D. 605 the Pope Sabinianus *iussit aperiri horrea ecclesiae* and their contents were auctioned at a fantastic price, an action which earned him severe censure. The grain stored in the church *horrea* was not intended to be sold at all, but to be distributed to the needy. In fact the church had taken upon itself, although in a smaller way, the distributions and *frumentationes* of the Roman Empire. The landed estates which the church owned in Africa and Sicily were administered by deputies who were expected to ship the produce to Rome. It is noticeable, for example, that *Horrea Caelia* in North Africa was the seat of a bishopric. In order to carry out the administration of this charity the church had early organised a system of deaconries,[2] but these were increased and largely reorganised in the seventh and eighth centuries A.D., a period when the church first began to take over and exploit certain ancient buildings in the centre of Rome.

Bartoli[3] in 1921 pointed out the possible connection between the late buildings in the central courtyard of the *Horrea Agrippiana* and the setting up of the *diaconia* of S. Teodoro immediately next to it, if not on top of part of it. He also, with justification, pointed to the significant positions of some of the other *diaconiae* associated with previous *annona* buildings: S. Giorgio in the *Forum Boarium*, S. Vito in the *Macellum Liviae*, and, most significant, S. Maria in Cosmedin in the ancient *Statio Annonae*. We may perhaps add to that list the *diaconia* of S. Maria in Via Lata which was placed in part of the great portico that flanked what is now the Via del Corso. An attempt has recently been made by Sjöqvist to identify this portico as the *Porticus Minucia Frumentaria*.[4]

Bartoli's suggestion, that the *horrea ecclesiae* known from this period were in fact largely the old *horrea* of Rome under new management, seems very plausible. How long they continued to exist and to be used is not so clear. If Valentini and Zucchetti[5] are right in supposing that

---

[1] *Lib. Pont.* I, p. 315. Cf. in general L. Ruggini, *Economia e società nell' 'Italia Annonaria'* (Milan, 1961). [2] *Dict. d'Arch. Chrét.* IV, p. 735, s.v. diaconies.
[3] Bartoli, 'Gli *Horrea Agrippiana*', pp. 399 ff.
[4] Sjöqvist, 'Gli avanzi antichi', pp. 48 ff.
[5] R. Valentini and G. Zucchetti, *Codice topografico della città di Roma* (Rome, 1953), IV, p. 475, line 9, and note 3.

the *horrea vicina vocantur in Aerario* mentioned by Francesco Albertini at the end of the fifteenth century are to be identified with the *Horrea Agrippiana*, then they at least survived till then, whether in use or not. However, we may doubt whether many ancient *horrea* survived the sack of Rome in A.D. 1084 by the Normans.[1] All previous sackings of the city were nothing to this vicious and comprehensive reduction of the city to ashes. *Horrea*, which because of their utility and lack of grandeur may have escaped serious damage in previous captures, when the invaders were intent on movable loot, were probably ruined at this time. At all events it was as a ruin, albeit a splendid one, that the Jewish traveller, Benjamin of Tudela,[2] saw the *Horrea Galbana* and its neighbouring buildings in the twelfth century. Fabretti's description[3] and drawings of the *Horrea Galbana* remains in the seventeenth century almost certainly do not refer to that building at all, but to the *Porticus Aemilia* nearby. However, they are interesting in showing the rise in the ground level by his time. The whole Aventine area, although it was still called *orrea* in the ninth and tenth centuries, must by this time have become completely ruinous. At all events, when Gregory XIII reopened the *horrea ecclesiae*[4] in 1566, it was in the ruined halls of the Baths of Diocletian, and not in a building which had been a proper Roman warehouse.

However long the physical structure of the *horrea* of Rome survived, and whether or not they had any effect on later architectural shapes and themes, there can be no doubt that their architecture was worthy of being copied and studied. Rome was preoccupied with the functional and the useful, and thus it is no surprise that in her architecture some of her greatest contributions were made in the building of functional structures. She may have copied Greek models for her temple designs and her ornamentation, but in her care for construction of buildings with utilitarian purposes she knew no master. With the revolutionary material, concrete, she built not only the daring vaults and domes of the great baths, but also in a simpler and no less satisfactory way the great

[1] R. Lanciani, *The Destruction of Ancient Rome* (New York, 1899), pp. 159 ff.
[2] H. Jordan, *Topographie der Stadt Rom im Alterthum* (Berlin, 1907), II, p. 68.
[3] Fabretti, *De Aquis* (1680), p. 165. Cf. D–S, s.v. *horrea*, p. 274, fig. 3893. The drawing there reproduced corresponds well with the known dispositions of the *Porticus Aemilia* and with a wall of that building which still survives in the area. Cf. Gatti, '"Saepta Iulia" e "Porticus Aemilia"', pp. 123 ff.
[4] R. Lanciani, *Pagan and Christian Rome* (London, 1895), p. 48.

horrea. They were constructed in the same materials, with the same care, with the same eye for simple monumentality and the lucid relationship of individual parts which characterises the best Roman architecture. The visitor to Ostia is not conscious when he enters the *Piccolo Mercato* (Fig. 2), the *Grandi Horrea* (Fig. 10) or the *Horrea di Hortensius* (Fig. 18) of a decline in architectural or structural standards, and has no sense of shoddy commercial architecture.[1] The remains of the fine arched entrance to the *Piccolo Mercato* (Pl. 5), the entrance to the *Horrea Epagathiana* with its framing pilasters and crowning pediment all in brickwork (Pl. 12), and the finely proportioned courtyard of the *Horrea di Hortensius* (Pl. 35) stand comparison with anything in Ostia. The building of warehouses was not regarded as an excuse for slapdash design and construction with inferior materials. Lanciani in 1888 wrote,

There is no doubt that, in ancient times, no hydraulic work was considered perfect unless it joined to the skill of engineering the beauty of architecture... For the storing of merchandise, we make use of wooden sheds, and, in exceptional cases when we want to impress the stranger with our magnificence, we build brick warehouses. I wish the reader could see, as it has been my privilege to see, the beauty of the docks and warehouses of Porto, the perfection of their reticulated masonry, their cornices and entablatures carved and moulded in terracotta, their mosaic pavements, their systems of drainage and ventilation.[2]

Similarly in modern Italy[3] an architect-engineer of the quality of Pier Luigi Nervi can contract to design and build tobacco warehouses at Bologna, and salt warehouses at Tortona for the government, while the Fish Market at Ancona can be designed and built by Gaetano Minnucci. These are buildings which use materials and methods, and are of a quality, that enable them to bear comparison with the best in modern Italian architecture.

The enduring factor which makes the modern analogy possible is the basic approach to design and structure. Even in the Greek world, at least during the fourth century B.C., there was the theory that utilitarian architecture should also have its κόσμος and by the time of Cicero one could theorise on the beauty which might be inherent in simple

[1] MacDonald, *The Architecture of the Roman Empire, passim.*
[2] R. Lanciani, *Ancient Rome in the Light of Recent Discoveries* (London, 1888), p. 247.
[3] G. E. Kidder Smith, *Italy Builds* (London, 1955), pp. 238 and 244 (Nervi); p. 216 (Minnucci).

functional things like the sails and rigging of a ship.[1] That this was still a philosopher's platitude rather than an architect's guide can be seen from Vitruvius, who under Augustus remarked sharply *horrea apothecae ceteraque quae ad fructus servandos magis quam ad elegantiae decorem possunt esse*.[2] However, a change was in the air.

After the fire in Rome in A.D. 64 and the rebuilding of large sections of Rome in the new town architecture of tall, plain, well-constructed concrete tenement houses with broader well-planned streets, Tacitus could remark *ea ex utilitate accepta decorem quoque novae urbi attulere*.[3] At the end of the century Frontinus[4] spoke with pride of the aqueducts which he supervised, and compared their *moles necessariae* with the *pyramides otiosae aut cetera inertia sed fama celebrata opera Graecorum*. The Romans had long known that they could do these structural things well[5] and now came the added feeling that a certain beauty was inherent in a functional structure well designed, in good materials, which did its job without fuss. The structure of the *horrea* was not disguised or ornamented, but its beauty depended simply on its strength, monumentality, and the excellence of its design. This drawing of beauty from structural elements has characterised the best Italian architecture at all periods, and it has now been recaptured by Nervi and his colleagues again after the Fascist interregnum.[6]

This functional architecture has given to the plan of Ostia a character of its own, remarkable for its clarity and proportion. On the ground, the *horrea*, wherever they are, although ruined, still retain their quality because, when all the inessentials are stripped away, good construction and apt design give unalterable distinction.

---

[1] Aristotle, *Politics* VII. 11 (1331 a–b); Cicero, *De Oratore* III. 46 (180). See A. Boëthius, 'Roman architecture from its classicistic to its late Imperial phase', *Göteborgs Högskolas Årsskrift* XLVII (1941), 8.

[2] Vitruvius VI. 5. 2. [3] Tac. *Ann.* XV. 43.

[4] Frontinus, *De Aquis*, 16. [5] Strabo V. 3. 8.

[6] Kidder Smith, *Italy Builds*, Preface, p. 10: 'One of the characteristics of Italian architecture is the balance in the constant relationship between the parts and the whole. This represents a desire for synthesis which seeks decorative values not so much through arabesques or ornamentation as in the interplay of volumes and surfaces by emphasizing structure and constructive feeling...'

CIVIL *HORREA*:
ORGANISATION

V

ROME AND THE PROVINCES

INTRODUCTION

The sources of evidence[1] for the organisation of civil *horrea* are three: the rescripts of the Emperors in the *Codex Theodosianus*, the inscriptions, and the papyri. The imperial rescripts in the *Codex Theodosianus* belong to a late period in the Empire, mainly the late fourth and early fifth centuries A.D., and were concerned with the detailed running, not only of the *horrea* of Rome, Portus and Constantinople, but also of the state storehouses in the provinces. The inscriptions range in date from the early Empire down to the fourth and fifth centuries A.D., although, so far as it is possible to estimate, the majority belong to the earlier period of the Empire. These inscriptions are mainly funerary in character and were set up by, or in honour of, men employed in some capacity in the *horrea*. The papyri concerning storehouses range in date from the earliest Ptolemaic rule until the Byzantine period and are concerned exclusively with the storehouses and arrangements for the organisation and transport of the corn supply in Egypt.[2] The fact that the organisation of the Roman period, as will be seen, seems to differ little in essentials from that of the pre-Roman period must make us cautious about inferring from arrangements in Egypt those in other parts of the Roman world. In this chapter the papyri will be used only where passages in the Theodosian Code are explained and illustrated by the Egyptian information.

There is no convenient dividing line in the civil organisation between early and late Empire, such as that supplied by the introduction of the regular *annona militaris* in the case of the organisation of military *horrea*. Nevertheless there is a strong case for dealing with the evidence of the *Codex Theodosianus* and certain late inscriptions separately, because they show an amount of state interference quite unlike what we know of the early Empire.

---

[1] Romanelli, pp. 975 ff. No consideration will be given here to 'horrea to let' and the conditions of *locatio–conductio*; separate treatment of these topics will be given in Chapter VI.

[2] See Appendix 2.

EARLY EMPIRE

The evidence for the organisation of civil *horrea* in this period consists largely of inscriptions concerning the *horrea* in Rome itself. It is therefore essential to establish what we can about these *horrea*.

I

Of the twenty or so *horrea* in Rome known to us by name, some are clearly irrelevant to our purpose. The *Horrea Ummidiana* and the *Horrea* of Q. Tineius Sacerdos seem to have been private '*horrea* to let'[1] which are discussed in Chapter VI. The *Horrea Candelaria* and the *Horrea Chartaria*,[2] known only from the Severan Marble Plan and the Notitia Regionum respectively, were probably founded in the period of the Severi or later. Of the *Horrea Aniciana, Postumiana, Peduceiana, Leoniana* and *Severiana*[3] we know nothing more than the names. With others we may go further. What we wish to establish, if possible, is to whom they belonged originally and whether and when they became public or imperial property.

The *Horrea Lolliana* are known not only from the inscriptions which refer to them, but also from their plan in the Severan Marble Plan of Rome.[4] It is clear from the name that they were founded by some member of the *gens Lollia*. The family had long had trade connections and the name is found among the Italian merchants on the island of Delos in the Hellenistic period.[5] Groag has suggested that these *horrea* were built by either Marcus Lollius, consul 21 B.C., or his son Marcus Lollius, the father of Lollia Paulina.[6]

Epigraphic evidence shows that the *horrea* had certainly become imperial property by the time of Claudius.[7] I think that we can pinpoint

---

[1] *CIL* VI. 37795 (*NSc* (1910), p. 90); *CIL* VI. 33860 = *ILS* 5913.

[2] *Candelaria*: *Pianta Marm.* frag. 44; *Chartaria*: *Not. Reg.* IV.

[3] *Aniciana*: *Not. Reg.* XIII; *Postumiana*: *CIL* XV. 4 = *ILS* 8667a; perhaps not in Rome, but apparently imperial property; *Peduceiana*: *CIL* VI. 33745; may not even be *horrea*. Hülsen restores *horti*, see Platner–Ashby, *A Topographical Dictionary*, p. 262; cf. *ILS* 1626 add.; *Leoniana*: *CIL* VI. 237 = *ILS* 3664; *Severiana*: *CIL* XV. 4807.

[4] *Pianta Marm.* frag. 25.

[5] *RE* XIII, col. 1375, s.v. *Lollius*.   [6] *RE* XIII, col. 1387, s.v. *Lollius*.

[7] *CIL* VI. 4226 and 4226a = *ILS* 1620. *Calamus Pamphilianus*, slave of the Emperor Claudius, *vilicus ex horreis Lollianis*. Frank, *ESAR* V, p. 233, uses these two inscriptions to show *Lolliana* was 'property of family of Livia and later of imperial house (VI. 4239)'. The fact that the inscriptions were found in the *columbarium Liviae* cannot

with more precision the particular context in the change of ownership. Since the property of the Emperor grew in two main ways, either by confiscation or by legacy,[1] we may see in the downfall of Lollia Paulina in A.D. 49 that change in ownership for which we are looking. Tacitus reveals[2] that her exile from Italy was accompanied by the seizure of her goods—*proin publicatis bonis cederet Italia*. It is certain that the word *publicatis* should not be pressed for any technical distinction of '*state* confiscation' as opposed to 'imperial confiscation' for we know that Claudius also got possession of the *Horti Lolliani*.[3]

It is true that we lack the final proof that Lollia Paulina did own the *Horrea Lolliana*. An inscription[4] does record a Q. *Lollius Hilarus, Lolliae libertus, horrearius* and this has been taken by Romanelli to belong to the period before imperial ownership. Since the stone has disappeared there is no means of confirming this early date, but the fact is likely enough. A more important difficulty is that there is no way of showing that the Lollia of the inscription is Lollia Paulina. The praenomen *Quintus* of the freedman is odd, in that all Lollia Paulina's nearest male relations seem to have borne the name *Marcus*.[5]

However, there is no doubt that Lollia Paulina was immensely rich. Tacitus refers to her *opibus immensis*[6] and Pliny tells of her fabulous pearls, alone worth forty million sesterces.[7] It is interesting that although the motive of Agrippina in engineering her downfall is stated in all sources to be jealousy and the desire to eliminate her ex-rival for the hand of Claudius, in Dio's epitome[8] it is placed in a chapter devoted to Agrippina's desire to build up wealth and property for her son Nero.

The *Horrea Galbana* have long been accorded the premier place among the *horrea* of Rome: they played a major rôle in the provisioning of the capital from the Republican period down to the fourth century A.D. The standard information in English upon this important

contradict the text of the inscription which proves that the man was a slave of Claudius. Inscriptions of other imperial *horrearii* were also found in the *columbarium Liviae* (*CIL* VI. 4240 and *CIL* VI. 3971 = *ILS* 1625).

[1] Frank, *ESAR* v, pp. 42 ff. and notes.
[2] Tac. *Ann.* XII. 22.   [3] *CIL* VI. 31284-5.
[4] *CIL* VI. 9467 (*not* found in the *columbarium Liviae*); Romanelli, p. 986.
[5] *RE* XIII, col. 1394, s.v. *Lollius* and cf. *AE* (1933), no. 85. Whether the freedman of a woman took as his *praenomen* that of one of her male relatives is, however, not certain.
[6] Tac. *Ann.* XII. 22. 2 (cf. Seneca, *ad Helv.* 12. 4).
[7] Pliny, *NH* IX. 35, 58, 116.   [8] Dio LX. 32. 3 (ed. Boissevain).

warehouse is given in Tenney Frank's *Economic Survey*.[1] There it is stated that they were also called *Horrea Sulpiciana* and *Horrea Caesaris*; that they were founded by some member of the Sulpician family in the Republic and restored by the Emperor Galba; that they were used as fiscal storerooms for grain, oil, marble, etc., and that space was let to private dealers; that they were a public warehouse by the time of Horace; and that they were located in the *Emporium* district.

This information is seriously misleading in certain respects. It quite ignores the sober remarks of Romanelli[2] as long ago as 1922 that the Zmaragdus inscription[3] cannot refer to a slave of Augustus but rather to one of Galba himself and that the passage of Horace's *Odes*, although the scholiast's identification of *Galbana* with *Sulpicia*[4] is valuable, shows only that the *Horrea Sulpicia* were very well known and cannot be used to prove that they were public property.

Thus the case for believing that the *Horrea Galbana* were public from the beginning of the Empire collapses.

Romanelli is cautious and confesses ignorance as to whether the *horrea* became public only with the accession of a member of the *Sulpicii Galbae* to the throne and the absorption of Galban property into the imperial *patrimonium*, or whether they became public at an earlier date.

I think we can go further than this without straining the evidence. The connection between Galba, the Emperor, and these *horrea* is very strong. Not only does the name *Galba* replace *Sulpicia*, but also a late chronographer[5] even states that *Galba domum suam deposuit et horrea Galbae instituit*. On the other hand the *Horrea Sulpicia* are known to have existed long before Galba came to the throne and were perhaps founded by the Ser. Sulpicius Galba whose tomb was found within the

---

[1] Frank, *ESAR* v, p. 233. *CIL* vi. 33886 = *ILS* 7539; *CIL* vi. 9801 = *ILS* 7500; *CIL* vi. 33906 = *ILS* 7584. Horace, *Odes* iv. 12. 17–18.

[2] Romanelli, p. 985.

[3] *CIL* vi. 30855 = *ILS* 1621.

[4] Horace, *Odes* iv. 12. 17–18 (published 13 B.C.):

> Nardi parvus onyx eliciet cadum
> Qui nunc Sulpiciis accubat horreis.

Porphyry *ad loc.*: (Sulpicii) Galbae horreis dicit; hodieque autem Galbae horrea vino et oleo et similibus aliis referta sunt.

[5] *Ad* A.D. 354. T. Mommsen, *Chronica Minora* i (1892), p. 146. The tradition continued into the Middle Ages, and the Jewish traveller Benjamin of Tudela speaks of the 'palace of King Galba'. (Jordan, *Topographie der Stadt Rom* ii, p. 68.)

area of the *horrea*;[1] it was remarked that its position was respected in later modifications of the *horrea*.

The generally proposed explanation of this anomaly is that Galba extensively modified and enlarged these *horrea* during his rule and thus the story grew up that he had built them.[2] In this connection is quoted an inscription[3] which, remarkably, is precisely dated to the period of his rule. It is a dedication upon a base which records *horriorum* [*sic*] *Ser. Galbae Imp. Aug.* and is dated by the two consuls *C. Bellicus Natalis* and *P. Cornelius Scipio Asiaticus*, who were in office from at least 15 October to 22 December A.D. 68.[4]

Such an explanation seems highly improbable. It is not likely that within a rule of seven turbulent months, not all of which were spent in Rome, Galba would have had time to indulge in such elaborate building, nor can one deduce such building from the dedication in the inscription. It is simply the remnant of a dedication to a protective deity by an unknown person. The wording of this dedication seems to me remarkable for its assertion of ownership; the adjective *Galbana* or *Galbiana* is not used. The *horrea* are stated unequivocally to be the property of *Ser. Galba*, with his proper imperial titles and this within a month or so at the most of Galba's arrival in Rome.[5] There is no reason to believe that at this period in the Empire the Emperor took over strictly *public* property for his own use. The conclusion seems to be inevitable that the *Horrea Sulpicia* belonged to Galba *before* he ever became Emperor.

This is of course nowhere explicitly testified, but there are certain pieces of corroborative evidence. The *Sulpicii Galbae* were not only an ancient and distinguished family, but also of immense wealth and with a great desire to make money.[6] It seems clear that they owned property

---

[1] Either the consul of 144 B.C. or of 108 B.C. *CIL* VI. 31617 = *ILS* 863 add. Cf. *NSc* (1885), 527; *BCom* XIII (1885), 165 ff. This must be regarded as completely uncertain in view of the fact that an excavation in 1955 revealed walls of the *Horrea Galbana* faced with *opus reticulatum* dated by Lugli between 50 B.C. and A.D. 50. See Lugli, *Tecnica* I, p. 508 and Tav. CXLI. 2. Of course, these walls may be part of a restoration of an earlier building.   [2] Lugli, *I monumenti antichi* III, p. 607.

[3] *CIL* VI. 33743 = 8680 = *ILS* 239. Cf. G. Gatti, 'Alcune osservazioni sugli orrei Galbani', *RM* I (1886), 72.

[4] A. Degrassi, *I fasti consolari dell'impero romano* (Rome, 1952), A.D. 68, p. 18.

[5] Tac. *Hist.* I. 6: *tardum Galbae iter*. Galba probably arrived in Rome in the late autumn.

[6] Tac. *Hist.* I. 49: *in familia nobilitas, magnae opes*. Appian, *Iberica* 60, of Servius Galba, cos. 144 B.C.: Λευκόλλου φιλοχρηματώτερος ὢν...καίτοι πλουσιώτατος ὢν ὁμοῦ τι

in the *Emporium* area outside the Porta Trigemina,[1] an area which must have been of immense value as the commercial quarters of Rome spread under the slopes of the Aventine. That the *Horrea Sulpicia* had been originally built to exploit this family asset can hardly be doubted.

As for the Emperor Galba himself, Plutarch[2] testifies that it was generally admitted that he was the richest private citizen who ever came to the imperial throne. Moreover it is fairly certain that the property of the *Sulpicii Galbae* had all been inherited by him, since his elder brother Gaius committed suicide under Tiberius.[3] We can also deduce that Galba had property either in Rome or very near it from the fact that Nero on hearing the news about Vindex and Galba declared that, although he could not do anything about the Gauls, he could sell up Galba's property.[4] This he did, and Galba retaliated by selling Nero's property in Spain—an incident which may help to explain the assertive nature of the dedication above. It would be an obvious piece of political tact to advertise the new Emperor's resumption of ownership.

It is more difficult to carry out a similar analysis with the other *horrea*. The *Horrea Petroniana* were presumably founded by some member of the *gens Petronia*. It is certain that they were imperial property by the time of Nero.[5] Bearing in mind that Nero acquired most of his property by confiscation, we might be tempted to connect the transfer to imperial ownership with the fall of Petronius, the *arbiter elegantiae* of Nero's court.[6] The temptation must be resisted. Although it would be fascinating to believe that the fastidious *arbiter* had connections with trade, the paucity of evidence concerning his life and connections, and the tightness of the chronology (his fall does not occur until A.D. 66) must forbid the attempt. However, it seems likely that it was only acquired by the imperial house in the course of the first century A.D.

The *Horrea Seiana* are even more puzzling. Founded supposedly by some member of the *gens Seia*, perhaps the aedile M. Seius, friend of Cicero,[7] they appear hired as a complete entity by a freedman with the

Ῥωμαίων. 'Galba, being even more greedy than Lucullus, distributed a little of the plunder...but kept the rest himself, although he was already one of the richest of the Romans.'
1 Jordan, *Topographie der Stadt Rom* I. 3 (Ch. Hülsen, Berlin, 1907), p. 175.
2 Plut. *Galba* 3.　　　3 Suet. *Galba* 3.　　　4 Plut. *Galba* 5. 5.
5 *CIL* VI. 3971 = *ILS* 1625.　　6 Tac. *Ann.* XVI. 17, 18–20.
7 Romanelli, p. 986.

name C. Iulius Hermes.[1] The name implies an early date in the century, although without any precision, and whether he was an imperial freedman is not clear. If he was, possible contexts for the change of ownership could be either the inheritance which the Emperor Tiberius received from Seius Strabo (Prefect of Egypt, and Sejanus' father), or the fall of Sejanus himself.[2]

It is possible that neither the *Horrea Volusiana* nor the *Horrea Faeniana* were founded until some time in the first century A.D. The generally accepted founder for the *Volusiana* is Q. Volusius Saturninus, consul of A.D. 56, because an inscription recording a *horrearius* belonging probably to this man has been found.[3] However, it seems to me more likely that the *horrea* were founded earlier. We know something about both the father and the grandfather of the consul of A.D. 56. It was the grandfather L. Volusius Saturninus (who died in A.D. 20) who gave distinction to this ancient family by holding the consulship. Tacitus also says of him *opumque, quis domus illa immensum viguit primus adcumulator*.[4] If he did found the *Horrea Volusiana* it would be perhaps at about the same period as the founding of the *Horrea Lolliana*. The fact that it was still in the hands of the *Volusii* as private property in the time of the grandson, the consul of A.D. 56, may be accounted for by the wiliness of his father, the L. Volusius Saturninus who died in A.D. 56, *cui tres et nonaginta anni spatium vivendi praecipuaeque opes bonis artibus, inoffensa tot imperatorum amicitia fuit*.[5] However, it was clear that the family property had not escaped the eye (at least) of Nero who could make a jibe to Seneca in A.D. 62 concerning *quantum Volusio longa parsimonia quaesivit*.[6] It may be worth noting that the Lollii were connected with the Volusii Saturnini: M. Lollius, the consul and father of Lollia Paulina, was married to Volusia, the sister of L. Volusius Saturninus, the grandfather of the consul of A.D. 56.[7]

The *Horrea Faeniana* were founded perhaps by L. Faenius Rufus, *Praefectus Annonae* in A.D. 55.[8] In neither the *Horrea Volusiana* nor the *Horrea Faeniana* is there any proof of imperial or state ownership.

The *Horrea Agrippiana* are thought to have been founded by Marcus

---

[1] *CIL* VI. 9471.
[2] Pliny, *NH* XXXVI. 197. Tac. *Ann.* VI. 2. 1.
[3] Romanelli, p. 988. Cf. *CIL* VI. 7289.
[4] Tac. *Ann.* III. 30 (A.D. 20). [5] Tac. *Ann.* XIII. 30. 4 (A.D. 56).
[6] Tac. *Ann.* XIV. 56 (A.D. 62). [7] Tac. *Ann.* XII. 22.
[8] Romanelli, p. 988. Cf. *AE* (1909), n. 93.

Agrippa before 12 B.C.[1] and the structure of the building, which has been partly excavated, confirms that dating approximately. There is no proof among the inscriptions which refer to them that they were state or imperial property. The chances are, however, that even if they were not public in his lifetime they were left among his property to Augustus or the Roman people.

The *Horrea Piperataria*[2] are a special case. They were created by the Flavians in the Neronian portico on the north side of the Sacra Via for the special purpose of storage and state control of oriental spices and peppers. They are of particular importance in that they may show for the first time imperial interest in controlling, not only the distribution, but also the storage of a certain type of goods and they presumably set the pattern for the later *horrea* named after the goods they stored rather than after the family of the founder. We know of the *Horrea Chartaria* and *Horrea Candelaria*: there may well have been others.

So much for this general survey of the named *horrea* known to us in Rome. The important point which I wish to stress is that in no case is there any proof that the *horrea* belonged either to the state or the Emperor from the beginning of the Principate. Of course there is a great need for caution in making such a proposition and in attempting to assess its possible consequences. The number of *horrea* whose names we know in Rome in the early Empire is not great, and in that number we can say little about many of them. However, caution should not become timidity. If the suggestions about the *Horrea Lolliana* and the *Horrea Galbana* alone have some truth in them, the consequences cannot be overlooked. Both these warehouses were of great importance. The *Horrea Lolliana*, as can be seen from the plan on the Severan Marble Plan, was an imposing building which commanded a stretch of the river bank; and the *Horrea Galbana* occupied an enormous area immediately behind the *Porticus Aemilia*, just in the position where one would expect to find state warehouses. Moreover it seems clear that in the first century A.D. other stretches of land in the Testaccio area were in the hands of the *Sulpicii Galbae*, since we hear in a second-century inscription about the *Praedia Galbana*,[3] which at that time were

---

[1] Romanelli, p. 987.

[2] Chronographer *ad* A.D. 354. Mommsen, *Chronica Minora* I, p. 146, says they were built by Domitian. Cf. Loane, *Industry and Commerce of the City of Rome*, pp. 137 ff.

[3] *CIL* VI. 30983 = *ILS* 3840. Cf. W. Henzen, 'Di una iscrizione rinvenuta presso il Monte Testaccio', *BCom* XIII (1885), 51 and Tav. VI.

under the control of the *Procurator Patrimonii* and had presumably passed into imperial hands at the same time as the *Horrea Galbana*.

The implications of all this are many and varied. It suggests that trade and storage of goods other than corn was in the hands of private enterprise. So much does the corn trade dominate our thoughts because of its political implications that it is difficult to remember the trade in other essential and luxury goods. In no case do we *know* whether these named *horrea* were used for storing corn; and even in the case of the *Horrea Galbana*, the scholiast on Horace's *Odes* simply says *hodieque autem Galbae horrea vino et oleo et similibus aliis referta sunt*. As a matter of fact excavation of the *Horrea Galbana* has revealed that *one* of its three great courts had raised floors similar to those in the corn-storing *horrea* at Ostia.[1] It may well be that the pattern of trade at Rome in this period was more like that of Hellenistic Delos, where the same people were both ἔμποροι, ναύκληροι and ἐγδοχεῖς—merchants, shipowners and owners or renters[2] of warehouses. Without wishing to deny that there must have been some state and imperially owned warehouses, we may still believe that even within the corn trade itself free enterprise may have played a bigger part than we suspect in the first century A.D. So much do the *frumentationes* dominate our thinking that we forget that they absorbed a small part of the mass of corn coming to Rome,[3] and that the basic worry was the maintenance of a stable price for corn on the open market. It has long been recognised that even tribute corn was *transported* by independent merchants, but we may go further. The independent merchants were all-important for Rome's corn supply. The Emperors' concessions and encouragements to them, as well as Cicero's and Tacitus' open admission[4] that if they sell elsewhere than in Rome famine results, all point the same way. That even the *granaries*

[1] Lugli, *I monumenti antichi* III, p. 608.
[2] M. Rostovtseff, *Social and Economic History of the Hellenistic World* (Oxford, 1941), pp. 228, 1628.
[3] Loane, *Industry and Commerce of the City of Rome*, p. 13, gives the following figures: 1,200,000 *modii* per month needed for *frumentationes*; 20,000,000 *modii* per annum came from Egypt; 40,000,000 per annum came from Africa, outside Egypt. Thus the *frumentationes* take less than a quarter of the corn from these two sources *alone*. See further Appendix 3.
[4] In the famine of A.D. 19, Tiberius kept the price normal by paying the grain merchants 2 *sesterces* the *modius* for the wheat they sold. Tac. *Ann.* II. 87. Cf. also Suet. *Aug.* 42. 3; Tac. *Ann.* XV. 39. 2; Suet. *Claud.* 18. 2–19; Cicero, *De Domo* 11 and Tac. *Hist.* IV. 38 for the necessity of ordinary merchants to sell at Rome.

of Rome in the Republican period could be run as private enterprise is hinted by Cicero.[1] He refers in a philosophical example to the granaries at Puteoli, the forerunner of Ostia as the great port of Rome, in a way which Madvig in his commentary and all subsequent commentators have taken to imply that they were privately owned and of great rental value.

A further implication is that some of the great senatorial families in the late Republic and early Empire were involved in trade. If they were not using their great warehouses for their own cargoes and estates produce, or not exclusively so, at least they were enjoying rents from traders and no doubt putting money into commercial ventures. They may not have been directly represented, but acted through freedmen: perhaps too they regarded their possession of warehouses merely as property and not involvement in commerce. This comes as a slight shock, but, as Cicero said,[2] there was nothing wrong in being in trade providing you were in it in a big enough way; the *Lollii* and the *Sulpicii Galbae* would, I suspect, have passed that test. There should perhaps be a rider added to the suggestion that free enterprise reigned and that the senatorial families continued to prosper directly or indirectly from trade. All the names of the *horrea* that have come down to us from this early period belong to families that were prominent in Augustus' cause and enjoyed continued imperial favour—until, of course, the moment when the Emperor grabbed the property for himself. The *Lollii* came to the fore under Augustus; the *Volusii Saturnini* were favoured; Galba was notorious for the favours he enjoyed; the *Seii* were prominent; and Agrippa was Augustus' right arm.[3]

Of course, it cannot have been only these men and these families which had princely wealth, and owned warehouses in Rome. Statilius Taurus, for example, became notoriously rich under Augustus, and the burial place of the Statilii in Rome has revealed over four hundred inscriptions of slaves including *horrearii*.[4] This may hint at Statilian-owned warehouses in Rome.

---

[1] Cicero, *De Finibus* II. 84 and 85.

[2] Cicero, *De Officiis* I. 151. Rostovtseff, *SEHRE* II, p. 545, note 10, rightly remarks on the lack of attention given to the sources of the income of the senatorial class: it probably took part in credit operations, despite prohibition of commercial activities.

[3] R. Syme, *The Roman Revolution* (Oxford, 1939), Index, *s.vv.* 'Lollius', 'Galba', 'Seius' and 'Agrippa'. Rostovtseff, *SEHRE* I, p. 57 and note 17.

[4] Syme, *op. cit.* pp. 380 ff. *CIL* VI. 6292 = *ILS* 7440[a]; VI. 6293 = *ILS* 7440[b]; VI. 6294, 6295.

Moreover, if we are right in thinking in terms of free enterprise, then renting and hiring, *locatio–conductio*,[1] and the offering of *custodia* on fixed terms assumes great importance. We are to think at this stage, not so much of state storehouses run by state officials as seen in the *Codex Theodosianus* and the massive bureaucracy of Roman Egypt, but rather of private contract. The action of Alexander Severus[2] in setting up *horrea* in all regions of the city where men might store valuables must be seen not as a new principle but as an extension of an old one.

With all this in mind it may be worth making a suggestion with regard to the work of the *Praefectus Annonae* and his staff. It seems to me possible that at this early stage the functions of the *Annona* office, although of great importance, were not quite so all-embracing as they were later to become; and that apart from the organisation of tribute corn their job was not unlike that of the ἀγορανόμοι[3] of the Hellenistic world, who checked weights and measures in the open market and saw to it that corn was not sold above a certain price.

It is certain that the functions of the *Praefectus* grew rapidly and that the State, even if it had not been over-industrious in providing *horrea* in Rome after C. Gracchus' legislation,[4] supplied in the building north of the *Decumanus* in Ostia, and around the Claudian and Trajanic harbours enormous storage capacity. But the fact remains that this was a slow business which did not reach its peak until Hadrian's time. Before that, I suggest, private enterprise played a great part.

2

We may now turn to the inscriptions concerning the *horrea* in Rome. There is one group, which has caused great difficulty.

It must be remembered throughout this discussion that the problem in Rome was not simply one of storage, but also of *distribution* of goods; this is the point at which the analogy with the Ostian *horrea*, so valuable for the general structure and design of the buildings, must break down.

---

[1] See Chapter VI.

[2] SHA (*Alexander Severus*) 39. 3: horrea in omnibus regionibus publica fecit ad quae conferrent boni hi, qui privatas custodias non haberent.

[3] *RE* I, col. 883. See further Appendix 3.

[4] Plut. *C. Gracchus* VI. 2 ἔγραψε...κατασκευάζεσθαι σιτοβόλια possibly confirmed by Festus p. 290: Sempronia horrea qui locus dicitur, in eo fuerunt lege Gracchi ad custodiam frumenti publici. But we hear of no further activity of this kind.

The problem in Ostia was predominantly one of storage and reshipment, *not* of distribution.

A Greek freedman from Bithynia, Μ(άρκος) Αὐ(ρήλιος) Ξενωνιανὸς Ἀκύλας, refers to himself as πρῶτος λιθενπόρων, στατίωνα ἴσχων ἐν ὁρίοις Πετρωνιανοῖς.[1] The freedman T. Aquilius Pelorus is described as *vestiarius de hor(reis) Volusianis*.[2] C. Iulius Lucifer was a *vestiarius de horreis Agrippianis*;[3] a man whose cognomen was Nectareus of unknown trade was similarly *—us de horreis Agrippia[nis]*; while M. Li[vius] [Herm]eros was *vestiarius de horreis Agrippinianis* (perhaps a stonecutter's error).[4] Similar inscriptions concern the *Horrea Galbana*: C. Tullius Crescens was *negotiator marmorarius de Galbes*; A. Cornelius Priscus was *sagarius de horreis Galbianis*; while a woman, Aurelia Nais, was *piscatrix de horreis Galbae*.[5]

So far as the dates of these inscriptions are ascertainable, they belong to a period after the property has passed into imperial hands. The names, Μάρκος Αὐρήλιος, of the freedman in the *Horrea Petroniana*, would indicate some date about the middle of the second century A.D. Similarly C. Iulius Lucifer and the wife of M. Livius Hermeros, whose name was Claudia Ti. f. Moschis, indicate an early first-century date (but the *Horrea Agrippiana* must have passed into state or imperial hands at least on the death of Agrippa if not before). We have no clue as to the date of A. Cornelius Priscus, at least so far as his name is concerned. It is clear, however, from the remainder of the inscription that several other freedmen of the same patron were associated with the *horrea* and thus it may not be impossible that the A. Cornelius Aphrodisius, known from a different inscription[6] to have been a *quinquennalis* of a *sodalicium* in the *horrea* in A.D. 159, may give us a general date for the whole group. There are no clues as to the date of C. Tullius Crescens or Aurelia Nais,[7] but the very fact that the *horrea* are described as Galban and not Sulpician would indicate that they lived in or after Galba's reign and therefore during a period when the building was imperial property.

[1] *SEG* IV. 106 = *RendPontAcc* III (1924/5), 191.
[2] *CIL* VI. 9973 = *ILS* 7573.   [3] *CIL* VI. 9972 = *ILS* 7571.
[4] (Nectareus) *CIL* VI. 10026; (Hermeros) *CIL* XIV. 3958 = *ILS* 7572.
[5] (Crescens) *CIL* VI. 33886 = *ILS* 7539; (Priscus) *CIL* VI. 33906 = *ILS* 7584; (Nais) *CIL* VI. 9801 = *ILS* 7500.
[6] *CIL* VI. 338 = *ILS* 3445.
[7] *CIL* VI. 9801 (Nais) is accented. The maximum use of accents, in Ostia at least, occurred in the Flavian period and early second century, cf. Meiggs, p. 556.

The basic problem about this group of inscriptions is, in what way were these people associated with the *horrea*? What does the formula *de horreis* mean?

An attempt has been made to suggest that these people all had shops flanking the *horrea* on the road and that they gave, as it were, their address in the sub-district named after the *horrea*. In short, the formula *de horreis* is to be regarded as a general reference to locality and not a specific reference to participation in the *horrea*.[1]

This is an explanation more convenient than satisfactory. First, so far as we know the plan of the *Horrea Galbana*, there were no shops flanking it.[2] Romanelli's suggestion with regard to the *Horrea Agrippiana* was made at a time when fragments 37 and 86 of the Marble Plan were regarded as the outline of those *horrea*. This is no longer considered to be the case and thus there is no reason to suppose that the *Horrea Agrippiana* were flanked by shops. Secondly, as a linguistic argument it is clearly unsound. Although certain officials in *horrea* do use a different phrase such as *ex horreis Lollianis*[3] to describe their place of work, there is an example of three workers inside the *Horrea Galbana*, who describe themselves as *hor(rearii) de H(orreis) C(aesaris)* or possibly *G(albanis)*.[4] Whatever the correct expansion of the phrase, there can be no doubt of their working inside the *horrea*, since we have another inscription[5] describing the same men even more specifically as attached to a certain part of the building. Furthermore it is certain that in the *Horrea Galbana* the *sagarii* were an integral part of some *internal* arrangements of the *horrea*.[6] Nor can there be any doubt that the Bithynian λιθέντπορος actually had his *statio* inside the *Horrea Petroniana*.

What then did these people do inside these *horrea*? Were they simply merchants who had hired storage space in imperially owned warehouses? On the whole this seems not to be a satisfactory explanation. The *statio* of the Bithynian implies more than storage space: some sort of office or headquarters of a firm seems to be involved. Moreover, in the case of the *vestiarii* and *sagarii* not only does the registering of the

---

[1] Romanelli, pp. 973, 987, makes such a suggestion for the *Agrippiana* inscriptions, cf. Loane, *Industry and Commerce of the City of Rome*, p. 115, note 8, and p. 130.
[2] Gatti, '"Saepta Iulia" e "Porticus Aemilia"', pp. 123 ff. *Pianta Marm.* frag. 42.
[3] *CIL* VI. 4226 and 4226 a = *ILS* 1620. Cf. also *CIL* VI. 37796 and 3971 = *ILS* 1625.
[4] *CIL* VI. 682 = *ILS* 1623.   [5] *CIL* VI. 30901 = *ILS* 1622.
[6] *CIL* VI. 30741: *cur(atores) collegi(i) Herculis salutaris c(o)hortis I sagariorum.* Cf. Loane, *Industry and Commerce of the City of Rome*, p. 131 and p. 132, note 70.

name of the *horrea* and their connection with them on stone seem to imply a more permanent arrangement than simply the hiring of storage space, but also these people give the impression of being rather small fry, retailers and craftsmen.

So far, I think, one can proceed with certainty: beyond this point nothing is clear. If these people really were small craftsmen and retailers, one has to face the problem of what they were doing in a *horreum* rather than in a *macellum*. A possible answer is to see in the organisation of the *Horrea Piperataria* a paradigm for the organisation of other *horrea* in Rome and to suggest that these people were involved in making up and retailing goods which were imperially owned. Thus Fiechter suggested a comparison between the *Horrea Agrippiana* with its *vestiarii* and the *Horrea Piperataria*:[1] Romanelli saw in the *sagarii* of the *Horrea Galbana* a possible connection with an imperial monopoly in Spartan wool;[2] and Loane a connection between two of the *vestiarii* of *Horrea Agrippiana* and fine linen from Egypt.[3] It is true that the *Horrea Agrippiana* has preserved in the entrances to its rooms thresholds of a type associated with shops and which has no parallel among the *horrea* at Ostia. Retail there must have been; but there is a serious difficulty in believing that the presence of small traders in *horrea* is the result of state monopolies in various goods, or the marketing of goods from imperial estates. How does the fish wife Aurelia Nais fit into such a scheme? Romanelli ignores her: Loane imagines her selling fish straight from the Tiber[4]—hardly an imperial monopoly, and not, one imagines, imperial property. Yet so far as we can tell she not only stored her stock in, but probably sold it from, the *Horrea Galbana*. The only honest answer to the problem in the present state of the evidence is one of *non liquet*.

3

Who was in charge of the individual *horrea* in Rome and how were they run? Attention has naturally been focused in the past almost exclusively on the *Horrea Galbana*, and in particular upon the threefold division of its *horrearii*.[5] An inscription set up by two imperial slaves,

[1] *RE* VIII, col. 2462 (Fiechter).
[2] Romanelli, p. 986. Cf. Statius, *Silvae* III. 3. 94 ff., but this passage may mean no more than that there were some imperial estates near Sparta.
[3] Loane, *Industry and Commerce of the City of Rome*, p. 130.
[4] *Ibid.* p. 32, note 95.
[5] Romanelli, p. 979 and earlier literature recorded there.

Maior and Diadumenus, an imperial freedman, T. Flavius Crescens, and the *operari Galbeses* in A.D. 128 includes the phrase *ex collatione horriariorum chortis II.*[1] An imperial slave called Anteros of unknown date calls himself *horrearius chortis III.* Zmaragdus, who was perhaps a slave of the Emperor Galba, refers to himself as *vilicus horreorum Galbianorum coh. trium.*[2]

Moreover this triple division seems to have affected more people than the actual *horrearii.* A. Cornelius Aphrodisius, whose job in the *horrea* is unknown (but he may be connected with the other freedmen of A. Cornelius, who were *sagarii*), set up an inscription recording a *sodalic(io) horr(eariorum) Galban(orum) cohort...* in A.D. 159.[3] The freedman Ti. Claudius Felix, his wife Claudia Helpis and their son Ti. Claudius Alypus, who seem to have come originally from Palmyra, describe themselves as *Calbiensies de coh. III.*[4]

The earlier explanations of this triple division, referring it to urban or praetorian cohorts,[5] were quickly and rightly dismissed. Thedenat's suggestion[6] that the workers in the *horrea* were organised because of the importance and size of the warehouse in a quasi-military way was more sensible. It has generally been combined with the view of Gatti,[7] who suggested a connection between the three 'cohorts' of the inscriptions and the three great cortili of the plan of the building. Hülsen alone has found this view artificial.[8] We must, I think, accept some sort of topographical division in order to make sense of the phrase *de cohorte*, inexplicable in purely military terms.

It is important for the previous questions we were asking about the *Horrea Galbana* to notice that people like the Palmyrene family and A. Cornelius Aphrodisius, who do not appear to have been actual *horrearii*, should be so closely knit into the organisation, Aphrodisius being even a *quinquennalis* of a *sodalicium* in the *horrea.*

However, for our present purpose we must note the fact that all the known *horrearii* are clearly designated as either imperial slaves or

[1] *CIL* VI. 30901 = *ILS* 1622.
[2] (Anteros) *CIL* VI. 588 = *ILS* 1624; (Zmaragdus) *CIL* VI. 30855 = *ILS* 1621.
[3] *CIL* VI. 338 = *ILS* 3445. [4] *CIL* VI. 710 = 4337.
[5] W. Henzen, 'Iscrizione relativa alle *Horrea Galbana*', *RM* I (1886), 42 ff. Cf. notes *CIL* VI. 30855 (= *ILS* 1621) and *EE* IV, n. 723 a.
[6] D–S III. 1, p. 271.
[7] Gatti, 'Alcune osservazioni sugli orrei Galbani', pp. 71 ff.
[8] Note to *CIL* VI. 30855 (=*ILS* 1621: Dessau accepts Gatti's view).

freedmen. Further, it looks as if the man in charge of the whole ware-house at one stage, Zmaragdus, was a slave of the Emperor and that he bore the title *vilicus*.

This evidence is supported by the inscriptions concerning the *Horrea Lolliana*. The only *horrearius* known to us in it was a slave of the Emperor and his inscription was found in the *columbarium* of Livia.[1] There was also a slave of the Emperor Claudius, Calamus Pamphilianus, known from two inscriptions also found in the *Columbarium Liviae*, who was *vilicus ex horreis Lollianis*.[2] Perhaps the slave of Nero, Phila-delphus, who is described simply as *ex horreis Petronianis* on an inscrip-tion similarly found in the *Columbarium Liviae*, was *horrearius* or *vilicus* of the Emperor.[3]

Thus the evidence from these *horrea* whose names are known to us is consistent in suggesting *imperial* slaves or freedmen as *horrearii*, presumably working under a slave (or freedman) *vilicus*. But in all three cases, if my hypothesis is right above, these *horrea* were originally privately owned and later became part of the Emperor's private prop-erty. Thus to find imperial slaves and freedmen as workers and imperial *vilici* in charge of them is no surprise: this would be just the way a man would run his own property.

What we would like to know is, Were imperial slaves and freedmen employed in other state *horrea*? There are a number of inscriptions referring to *horrearii* or *vilici* of unnamed *horrea* but analysis of them reveals very little. Presumably the *horrearii* Saturninus and Successus who made a dedication to the *genius* of their *horrea* in A.D. 75[4] were imperial slaves—at least that is a possible implication of the dedication *pro salute dominorum*: certainly the *horrearius* Zosimus was a slave of the Emperor, as was Primus the husband of Titinia Saturnina.[5] It is more difficult to be certain about Ti(berius) Claudius Dapnio [*sic*] and Felix, the father of Ti(berius) Claudius Secundinus, although the names perhaps suggest imperial freedmen.[6] As for the *horrearius* Apsyrtus, we have no evidence at all;[7] the *vilici horreorum* Cocceius Cosmus, Pyramus, Eutyches and Vinicius Dius seem to be rather different.[8] Despite the fact that we do

---

[1] *CIL* VI. 4239. [2] *CIL* VI. 4226 and 4226*a* = *ILS* 1620.
[3] *CIL* VI. 3971 = *ILS* 1625. [4] *CIL* VI. 235 = *ILS* 3663.
[5] (Zosimus) *CIL* VI. 8682; (Primus) *CIL* VI. 33746.
[6] (Dapnio) *CIL* VI. 9460; (Felix) *CIL* VI. 9463.
[7] *CIL* VI. 9108.
[8] G. Mancini, 'Le recenti scoperte di antichità al Testaccio', *BCom* XXXIX (1911), 258.

not know to which *horrea* they refer (although the Testaccio area was the place of discovery), the notion of *vilici* as opposed to *vilicus* may be significant and the men certainly did not belong to the Emperor.

To settle the question we would need a series of early inscriptions from somewhere like Ostia or Portus; but it is a remarkable fact that among the mass of Ostian inscriptions there is no reference to the workers and managers of *horrea*.

An attempt to settle the question by studying the evidence concerning *custodiarii*, *apothecarii*, *mensores frumentarii* and other supposed workers in *horrea* is useless. Despite Loane, *custodiarii* were not warehouse guards but prison officers.[1] Similarly *apothecarii*[2] are referred to only once in a legal text which classes them with *institores...mercium*: thus even if their place was in the *horrea* they were not a part of the staff. *Mensores frumentarii* were clearly important for the measuring of corn that was to be stored in the *horrea*, but it also seems clear that they formed no part of the staff of individual *horrea*. In Ostia the inscriptions concerning them come from an area around their *aula* and Temple.[3] Moreover the unique plan of the so-called *horrea dei Mensores*, of which the *aula* formed a part, with its unusually spacious halls, seems to have been designed to allow freedom of movement and thus may have been the central depot at which corn was measured and organised before being despatched in sacks to the earmarked *horrea*. Similarly in Rome the inscriptions concerning the *mensores machinarii frumenti publici*[4] have *not* been found in association with the great *horrea* of the Testaccio area. Although, therefore, we may believe that an immense number of different workers must have been involved in unloading, loading, carrying, recording, measuring and checking goods for the *horrea*, within the *horrea* themselves we only have unimpeachable evidence for *horrearii* and *vilici horreorum*. Their job must have been predominantly one of guarding not only against theft but also against the deterioration of the goods stored. Liability must have been their

---

[1] Loane, *Industry and Commerce of the City of Rome*, p. 14, note 13; contrast J. Waltzing, *Étude historique sur les corporations professionnelles chez les romains* (Louvain, 1900), IV, p. 15.

[2] Romanelli, p. 979, relying on Waltzing, *Corporations professionnelles* IV, p. 7, seems to regard *apothecarii* as equivalents of *horrearii*. But there is no evidence for this; only reference in *Cod. Iust.* XII. 57. 12. 3.

[3] Waltzing, *Corporations professionnelles* IV, p. 30. Cf. H. Bloch, 'Ostia: iscrizioni rinvenute tra il 1930 e il 1939', *NSc* (1953), p. 297. *Aula dei Mensores* (Reg. I. Is. XIX. 2–3).

[4] Waltzing, *Corporations professionnelles* IV, pp. 29 ff.

12-2

main worry and an elaborate system of receipts, signed and counter-signed on acceptance and discharge of goods, must have existed whatever the purpose of the *horrea* and whether state or private goods were stored.[1]

Within the *horrea*, as has been noted, there were *sodalicia* and *collegia* probably funerary in character.[2] Each college had its own officials: we hear of *magistri, magistri quinquennales* and *curatores*.[3] Probably because of their purely funerary character people other than the actual staff of the *horrea* were admitted to membership.[4] It is likely that the *immunitas* of the *negotiantes* on the inscribed base in the centre of the excavated courtyard of the *Horrea Agrippiana* is to be referred to such a *collegium* and its *munera*.[5]

4

Outside Rome, although the evidence is considerably less, the problem is simpler. Both in Italy and in the provinces the problem is one of storage alone and not of distribution. The administration of public *horrea* at least from A.D. 8 onward must ultimately have been the charge of the *Praefectus Annonae*. Seneca, writing in A.D. 49[6] to Pompeius Paulinus, *Praefectus Annonae*, can say: *cures ut incorruptum et a fraude advehentium et a neglegentia frumentum transfundatur in horrea, ne concepto umore vitietur et concalescat ut ad mensuram pondusque respondeat.* This clearly indicates his responsibility for *grain* which was stored, but he exercised a general supervision over other imports as well. The C. Pomponius Turpilianus, who in the reign of Antoninus Pius had the unusual title *proc(urator) ad oleum in Galbae Ostiae Portus utriusque*,[7] was probably a special official of his department in charge of oil at Ostia, Portus and the *Horrea Galbana* in Rome. Whether the administration and upkeep in Italy of the public *horrea* themselves as opposed to what was stored in them was also the responsibility of the *Praefectus Annonae* is not certain, but it is probable.

In the provinces it is certain that, as in the late Empire, the upkeep

[1] Cf. *CIL* VI. 33747 = *ILS* 5914, and *Cod. Theod.* XII. 6. 16 (A.D. 375).
[2] Waltzing, *Corporations professionnelles* II, p. 68.
[3] (*magistri*) *CIL* VI. 188 = *ILS* 3721; 236 = *ILS* 3668; (*magistri quinquennales*) *CIL* VI. 30740; (*curatores*) *CIL* VI. 30741.
[4] Cf. *CIL* VI. 30741.
[5] G. Schneider Graziosi, 'Genius horreorum Agrippianorum', *BCom* XLII (1914), 29. Cf. L. Wickert, *RM* XL (1925), 213–14 and *RM* XLI (1926), 229.
[6] Seneca, *De Brevitate Vitae* 19. 1. See Appendix 3.
[7] *CIL* XIV. 20 = *ILS* 372. Cf. Meiggs, p. 302.

and control of the *horrea* within the province seem normally to have been the responsibility of the governor. At Djemila[1] in North Africa the dedication of the *horrea* constructed by the *respublica Cuiculitanorum* (and now fully excavated) was made to Septimius Severus by Q. *Anicius Faustus, leg. Aug. pr. pr. vir amp. consularis, pat. coloniae*. Again in Sardinia the *horrea* at Cagliari[2] were restored by the governor.

What officials were employed in *horrea* in the provinces, what were their status, titles and duties, are not known to us in detail except in Egypt. An inscription from Carthage,[3] which is undated but probably belongs to the early Empire, reads *Dis manibus sacr(um), Chrestus Aug(usti servus) custos Utika horreorum Augustae, pius vixit annis LXXX*. This would suggest imperial slaves working in public *horrea* in the provinces. (This is what the *horrea* at Utica must have been.) The title *custos* is slightly unusual. We know of *horrea* officials called *custodes* mostly from legal texts concerning the regulation of '*horrea* to let',[4] where they are responsible for protecting the building from theft. The man Eutychus,[5] who is described on an inscription from the cemetery of Callistus on the Via Appia as *[cu]stos horrei...[qu]i fuit ad Ludum G[allicum]*, may have been employed in just such a capacity. It is possible that we may have a more apt parallel for the Utica inscription in an inscription from Maxula and in the altars set up at Djemila and Bone also in North Africa.[6] The inscription from Maxula refers to *Caeler Caesaris nostri servus custos horreorum*. The Bone inscription reads *Genio et Numini horreorum Sabinus Aug. lib. c. s. h. Hipp. R. item cura cancellorum*. At Djemila the inscription is *Veneri Aug. Sac. Marcellus Aug. N̄. Lib. c. s. h. Chrestus Aug. N̄. verna vilicus Cuiculi IIII Publicu. Afric. posuerunt*. Albertini in his publication of these last two inscriptions has suggested the expansion *c(ustos) s(acrorum) h(orreorum)* for both these inscriptions. This seems very plausible, and if it is right, we begin to have a picture of the administration of public *horrea* in the hands of imperial slaves and freedmen with the title *custos*, at least in North Africa. At Caesaraugusta[7] in Spain a freedman made a dedication to the *Genio tutelae horreorum*, but what position he held, if any, is not specified.

[1] *AE* (1911), no. 106. Cf. Allais, *RAfr* (1933), 259.
[2] *NSc* (1909), pp. 183 ff.
[3] *CIL* VIII. 13190. The *Dis Manibus* formula would suggest an early date.
[4] *Iust. Cod.* IV. 65. 4.   [5] *CIL* VI. 9470.
[6] M. Poinssot, 'Inscriptions de Suo et de Maxula', *CRAI* (1936), p. 285. Albertini, *CRAI* (1924), 253.   [7] *CIL* II. 2991 = *ILS* 3667.

In Italy itself there is certain evidence for officials in towns with the title *horrearius*. At Beneventum a certain Concordius, presumably a slave, describes himself as *Co[l](oniae?) horr(earius)*.[1] At Luna a dedication was made by Abascantus, *imperatorum hor[r]earius*,[2] while at Ravenna, probably considerably later, a stone was set up to a man described as *orrearius*.[3] These men all seem to have been slaves and in public buildings. At Ariminum, however, two freedmen, L. Lepidus Politicus and C. Pupius Blastus,[4] made a dedication to the *Genio larum horrei Pupiani*—seemingly a private venture owned either by them or the patron of one of them, who employed them in some capacity in it.

5

It is always dangerous to argue from silence, but in view of the paucity of inscriptions recording *horrea* officials and the even greater scarcity of material remains of *horrea* in the townships of Italy, it is very probable that not every town had *horrea* of its own and that those which did owed their possession of them to the fact that they were ports or central collecting dumps set up by the Emperor for imperial purposes.

Moreover it does appear from what little evidence we have that with the gradual breakdown of private ownership and the confiscation of property and the building of new establishments, for example at Ostia, by the Emperor, the staffing of public *horrea* was done by imperially owned slaves or freedmen. With the ever-spreading growth of imperial power it is very doubtful whether any of the important *horrea* which were built in the Empire could be regarded as State or public property. The Emperor owned everything. The inscriptions recording the building of *horrea* feature the Emperor's name prominently and the *horrea* at Myra and Patara in Lycia state simply *horrea Imp. Caesaris Divi Traiani. Parthici F. Divi Nervae Nepotis Traiani Hadriani Augusti cos. III*.[5] So far as we can judge from our scanty evidence, the process continued and was intensified, and the *horrea fiscalia* of the late legal codes were all imperial property.

At the beginning of the first century A.D., if I am right, the Emperor owned no *horrea* and free enterprise was dominant. By means of con-

---

[1] *CIL* IX. 1545.
[2] *CIL* XI. 1358. We may suspect some connection with marble working.
[3] *CIL* XI. 321.
[4] *CIL* XI. 357 = *ILS* 3666.   [5] *CIL* III. Suppl. 12129.

fiscation of important warehouses in Rome and the building of vast new warehouses at Ostia, Portus, elsewhere in Italy, for instance at Aquileia,[1] and in the provinces, the situation came about that the Emperor ultimately owned all *horrea* which had any public or imperial purpose and was responsible for their administration and staffing. This led to the situation in the late Empire, which we must now examine.

LATE EMPIRE

I

The organisation of the higher administrative posts in control of the great storehouses of state at the time of the rescripts in the Theodosian Code is not in doubt. The *Praefectus Annonae*, who had been the head of the whole administration under the early Empire, was now subordinate in Rome itself to the *Praefectus Urbi*. These two officials worked together, but the orders were given by the *Praefectus Urbi* and carried out by the *Praefectus Annonae* and his staff. Great care was to be taken that the staff of the city prefect should *not* become involved in the minutiae of the *annona* organisation.[2]

In the case of the *horrea* at Portus, the *Praefectus Annonae* was again made subordinate, to the *Praefectus Praetorio*, to whom all the rescripts concerning the organisation of *horrea* at Portus were addressed. The subordination is proved in a rescript to the *Praefectus Praetorio* concerning Portus where a certain limit was placed upon the jurisdiction of the *Praefectus Annonae*.[3]

Moreover we know of specialised men such as the *Praefectus Annonae Africae*, who was subordinate to the *Praefectus Praetorio*, and the *Praefectus Annonae Alexandrinae* under the *Praefectus Urbi Constantinopolitanae*.[4] The very existence of such distinct posts controlling the organisation of the two great corn-producing areas of the Empire must have meant further localisation of the powers and influence of the *Praefectus Annonae* at Rome.

In the provinces in general the provincial governors, as at all times

---

[1] A. Calderini, *Aquileia Romana* (Milan, 1930), Introd. p. cxix.
[2] *Cod. Theod.* XI. 14. 1 (A.D. 365).
[3] *Cod. Theod.* XIV. 23. 1 (A.D. 400) and XIV. 4. 9 (A.D. 417).
[4] *Not. Dign.*, ed. Seeck. From A.D. 330 Egyptian corn went not to Rome but to Constantinople. Cf. *Cod. Theod.* XII. 6. 3. (A.D. 349).

under the Empire, had the customary responsibility for tax collecting and the care and administration of the *horrea* within their areas. They in their turn were subordinate to the vicars and to the *Praefectus Praetorio*.

At Rusicade in Numidia the famous inscription[1] of the time of Valentinian and Valens recording the *horrea ad securitatem populi Romani pariter ac provincialium constructa* was dedicated by Publilius Caeonius Caecina Albinus who is described as *v(ir) c(larissimus), cons(ularis) sexf(ascalis) p(rovinciae) N(umidiae) Cons(tantinae)*. In short, the governor of the province.

Similarly the inscription from the territory of Megara,[2] concerning arrangements for the supervision of *horrea* in the time of Arcadius, Honorius and Theodosius, records as the man in charge of the proceedings the proconsul Claudius Varius.

However, from Savaria in Pannonia is an inscription[3] to the Emperor Constans concerning the founding of some *horrea* which were dedicated *in securitatem perpetem rei annonariae* by Vulcacius Rufinus *v.c. praef. praet.* This man is known to have been *cos. ordinarius* in A.D. 347 and *praefectus praetorio Illyrici* in A.D. 349.

Moreover on a stone embedded in the wall of the Hadrianic *horrea* at Myra[4] in Lycia is an inscription (probably of fourth-century A.D. date), concerning various weights and measures that are to be used, which, although the name of the particular praetorian prefect has been erased, makes clear his responsibility and overall supervision even of *horrea* in the provinces.

This evidence for the importance of the *Praefectus Praetorio* is borne out and given ample illustration by the legal texts to be quoted later. In almost every case the rescripts are addressed either to the *Praefectus Urbi* or the *Praefectus Praetorio*, and of the two those addressed to the Praetorian Prefect form by far the larger group.

---

[1] *CIL* viii. 7975 (cf. viii. 19852 for complete version, = *ILS* 5910). Romanelli, p. 976, expands the abbreviation of the man's office wrongly. The right interpretation is given in *ILS* 5910, note 1.

[2] *IG* vii. 24 = Dittenberger, *Sylloge*³, 908.

[3] *CIL* iii. 4180 = *ILS* 727. Cf. *Cod. Iust.* vi. 62. 3 (A.D. 349) for dates.

[4] E. Petersen and F. von Luschan, *Reisen im Südwestlichen Kleinasien* ii (Vienna, 1889), p. 42, No. 77 a.

2

So far as the organisation of individual *horrea* is concerned, the important men seem to have been the *praepositi horreorum*. The nucleus of the
evidence concerning them is to be found in *Codex Theodosianus* XII. 6,
where they are grouped together with the *susceptores* and *praepositi
pagorum*.

The evidence for the appointment of *praepositi horreorum* is some-
what confusing. A change in the type of person who was to be eligible
for the office took place in the fourth century A.D. The most explicit
pieces of evidence as to the people eligible are unanimous in stating
that the *praepositi horreorum* must be chosen *ex praesidali officio*—from
the office staff of the governor.[1] The implication of these passages is,
however, that this had not been the case in the past, when the appointments had been made from among the *curiales*, the local senators.
Moreover the vehemence and repetition of the imperial order that the
susceptores and *praepositi horreorum* must be chosen from the office staff
of the governors suggest that the change might have been a recent one.
Perhaps some confirmation of this is given by the fact that, in the first
reference to this mode of appointment, it is admitted that the governor
of Cilicia says that no such men are available and thus the *vetustum
morem consuetudinemque sectabitur*. Further, a slightly earlier rescript to
the *concilium* of the Province of Africa[2] orders that *sacerdotales*,
permanent *flamines* and *duumvirales* shall have immunity from *annonarum praeposituris* and other inferior *munera*—implying that the other
curiales did *not* have such immunity. This, however, is not quite so
conclusive as it may appear, because there is reason to believe that Africa
was a special case in this matter and was allowed to retain the method
of election from the *curiales* after it had been abolished elsewhere. In a
rescript to the vicar of Africa at this period[3] concerning *susceptores* it is
stated that orders have been given for their election, throughout the
provinces of Illyricum, from office staffs, because such men were
proved to be more suitable and trustworthy than the *curiales'* appointments; but in the province of Africa the old system is to remain, with
certain safeguards against fraud. In a later rescript to the *Praefectus*

---

[1] *Cod. Theod.* XII. 6. 5 (A.D. 365); XII. 6. 7 (A.D. 365); XII. 6. 9 (A.D. 365? or 8?). The two
latter passages refer to *susceptores* alone.
[2] *Cod. Theod.* XII. 5. 2 (A.D. 337).   [3] *Cod. Theod.* XII. 6. 9 (A.D. 365 or 368).

Praetorio[1] it is revealed that the province of Byzacium in Africa had for a long time possessed the right that the *curiales* of its cities should undertake the *custodia* and *cura* of the *horrea*, but that in the proconsular province of Africa no local magistrate should exercise such a function.

The system thus seems to have been changed in general, although an exception was made for some reason in Byzacium. Romanelli,[2] however, relying on a rescript dated A.D. 386, which describes the election of *exactores* and *susceptores in celeberrimo coetu curiae*, states that it was not long before there was a reversion to the old system. Whatever the truth may be concerning the election of *exactores* and *susceptores*, the clear implication of the rescript concerning Byzacium (A.D. 430) just quoted, is that the *horrea* officials at least were not appointed from the *curiales* in general.

Until about the middle of the fourth century A.D., however, there is no doubt that the *praepositura horreorum* was a liturgy or *munus* which devolved upon the local communities. That it was a *munus*, and that people liable for the obligation tried to avoid it, is clear.[3] The term of office normally lasted one year, but, at least in Rome and the suburban area, if the man proved satisfactory it could be prolonged for a five-year period.[4] Again, a rescript to the *Comes Rerum Privatarum* reveals that before taking up office, a public declaration of the property and securities of the person chosen had to be made and the information lodged in the office of the *Comes*.[5] The man chosen had to be 'nominated' by certain of his fellows and they and their property, publicly declared, were held as surety for his efficiency and honesty in office.[6] No part of this property was allowed to be disposed of secretly through a third party[7] and in some cases it seems as if the whole *ordo* of the local senate was held responsible as *nominatores*.[8] At the end of the term of office accounts had to be rendered to the office of the provincial governor[9] or before the vicar and the prefect of the *annona* at Rome.[10]

These rescripts of the Theodosian Code are illustrated by certain papyri from Egypt which record the election of such local storehouse

---

[1] *Cod. Theod.* XII. 6. 33 (A.D. 430).
[2] Romanelli, p. 978. Cf. *Cod. Theod.* XII. 6. 20 (A.D. 386).
[3] *Cod. Theod.* XII. 6. 5 (A.D. 365); XII. 5. 2 (A.D. 337); XII. 1. 49 (A.D. 361).
[4] *Cod. Theod.* XII. 6. 24 (A.D. 397).   [5] *Cod. Theod.* XII. 6. 25 (A.D. 399).
[6] *Cod. Theod.* XII. 6. 8 (A.D. 365); XII. 6. 20 (A.D. 386).
[7] *Cod. Theod.* XII. 6. 8 (A.D. 365).   [8] *Cod. Theod.* XII. 6. 9 (A.D. 365 or 368).
[9] *Cod. Theod.* XII. 6. 7 (A.D. 365).   [10] *Cod. Theod.* XII. 6. 24 (A.D. 397).

supervisors. A return from two *Komarchs*[1] of the village of Ibion addressed to the *praepositus* of the *pagus* lists the persons qualified for certain offices including those of *sitologi*, which was the title of the granary keepers in Egypt. Ten men are named for *sitologi* as persons of means and suitability (although their means are not expressly stated) and the *Komarchs* and the whole village are regarded as responsible for their good behaviour.

Two earlier examples may be quoted. A papyrus from Oxyrhynchus,[2] dated A.D. 209–10, gives a list of officials for two villages in the Arsinoite nome submitted by a *Komarch*. These officials consist of village elders, a chief of police, guards, inspectors, night watchmen, policemen and persons to see to the safety of the deliveries to the public granaries. These men are named, their ages given and the property qualification, 600 drachmae, stated. Even more explicit is a papyrus in the Rylands collection[3] which is also a presentation of names for office in two villages. The duties were such things as clearing canals and guarding crops, but only the last two duties concern us. They are described as τὸ πρόνοιαν ποιήσασθαι τοῦ καθαρὸν εἶναι καὶ ἄδωλον τοῦ μετρουμένου δημοσίου πυροῦ and τὸ προστῆναι τοῖς δημοσίοις θησαυροῖς καὶ συσφραγίζειν ἅμα τοῖς σιτολόγοις ('To ensure clean grain and honest weight at the measuring of the public corn' and 'to exercise surveillance over the public granaries and to co-operate with the *sitologi*.') The names of two men are put forward for each of these duties, although the list is not complete. The heading of the whole list states that the men are suitable candidates and of means, and after their names are given their ages, 35 and 40 years old, and their property: 600 drachmae, in the former duty, and 1,000 drachmae in the latter. It is even specified in one case that the property is in building sites. The candidates are put forward 'for the services of the year at our own risk'—τῶν ἡμῶν κινδύνων. These papyri give vivid illustration of the system of election outlined in the Theodosian Code.

The important inscription from Megarian territory,[4] already referred to, has been taken by Romanelli to have some bearing on the election of *praepositi horreorum*. The inscription records how in the reign of Arcadius, Honorius and Theodosius, arrangements were made by the

---

[1] *P. Amh.* 139 (A.D. 350). [2] *P. Oxy.* 2121.
[3] *P. Ryl.* II. 90 (early third century).
[4] *IG* VII. 24 (A.D. 401–2) = Dittenberger, *Sylloge*[3], 908.

Greek cities meeting at Corinth as to how much (or how) each city should pay and when [εἰς] τὴν ὁρρεοπραιποσιτίαν, the cities of Boeotia, Euboea and Aetolia being associated with the *horrea* at Scarphia, those of the Peloponnese with the *horrea* at Corinth. At a point just after the statement that the following decision had been taken and that 'into the *horrea* at Scarphia...' the inscription unfortunately breaks off. Further, in the earlier part of the inscription it is possible to restore ὅπ[ως] χρὴ ἑκάστην πόλιν...λύειν (as Foucart and Romanelli) or ὁπ[όσα] χρὴ ἑκάστην πόλιν...λύειν (as Dittenberger does). Romanelli, adopting the former reading, wishes to interpret the passage as decisions taken concerning the method and order in which the *curiales* of the different cities should be responsible for electing the *praepositi* of the central *horrea*. Apart from the fact that, as has been shown, it is very likely that at this date, A.D. 402, the elections of the *praepositi* were not made from the *curiales* but from the office staffs of the governors, such an interpretation puts a curiously loose and unnatural meaning on the word λύειν. Some means of payment seems to be involved towards the maintenance of the *praepositi horreorum* and the natural restoration would be ὁπ[όσα]. It would be natural that, although the *munus* of providing *praepositi horreorum* should be taken away from the local communities because of inefficiency and fraud, the cost of maintaining the system should still remain as their burden.

The existence of the *praepositi* in Asia Minor is revealed also in the late inscription on the wall of the Hadrianic *horrea* at Myra[1] and some hint as to a part of their duties is given. The inscription is concerned with the sending of certain weights and measures, and with the cities to which they are to be given—so much to the metropolis of the Myrians, so much to the people of Arneae, ἐπὶ τῷ φροντίδι τῶν κατὰ καιρὸν πρεποσίτων φυλάττεσθαι τά τε μέτρα καὶ τὰ σταθμὰ ἀνεπιβούλευτα τοῖς ὁρρίοις. 'It is the responsibility of the *praepositi* at the time to look after the measures and weights allotted to the *horrea*.'

At Portus, which had by the late third and fourth centuries A.D. outgrown Ostia, of which it had been simply an offshoot under the early Empire, we find men with the title *patroni horreorum Portuensium*. Although the title may differ, *patroni* instead of *praepositi*, they seem to be exactly similar offices. Such *patroni* were to hold their post for only one year, during which time no fraud was to be practised, such as

[1] E. Petersen and F. von Luschan, *Reisen im Südwestlichen Kleinasien* II, p. 42, No. 77 a.

inserting the accounts of old issues of public supplies into the new accounts. No *patronus'* tenure of office was to exceed one year unless the accounts of the previous year were rendered and he should be chosen for another year, because of the probity of his conduct.[1] In a rescript dated seventeen years later, A.D. 417, we hear of a *patronus Portuensium conditorum*.[2] It is quite clear that this office, which seems to have been concerned solely with the safe passage of corn upstream to Rome, was distinct from that of the *patroni horreorum Portuensium*. There seems to have been only one *patronus conditorum* elected from the *patroni* of the whole guild of *caudicarii* and *mensores* at Portus for a period of five years. His whole purpose was to undertake the *custodia* of the stores at Portus, so as to prevent frauds by the *caudicarii* and thefts by the measurers. A particular way in which he was to prevent frauds by shippers was to send a sealed sample (*digma*) to his colleagues of the quality of supplies in kind. If on completion of his term of office, he was shown to have acted honestly, he was to be rewarded with the honour of count of the third order; if dishonestly, he was to be demoted to the lowest orders of breadmaking. Clearly his was a special office apart from and in addition to the normal *patroni*.

The particular method of avoiding fraud by shippers advocated in this rescript is interesting in that it seems to have been copied from a method practised in Egypt from at least the third century B.C. to the third century A.D.[3] The name itself, *digma*, which is simply a transliteration of the Greek word, δεῖγμα, found in the Egyptian papyri, reinforces this suggestion. The system as practised in Egypt was designed to check any attempt at substitution of grain on the voyage down the Nile from the harbours and *metropoleis* up river on its way to Alexandria. A sample of the type and quality of the grain cargo of the ship was placed in a small pot or even in a leather wallet and carefully sealed and labelled. Examples of both kinds of container used for this purpose have been found recently[4] and illustrate for the first time what

---

[1] *Cod. Theod.* XIV. 23. 1 (A.D. 400).   [2] *Cod. Theod.* XIV. 4. 9 (A.D. 417).

[3] *P. Hib.* 39, lines 15–16 (265 B.C.); 98, line 17 (251 B.C.); *P. Oxy.* 1254 (A.D. 260).

[4] O. Guéraud, 'Un vase ayant contenu un échantillon de blé', *JJurP* IV (1950), 107 ff. Cf. H. Zilliacus, 'Neue Ptolemäertexte zum Korntransport und Saatdarlehen', *Aegyptus* XIX (1939), 62. O. Guéraud, 'Sachet ayant contenu un échantillon d'orge', *Ann.Eg.* XXXIII (1933), 62–4: a leather bag for a barley specimen carrying in ink the legend *exemplar / hordei missi per Chae/remonam Anubionis / gubernatorem ex no/mo memphite a metro/poliu.*

such *digmata* were really like. Upon the sides of these containers were sometimes given such details concerning not only the sample but also the cargo of the boat so that they formed almost a duplicate receipt. On the side of a pot for a *digma* in 2 B.C. is given the name of the two κυβερνῆται, the emblem of their boats, the name, rank and unit of the soldiers acting as ἐπίπλοοι. Then follows the statement that this pot is a *digma* of cargo of grain of specified kind of a certain year measured to them by the *granary* officials of a certain district, and which formed the tax payable for a certain period. Next follows the declaration that the cargo has been sealed with the seals of both men and the date. A second hand records the sealing of the *digmata* and the date.

It would seem that the *digmata* were carried sometimes on the boat concerned in the care of the ἐπίπλοοι (soldiers, in the first century A.D. at least, who accompanied the grain), and were sometimes sent separately.[1] That they could be effective in revealing a fraud is shown by the papyrus from Oxyrhynchus[2] dated A.D. 188, which is a letter to the *strategos* of a nome from which a cargo of wheat had come and which was found to be adulterated with earth and barley.

3

Despite such devices to avoid fraud it is clear that the Emperors found it a matter of major concern to resist the rising tide of mismanagement and trickery in the running of the *horrea*. Explicit instructions were given to the *Praefectus Urbi* that no distribution should take place from the *horrea* in Rome until the taxes were entirely paid in.[3] Heavy penalties, including deportation and the forfeiture of all property, were threatened against those tampering with supplies in state storehouses.[4] There had been apparently even cases of public *horrea* in Rome and Portus converted to private use: the *Praefectus Urbi* was urged to convert them back, with the interesting instruction that grain was not to be stored in the lower storeys because it was spoiled by the 'nature of the place and moisture'; appropriation of supplies from them was to be punished and restoration made; and any destruction of buildings was to be made good.[5] The breadmakers in particular were accused of

---

[1] *P. Oxy.* 1254 (A.D. 260) records the appointment of an official to accompany *digmata* of wheat to Alexandria. In the third century A.D. some of the *digmata* were being sent separately.

[2] *P. Oxy.* 708 (A.D. 188).   [3] *Cod. Theod.* XI. 14. 2 (A.D. 396).

[4] *Cod. Theod.* XI. 14. 3 (A.D. 397).   [5] *Cod. Theod.* XV. I. 12 (A.D. 364).

taking supplies without warrant from the state *horrea*.[1] A record of all grain deposited in public warehouses was to be made immediately and receipts given for it, although only fiscal grain was to be so placed in public storehouses.[2] How effective these measures were is not known, but the repeated commands hint that all was not well. It is a measure of the times and not without irony that the Emperors Valentinian and Valens order that no new corn is to be distributed before whatever old corn there was already in the storehouses: if the old corn proved to be bad, then it must be mixed with the new to disguise this fact and a man of *integrity* was to be chosen to carry out this task and make an inventory of the storehouses.[3]

Side by side with this constant preoccupation with mismanagement is a concern for the physical structure of *horrea*. An area of one hundred feet adjacent to *horrea* was to be kept vacant, according to an order of A.D. 326, as the result of recent experiences with fires. Anything constructed in that area was to be torn down and the whole property of the offending builders was to be forfeit.[4] Later, in A.D. 398, the Praetorian Prefect was given orders to tear down all private buildings adjoined to state storehouses, so as to leave them free on all sides 'as they were built from the beginning'.[5] Similarly, in a rescript concerning the amount of free space to be left between opposing balconies, while 10 feet is the usual standard, in the case of private buildings adjoining *horrea* an open space of 15 feet is the minimum required.[6]

But the Emperors' concern at the end of the fourth century A.D. was not only for the encroachment by private jerrybuilding upon the *horrea*, but also for the collapse of existing *horrea* and the general diminution of the storage capacity available. Instructions were given to the *Praefectus Praetorio* that if any palace (*palatium*), residence of a governor (*praetorium iudicum*), state storehouse (*horrea*) or stable for public animals (*stabula et receptacula animalium publicorum*) fell into ruin, it must be repaired from the resources of the governors.[7] This curious mixture of buildings mighty and humble indicates the importance of the *horrea* at this period and the priority the Emperors gave to their upkeep. This is confirmed by a rescript of similar date which threatens heavy penalties for *iudices* who start new public works without consulta-

[1] *Cod. Theod.* XIV. 3. 16 (A.D. 380). [2] *Cod. Theod.* XII. 6. 16 (A.D. 375).
[3] *Cod. Theod.* XI. 14. 1 (A.D. 364 or 365). [4] *Cod. Theod.* XV. 1. 4 (A.D. 326).
[5] *Cod. Theod* XV. 1. 38 (A.D. 398). [6] *Iust. Cod.* VIII. 10. 11 (A.D. 423).
[7] *Cod. Theod.* XV. 1. 35 (A.D. 396).

tion, or take ornaments and material from existing public works: similar penalties are threatened for local councils who do not protect their buildings. But *iudices* have the right to construct *horrea* and *stabula* on their own initiative and are encouraged to do so.[1] The implication of these rescripts, that there were not enough *horrea* throughout the Empire and that even these were falling into disrepair, is clear. That these efforts by the Emperors to rectify the situation were *not* successful can be seen in the much later rescript from the Emperor Leo (A.D. 471?): the *iudices* were not to abandon their *palatia* and *praetoria* and requisition private houses for themselves, but to live in their *palatia* and *praetoria*, since thus they would be forced to repair them. A special case, however, is made when the *praetorium* is being used for the collection and preservation of public supplies *horreorum vice*.[2] This rescript conjures up a picture of the dissolution of the whole system.

4

That system, as we have seen, consisted of an Empire-wide organisation with the *Praefectus Praetorio* at the summit, administering *horrea* scattered throughout every province. It seems that often cities shared their storage depots and that until the middle of the fourth century A.D. at least the local *curiales* were responsible for the election of the *praepositi* who superintended the local storehouses. Acting as their assistants no doubt were the *horrearii*,[3] guards and workmen attested more frequently under the early Empire, but whose employment would be needed at all times. The duties of the *praepositi* and their assistants must have been concerned with the protection and registration of whatever was actually consigned to the storehouses from the moment it was officially delivered to them and they signed a receipt to that effect, acknowledging the amount and quality received, until the moment when they delivered it to shippers, breadmakers or others, from whom

---

[1] *Cod. Theod.* XV. 1. 37 (A.D. 398).

[2] *Iust. Cod.* I. 40. 15. 1 (A.D. 471?). A similar breakdown can be seen much earlier in the military sphere when in the restoration of the forts on Hadrian's Wall in Britain after the *barbarica conspiratio* of A.D. 367–9 (Ammianus Marcellinus XXVII. 8. 1) headquarters buildings came to house granaries and forges. See E. Birley, I. A. Richmond and J. Stanfield, 'Excavations at Chesterholm—Vindolanda, Third Report', *AA*[4] XIII (1936), 225–7.

[3] For Rome itself see two late inscriptions, *CIL* VI. 9461 (A.D. 530), tombstone of Constantinus, *horrearius*; and *CIL* VI. 9464 (A.D. 513), tombstone of *M. Vir. Fringyllus, horr(earius)*.

they in their turn demanded a receipt to protect them from liability. The details of these receipts for at least one part of the Empire will be seen in the section on Egypt.

Within Rome itself and the surrounding area the *Praefectus Urbi* was the summit of the organisation. Although there were variations, particularly in the titles of the officials of the *horrea* at Portus, there is no reason to suppose that the organisation was in any essential way different from that in the remainder of the Empire. The *Notitia Dignitatum* does, however, reveal that the head of the great *Horrea Galbana*, which played a major rôle in the storage capacity of the city of Rome from the early Empire onwards, had the title of *curator horreorum Galbanorum*[1] and was directly responsible to the *Praefectus Urbi* himself.

[1] *Not. Dign.*, ed. O. Seeck, p. 114. The title *comes horreorum* revealed in *Iust. Cod.* XI. 16. 1 perhaps belongs to an official at Constantinople.

VI

HORREA: LOCATIO–CONDUCTIO

The process whereby warehouses or parts of warehouses, in Rome at least, were hired out for storage purposes is known from two sources: legal texts, mainly Justinian's *Digest*, and a few inscriptions. Neither source is entirely satisfactory. The legal passages are often open to more than one interpretation, and at some points later interpolations may have found their way into the texts. The inscriptions are in almost every case severely mutilated. However, a careful combination of the two types of evidence can be made to yield a general picture of the organisation. There is also the further difficulty that the contract under which all this falls, *locatio–conductio*,[1] has a number of disputed features in general, and in particular the rules about liability for safe-keeping, *custodia*, which is naturally fundamental for warehouses or repositories, are the subject of long-standing and unresolved controversy.

First, what were these *horrea* which were to let? Hülsen[2] was unwilling to admit that the part of a *lex horreorum Caesaris* found in 1885, which laid down provisions for hire, could have applied to the ordinary commercial *horrea* of Rome. He saw in it the provisions of 'safe-deposit *horrea*' of a type for which the first unequivocal evidence is in the reign of Alexander Severus, but which almost certainly had existed before then.[3] It seems to me, however, that no distinction in this respect can be drawn between 'safe-deposit *horrea*' and *horrea* for the

---

[1] Romanelli, p. 981. J. A. C. Thomas, '*Custodia* and *Horrea*', *RIntDroitsAnt*³ VI (1959), 371. F. Wubbe, 'Zur Haftung des *Horrearius*', *ZSavignyStift* LXXVI (1959), 508. Alzon, *Problèmes relatifs à la location des entrepôts*. C. A. Cannata, 'Su alcuni problemi relativi alla *locatio horrei* nel diritto Romano classico', *SDHI* XXX (1964), 235 ff. J. A. C. Thomas, 'Return to *Horrea*', *RIntDroitsAnt*³ XIII (1966), 353 ff. Reference to the extensive earlier literature will be found in these works.

[2] Hülsen, 'Di una pittura antica', p. 225.

[3] SHA *Alexander Severus* 39. 3: Horrea in omnibus regionibus publica fecit ad quae conferrent bona hi, qui privatas custodias non haberent. *Digest* I. 15. 3. 2 refers to *horrea, ubi homines pretiosissimam partem fortunarum suarum reponunt*, and to the instructions of Divus Antoninus about these. This is more likely to be the Emperor Antoninus Pius than Caracalla. Cf. another reference to rescript of Antoninus Pius on this matter in *Iust. Cod.* IV. 65. 4. (See G. Gualandi, *Legislazione imperiale e giurisprudenza* II (Milan, 1963), p. 175.)

storage of grain, wine and other commercial goods. If it is true, as I have argued elsewhere,[1] that the *Horrea Lolliana* and *Horrea Galbana* were even in the first half of the first century A.D. run as private commercial enterprises, and if it is true that the general methods of Roman trade in this early period were those of free enterprise, then it must follow that the renting of warehouse space for private merchants was a possibility. Perhaps this was not permitted in some state-owned warehouses, for example at Ostia, but in the Testaccio district in Rome where the development in the late Republic had, I suspect, been largely in the hands of private families, whose *horrea* were later absorbed into the imperial property, the renting and hiring of warehouse space must have been the regular procedure for ordinary merchants in the practice of their trade.

That the Emperor had warehouses to let is clear enough, not only from the part of the *lex horreorum Caesaris* but also from the record in the *Digest* of a *negotiator marmorum* who was a *conductor horreorum Caesaris*.[2] Moreover it is clear that such *horrea* hired as a whole by a contractor could be in the heart of the commercial quarters of Rome, for a certain C. Iulius Hermes was *conductor Horreorum Seianorum*, which are believed to have been near the Tiber in the Testaccio area.[3] However, it is equally true that space was for hire also in private warehouses. Whether the *Horrea Ummidiana*[4] were still in private hands when their *lex* (which is still partly preserved) was published we do not know. But the notice to let for the *horrea* of Q. Tineius Sacerdos,[5] probably the consul of A.D. 158, clearly labelled them as *horrea privata*.

It seems that the owners of these warehouses, whether the Emperor or private individuals, at least in the early Empire were not directly involved in the letting of space within the warehouses, although in the case of private individuals there was presumably no reason why they should not have been involved if they wished. The customary method was to rent the whole warehouse to a contractor who was then responsible for running it. Such a contractor was C. Iulius Hermes, who

---

[1] Chapter V (p. 171).   [2] *Digest* XX. 4. 21. 1 (Scaevola).

[3] *CIL* VI. 9471, cf. Platner–Ashby, *Topographical Dictionary*, p. 263. 'Contractor' is perhaps not an adequate word for this man who actually ran the *horrea*. But 'hirer' and 'entrepreneur' seem clumsy; 'contractor' therefore will be retained, although the overtones which this word may have in English, concerning the nature of the legal agreement, should be ignored.

[4] *CIL* VI. 37795.   [5] *CIL* VI. 33860 = *ILS* 5913.

rented the *Horrea Seiana*, and the marble merchant, *conductor horreorum Caesaris*, who was responsible for his rent to a *procurator exactioni praepositus*, presumably an official of the *Procurator Patrimonii*.

Before we go further, certain confusions of terminology must be explained. The terminology of *locatio–conductio* is consistently ambiguous in that the same man may be regarded, from different points of view, as both *locator* and *conductor*. Thus the contractor of a whole warehouse was, in relation to the owner, the *conductor*, as we have seen; but in relation to those hiring individual parts of the building he was the *locator* and they the *conductores*.[1] The use of the word *locator* or *conductor* therefore can only be understood properly in the context of each individual passage. A further confusion in the case of *horrea* is that the contractor is often referred to as the *horrearius* in legal texts and once in the *lex horreorum Caesaris*[2] and is clearly distinguished from the *custodes*, whereas in the rest of the epigraphic evidence the *horrearii* seem to be simply the workers in the warehouses.[3]

C. Alzon, relying on this epigraphic evidence, has tried to interpret the references to *horrearius* in the legal texts as if they were to a foreman of the staff of the *horrea*, an employee of the *dominus*, who was the actual lessor of warehouse space. But as J. A. C. Thomas has pointed out,[4] this raises intolerable problems in the legal texts and it seems better to admit simply that there was a difference of usage of the word *horrearius*. It certainly seems dangerous to base sweeping conclusions about *horrearii* in general on the epigraphic evidence, which is scrappy, unclear and perhaps untypical in that so much of it comes from the *Horrea Galbana* in Rome.

The length of the lease held by the contractor from the owner no doubt varied, but so far as the *Horrea Seiana* were concerned, a five-year period seems to have been customary since C. Iulius Hermes was *conductor . . . lustri terti*.

The exact nature of the agreements between the owner and the

---

[1] The complication is even greater than this in that the contractor might be regarded as letting empty storage space and therefore be a *locator*; or he might be regarded as the person who contracted to perform certain obligations and provide services, in which case he was a *conductor*. Wubbe, 'Zur Haftung des *Horrearius*', p. 511.

[2] *Digest* IX. 3. 5. 3; *Digest* X. 4. 5 pr.; *Digest* XIX. 2. 60. 9, etc. Cf. *CIL* VI. 33747 = *ILS* 5914, last line.   [3] Chapter V (p. 176).

[4] Alzon, *Problèmes relatifs à la location des entrepôts*, pp. 8 ff.; Thomas, 'Return to *Horrea*', *RIntDroitsAnt*[3], XIII (1966), 357. Cf. Romanelli, pp. 974, 979.

contractor on the one hand, and the contractor and the individual *conductores* on the other, has been the subject of dispute among modern students of Roman law. There is no doubt, however, that the important agreement lay between the contractor and the *conductores*. Since it is the provisions of this agreement which were laid down and publicly exhibited in the individual *leges horreorum*, it seems best to examine these inscriptions before turning to the controversial legal passages.

The inscription concerning the private *horrea* of Q. Tineius Sacerdos[1] is not a *lex horreorum* but rather a notice of lease. It is stated that within these *horrea* there are for hire *horrea, apothecae, compendiaria, armaria, intercolumnia et loca armaris.*

The meaning of these terms is not clear, except that they clearly designate parts of the building and that the size of the storage space diminishes towards the end of the list. *Horrea* must mean an ensemble of rooms, if not the whole building. *Apothecae* is normally used to indicate storerooms, with perhaps a particular reference to the storage of wine. When used for storing other goods it was necessary to indicate the fact clearly by stating *apotheca olei* or *apotheca frumenti.*[2] *Compendiaria* are not known in any other context than as parts of *horrea*, where they must mean 'safe deposits'. Normally the word was used as an adjective, *compendiarius*, and was particularly used for qualifying the noun *iter.*[3] Whatever was designated by *compendiaria* was presumably smaller than either *horrea* or *apothecae*, but larger than the *armaria*, which are listed next. They may be either divisions within rooms or perhaps small groups of rooms. *Armaria* is used quite normally in Latin to describe large lockers or chests. What the final two divisions were is again obscure. *Loca armaris* must mean a series of individual compartments within the *armaria*. In short, one need hire not necessarily even a whole *armarium*. But what is the significance of the *intercolumnia*? Romanelli[4] suggested that they too were subdivisions of the *armaria* which were divided vertically by tiny columns into pigeon holes. This may be right, but it is then difficult to see any distinction between *intercolumnia* and *loca armaris*. *Intercolumnia* would normally mean simply the space between two columns. But in the *horrea*, whose ground

---

[1] *CIL* VI. 33860 = *ILS* 5913. Cf. C. Bruns, *Fontes Iuris Romani Antiqui*[7] (Tübingen, 1909), p. 371; P. Girard, *Textes de Droit Romain*[6] (Paris, 1937), p. 857; S. Riccobono, *Fontes Iuris Romani Anteiustiniani* III (Florence, 1941), p. 457.
[2] *Thesaurus Ling. Lat.*, s.v. *apotheca*.   [3] *Thesaurus Ling. Lat.*, s.v. *compendiaria*.
[4] Romanelli, p. 973.

plan we know, goods placed between the columns of the cortile would not be safe and would interfere with the running of the whole building.

Whatever the precise meanings of some of these divisions, it is clear that the terminology was almost standardised. The half of the *lex horreorum Caesaris*[1] which is preserved clearly includes *armaria et loca*, and since the word preceding *armaria* ended in -AR, it may well have been *compendi* -AR. Similarly the inscription concerning the *Horrea Ummidiana*, although only the middle section is preserved, records that [*comp*]*endiaria* and *ar*[*maria*] are for hire.[2] In *Digest* I. 15. 3. 2 comes further confirmation—*vel cella effringitur vel armarium vel arca*. *Cella* is presumably equivalent to *apotheca*, although there is no suggestion that wine in particular should be stored there. *Arca* introduces a division smaller than an *armarium*, most probably a strong box used for storing money.

After the spaces for hire in the private *horrea* of Q. Tineius Sacerdos have been listed, there is the formula *ex hac die et ex K. Iulis*. This again was a standard formula occurring in both the other *leges horreorum*, although in their cases the precise date is lost. The rooms were for hire 'from this day', that is, either from the day on which the *horrea* were opened, or, alternatively, from the day on which the prospective *conductores* read the notice and wished to hire space. The significance of the second part of the formula was that it fixed the financial year of the *horrea*, the date on which the rents for the year fell due. The Kalends of July had a general significance in this respect in that it was the day on which rents of all kinds fell due. The obvious illustration is the famous epigram of Martial,[3] beginning with the line O *Iuliarum dedecus Kalendarum*, which describes the eviction of a family two years behind with their rent.

The famous fragment of a *lex horreorum Caesaris*,[4] a marble plaque 98 centimetres by 88 centimetres preserving almost precisely the right half of the whole inscription, was found in 1885 by the Porta Salaria in north Rome. It has been published many times, and with many

---

[1] *CIL* VI. 33747 = *ILS* 5914. Mommsen's restoration [*mercatoribus frument*]*ar*(*iis*), retained by *FIRA* III, p. 455, seems to me implausible in that it leaves only *armaria* and *loca* as the spaces listed for storage; hardly suitable for storage by corn merchants. Hülsen and *CIL* VI. 33747 restored [*horrea compendi*]*ar*(*ia*).   [2] *CIL* VI. 37795.

[3] Martial XII. 32. Cf. Petronius 38; Suet. *Tib.* 35; Bruns, *Fontes*[7], pp. 290 ff. (*Lex Metalli Vipascensis*).

[4] *CIL* VI. 33747. Cf. *ILS* 5914; Bruns, *Fontes*[7], p. 371; Girard, *Textes*[6], p. 856; Riccobono, *FIRA* III, p. 455; G. Gatti, 'Frammento d'iscrizione contenente la *lex horreorum*', *BCom* XIII (1885), 110–29.

different restorations of the missing half. However, there is enough agreement concerning the sense, if not always concerning the wording, of the inscription, to extract much information about the conditions listed.

The date of the inscription is not known, since the Emperor's name is missing. The lettering is of good quality and the inscription has accents.[1] Gatti thought that the inscription probably dated from the time of Hadrian and accordingly restored his name in the title. Mommsen, however, pointed to the position of the word *Caesar* in the title, which was not placed after the name of the Emperor at the time of Hadrian, and he judged from the letter forms that the inscription belonged to the time of Nerva. This date and identification has been accepted *with reservations* by all subsequent editors.[2]

After the list of spaces for hire, there stands the usual formula *ex hac die et ex*: the date is missing. Mommsen not unnaturally restored *K. Iulis*,[3] but because in the first clause of the *lex* proper the Ides of December are given as the date by which rent must be paid and intentions for the following year declared, Hülsen's *Kal. Ian.* has found greater favour. It is clear that almost any date could be used in the fixing of contracts, so the point is not of great importance.[4]

The *lex* itself seems to contain seven clauses, now all in a more or less fragmentary state. First, if the *conductor* wished to retain what he had hired for a further year, he should report this before the Ides of December after paying his rent. In the case of a man not making arrangements for the following year, his tenancy would be prolonged for the same amount of rent if his goods remained, provided that his place was not let to someone else. Secondly, whoever had hired space in these *horrea* was not allowed to sublet. (Scialoja has objected to this restoration by Gatti and Mommsen.[5] He held that the *conditions* of subletting must have been set out in this clause. While it was possible for parties to a contract to make what terms they liked in individual

---

[1] Photograph in Bruns, *Simulacra*, p. xx, no. 22.

[2] No editor has proposed another candidate, although Riccobono, *FIRA*, and Dessau do not print Mommsen's restoration in their texts. The matter is not really important, since the lettering and accents fix the date to the first or early second century A.D.

[3] Bruns, *Fontes*[7], p. 372.

[4] Hülsen *ad CIL* vi. 33747 (*ILS* 5914), cf. Riccobono, *FIRA* iii, p. 455. The dates for leases in the Pompeian inscriptions have great variation, see *FIRA* iii, pp. 453 ff.

[5] V. Scialoja, 'Di una *lex horreorum* recentemente scoperta', *Studi giuridici* i (1933), 288.

cases, it is unlikely that subletting would have been allowed in any *lex horreorum*, and that responsibility would automatically extend to the goods of a sub-tenant.) The precise point of the third clause, if it is indeed distinct from the second, is not clear. All that remains is . . .*cu*]*stodia non praestabitur*. Mommsen restored *invectorum in haec horrea* before *custodia*. But Mitteis has suggested *auri argentive* before *custodia*, drawn from an example in the *Digest*.[1]

The fourth clause lays down that whatever goods of the *conductores* were brought into the *horrea* were to be regarded as security for the payment of the rents.

The fifth clause is difficult to restore and was left blank by Mommsen, Hülsen and Dessau. But it is possible that the sense of it was the same as that of the second clause in the *lex* of the *Horrea Ummidiana*, namely that any alterations made by the *conductores* to their hired space were not allowed to be dismantled and taken away without permission.

The sixth clause seems to stipulate that upon payment of their rent the *conductores* were to be given a receipt for it (*chirographum*), but there may have been more in this clause than such an elementary regulation.

The final clause lays down that if anyone, having hired space within the *horrea*, left his goods without properly assigning them to a *custos*, the *horrearius* (contractor) should be free from the responsibility.

The *lex* concerning the *Horrea Ummidiana*[2] is even more fragmentary. We have perhaps the middle third of the upper part of the inscription. It was discovered in 1910 on the Aventine. Comparison with the other *lex horreorum* quickly revealed its nature. Gatti first suggested the full name of the *horrea* was *Ummidiana*, or perhaps *Ummidiana Cornificiana*. In the first case the *horrea* belonged to the family of M. Ummidius Quadratus, consul in 167, in the second to the descendants of him and his wife, Annia Cornificia Faustina, younger sister of Marcus Aurelius, whose family property was on the slopes of the Aventine away from the Tiber. After the usual list of spaces for hire within the warehouse we have preserved only the remains of two clauses. The first probably made

---

1 Bruns, *Fontes*[7], p. 372. U. Wilcken and L. Mitteis, *Grundzüge und Chrestomathie der Papyruskunde* (Leipzig, 1912), II, p. 259, note 3. Cf. *Digest* XIX. 2. 60. 6. But Riccobono, *FIRA* III, p. 456, retains Mommsen's reading. Mitteis' suggestion seems preferable in that such refusal of *custodia* is illustrated by the *Digest* text and it avoids any redundancy in the final clause of the *lex*.

2 *CIL* VI. 37795. Cf. Girard, *Textes*[6], p. 857; Riccobono, *FIRA* III, p. 457; G. Gatti, 'Frammento di una nuova *lex horreorum*', *BCom* XXXIX (1911), 120.

the point that whatever was deposited was a security for rent payment. The second has preserved only the words *aedificaverit* and in the line below *ei refigendi*, but it is almost certain that the point at issue was whether additions and alterations to the storage space were allowed to be removed.[1]

So much for the inscriptions. A proper understanding of the legal texts depends above all else upon the understanding of the terminology involved. The kernel of the problem is given by six texts which are worth reproducing in full:

Digest XIX. 2. 55 pr. (Paulus): Dominus horreorum effractis et compilatis horreis non tenetur, [nisi custodiam eorum recepit] :[2] servit amen eius cum quo contractum est propter aedificiorum notitiam in quaestionem peti possunt.

Digest XIX. 2. 60. 6 (Labeo): Locator horrei propositum habuit se aurum argentum margaritam non recipere suo periculo: deinde cum sciret has res inferri, passus est. Proinde eum futurum tibi obligatum dixi ac si ⟨propositum non habuisset, quoniam quod⟩[3] propositum fuit, remissum videtur.

Digest XIX. 2. 60.9 (Labeo): Rerum custodiam, quam horrearius conductoribus praestare deberet, locatorem totorum horreorum horreario praestare non debere puto, [nisi si in locando aliter convenerit].[4]

Collatio 10. 9: Paulus libro responsorum V. sub titulo ex locato et conducto: Imp. Antoninus Iulio Agrippino. Dominus horreorum periculum vis maioris vel effracturae latronum praestare non cogitur. His cessantibus si quid ex depositis rebus inlaesis extrinsecus horreis perit, damnum depositorum sarciri debet [a. 213].	*Codex* 4. 65. 1 (Antoninus a. 213) Dominus horreorum periculum vis maioris vel effracturam latronum conductori praestare non cogitur. His cessantibus, si quid extrinsecus ex depositis rebus inlaesis horreis perierit, damnum depositarum rerum sarciri debet.

---

[1] G. Gatti, 'Frammento di una nuova *lex horreorum*', BCom XXXIX (1911), 127. Cf. *Digest* VII. 1. 15 pr. (Ulpian): si quid inaedificaverit, postea eum neque tollere hoc neque refigere posse: refixa plane posse vindicare.

[2] Regarded as an interpolation by Haymann, Arangio-Ruiz and Vazny. *Index Interpolationum* I, p. 366.

[3] Mommsen's emendation. *Index Interpolationum* I, p. 367.

[4] Interpolation? *Index Interpolationum* I, p. 368.

Paulus respondit: satis
praepositam constitutionem
declarare his, qui horrea
locant, maiorem vim imputari
non posse.

Codex 4. 65. 4 (Alexander a. 222). Ex divi Pii et Antonini litteris certa forma est, ut domini horreorum effractorum eiusmodi querellas deferentibus custodes exhibere necesse habeant nec ultra periculo subiecti sint.

1. Quod vos quoque adito praeside provinciae impetrabitis. Qui si maiorem animadversionem exigere rem deprehenderit, ad Domitium Ulpianum praefectum praetorio et parentem meum reos remittere curabit.

2. [Sed qui domini horreorum nominatim etiam custodiam repromiserunt fidem (idem?) exhibere debent.][1]

The problem in these texts is to unravel how many parties were involved and what precisely the relationships between them were in law. Labeo (*Digest* XIX. 2. 60. 9) seems to settle the matter by his clear distinction between *locator totorum horreorum*, *horrearius*, and *conductores*. The *conductores* were clearly the depositors, the *horrearius* the contractor, with whom they dealt, and *locator totorum horreorum* presumably the owner who let the whole warehouse to the contractor.

Are there traces of this threefold division detectable in the other texts? At first sight this appears to be the case. The *locator horrei* (*Digest* XIX. 2. 60. 6), who made it clear that he would not accept responsibility for gold and silver, is clearly a contractor (*horrearius*). In the passage of Paulus (*Digest* XIX. 2. 55) the *dominus horreorum* seems on first reading to be the owner of the warehouse and to be a different person from *is cum quo contractum est*, the contractor, who dealt with the *conductores*. This is in fact how J. A. C. Thomas has interpreted it.[2] It is possible, however, that in this passage *dominus horreorum* and *is cum quo contractum est* are different ways of describing the same man, who was both owner and contractor. The phrasing of the passage suggests to me that this is the more likely interpretation. It is reinforced, for what it is worth, by the *Basilica* (20. 1. 54) and its scholia which understood it in this way, although this, of course, only shows how the passage was

---

[1] Interpolation? Cf. Wubbe, 'Zur Haftung des *Horrearius*', p. 519.
[2] Thomas, *RIntDroitsAnt*[3] VI (1959), 379; *RIntDroitsAnt*[3] XIII (1966), 354.

understood in the sixth century and later, and does not prove that this is the correct interpretation.

Whatever the interpretation of this passage, it cannot be denied that the legal writers from the third century A.D. onward concentrate on the liabilities of the *domini horreorum*. The word *horrearius* in the sense of a contractor of a warehouse is used only five times in the *Digest* and once in an inscription.[1] Four of the references in the *Digest* and the reference in the inscription are all early, either of the first century, or early second century A.D. Even the other passage of Paulus (*Digest* I. 15. 3. 2), from which Thomas tries to wring evidence for a threefold division in the third century, is based on a rescript from Antoninus Pius in the second century and therefore perhaps not to be relied upon for third-century conditions.

It seems clear that under the early Empire the *horrearius* (contractor), from whom the *conductor* (depositor) hired his space, need not be, and very often was not, the *dominus horreorum* (the owner). From the third century A.D., on the other hand, the *horrearius* (contractor) probably need not be, but almost always was, the *dominus horreorum* (owner). The reasons for this are perhaps more to be sought for in the changing social and economic conditions of the developing Roman Empire. These favoured the existence of the owner-contractors of small private warehouses in an insecure age. The great warehouses once owned by aristocratic families or the Emperor, and earlier let by them to contractors, were now all absorbed into the bureaucratic state system and administered directly by state officials.

However that may be, it is clear that it is the relationship between the contractor (or the contractor-owner) and the *conductores* that was at all times important and complicated. The only certain reference to the legal relationship between the owner and the contractor states that the owner had no responsibility for *rerum custodia* towards the contractor.[2]

The question used to be asked whether the relationships between the owner and contractor, on the one hand, and the contractor and the *conductores* on the other, were regarded as falling under *locatio rei*, *locatio operis* or even *locatio operarum*.[3] This question is now rightly

---

[1] *Digest* IX. 3. 5. 3 (Ulpian); X. 4. 5 pr. (twice) (Celsus); XIX. 2. 60. 9 (twice) (Labeo); *CIL* VI. 33747 = *ILS* 5914.

[2] *Digest* XIX. 2. 60. 9 (Labeo).

[3] Thomas, *RIntDroitsAnt*[3] VI (1959), 373. Wubbe, 'Zur Haftung des *Horrearius*', p. 512.

regarded as an improper one by all authorities. The attempt to squeeze every contract of the Roman world into the modern division into three classes gave rise to a series of spurious problems. The *locatio–conductio* relationship is now regarded as a general one which could and did cover a multitude of variations.[1]

The problem of *custodia*[2] is more fundamental for the study of *horrea*, but probably not susceptible of complete solution. The concept of *custodia* in general covered great differences. In some texts it seems to be an absolute liability for safety quite irrespective of negligence, while in others it seems to be no more than *maxima diligentia in custodiendo*. Theories produced to fit the texts have ranged to two extremes. On the one hand, it has been suggested that in classical law *custodia* was an absolute liability, and this was weakened by interpolation to fit the milder form under Justinian; on the other hand, it has been suggested that originally *custodia* was simply *maxima diligentia* and that this concept was tightened up by the interpolations to fit the stricter legal position under Justinian. Neither theory in fact fits all the texts, and it seems possible that there were differences of opinion about the extent of liability among jurists of the same period. Here, of course, it is possible only to investigate the limits of *custodia* in the particular case of the warehouse contractor.

That his responsibility towards the *conductores* was regarded precisely as *custodia* is clearly proved by the passage of the first-century jurist Labeo and the *Lex Horreorum Caesaris*.[3] In both cases the word *custodia* is used and in such a way as to indicate a definite legal responsibility *rerum custodiam praestare*.[4]

Whether this *custodia* be interpreted as otherwise a strict liability for safety or not, the one general exception granted by the law would be in cases of *vis maior*—fire, flood, tempest and robbery with violence. This exception is clearly attested with regard to *horrea* in the second- and third-century texts. Warehouse contractors were regarded as free from liability in cases of *vis maior vel effractura latronum*, but were

---

[1] F. Schulz, *Classical Roman Law* (Oxford, 1951), pp. 542 ff.; cf. *De Furtis*, ed. Jolowicz, p. xlvi.

[2] W. Buckland, *A Text-Book of Roman Law*, 3rd ed. (Cambridge, 1963), p. 560.

[3] *Digest* XIX. 2. 60. 9; *CIL* VI. 33747 = *ILS* 5914.

[4] The significance of this must be that whatever the similarities between the legal position of *horrearius* and those of *nauta* and *stabularius*, whereas they received *mercedem pro arte* (*Digest* IV. 9. 5), the *horrearius* received *mercedem pro custodia*.

bound to surrender their *servi* or *custodes* for questioning by the Prefect of the Vigiles, on the general principle that their knowledge of the building made them suspect. This was done even when the slaves formed part of the household of the Emperor and they were often punished.[1]

The rescript of Caracalla on this point continues that if, in the absence of *vis maior* and *effractura latronum*, any of the goods deposited 'perished', the contractor had to make good the loss. What could be included within the word *perire* is made clear by another passage of the *Digest* (L. 16. 9). Within its terms were included both damage and simple theft.

We have two versions of the legal point in this rescript, one preserved in the *Collatio Mosaicarum et Romanarum Legum*, the other a more condensed version in Justinian's *Codex*.[2] The wording of these versions, although having an overall similarity, is not precisely the same; in particular the word *extrinsecus* is differently placed. In the *Collatio* text it is placed within the ablative absolute, *inlaesis extrinsecus horreis*; in the *Codex* text it is placed outside it, *si quid extrinsecus ex depositis rebus inlaesis horreis perierit*.

Wubbe has objected to the *Collatio* text that the placing of *extrinsecus* is pleonastic, that *horrea* cannot be broken into from inside and that therefore the *Codex* text is to be preferred.[3] The meaning he would give to the word *extrinsecus* in that text is 'if any of the deposited goods perishes for an external reason (that is, a reason not inherent in the object itself) when the *horrea* have not been broken into'. In short, the use of the word *extrinsecus* placed yet another restriction upon the general liability of the warehouse contractor.

This is very difficult to believe. If that was really the meaning of the *Codex* text, it was very clumsily and imprecisely expressed in the Latin. Moreover it is not clear to me that the slight pleonasm of the *Collatio* text *inlaesis extrinsecus horreis* is without justification. Since the Emperor was trying to make clear the legal position in cases where no *vis maior* or robbery with violence had occurred, *inlaesis extrinsecus horreis* expresses with great precision the conditions under which loss by damage and simple theft had to be reimbursed.

---

[1] *Digest* XIX. 2. 55 (Paulus); *Collatio* 10. 9 (*Iust. Cod.* 4. 65. 1) (A.D. 213, rescript of Caracalla); *Iust. Cod.* 4. 65. 4 (A.D. 222); *Digest* I. 15. 3. 2 (Paulus).

[2] *Collatio* 10. 9; *Iust. Cod.* 4. 65. 1.

[3] Wubbe, 'Zur Haftung des *Horrearius*', p. 514.

What would be meant by damage and simple theft *inlaesis extrinsecus horreis*? Is it probable that the warehouse contractor could be held liable for them?

It must be regarded as certain that damage or simple theft by the employees of the warehouse contractor would be regarded as his liability, if the warehouses had not been broken into from outside. It is more difficult to be certain that he would be held liable for the theft of goods belonging to one depositor by another. Wubbe becomes very much confused upon this issue,[1] because of his conviction that apart from the main entrance to the warehouse there was no locking or barring of access to anyone who had goods stored anywhere within the building. Apart from the fact that this is inherently very unlikely, a passage of Paulus expressly shows that the individual parts of *horrea* were locked, *cum vel cella effringitur vel armarium vel arca.*[2] Moreover, if the *Horrea Epagathiana et Epaphroditiana*[3] at Ostia were used as a safe deposit, as has been suggested elsewhere, then we have structural proof of internal locking. Not only was the main entrance locked at two points in its entrance corridor, but also each room was locked and even the bottoms of the staircases leading to the upper storeys. In all these cases the locking devices enabled the entrances to be not only locked but barred by a wooden beam slipped into slots in travertine blocks set in the door jambs. Although smaller, they are to be compared with the devices for barring the gates of Rome itself in the Aurelian Wall and the fort gateways on Hadrian's Wall.

In view of this locking of individual parts of the building and of the fact that the contractor very often provided *custodes* (although not *cellararii* and *librarii*, as Thomas states[4]) for the safe keeping of the goods, we must suppose that he was responsible for protection against other depositors.

Again, whether *custodia* be regarded as a strict liability or not, it is clear that it could be limited and clarified by the specific provisions dictated and publicly displayed by the warehouse contractor. In the case of the *lex horreorum Caesaris* it was not simply painted on a wall, but inscribed on marble as an abiding record.

Thus for example in the *lex horreorum Caesaris* one clause stated

---

[1] *Ibid.* p. 517; cf. p. 512.   [2] *Digest* I. 15. 3. 2.
[3] Chapter I (p. 30).
[4] Thomas, *RIntDroitsAnt*[3] VI (1959), 373, note 13. The word *cellararii* in the *lex horreorum Caesaris* is a restoration of a word ending in *-rar. Librarii* in *Digest* L. 6. 7 were associated with military not civil *horrea*.

...*cu*]*stodia non praestabitur*. We do not know what it was that was thus refused. In *Digest* XIX. 2. 60. 6, however, a *locator horrei* refused to accept liability for gold, silver and pearls in the technical phrase *non recipere*, and there can be little doubt that some such precious or unusually valuable objects were mentioned here.

In the final clause of the *lex horreorum Caesaris*, which is almost completely preserved, it was stated that unless a proper assignation of the goods left had been made to the *custos*, the *horrearius* would be *sine culpa*. This again is an example of the defining and restricting of the *custodia* offered.

So far we have concentrated upon the liabilities of the warehouse contractor, but no account of the organisation of the renting of *horrea* would be complete without some mention of his rights and the general conditions for the sale of property stored in *horrea*.

The conditions listed in the *leges horreorum* not only defined and limited the *custodia* offered by the contractor, but also prescribed some of his rights. Thus in the *lex horreorum Caesaris* the first clause prescribed the procedure for re-renting and the right of both the contractor and the depositor to prolong tacitly the agreement in the case of a depositor not appearing to renew the contract. Probably the second clause forbade subletting within the *horrea*. The fourth clause made it clear that the goods of the depositors could be seized as security for the payment of the rent.

Such rights as these are further defined in the legal texts. If the *conductores* failed to make an appearance for a considerable time and thus failed to pay their rents, the contractor had the right to open up their deposits in the presence of *publicae personae* in order to *describere* their contents, that is, to make a catalogue of the debtors' assets prior to confiscation. A two-year period was normally the limit for the payment of rent.[1]

The goods of a depositor in a warehouse could be regarded as security not only for the payment of rent to the warehouse contractor but also for the payment of debts to other creditors. Thus the marble merchant *conductor horreorum Caesaris*,[2] who was in arrears with his rent and had his stones seized by the *procurator exactioni praepositus*, had other creditors for whom the *pignus* was those same stones. Neratius stated

---

[1] *Digest* XIX. 2. 56. Eisele regarded the two-year limit as an interpolation, but it agrees with the ejection of Martial's couple for the failure to pay two years' rent (Martial XII. 32). For the use of *describere* cf. *Digest* XLII. 5. 15.

[2] *Digest* XX. 4. 21. 1 (Scaevola).

the position simply by saying that there was a *tacita conventio* that all goods brought into *horrea* could be seized in cases of debt.[1] While the goods were in the *horrea*, although being used as security, they were still the property of the debtor and not the creditor, so that any damage or loss which occurred (without the fault of the debtor) was still regarded as loss to the debtor.[2]

In the case of an action being brought for the production of some goods deposited in *horrea*, the action in the first instance would be brought against the depositor: if he had died, then his heir was liable. If there were no heir, then the action was brought against the warehouse contractor himself, who was regarded as the *possessor* of the goods in that at least he had the ability to produce them.[3]

It was possible for the depositor to sell to another man goods stored in *horrea*. The fullest text that we have describing the process states that the transfer of the ownership of the goods was completed at the moment when the keys to the deposit changed hands, providing that this transaction was carried out at the warehouse concerned.[4] The other two shorter texts[5] make the same point, but do not include the condition that the ceremony had to be performed at the actual *horrea*. The legal process involved was that of *traditio*[6] which originally seemed to require a transfer of physical control. In classical Roman law it appears that delivery of keys away from the warehouse did not satisfy this requirement. Later 'symbolic *traditio*' seems to have allowed the transfer of the keys at any place, not necessarily at the warehouse itself.

Apart from the legal problems involved in *traditio*, there is also the practical problem of what keys are being referred to and, indeed, who held the keys to deposits in warehouses. Clearly if a depositor left a locked chest he is likely to have retained *its* key. Equally clearly the *horrearius* (contractor), and not the depositor, had the keys to the main entrance to the whole building and it was possible, although rare, for the depositor to find himself shut out of the whole building.[7] It is also clear, I think, that the *horrearius* (contractor), although he had no general right of entry into locked *cellae*, nevertheless had the means to

[1] *Digest* xx. 2. 3.
[2] *Iust. Cod.* IV. 24. 9 (A.D. 293).
[3] *Digest* x. 4. 5 pr. (Celsus).
[4] *Digest* xvIII. 1. 74 (Papinian).
[5] *Digest* xLI. 1. 9. 6 (Gaius). Iust. *Inst.* 2. 1. 45.
[6] Buckland, *A Text-Book of Roman Law*, p. 227, and p. 232, n. 1. J. K. B. Nicholas, *An Introduction to Roman Law* (Oxford, 1962), pp. 119 ff.
[7] *Digest* xvI. 3. 1. 21 (*horreis forte clusis*); *Digest* xL. 7. 40 pr.

get in, if necessary.[1] It was only common sense that he should have such means. The insoluble question is therefore whether the *horrearius* kept the only keys to the *cellae* in his office, to which the depositors came when they wanted entry, or whether the *horrearius* simply kept duplicate keys or some master key which would allow him entrance, while the depositors held their own keys to locked *cellae*. I think the latter is more likely, but the former would give a practical, as well as a legal, reason why the handing over of the keys had originally to be carried out at the warehouse itself.

To sum up, then, we may say that the renting and hiring of *horrea* or parts of them was probably of fundamental importance to Roman trade in general. Later the emphasis came more and more to be put upon those *horrea* which acted simply as safe deposits for ordinary people in uncertain times. The general pattern of the organisation was originally that the owner let the whole building to a contractor, who sublet parts of it to individual depositors. Later it was more common for the owner to be himself the contractor who dealt with individual depositors. So far as the evidence goes, there is no reason to suppose that the owner, unless he was also the contractor, was regarded as having any liability towards either the contractor or the depositors.

The contractor, or owner-contractor, however, not merely offered to the depositors the use of an empty room or coffer within the building, but also undertook to protect whatever was deposited. He was therefore liable in the case of loss or damage to the goods. This, however, was no absolute liability. He was automatically free from liability in cases of *vis maior* and robbery with violence, and he could further define and limit the protection he offered in the conditions listed and publicly displayed in the *lex horreorum*.

Whatever may be the truth on the technical legal problems, the number of references in the *Digest* to the depositing of goods in *horrea*, and the variety of contexts, from sale of goods to theft and inheritance problems,[2] show that they were a common feature in the life and business of ordinary men in the city of Rome.

---

[1] *Digest* XIX. 2. 56.

[2] For example, *Digest* XLVII. 2. 21. 5 (Paulus) (theft); *Digest* XL. 7. 40 (Scaevola) (theft and inheritance); *Digest* XXXVI. 4. 5. 22 (Ulpian) (inheritance); *Digest* XXXIV. 2. 32. 4 (inheritance). There are many more such examples.

MILITARY *HORREA*

VII

DESIGN AND STRUCTURE

INTRODUCTION

This subject has attracted a certain amount of attention in print within the last fifty years, not least because in most of the Roman military sites excavated in Britain and Germany, *horrea* together with the *principia* (headquarters building) often form the most notable remains. Thus, in addition to the actual descriptions in excavation reports, there have been attempts at collection and comparative study—notably in John Ward's *Romano-British Buildings and Earthworks*, and Nash-Williams's *The Roman Frontier in Wales*.[1] But the former was simply a small section of a general book, which took no account of the examples in other parts of the Roman Empire, and was published as long ago as 1911, while the latter, although more up to date, is obviously even more restricted in the area from which examples are drawn. Apart from these there are only the citing of some examples for comparison in the later excavation reports in Britain and Germany and the bare enumeration of sites in which military *horrea* have been found, with a few basic data about planning and structure in the encyclopaedia articles—often published a considerable time ago.[2]

The difficulties of making a comparative study are even now not small. For although it is true that over the years the number of examples known to us has increased, while refined archaeological techniques[3] and greater experience have ensured the closer dating of buildings, and, perhaps even more important, have permitted the detection of traces of early timber buildings, the fact remains that the bulk of our examples were excavated at a period when archaeologists were fortunate if they

---

[1] J. Ward, *Romano-British Buildings and Earthworks* (London, 1911), pp. 91 ff. V. Nash-Williams, *The Roman Frontier in Wales* (Cardiff, 1954), pp. 128 ff.

Note: In order to reduce the number of footnotes, a separate bibliography for the forts and fortresses of Britain and Germany, with particular reference to their *horrea*, has been compiled and can be found on p. 336.

[2] Romanelli, p. 972 (1922); *RE* VIII. 2458 (Fiechter) (1913); D–S III (1), p. 275 (H. Thédenat) (1900).

[3] J. K. St Joseph's air photograph of Beckfoot in Cumberland reveals the granaries of the fort quite clearly, *JRS* XLI (1951), Pl. IV. 2.

could make out the main structures, and their attempts at dating concerned the whole fort or fortress and not individual buildings within it. Even in Germany the desire to be exhaustive and precise led often to plans containing an inextricable mass of post holes and walls of every period. Thus in some examples, excavated more than half a century ago, not only will the dating be difficult, if not impossible, but also the plan of the structure may need to be 'interpreted' in the light of other later excavated examples. Be that as it may, it does seem possible, as I hope to show, to trace a certain development in the structural planning of the flooring of these buildings in Britain at least, although it may yet be impossible to fix the stages of that development to certain absolute periods. Moreover, the *horrea* in German forts or fortresses, while certainly distinct in type, will be shown to be basically not so different from the British examples as has sometimes been imagined.

Although it is natural to concentrate on the *horrea* in the forts and fortresses of Britain and Germany, it must not be forgotten that they are simply the best and best known examples of buildings which certainly existed elsewhere in the Roman world. Wherever the Roman army went, the form of the granary will not have been too dissimilar, as can be seen from the *horrea* in the military outpost at Mons Claudianus in Egypt near the Red Sea[1] or the fort at Drobeta on the Danube.[2]

Finally, it will be suggested that quite apart from these generally recognised *horrea*, there is now evidence for at least two other distinct types of building associated with military storage. First, a growing body of evidence suggests that within legionary fortresses, or at least in some of them, in addition to the normal granaries with raised floors, there existed a large courtyarded storehouse of a type which owed nothing to the normal military *horrea*, but which bears a marked similarity to the civil *horrea* of Rome and Ostia. They may perhaps be regarded as baggage stores. Secondly, some recent excavations in Germany indicate that under the late Empire another type of military *horrea* was current, distinct from both of the main types mentioned above, which may have served as the frontier supply bases whose existence is implicit in some edicts of the *Codex Theodosianus*.

---

[1] T. Kraus and J. Röder, 'Mons Claudianus', *MDInstKairo* XVIII (1962), 89–91 with Abb. 1 and Taf. XIIa.

[2] R. Florescu, 'Les phases de construction du castrum Drobeta (Turnu Severin)', *Studien zu den Militärgrenzen Roms* (Köln, 1967), pp. 144 ff.

The basic shape of the Roman *horrea* in British military forts is well known. They were long, narrow, rectangular hall-like buildings with walls of remarkable thickness, heavily buttressed and very often with their floors raised. Yet despite the fact that these buildings clearly were constructed to a standard pattern, there are differences between them in dimensions, in grouping, in position and in structural details.

Flooring arrangements

The purpose of raising the floors is not in doubt: clearly the idea was to allow a free current of air to pass between the ground and the floor of the building to counteract the evils of damp, overheating, and the attacks of insects and rodents to which grain is particularly prone. But the way in which this purpose was accomplished varied.

The increased attention paid in recent years to the disentangling of the traces of wooden buildings characteristic of the earliest phase of Roman occupation has yielded important results for the study of raised floors. We now have examples of wooden *horrea* in supply bases, in auxiliary forts, and in a legionary fortress, all of the first century A.D., where previously there had been nothing before the first stone *horrea*, dated to the reign of Trajan.

Three methods seem to have been used for raising the floors of wooden *horrea* in Britain, although the differences between the methods are slight. The floor was carried by upright posts in all cases. But the posts themselves were either carried on a grid of timber sills let into the ground, or secondly set in post holes as individual uprights, or thirdly set in post holes aligned in long shallow trenches.

Examples of the first method were excavated in the auxiliary forts at Pen Llystyn and Fendoch (Fig. 35), and the legionary fortress at Inchtuthil. An example of the second method was discovered in the small fort at Hod Hill (Fig. 36), while examples of the third method have long been known at Richborough (Fig. 37) and have now been added to by the excavations at Fishbourne and at Rödgen (Fig. 38) in Germany.

At Richborough in Kent, the military position which covered the disembarkation of the Roman invasion forces was turned into a military

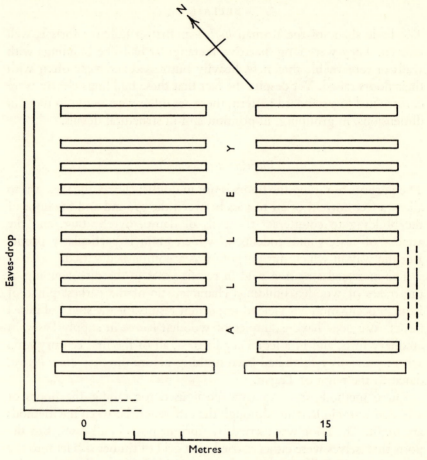

Fig. 35   Fendoch, sleeper-trenches for support of wooden *horrea*

supply base about A.D. 44 and continued to be used for this purpose until A.D. 85. The site was excavated in the 1920s and 1930s, but the final publication was delayed until 1968.[1]

It is now apparent that a rectangular street grid was imposed on the site and in the excavated area the main road ran from east to west. To the south of this road the area was divided into three *insulae* by two side roads running from north to south. In these three *insulae* were

[1] J. P. Bushe-Fox, *Richborough, Report IV* (Oxford, 1949), pp. 26 and 34. B. Cunliffe, *Richborough, Report V* (Oxford, 1968), pp. 7, 10, 11, 235–7, Fig. 3 and Fig. 28.

groups of wooden military storehouses. In the most easterly *insula* was a group of four storehouses, positioned with their long axes at right angles to the side road, running from north to south. Each of these storehouses was 123 feet long and 26 feet wide.

In the central *insula* was again a group of four wooden storehouses, again 26 feet wide, but only 93 feet long.

In the most westerly *insula* the ends of two more storehouses, again 26 feet wide, have been discovered. Clearly there were more wooden

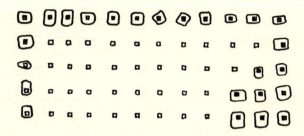

Metres

Fig. 36   Hod Hill, post holes for support of wooden *horrea*

storehouses not only in this area, but no doubt also in other areas of the supply base.

The buildings in each block were separated by gaps of 8 feet and there were post holes for porticoes and loading platforms at one end of each building.

The storehouses were built predominantly to one pattern. For each building there were six parallel longitudinal sleeper trenches, 1 foot 6 inches–2 feet wide, and 10 inches–1 foot 10 inches deep, which were 4–5 feet apart (Fig. 37). In these trenches at irregular intervals (but approximately 3–4 feet) were traces of post holes 9–10 inches in diameter. The original excavator, Bushe-Fox, calculated that these posts were to carry a raised wooden floor. It was suggested that the longitudinal sleeper trenches were not to be considered as having any bearing on the detailed design of the superstructure, but were dug merely for the convenience of the upright supports, on which were laid timber beams which ran *transversely* across the width of the building. Thus the system for raising the floor was essentially one of transverse supports. The irregularity in the spacing of the post holes was explained by the difficulty of finding straight timber beams for these transverse supports.

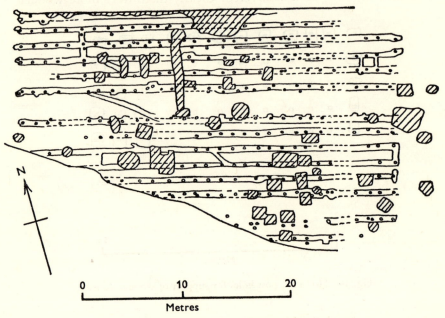

Fig. 37 Richborough, sleeper trenches with post holes for support of wooden *horrea*

The foundations of one of the buildings discovered revealed what seemed to Bushe-Fox to be a different plan. The sleeper trenches were arranged in a grid system; those running east–west (that is, longitudinally) were 1 foot 8 inches wide and 1 foot 6 inches–2 feet deep, while those running from north to south (that is, transversely) were 10 inches wide and only 6 inches deep. Bushe-Fox's suggestion was therefore that the floor was not raised significantly above ground level but rested on a massive timber grillage laid in the soil itself in order to store supplies of great weight. Professor Cuncliffe's restudy of the site has now revealed that the foundation trenches are those of two different buildings superimposed on each other. The wooden granaries at Richborough were therefore, so far as we know, all of one structural type.

At Fishbourne[1] a similar supply base of Claudian date, probably to be associated with the campaigns of the second legion under Vespasian

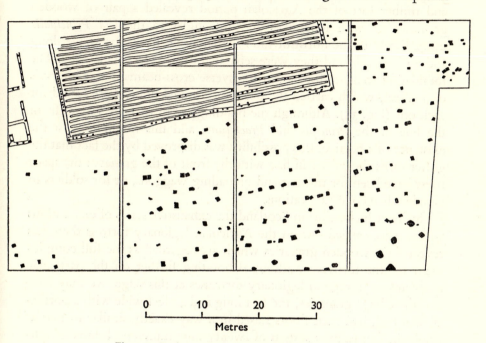

Fig. 38 Rödgen, sleeper trenches with post holes
for support of wooden *horrea*

in the south-west, has come to light beneath the later Roman palace there. Two buildings of a type similar to those at Richborough have been discovered, one measuring 23 feet by more than 72 feet. Yet another timber building seems to have had a raised floor supported by individual posts set in pits 8 feet apart, giving rise to a building measuring 40 feet by 96 feet.

Although rather bigger, this building is similar to the granary in the

[1] B. Cunliffe, 'Excavations at Fishbourne, 1962', *Antiquaries Journal* xliii (1963), 1; cf. *Antiquity* xxxix (1965), 178; *JRS* liii (1963), 151.

Claudian fort at Hod Hill.[1] There the granary was carried on sixty posts, five rows of twelve posts apiece (Fig. 36). The post holes varied in size, shape and position but the posts themselves seem to have been from 9 to 10 inches square, that is, they were more massive than those of the timber-framed walls elsewhere in the fort.

At Fendoch[2] in Scotland the excavation of a complete auxiliary earth and timber fort of the Agricolan period revealed a pair of wooden granaries set with long axes at right angles to the *Via Principalis* immediately to the north of the *Principia* itself. Each was 56 feet long and 30 feet wide and they were separated by a 10-feet-wide alley. The foundation trenches for eleven transverse cross-beams, set at intervals of 3–5 feet, which carried the posts for a raised floor, were found for each one (Fig. 35). Although the buildings were set back 10 feet from the line of the *Principia* and *Praetorium*, and this might suggest the existence of a portico, this possibility was disproved by the fact that the gutter turns the corner in line with the front of the granary: the space must have been for turning and unloading waggons, or for soldiers to parade when collecting rations.

Finally at Inchtuthil[3] in Scotland the exhaustive series of excavations which were carried out on the Agricolan legionary fortress there has revealed six wooden granaries which are regarded as the full complement for the fortress. Without elaborating further on the particular problems of storage in legionary fortresses at this stage, we may note that these huge granaries, 136 feet long and 42 feet wide with a portico at each end, had their floors raised in a way exactly similar to that at Fendoch, that is, by a system of twenty-nine transverse beams set into the ground to carry the posts for a raised floor.

There can be no doubt that from now on increasing numbers of these wooden granaries will be identified in excavations. Already in the last five years there has been discovered in the Roman fort at Wall in Staffordshire traces of a wooden granary similar to those at Rich-

[1] Sir Ian Richmond, *Hod Hill* II (London, 1968), p. 84.
[2] Richmond, *PSAS*, LXXIII (1938/9), 129 ff.
[3] Because of the untimely death of Professor Sir Ian Richmond, the full publication of these excavations has not yet taken place. Interim reports were published in *JRS* 1953–66, and the last plan of the fortress published in *JRS* LI (1961), 158, fig. 9 is not as complete as that in R. M. Ogilvie and I. A. Richmond, *Tacitus, 'Agricola'* (Oxford, 1967), p. 72, fig. 9. For a brief discussion of the fortress, I. A. Richmond, 'The Agricolan legionary fortress at Inchtuthil', *Limes-Studien* (3rd International Limes Congress) (Basel, 1959), pp. 152 ff.

borough, while the forts at Castleshaw and Pen Llystyn have produced granaries like those at Fendoch. Wooden granaries are reported from forts at Longthorpe in Northamptonshire and Baginton in Warwickshire. The study of wooden granaries is only just beginning.

The earliest stone *horrea* known to us, in the Trajanic auxiliary forts in Wales, have—where evidence for raised floors is preserved at all—a system not dissimilar to that in the wooden granaries for the support of the floor. At Pennydarren (60 feet+ by 34 feet) there were at least eleven transverse dwarf walls 1 foot 6 inches wide and 3–6 feet apart;

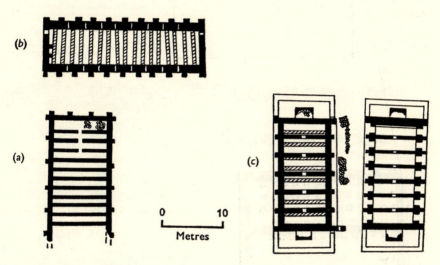

Fig. 39   *Horrea* at (*a*) Pennydarren, (*b*) Castell Collen, (*c*) Gellygaer

at Castell Collen (93 × 32 feet) seventeen transverse dwarf walls 22–8 inches wide and approximately 2½ feet apart; at Gellygaer (59 × 34 feet) six or five transverse dwarf walls (Fig. 39).[1] These masonry transverse supports, appearing at a time when the changeover from timber to stone construction was taking place, seem to be copies in stone of the system which prevailed in wooden granaries. They are characteristic of this interim period and were not to be repeated. Wooden granaries with raised floors did persist, as at Old Kilpatrick

[1] It seems that one of the granaries at Gellygaer, Building VIII, was modified at an unknown period so that the eight original dwarf walls were reduced to five. The other granary, Building V, had six transverse dwarf walls throughout its history.

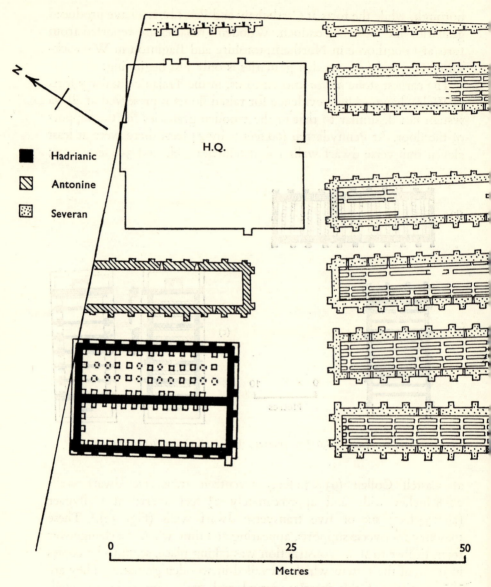

N

■ Hadrianic

▨ Antonine

▦ Severan

H.Q.

0   25   50

Metres

Fig. 40   South Shields, Severan supply base

(Buildings VII, VIII and IX), beside stone buildings, but wherever stone granaries with raised floors were built after this interim period the system of transverse supports seems not to have been used.

Instead we find two methods of supporting a raised floor: either by rows of dwarf piers, similar to those well known in hypocausts, or by a series of longitudinal dwarf walls which ran parallel with the long axis of the building. There can be no doubt as to which of these methods was the more common or which was the more persistent and became the standard type. The use of stone piers is known so far in

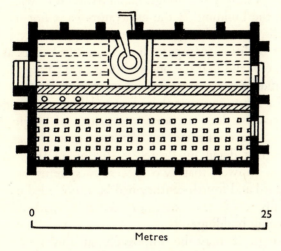

0   25
L_____J
Metres

Fig. 41 Housesteads, *horrea*: originally divided axially by columns, later divided into two distinct buildings

only four examples in Britain: at South Shields in the Hadrianic double granary (Fig. 40); at Housesteads on Hadrian's Wall, where one of a pair of granaries has stone piers, while the other has longitudinal walls (Fig. 41); at Castlecary on the Antonine Wall; and at Ribchester in Lancashire, where again the two granaries of the fort have different systems, one with piers, the other with an axial dwarf wall supporting a wooden floor.

The number of examples on the other hand with a system of longitudinal dwarf walls is far greater and they seem to belong to all periods from Hadrian onward. A multiple system of longitudinal dwarf walls has been found at Housesteads (Fig. 41), Chesters, Rough Castle,

Mumrills, Old Kilpatrick, Bar Hill, Balmuildy, Birrens (Fig. 45), Newstead, Ambleside and the legionary fortress at Chester. In certain of these cases, for example at Birrens, it was established that these walls were interrupted at intervals corresponding to the ventilators in the side walls of the building to form transverse air shafts in order to ensure a good current of air, and this is the case in the Antonine and Severan granaries at South Shields (Fig. 40). On the other hand, if we can believe the excavation reports, there are a few examples, at Old Church, Brampton, Cadder and Ribchester, and perhaps Hardknott[1] (Fig. 43), where there was simply one longitudinal dwarf wall which ran down the centre of the building. If the excavators have not merely missed the other walls, it would seem that these examples may belong to an older, simpler tradition (compare the Scipionic granaries at Numantia in Spain, Fig. 60), and that the one wall was used to support a wooden floor in the middle.

The case for supposing that there was a deliberate change from the system of transverse floor supports to a system of longitudinal dwarf walls seems to be confirmed by the two granaries at Corbridge, excavated in great detail by Professor Richmond (Fig. 42; Pl. 52).[2] Both granaries showed that two successive systems of longitudinal walls in the third and fourth century had been preceded by a system of transverse walls which the excavator connected with an earlier, but similar, Antonine building.

Thus although it may be impossible at this moment to date the changeover in systems precisely, we can be sure that such a development did take place, probably by the mid-second century, and we can see that the transverse system seen in the earliest stone examples is perhaps an inheritance from the earth and timber period.

In 1961, however, excavations at Haltonchesters[3] on Hadrian's Wall revealed a large granary, 134 × 34 feet, with sleeper walls to support the floor which ran from north to south in the north part of the building,

---

[1] See re-examination of the Hardknott granary by D. Charlesworth, 'The granaries at Hardknott Castle', *CW*[2] LXIII (1963), 149.

[2] I. A. Richmond, and J. P. Gillam, 'Excavations on the Roman site at Corbridge 1946–1949', *AA*[4] XXVIII (1950), 152; on *horrea* in Hadrian's Wall forts in third and fourth centuries A.D. see J. Wilkes, 'Early fourth-century rebuilding in Hadrian's Wall forts', *Britain and Rome* (M. Jarrett, ed.) (Kendal, 1966), p. 126.

[3] Not fully published yet, but see *JRS* LI (1961), 164; *JRS* LII (1962), 164; *Durham Univ. Gazette* (Dec. 1961), 6.

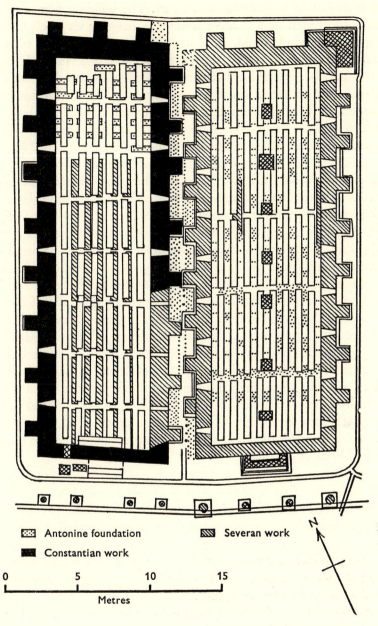

Antonine foundation   Severan work

Constantian work

0   5   10   15

Metres

Fig. 42   Corbridge, *horrea*, showing changes in methods of floor support

and from east to west in the south part. The building was very substantial and rested on a massive stone raft, flagging set in clay, which
lay under the whole building. It survived the attacks of the northern
tribes at the end of the second century A.D. and lasted with only minor
repairs until late in the third century A.D. when its wooden floors and
the grain which stood on it were charred, and the sandstone roof
collapsed. It was the opinion of the excavator, Mr J. P. Gillam, that
the two systems of floor support were contemporary and that the
granary was constructed in the Hadrianic period.

It should also be stressed at this point that the need to raise the floor
of a granary was in the first place because of its wooden floor. This
explains the precautions taken in wooden buildings and in those stone
buildings which clearly retained wooden floors: gaps of 5 feet and
more between dwarf walls must make it unlikely that they were
bridged in any other way than with timber. But there was *prima facie*
no reason why a stone building with *flooring* of stone or concrete should
have to have a raised floor. We find some examples where no trace of a
raised floor has been preserved in the early second century in forts such
as Caerhun (Fig. 44), Caersws and Brecon Gaer. It is possible that the
evidence was simply missed or has been destroyed by time. But it is
also possible that the system of *raising* floors made of flagstones and
materials other than wood may be a development which was not
widely practised until well into the second century A.D. Such a view
would harmonise well with the fact that all raised floors of this type in
Ostia date from the middle of the second century, if not a little later,
and in one case at least the flooring which preceded the raised floor of
tiles had been of *opus signinum*.[1]

Types

In general the military *horrea* in Britain may be divided into four types:

A Single *horreum*: narrow rectangular building consisting of a single
room with buttresses along the sides. This type is the most common.

B Double *horrea*: rectangular buildings of double width with buttresses along the sides *but divided axially* by a wall into two long rooms.
The Hadrianic granary at South Shields (Fig. 40) is of this type, and
other examples were found at Brecon Gaer and Benwell. Cf. Housesteads (Fig. 41) and Hardknott (Fig. 43).

[1] The so-called *Grandi Horrea* at Ostia, see Chapter I (p. 47) and Appendix I.

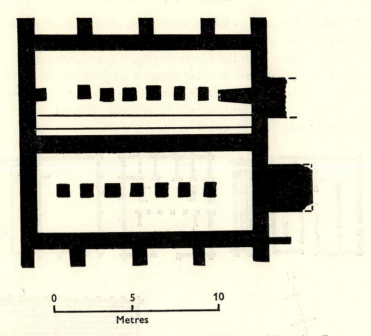

Fig. 43 Hardknott, *horrea*, centre strengthened by an additional wall

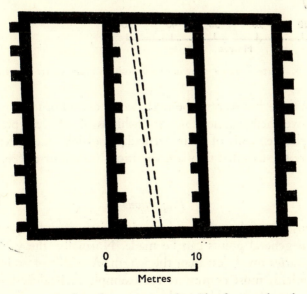

Fig. 44 Caerhun, *horrea*, set on either side of a central yard

C Paired *horrea*: two *horrea*, set one on either side of a central yard. The whole ensemble has been planned and built as one unit. Examples of this type were found at Caerhun (Fig. 44) and Ambleside.

D *Horrea* placed end-to-end: there is only one example in Britain of this type—one of the three granaries at Birrens has double length (120 feet compared with a width of only 32 feet) and is divided *transversely* into two rooms (Fig. 45).

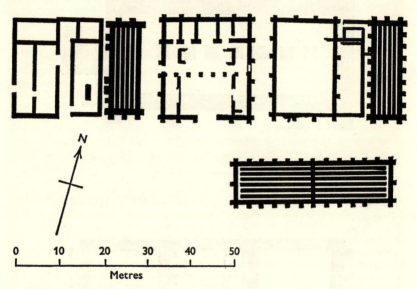

N

0   10   20   30   40   50
Metres

Fig. 45   Birrens, *horrea*, showing their position in the centre of the fort

The last three types are to be regarded as exceptions to the rule and seem to owe their creation, not to fashions of different periods, but rather to the demands of their particular location; the differences do not obscure the fact that they are variations on the first type.

Proportions

The dimensions of the military *horrea* in Britain vary from site to site, but certain general points can be made. Normally, the width of the buildings varies much less than the length. A width of 20 feet or just over is perhaps most common: for example at Rudchester, Housesteads (Fig. 41), Balmuildy, Cadder, Castlecary, Cappuck and Lyne,

0   25
Metres

Fig. 46 Chester, *horrea*, simplified plan of three legionary granaries

but there is a group of examples where a width of approximately
30 feet is preferred: for example at Fendoch (Fig. 35), in most of the
Welsh forts (Fig. 39), at Chesters, Bar Hill, Stanwix and Templeborough. The exceptions from these two most common widths can
easily be explained: the granaries at Chester (Fig. 46) (45 feet wide) and

at Inchtuthil (42 feet wide) were larger buildings altogether, understandable in legionary fortresses: other exceptions at Brecon Gaer (48 feet wide), at Benwell (60 feet wide) and Hardknott (44¼ feet wide) (Fig. 43), are explained when we see that they are double granaries, and thus conform essentially to the 20 or 30 feet standards.

The length of the buildings is more variable and ranges from 50 feet at Cappuck to 150 feet at Benwell.[1] One of the deciding factors in fixing the length was the distance between the *Via Principalis* and the *Via Quintana* of the fort concerned, for the most common position for granaries, at least in auxiliary forts, as we shall see, was next to, and parallel with, the *Principia* building.

In general, the proportions of the British *horrea* tend to be slimmer than the examples in Germany and, although there are obvious exceptions, an average proportion of 3:1 for the length to the width will not be too misleading.

Structure

The foundations of military *horrea* were often constructed of cobbles set in stiff clay (for example, at Cadder, Templeborough and Balmuildy). But other types of foundations were used: concrete and gravel at Chester; a bed of boulders at Mumrills; and large stones set in clay covered by a layer of flagstones at Ambleside. In some cases, as at Newstead, Balmuildy and Old Church, Brampton, the foundations were carried out to the line of the buttresses throughout (making the foundations 5–6 feet wide) so as to form a complete platform, but more often the foundations followed strictly the contours of the buttresses and wall.

Above these foundations the walling could be of two types: either (*a*) squared blocks of stone throughout (as at Newstead, Chester, Ambleside, Mumrills, Castell Collen, etc.); sometimes the masonry was dry-stone, sometimes set with mortar; or (*b*) facings of squared stones with a core of rubble and chips set in mortar (as at Castlecary, Drumburgh and Corbridge, Plate 52).

The type of stone used varied and depended largely upon local

---

[1] Benwell with double granary of unusual length had a storage capacity beyond what was necessary for a fort of its size. As the first large fort on Hadrian's Wall positioned at the last point accessible to river-borne traffic on the Tyne, it seems to have held extra reserves of corn. See F. G. Simpson and I. A. Richmond, 'The Roman fort on Hadrian's Wall at Benwell', *AA*⁴ XIX (1941), 18.

supplies. Brathay stone was used at Ambleside, grit and magnesian limestone at South Shields. But sandstone of one kind or another seems to have been particularly favoured, as at Newstead, Chester, Cappuck and Drumburgh. At South Shields it is possible to see in the series of granaries of different periods how an increasing knowledge of the local resources affected the choice of building material. The first twin granary of Hadrianic date was built of magnesian limestone. The second single granary of Antonine date was built, not of magnesian limestone, a hard rock to work, but of pinkish sandstone obtainable in the Dean Quarries between South Shields and Tyne Dock: this is a good building stone but not used by the first builders on the site and presumably not known to them. The large series of Severan granaries again used different stone—Gateshead Fell sandstone. Whatever the type of stone or the method of construction employed, the walls of these buildings, buttresses disregarded, were of remarkable thickness and solidity, only rarely falling below 3 feet in width and often approaching 4 feet.

Buttresses

Despite the unusual thickness of their walls, military *horrea* were as a rule heavily buttressed, particularly along their sides. The exceptions to this rule, as at Caernarvon and Bar Hill, were very few indeed. If a granary had buttresses at all at the ends, and this was not always the case, they appear only rarely to have exceeded two in number, as at Chesters, Housesteads (Fig. 41), Cadder and Mumrills, although the extraordinary double granary at Birrens (Fig. 45) does have three buttresses at the ends. The number of buttresses along the sides naturally varied in accordance with the length of the building, the distance between buttresses remaining fairly constant, between 7 and 15 feet. The buttresses themselves were most often either $2\frac{1}{2}$ or 3 feet square, although there are examples where the projection exceeds the width or *vice versa*. At Brecon Gaer the buttresses projected 3 feet and were only 2 feet wide, while at Benwell the projection was only 2 feet compared with a width of 4 feet. Whatever the size of the buttresses, they were always incorporated into the main wall structure and were not merely juxtaposed.

Ventilators

The floors of military granaries were raised to protect the contents from damp and overheating. To maintain a strong current of air under these floors was therefore essential, and to achieve this ventilators were introduced in the side walls. These took the basic form of vertical narrow openings in the masonry, at ground level, which were crowned with a flat lintel. There were two types: (*a*) with splay (e.g. Fig. 42); (*b*) without splay (e.g. Fig. 39). In the first case, the openings were very narrow in the outer face of the wall, but broadened inwards, while in the second case the openings maintained a uniform width throughout.

The amount of splay varied, just as the general dimensions of the openings varied. At Balmuildy an opening 18 inches wide was reduced to 9 inches; at Mumrills from 12 to 7 inches. But at Castlecary 30 inches was reduced to a mere 6 inches, while at Castell Collen the splay was very slight, from 16 to 12 inches. The purpose of the splay was no doubt to maintain the best possible air current, while at the same time attempting to exclude all but the smallest animals from penetrating under the floor itself. In cases where, despite the splay, the width of the ventilator on the outside remained large, it is very probable that a central stone mullion was inserted, the ends of which were let into the sill and the lintel, as in the example preserved in the east granary at Corbridge.

In the Trajanic fort at Gellygaer (Fig. 39) the ventilators of the granaries were without splay and of an unusual width of 3–4 feet, which had been reduced at some period to 2 feet by the insertion of masonry cheeks. As we have seen, there is reason to believe that this granary was built during a transition period and it is certain that, although there are later examples of granaries with ventilators that have no splay, none of them are of such width. Even the ventilators of the granaries in the legionary fortress at Chester, built early in the second century A.D., were only 2¼ feet wide, and the ventilators of the Severan granaries, which filled the fort at South Shields, had a much smaller width of approximately 1 foot.

The position of the ventilators, of whatever type, was naturally between the buttresses, generally in the middle of the space available. Often they were located in all the bays between the buttresses, but

there were exceptions. At Chester in the legionary fortress the ventilators were between every *other* pair of buttresses; at Castell Collen
they were positioned in all but the last bays at either end of each side.

Entrances, porticoes and loading platforms

Evidence for the point at which the granaries were entered is only
rarely in the explicit form of preserved doorways: more often it is the
case that remnants of a loading platform or portico will indicate where
the doorways once had been.

At Housesteads (Fig. 41), however, doorways reached by steps were
found at the west end of the granaries and a perfectly preserved
threshold was still situated in the north building. It had a marginal check,
bolt holes and pivot holes for two doors opening inwards: in short,
it was the kind of threshold that is typical of the civil *horrea* in Ostia.

More often we find evidence for loading platforms built against one
or both ends of the granary. Sometimes this evidence is merely the
traces of foundation at the end of the granary, without any details
preserved for study, as at Cadder, Balmuildy, Ribchester and Corbridge
(Fig. 42), or the strengthening of the end walls as at South Shields. But
there are explicit examples. At Newstead at the west end of the southern
granary was a loading platform 10 feet long and 14 inches high; at
Rudchester the loading platform for a large granary measured 32 feet
by 10 feet; while at Rough Castle, for a much smaller building, the
loading platform of flagstones bedded on stone foundations was only
$3\frac{1}{2}$ feet wide, projected a mere 21 inches from the building and was
approached by two steps.

At Gellygaer (Fig. 39) there is the suggestion that here a veranda and
loading platform were combined. At each end of the granaries a
veranda the width of the building was formed by walls 3 feet thick
which were capped at a height of 1 foot above street level by flagstones.
These verandas appear to have had a row of four columns along the
edge parallel to the building and were entered from either side. Within
this veranda area a loading platform was built against the end wall,
$9\frac{1}{2}$ feet in width with a projection from the building of 6–7 feet.

As for porticoes, there is a growing body of evidence to suggest that
these were more common than has been apparent; and it is possible
that their traces may have been missed in earlier excavations. At all

events, at Benwell the south end of the granary had a portico of six rectangular piers on splayed bases so disposed that the three central bays were 10 feet wide, while the lateral bays were only 7 feet in width. The two granaries at Corbridge (Fig. 42) each had a tetrastyle portico, again with the central intercolumniations of extra width. There was possibly a portico at Newstead. Certainly at Templeborough the granaries which were set transversely along the *Via Principalis* not only had a portico fronting their ends on the intervallum road, but also had a slighter colonnade on the side, masking their length along the *Via Principalis*.

It is likely that these porticoes were of fairly simple construction. At Corbridge the portico of the west granary, with column drums 19 inches in diameter and simplified Attic bases, probably supported, not stone architraves, but a timbered roof carried forward from the granary roof. At Inchtuthil the presence of post holes marking the entrances to the great timber granaries of the legionary fortress seem to indicate that at each end there were two entrances. In view of the enormous size of these granaries (136 feet long × 42 feet wide) it may have been the case that, not only were they divided transversely into two halves, but perhaps, as the double doors suggest, divided longitudinally also to make four compartments.

All the evidence, however, leads to one conclusion, that the means of access in military granaries was always at the ends and not in the sides. Whether both ends were used, or which of the two ends, seems to have been a matter of choice, but it is sometimes the case that the end facing on to the important and busy *Via Principalis* has been deliberately avoided and the other end, facing on to an open square or quieter subsidiary street, has been chosen, for example as at Housesteads.

Position

Since it is clear that in many cases the full number of granaries necessary for the garrison has not been discovered, or that sometimes the granaries were a late insertion,[1] a certain caution is necessary in discussing the positions chosen for military *horrea*.

[1] At Chesters two granaries were discovered in the *retentura* of the fort behind the *Principia* and were removed (as being late insertions) by their excavator John Clayton in the late nineteenth century! E. Birley, *Research on Hadrian's Wall* (Kendal, 1961), p. 175.

In auxiliary forts the most favoured position seems to have been beside the *Principia* itself. Orientated in the same direction as the *Principia* building, with which it was parallel, the granary stretched between the *Via Principalis* and the *Via Quintana*. For brevity's sake the orientation may be described as longitudinal (that is, parallel with the long axis of the fort as a whole). Examples of either one single or double granary in such a position beside the *Principia*, or of two granaries in such a position one on either side of the *Principia*, occur at Caerhun, Benwell, Newstead, Rudchester, Housesteads, Balmuildy, Bar Hill, Cadder, Old Kilpatrick, Camelon, Mumrills, Castlecary, Rough Castle and Lyne. At Brecon Gaer and Gellygaer the granaries were in a similar position, but were separated from the *Principia* by one intervening building (cf. Fig. 45).

Other Welsh forts, however, show distinctly different positions for their granaries. At Pen Llystyn, Caernarvon and Castell Collen the granaries, although placed beside the *Principia*, were orientated transversely, not longitudinally, so that the long side of the building flanked the *Via Principalis*. A similar position is adopted for the granaries at Birdoswald. At Templeborough the granaries, although located side by side and set transversely on to the *Via Principalis*, were positioned, not by the *Principia*, but close to the south-east gate of the fort. In the Claudian fort at Hod Hill the wooden granary was situated on the *Via Praetoria* beside the main *Porta Praetoria* itself.

In the legionary fortresses at Chester and Inchtuthil the granaries so far laid bare seem to reveal a similar tendency for positions near a gateway into the fortress. Only at Inchtuthil has the full complement of six *horrea* been discovered: there are so far only three at Chester. At Inchtuthil two *horrea* are positioned near the *Porta Decumana*, one near the *Porta Praetoria*, two in the eastern part of the *Retentura*, and one near the *Porta Principalis Sinistra*. At Chester all three *horrea* so far discovered are in a row running north–south and positioned close to the western gate of the fort. In this case the position was probably dictated, not only by the desire to be near a gateway, but in particular to be near the gateway which led to the harbour. The choice of a position near a gateway must be linked with problems of transport, loading and unloading of goods, and in that case the importance of transport by water, wherever it was possible, cannot be overestimated. As we shall see, the position of *horrea* in some German legionary fortresses indicates a similar interest in and use of water transport. With this in mind it may not be out of place to predict that in the legionary fortress at Caerleon, for example, where no *horrea* have so far been discovered, at least some granaries are likely to be found, if and when opportunity occurs, on one side or other of the present High Street, near the gate which leads down to the River Usk.

Superstructure and storage capacity

We have little direct evidence for the arrangements of the superstructure of military *horrea*, but much can be intelligently deduced as highly probable. Conjectural restorations of wooden granaries have been given by Bushe-Fox for Richborough and by Richmond for Fendoch (Fig. 47). Arrangements in stone granaries will have been much the same, except for the presence of side buttresses unnecessary in wooden buildings.

We are to think of them as one-storeyed buildings, as there is a complete lack of evidence for any arrangements for supporting or reaching a second storey. Only in a late restoration of the east granary at Corbridge, when a series of massive central piers was introduced, is there a slight possibility of a second storey.

The roofing arrangements are clear. Roofs were always remarkably well constructed from tiles, whatever material was used in the lower part of the building, as the consistent discovery of masses of roof tiles on the site of *horrea* proves. The natural form for the roof would have been a gable, no doubt of timber covered by tiles, and this is shown to have been the case in such examples as at Fendoch, where drip lines or gutters have been found on either side of the building. Such evidence also shows that the eaves of the roof had a wide overhang and we are perhaps to think, in the case of the stone granaries, that the buttresses were not only to support a lateral thrust of goods stored inside but also to run right up to the roof and help to support the wide overhang of the eaves. Such an overhang is easily explained by the desire to shelter grain sensitive to heat and damp, and no doubt in the case of wooden granaries to protect the wooden structure of the building from the elements and attacks with fire arrows by the enemy.

In the side walls we must assume a series of shuttered louvres, which were weather-proof but provided ventilation. Light must have been admitted by such louvres and perhaps by windows at the ends of the building and the doorways. In the stone granaries it may be that the light and air were admitted by tall narrow splayed windows which are characteristic of the civil *horrea* in Ostia.

The presence of buttresses, particularly along the sides of *horrea*, has naturally suggested that the grain was stacked laterally, presumably in bins. If this is accepted and certain other assumptions are made, for

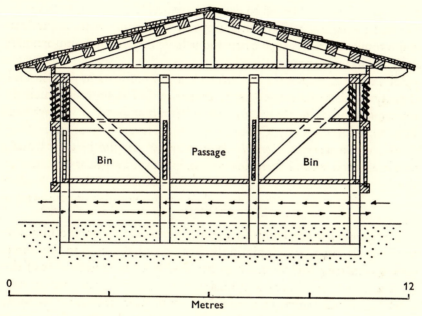

Fig. 47 Fendoch, reconstruction of wooden *horrea*

example that there was a central gangway of so many feet, and that the bins were of such-and-such a height, it becomes possible to estimate the storage capacity of the buildings. With further assumptions about men's rations in the Roman army, it becomes possible to estimate the space needed to store a year's corn ration for one soldier. Finally, by a judicious comparison it is possible to see how far the granaries within a given fort provided sufficient storage capacity for the garrison.[1]

[1] R. G. Collingwood and F. Haverfield, 'The provisioning of Roman forts', *CW*[2] xx (1920), 127. Richmond, *PSAS*, LXXIII (1938/9), 129 ff. For inaccuracy in Collingwood's figures see Simpson and Richmond, *AA*[4] XIX (1941), pp. 18 ff.

So long as the storage capacity of all *horrea* is calculated in the same way, the results have a certain value for a *comparative* study of the capacity of those *horrea* (the question as to whether the calculations are right in an absolute sense being irrelevant). Moreover, if the calculations are regarded as a very *approximate* indication of the ability to feed the garrison for a certain period, they are not without a certain importance. But already the large number of assumptions in the calculations and other imponderables such as the difference of space taken up by vegetables and meat as opposed to cereals in general, and even by wheat as opposed to barley, remove much of any confidence one might have in the results. Further, such calculations have in general an unfortunate tendency to be inaccurate.

All in all, the attempt to extract *detailed* information of storage capacity by these methods seems hardly worth the effort. Fortunately a *general* trend is not hard to establish, and it has the importance, recognised long ago by Collingwood and Haverfield, of supporting the passage in Tacitus, *Agricola* 22. 2, namely that the forts in Britain could maintain within their defences supplies sufficient for a year.

GERMANY

The evidence for the *horrea* in the auxiliary forts along the Limes in Germany is often disappointingly vague and difficult to interpret. This is primarily because most of them were excavated as part of the great work of the Limes-Kommission in the early part of this century. Important as this work was in its day, by present standards it is poor, particularly in the disentangling of different periods, in the precise dating of individual buildings and in the fullness of the structural information. The work of re-examining these sites with a view to establishing detailed chronology has barely begun, although von Petrikovits has recently been re-examining the legion fortresses excavated during this period, for example Novaesium. The result is that we have no chronologically precise re-examinations of *horrea*, such as Professor Richmond has carried out at South Shields and Corbridge in England.

Thus it is impossible to establish any sequence of building methods comparable to what has been attempted in the different methods of supporting raised floors in the British *horrea*.

Very few wooden *horrea* were known earlier in the century and the examples at Haltern (Fig. 48), Hofheim and the earliest granary at Saalburg all seemed to be constructed with their floors raised by posts set in individual post holes, as at Hod Hill.

More recently, however, early granaries have been discovered at Vindonissa and at Rödgen (Fig. 38) in the Wetterau area north of the River Main, which are more closely paralleled by the granaries at Richborough and Fishbourne. The posts for supporting the raised wooden floors were set in post holes in sleeper trenches.

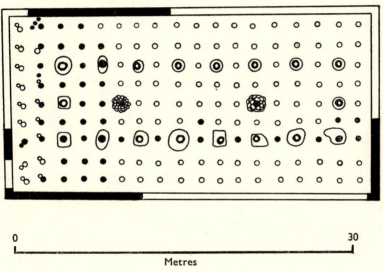

0   30

Metres

Fig. 48   Haltern, *horrea*, post holes for support of wooden floor

At Vindonissa in the early Julio-Claudian period long rows of sleeper trenches with post holes in them were arranged in three groups to make a U-shape around a long narrow central space. The overall dimensions of the ensemble were 19 × 43 metres, and each 'wing' was about 6–7 metres broad.

At Rödgen even more remarkable discoveries have been made. The fort was of great oval shape and enclosed by a double ditch (Fig. 49). Almost none of the buildings are yet known inside it, but it has already yielded three enormous wooden granaries. The excavators suppose that it was a depot and communications centre, built about A.D. 11, and is to be

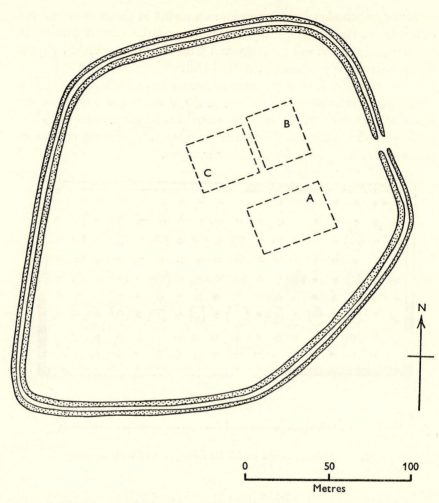

Fig. 49   Rödgen, sketch-plan of camp showing size and position
of wooden *horrea* so far uncovered

associated with Drusus' campaigns across the Rhine. *Horrea* A measured
some 47·25 × 29·25 metres; *Horrea* B 29·50 × 30 metres; *Horrea* C 33·50
× 30·70 metres. These buildings are therefore both the largest and the
oldest granaries so far known in Germany. Their floors were raised on
posts set in post holes in sleeper trenches running longitudinally, and
the excavator, H. Schönberger, supposed that the horizontal beams that

240

carried the flooring must have run in the same direction as the sleeper trenches (Fig. 50); indeed, he thinks the beams were placed on the ground, the trenches were then dug and the posts put in them to suit the beams which were then lifted on to them. If this is true, then the system was different from the transverse supports postulated in Britain.

Whatever the truth about these hypotheses, it remains a fact that the system of supports resting on sleeper beams let into the ground (as at Fendoch, Inchtuthil and Pen Llystyn) has not so far been found in Germany.

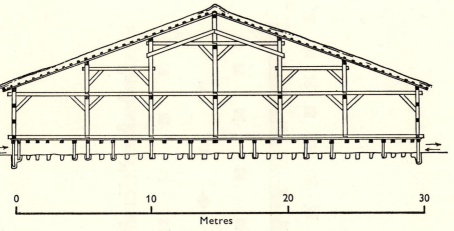

Fig. 50   Rödgen, reconstruction of large wooden *horrea*

When we come to the stone-built granaries, the pattern again seems slightly different from that of the buildings in Britain. First, the method for supporting a raised floor, which on the present evidence seems to have been least popular in Britain, proves to have been most common in Germany and sometimes in a form unknown in Britain. At Hüfingen the floor was supported by stone piers set in three rows approximately 5 metres apart, which ran the length of the building (Fig. 51); a similar system of stone piers was used in the conventional granaries in the legionary fortress at Neuss (buildings 13 and 14) and in the newly excavated granaries of the legionary fortress at Bonn (Fig. 52). In other auxiliary forts the same system was used, but although the outer walls of the buildings were of stone, the support for the floor was carried out in wood. Thus at Niederbieber the interior of a large granary was filled with post holes approximately 2 metres apart, in such a way that they form twenty-five transverse rows of seven holes each (Fig. 53); similarly at Weissenburg posts of pinewood, bedded 80 centimetres deep into the ground, carried the raised floor (Fig. 56).

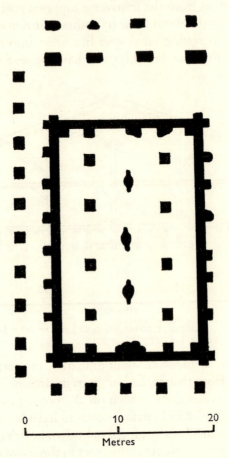

Fig. 51 Hüfingen, *horrea*

Nowhere have the transverse sleeper walls, characteristic of the floor supports of some of the Trajanic Welsh forts, been found in Germany, unless the three transverse walls reported in the granary at Gnotzheim were not, as suggested, division walls, but rather sleeper walls for floor support.

On the other hand, longitudinal dwarf walls have been found in the stone granaries at Saalburg (Fig. 54), five in the north building and only four in the south, and at Benningen, where there were four such walls.

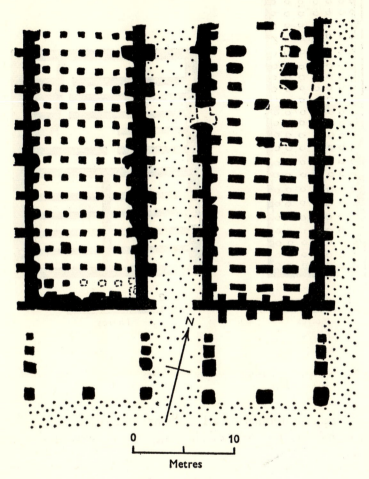

Fig. 52   Bonn, *horrea*

It is possible that the rows of foundation walls 70 centimetres wide, with a length of 41·5 metres at least, reported at Okarben, may be the remnants of this support system for a granary, and that the two axial walls reported at Wiesbaden were not division walls but floor supports. In the newly excavated *horrea* of the legionary fortress at Nijmegen

16-2

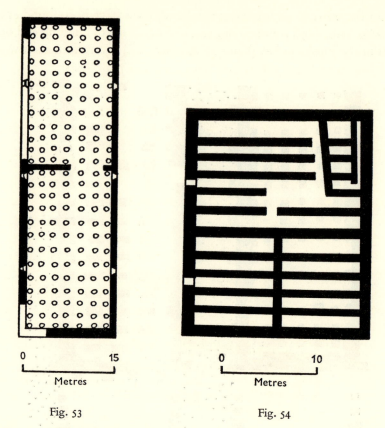

Fig. 53

Fig. 54

Fig. 53 Niederbieber, *horrea*, showing post holes for support of wooden floor
Fig. 54 Saalburg, *horrea*

(Fig. 55) the longitudinal dwarf walls are interrupted at regular intervals to increase the flow of air under the floor as in the British examples.

Types and proportions

The fourfold division of types applied to British military *horrea* is not really applicable to the German examples. It is just possible to compare the double *horrea* at Saalburg (Fig. 54) with the Hadrianic granary at South Shields (Fig. 40) and with the granaries at Brecon Gaer and Benwell, but all that they really have in common is that two storehouses are accommodated within one main building. Similarly the

244

nearest approach to the extra long building at Birrens (Fig. 45) in Britain, which is divided transversely into two *horrea*, is the west granary at Niederbieber (Fig. 53), but there is a real possibility that this building was divided thus into two only after the similarly large east

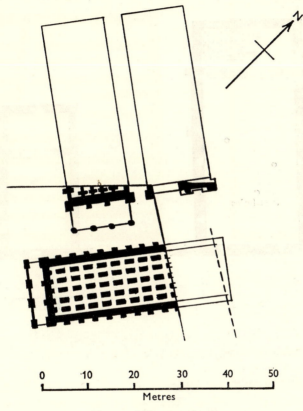

Fig. 55   Nijmegen, *horrea*

granary had been converted into a *fabrica*, and thus the comparison is not to the point.

Predominantly, the *horrea* of the German auxiliary forts fall into the category of single rectangular buildings (compare British *horrea* type A), but within this general category there is great variety in detail. Perhaps the most characteristic and developed type of these buildings is that in which the main rectangular buttressed hall has the end opposite the entrance cut off by a transverse wall and in the unit so formed is created a tiny suite of two rooms, one of which sometimes has a hypocaust. Such is the case at Weissenburg (Fig. 56) and probably at Ruffenhofen. In certain other places, such as Wiesbaden (building B), Saalburg (north granary) and Kapersburg (Fig. 57), the granaries,

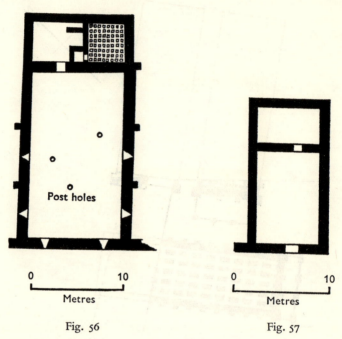

0   10
Metres

0   10
Metres

Fig. 56   Fig. 57

Fig. 56 Weissenburg, *horrea*, with post holes for support of wooden floor and small suite of rooms at one end
Fig. 57 Kapersburg, *horrea*

although very similar to the Weissenburg example, lack buttresses and seem to have only a single room at the end created by the transverse wall. On the other hand, the *horrea* at Urspring (Fig. 58), Theilenhofen and Hüfingen (Fig. 51), although they have buttresses, show no signs of any end rooms. Where they exist, such rooms at the ends of *horrea* have naturally been regarded as the quarters of the *librarii horreorum* known from the *Digest*.[1]

The dimensions of these buildings, even discounting the unusual

[1] *Digest* L. 6. 7.

long examples at Niederbieber (Fig. 53) (53 × 16 metres) and the unusual wide examples at Benningen (22·90 × 17; 21·10 × 17·55 metres), show no standardisation. As usual, the width of the buildings tends to remain more constant than the length. Most of the German *horrea* have a width of more or less 10 metres, although at Theilenhofen the width is 14 metres and at Hüfingen (Fig. 51) as much as 16 metres. Despite these exceptions, the fact remains that the width is not very different from the 30 feet standard in Britain.

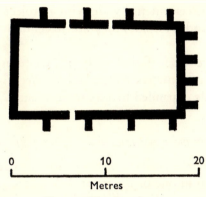

0   10   20

Metres

Fig. 58   Urspring, *horrea*

In length the figures range from as little as 14·80 metres at Wiesbaden to 31 metres at Ruffenhofen, a variation not dissimilar to that of the British examples. Since, however, the majority of the German examples have a length of approximately 20 metres or less, the general proportions of the buildings' length to breadth is 2:1, rather than the proportion 3:1 characteristic of the longer narrow *horrea* in British forts.

Structure, buttresses and ventilators

As in Britain, the *horrea* of the German forts were remarkable for the thickness of their walls. Only rarely did the width of the main walls fall below 90 centimetres, and they were always carefully constructed, often of limestone and mortar, as at Urspring.

Despite this thickness the buildings were often reinforced by buttresses, while this was not so universal as in Britain. These buttresses, where they occur (at Urspring (Fig. 58), Ruffenhofen, Theilenhofen,

Weissenburg (Fig. 56), Pfünz and Benningen), were ranged pre-dominantly along the side walls of the buildings, although buttresses do occur also at one end of the *horrea* at Ruffenhofen, Urspring and Pfünz. Even along the sides of the buildings the number of buttresses was usually only four, although Ruffenhofen has five, and thus the intervals between buttresses are greater than in Britain. The dimensions of the buttresses vary. They can be small and almost square, as at Benningen (60–90 centimetres wide × 60–80 centimetres projection), or larger and rectangular, as at Urspring (on the south side the four buttresses are 80–90 centimetres wide with a projection of 1·50 metres, while on the east and west sides they are 70 centimetres wide and pro-ject 1·20 metres).

Ventilators have been found only at Urspring (without splay, approximately 40 centimetres wide), and at Niederbieber (with splay, 40 centimetres wide expanded to 1·25 metres) and Weissenburg (again with splay).

Entrances, porticoes and loading platforms

Where evidence for the position of the entrances is preserved, it always points to a position in one of the short ends of the granaries, just as in Britain. Although, as at Kapersburg, the end which gave on to the main *Via Principalis* could be chosen for the entrance, the position of the buttresses at the south end of the *horreum* at Urspring would suggest that the main street was avoided and the entrance must lie at the other end.

Porticoes sheltering the entrance seem to have been a rarity in the German auxiliary forts, and loading platforms are unknown. The only example of a portico, at Hüfingen (Fig. 51), extends around three sides of the building and is not therefore comparable even with the portico at Templeborough. Not only is it a fact that porticoes were not reported in front of the German *horrea*, but also it seems unlikely that they were missed by the excavators, since in the majority of cases where granaries were situated on the *Via Principalis*, there could have been no room for them, in that the granaries were not set back to accommodate them.

In the legionary fortress at Novaesium, however, the granaries (buildings 13 and 14) (Fig. 59) *were* fronted by porticoes and thus con-form to the type already discussed in Britain.

Position

The position favoured for *horrea* in British auxiliary forts has been seen
to be near the *Principia*, with the long axis of the building at right
angles to the *Via Principalis*. This is true also of the *horrea* in German
auxiliary forts, for example at Niederbieber, Urspring, Gnotzheim,

0   25

Metres

Fig. 59   Neuss, *horrea*

Weissenburg, Pfünz and Wiesbaden. At Ruffenhofen, although the
orientation and general position have not changed, the *horreum* has been
placed closer to the *Porta Principalis Dextra*. But at other of the German
forts the position is quite different. At Saalburg and Benningen a

position on the *Via Praetoria*, close to the *Porta Praetoria*, has been chosen, and the reason is not difficult to understand. At Theilenhofen, however, the *horreum* is placed in the *retentura*, behind the western half of the *Principia* building, and at Kapersburg the *horreum* is in the *Praetentura*, opposite and to the east of the *Principia*. The explanation of these positions is difficult to find, and may lie in some reorganisation of the layout of the fort after their construction.

In the legionary fortresses at Neuss and Bonn the *horrea* are situated in both cases on the *Via Praetoria*, close to the *Porta Praetoria* of the fortress in question. The advantages of positioning the granaries near the gates, apparent in any legionary fortress, were rendered even greater at both places by the proximity of the Rhine and its water transport.[1]

Summing up

The superstructure of these buildings must have been not dissimilar to that of the *horrea* in Britain and the same principles apply in making any conjecture about it.

What Collingwood, Haverfield and Richmond have done for the conjectural calculation of storage capacity in British *horrea*, has been carried out, it is claimed, for the German examples by Herr Wahle.[2]

The important point to remember about the German military *horrea* is that despite their points of difference from their British counterparts, in their flooring arrangements, their proportions, their use of buttresses and their two-room suites, they are in essentials not very dissimilar. The differences that there are between the *horrea* in the auxiliary forts in the two countries must not blind us to the overall similarity to the British types shown by the buttressed *horrea* in the legionary fortresses at Neuss and Bonn.

The differences may be attributed to that flexibility in different environments shown by the Romans in their building, as in all other things. These cannot obscure the fact that both British and German military *horrea* derive from one tradition.

[1] H. Aubin, 'Der Rheinhandel in römischer Zeit', *BonnJb* cxxx (1925), pp. 1 ff. Cf. C. Cichorius, *Die Reliefs der Traianssäule* (Berlin, 1896–1900), Taf. 35.

[2] *Die Saalburg, Mitteilungen der Vereinigung der Saalburg-Freunde II*, Nr. 2 (10 April 1920), 29 ff. (I have not managed to find or consult this book.)

THE TRADITION

In any attempt to trace back this tradition, it is clear that the first question is whether there are any excavated examples dating from the Republican period of Roman history. In the excavations carried out between 1905 and 1912 in and around Numantia[1] in Spain, Dr Adolf Schulten revealed examples of military *horrea* in two places—in the fifth camp at Renieblas, dated by him to approximately 75 B.C., and in the camp of Scipio at Castillejo, dated *circa* 134 B.C. In both cases the resemblance to the later examples under the Empire is startlingly close.

At Renieblas in the fifth camp on the site, two *horrea* were situated close to each other just south of the *Via Principalis*, not far from the *Porta Principalis Sinistra* (another possible *horrea* is situated away in the north-west corner of the camp). The western one measured some 28–30 metres in length and 17·40 metres in width, with walls 90 centimetres thick. At least three buttresses 80 × 60 centimetres were found along one of the side walls. The interior of the building was divided longitudinally by three walls, only 60 centimetres thick and 2·95–3·20 metres apart. The eastern building measured 29·10 metres in length and 19·60 metres in width, with the same wall thicknesses as its neighbour. In this case, however, there were four internal walls dividing the building longitudinally; and in addition to the usual buttresses along the outer walls these internal walls had a series of minor buttresses. The overall design of these buildings and their proportions and flooring arrangements (presumably timber beams supported on the widely spaced internal walls) strongly recall the examples in the German auxiliary forts.

A certain anomaly in their position demands attention. Not only is each slightly differently orientated from the other, but neither has quite the right orientation for the *Via Principalis* on to which they are supposed to front. Moreover, both of them project awkwardly into the *Via Principalis*, quite out of line with the Tribunes' houses to the west. Perhaps the full truth is not yet revealed about these buildings and their date.

At Castillejo, three *horrea* constructed all as one group were placed on the *Via Praetoria* not far from the *Porta Praetoria* (Fig. 60). This

[1] A. Schulten, *Numantia* III (Munich, 1927), p. 207 and pl. XXIX; IV (1929), p. 177 and pl. XX.

group consists of three buildings with a constant length (internal) of
17·80 metres but of slightly varying widths (internal)—5·60, 6·80 and
6·10 metres. The buildings were separated by alleys 2 metres wide
into which projected six buttresses along each side, but they seem to
have had a common façade. The walls were 60 centimetres thick and
they were built of limestone; each granary was divided axially by one
wall, certainly to support a raised wooden floor. As a group they were
isolated from the surrounding buildings. In
this case the more apt comparison seems to
be with the later British military *horrea*, both
for the general proportions of the building
and the buttressing.

So much for earlier Roman examples. But
it is possible to carry the search still further
back and to suggest that this tradition of long
narrow buildings with raised floors for
storage purposes was part of that heritage
which Rome absorbed from the Greek East.
The possibility that as early as 134 B.C. the
Roman military granary was in its essentials

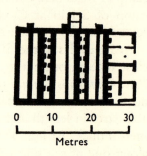

Fig. 60 Numantia, *horrea* in
the camp at Castillejo

a fixed type would in itself suggest that the Romans were drawing on
an older tradition. That this was so is seen from the series of so-called
arsenals discovered on the Burg at Pergamon by German excavators
in 1927,[1] and even more spectacularly in the great granary at Harappā
in the Indus Valley[2] excavated at the same time.

In a special area given over to this purpose alone on the acropolis
at Pergamon were grouped at least five rectangular storehouses
(Fig. 61); the lower parts of these buildings with the arrangements for
supporting the floor are very well preserved.

Arsenal I, placed on the highest available ground level, measured
36·52 × 12·97 metres, and had walls 70 centimetres thick. It was built
of cut trachyte stones, the outside surfaces of which were smoothed,
and the whole was bonded by lime mortar. The corners were strengthened by great squared blocks. Within the building a system of transverse dwarf walls and later longitudinal dwarf walls, both only

[1] A. von Szalay and E. Boehringer, *Altertümer von Pergamon*, x, *Die Arsenale* (Berlin,
1937).
[2] M. S. Vats, *Excavations at Harappā* (Delhi, 1940), I, pp. 15–16; II, pls. III–VI.

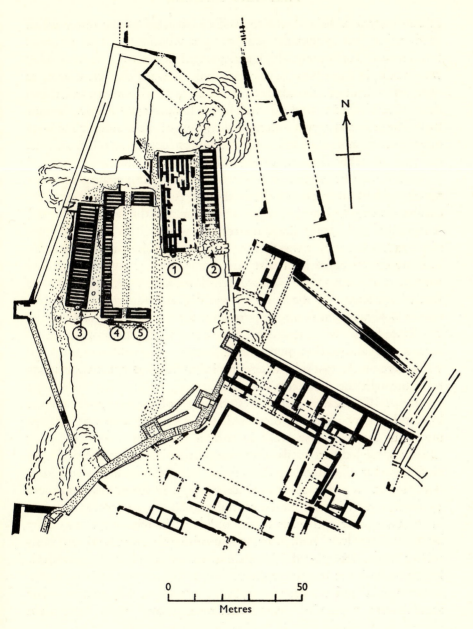

Fig. 61 Pergamon, arsenals on the acropolis

253

45 centimetres wide and not so well constructed as the outer walls, produced a grid system for supporting a wooden floor. A series of ventilators 110 centimetres high and 40 centimetres wide without splay were made in the centre of the longitudinal walls of each transverse compartment of the foundations in connection with a series of ventilators cut only in the west side wall of the building as a whole. There is no evidence for any partitioning of the inside of the building. The roof must have been gabled and tiled, the superstructure wooden, and the entrance probably at the south end of the whole building.

Arsenal II to the east, which was constructed flush against the perimeter wall of the whole area, is shorter and thinner, although the excavators believe it to have been constructed at the same period as I. It measured only 30·93 × 6·62 metres and was built in the same technique as I. The interior was divided only by a series of transverse walls at more or less equal intervals: however, after each two thin sleeper walls 30 centimetres wide is placed a thick division wall, 70 centimetres wide, indicating that the building was divided transversely into five rooms with wooden floors supported on thinner sleeper walls. All the transverse walls were pierced by centrally placed ventilators 40 centimetres wide and 90 centimetres high. The only ventilators in the outer walls were on the east side, where special provision for them was made right through the perimeter wall itself.

Arsenal III, situated at the western edge of the area, was on the lowest level available. It measured 39 × 8 metres, and was divided internally by transverse walls in such a way that after every four equally spaced dwarf walls, there are two thicker division walls set close together, thus dividing the building transversely into five rooms with raised wooden floors. Ventilators 100 centimetres high and 45 centimetres wide are placed centrally in all the transverse walls and in the two outer end walls of the building: in the long sides of the building narrower ventilators, 100 centimetres high and 20 centimetres wide, are placed 1½ metres from each other admitting air between the inner transverse walls.

Arsenals IV and V measure 48·70 × 8 metres, and thus accommodate six transverse rooms, but in all other respects conform to the pattern set by Arsenal III.

In all the last four examples it seems clear that the entrances to the individual rooms must have been at the side.

The excavators suggest three building periods:

A. Arsenals I and II   283–261 B.C.?

B. Arsenal III   ⎫ Two periods within

C. Arsenals IV and V   ⎭ 230–160 B.C.?

The importance for us is that here, in the Hellenistic period, are many of those features of the later granaries of Roman forts.

What is even more astonishing is that at Harappā[1] in the Indus Valley we have exact parallels for the Pergamene arsenals, but built more than 1,500 years before them. Between the citadel and the river were discovered two great buildings (Fig. 62) approximately 150 feet long and 50 feet wide, parallel with each other but divided by a 23 feet passage between them. Each of these building blocks was divided transversely into six halls or granaries, each about 52 feet by 17 feet, divided by five narrow corridors which opened only on the sides of the buildings away from the central passageway. There were thus two sets each of six granaries apiece. Within each granary the floors were carried by three dwarf walls set equidistant from the division walls and from each other, running transversely across the building but longitudinally within each of the individual granaries. The whole structure was built in a mixture of burnt and sun-dried brick, and was constructed, in the opinion of the excavators, to withstand great weights. A free current of air was created under the floors by ventilators set in the long sides of each building, and even when later alterations restricted the size of the ventilators, additional triangular air-holes were cut in unusual projecting buttresses in order to maintain the flow of air.

The Romans therefore in their standard military granaries were drawing upon a tradition of building that stretched back for 2,000 years or more, at least in the East.

So much for the standard type of military granary. No survey, however, of the *grain* storage facilities of Roman forts would be complete without some mention of the two superimposed buildings (21 and 22) at Neuss.[2] The legionary fortress there had, as we have seen, at least two examples of the standard type of granary, rectangular and heavily buttressed. But in addition to these, and on the opposite side

---

[1] Vats, *Excavations at Harappā* I, pp. 15–16, 17–22; II, pls. III–VI; R. E. M. Wheeler, *The Indus Civilization*³ (Cambridge, 1968), p. 33; pl. V (from M. S. Vats); R. E. M. Wheeler, *Civilizations of the Indus Valley and Beyond* (London, 1966), pp. 26–8, figs. 29 and 32.

[2] C. Koenen, 'Beschreibung von Novaesium', *BonnJb* CXI–CXII (1904), 186 ff.

of the *Via Praetoria* from them, was a courtyard building in which was found a layer of carbonised wheat. As described by the excavators, the building formed roughly a square measuring externally 78·40 × 66·05 metres around an open central courtyard 47·75 × 37·35 metres.

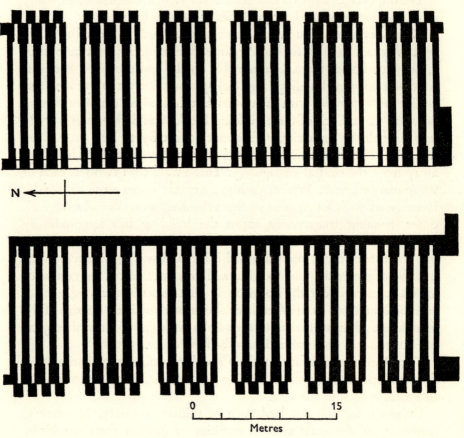

N ←

Fig. 62   Harappā, granaries. Air vents were cut through the added buttresses

Both the outside walls of the square and those around the central court-yard were buttressed on the outer side. There were no other walls of any kind, according to the excavators, and thus the four ranges around the courtyard had no divisions. The entrance may have been on the north side on the *Via Sagularis* where the drain leading out of the building was found. No parallel for such a *grain* store exists elsewhere;

but it seems that even when this building was destroyed, another was superimposed of almost precisely the same plan, although with a different orientation and a more regular shape—86·10 × 45·20 metres round an internal courtyard 72·50 × 19·60 metres. This building was more massively constructed and had buttresses on both sides of its walls.

If we accept these buildings as the excavators have reported them, and do not suppose that something has been missed or unwittingly misrepresented, in order to understand them we must look at them not alone, but in conjunction with the other corn stores in the fortress, namely the two already mentioned. It is possible in this way to see them perhaps as four large rectangular granaries disposed around a central courtyard, which could be used for stacking baggage or some similar purpose. While there is so far no parallel for such an arrangement elsewhere, this way of looking at the building makes it understandable.

BAGGAGE STORES

Even a brief acquaintance with a modern army reveals that storage problems are not concerned solely with food. The quartermasters have to provide adequate space and protection for a vast amount of impedimenta of all kinds, ranging from items of equipment, through blankets and bedsteads, right down to thick china mugs. This, we may suppose, was the case in the Roman army; and our supposition is borne out and illustrated by the scenes of army activity on the columns of Trajan and Marcus Aurelius.[1] Leather tents done up in bundles, entrenching tools and baskets for carrying earth, cooking pots and 'haversacks', and weapons of all kinds are depicted. Even granting the obvious fact that individual soldiers would be responsible for their own kit and would keep it in the anterooms of their barrack blocks, the point remains that spares of all kinds and such things as tents had to be stored somewhere.

This aspect of the problem has been rather ignored, because of the attention paid exclusively to food storage. There were several possibilities open for storage of this kind, and at Inchtuthil it has been shown that at least some of the rooms which line the main streets of the fortress were used for the storing of utensils such as Samian ware and glass,

[1] C. Cichorius, *Die Reliefs der Traianssäule* (Berlin, 1896–1900), Taf. VII and XXXV. E. Petersen, *Die Marcus-Säule* (Munich, 1896), Taf. 119.

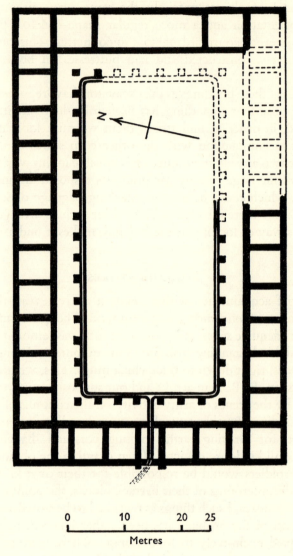

Fig. 63   Vindonissa, courtyard building

which were systematically taken out and smashed when the fortress was abandoned.

In 1959 during excavations in the legionary fortress at Vindonissa,[1] in the southern part of the fortress a large courtyard building was found to have been constructed in the period A.D. 75–80 above some demolished barrack blocks. This rectangular building (Fig. 63) measured 81 × 48 metres and had an open court in the centre 24 metres wide. The courtyard had been surrounded by an arcade resting on square piers 2·40 metres apart, except on the west side, where the distance between the two central piers corresponding to the entrance to the building was 2·80 metres. At this point, too, the drain from the court debouched, and a further indication that an entrance to the whole building was here was given by the strengthening of the gravel by a limestone bed as in a roadway. The gateway was marked by two projecting pilasters which framed it on the outside. The ranges were divided into regular, almost square, rooms 5·20 × 5·80 metres: only in the western range were there two narrow rooms only 2·40 metres, probably for staircases.

The solidity and depth of the foundations (1·20 metres wide and 2 metres deep) and of the piers in the court led the excavators to suppose that the building was two-storeyed and that the piers supported, not a lean-to roof, but a gallery giving access to the first floor rooms. The partition walls of the rooms were less deeply founded.

The excavators suggested that it was a magazine of some kind, although not the corn store, which probably lay further to the west.

The similarity of this building to the *horrea* of Rome and Ostia, for example the *Horrea Lolliana* on the Marble Plan[2] (Fig. 23) or the *Horrea di Hortensius* at Ostia[3] (Fig. 18), is most marked and there can be little doubt that the identification as *horrea* of some kind is attractive.

A close inspection of the complete plans of earlier excavated legionary fortresses soon reveals interesting parallels which existed in addition to the normal corn storehouses. At Carnuntum[4] two buildings with courtyards surrounded by ranges of rooms (buildings C and D) were identified by the excavators as examples of *fabricae*. They are not

[1] R. Moosbrugger-Leu, *Jahresbericht Pro Vindon.* (1959/60), particularly pp. 16 ff. Plan, Abb. 7. Reconstructions, Abb. 8 and 8 *a*.
[2] See Chapter II (p. 109).   [3] See Chapter I (p. 64).
[4] *Der Römische Limes in Österreich* x (1909), Taf. II, and pp. 35 ff.

entirely similar to one another: whereas building C, with only three ranges of irregular rooms, may well have been a *fabrica*, it is tempting to see in building D (Fig. 64) a parallel to the Vindonissa storehouse.

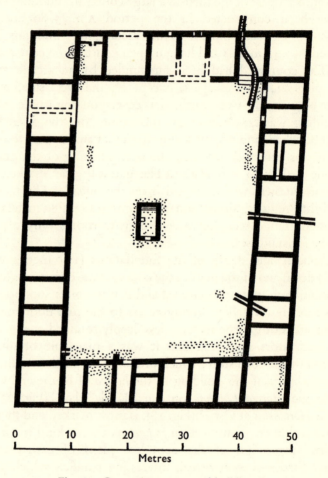

Fig. 64 Carnuntum, courtyard building D

Haverfield[1] indeed regarded both Carnuntum buildings as storehouses, when he cited them as parallels for the great unfinished courtyard building at Corbridge in Britain, but this is to ignore the differences between the two buildings. Building C does not really compare with the

[1] F. Haverfield, 'Corbridge excavations, 1910', *PSAL*[2] xxiii (1911), 478.

civil *horrea* of Rome and Ostia, whereas building D, a tilted parallelogram 67 × 49 metres with four ranges of regular rooms, does compare well. Haverfield's main point, however, was that the great courtyard building at Corbridge, measuring 222 × 216 feet with a central court 165 × 160 feet which was left unfinished, was a storehouse. Recently Professor Birley[1] has tried to identify the building as an unfinished legionary headquarters. Such a thesis can only be refuted finally by a further excavation on the site to the north of the building, but as the evidence stands at present, it is implausible, even if there was a whole legion at Corbridge, as Birley suggests. The discovery of the Vindonissa building strongly reinforces Haverfield's idea that it was intended as a storehouse and even the new date for the structure made by Birley, that is, the Severan period, brings to mind the great massing of ordinary *horrea* at South Shields and the reconstruction of storehouses at Corbridge itself for the Scottish campaigns.

Not only the identification of the Corbridge building, but the whole theory that the Roman army used a type of courtyard *horrea* in addition to the one-roomed buttressed buildings, receives further support from the legionary fortresses at Lambaesis and Bonn. In the west corner of the *praetentura* at Lambaesis is a large courtyard building consisting of four ranges of regular rooms (10 metres deep and 8–10 metres wide) which open on to a portico. This portico certainly surrounds the central court on the west, south and east sides and may well do so on the north. The room entrances were wider than is usual, measuring more than 2 metres. Cagnat[2] remarked the building's resemblance to known examples of *horrea* in Rome and Ostia, but also suggested that it resembled the *valetudinarium* at Novaesium. With all the evidence which has now accumulated about hospitals in legionary camps, the latter is an impossible identification.

At Bonn the recent excavations of von Petrikovits[3] have uncovered a large courtyard building in the legionary fortress between the intervallum road and the *valetudinarium*. The courtyard is surrounded on all four sides by ranges of more or less equal rooms, and the resemblance to the Vindonissa building is striking.

[1] E. Birley, 'Excavations at Corstopitum 1906–1958', *AA*⁴ xxxvii (1959), 12 ff.

[2] R. Cagnat, *L'armée romaine d'Afrique* (Paris, 1913), p. 510.

[3] H. von Petrikovits, *Das Römische Rheinland, Archäologische Forschungen seit 1945* (Cologne, 1960), p. 44 and Taf. 3.

The buildings at Carnuntum and Corbridge already mentioned are quoted by von Petrikovits as parallels for his new building at Bonn, and he adds building 141 at Novaesium, hitherto supposed to be a *schola* or *fabrica*. As an identification for all these buildings he suggests *veterinaria*—horse hospitals. His identification is based upon Pseudo-Hyginus 4:

et si res exiget, cohors peditata quingenaria loco vexillariorum solet superponi, et, si strictior fuerit pedatura, cohors legionaria dari debet, sed numero suo, ut LXX pedes valetudinarium et reliqua, quae supra tendent, accipiant, hoc est veterinarium et fabrica, quae ideo longius posita est, ut valetudinarium quietum esse convalescentibus posset.

Further, he suggests that the buildings are not unlike ordinary hospitals in plan.

The first objection to von Petrikovits' identification is that even within his chosen group the buildings are not entirely similar to each other. Within his group it is possible to make two groups, the first consisting of building D at Carnuntum and the unfinished storehouse at Corbridge, the second consisting of building C at Carnuntum and building 141 at Novaesium. The regularity of disposition and dimensions of the four ranges of rooms cannot be ignored. The buildings of the second group are more likely to be *fabricae* or *scholae* than anything else. However, this would still leave the first group open for identification.

Neither of the two specific arguments brought by von Petrikovits seems to me sound. He seems to argue thus: Hyginus enumerates in close proximity to the *valetudinarium* the *fabrica* and the *veterinarium*: we have identified all of these except the *veterinarium*: therefore the building we have left must be the *veterinarium*. This argument has only to be expressed nakedly to be seen to be weak. Further, Hyginus is particularly concerned to solve a hypothetical problem: what happens when, with only a limited amount of space for disposal, more than one legion is to be accommodated? This results in crowding together elements which were not necessarily normally so placed.

Moreover, the attempt to reinforce the argument by pointing out that the building to be identified as a *veterinarium* is similar in plan to a *valetudinarium* cannot succeed. There are two points here. First, on this reckoning, any and all courtyard buildings without further ado might be said to resemble *valetudinaria* on military sites. Secondly, why should it be supposed that the ground plan of a horse-hospital should resemble that of an ordinary hospital?

The strength of von Petrikovits' position seems then to lie, not in the arguments he presents, but in the fact that since we have no proven examples of *veterinaria*, it seems impossible for us to prove conclusively that these buildings were not *veterinaria*. But this would be true if he had made the suggestion about any type of building, not firmly identified, of any shape or size. Thus the onus of proof for identifying these buildings in this way still lies with him.

It is possible, as I have shown, to gather together a series of buildings from Vindonissa, Lambaesis, etc., on much stricter principles of similarity than those employed by von Petrikovits, and to show that these buildings reveal a striking resemblance to the ground plan of the civil *horrea* of Rome and Ostia. The need for baggage stores is obvious, and in these buildings we have the typical Roman ground plan for such storehouses.

Moreover, it seems possible that the adoption by the military authorities of a storehouse of this civil pattern may have helped to spread it through the Empire. Thus we find it, although probably introduced at military instigation, not always in specifically military locations. At Dura Europos[1] on the Euphrates is a building labelled on the plan by the excavators as a Caravanserai, which resembles the Vindonissa type. Moreover, at Karanis[2] in Egypt, in marked distinction to the typical local storehouses of the place, is a building clearly inspired by Roman planning, with a colonnade round the courtyard, on to which open rooms on four sides and which supports a gallery for the first floor rooms. In this case the building was clearly used as an immense storehouse for grain, some three storeys high. As far as the excavators could estimate, the building started its life at least as early as the end of the first century A.D., and was probably under military control.

[1] M. Rostovtseff, F. E. Brown, C. B. Welles, *Dura Europos: Report on 7th and 8th Seasons* (New Haven, 1939), Plan, Block L 4.

[2] A. Boak and E. Peterson, *Karanis, Topographical and Architectural Report, 1924–28*, University of Michigan Studies, Humanistic Series xxv (1931), pp. 55–7.

FRONTIER SUPPLY BASES IN THE LATE EMPIRE

A careful reading of the edicts concerning the military *annona* in the *Codex Theodosianus*[1] reveals that at least under the late Empire a system had grown up whereby supplies were organised by *primipilares* (commissary officers) for whole sections of the frontier-garrisons, and that these officials had at their disposal, outside the military fortresses and forts, *horrea* which were central collecting dumps for stores and from which they could make their issues. Some of these *horrea* were located in the neighbouring towns of the frontier area, but others are known from Ammianus Marcellinus[2] to have been distinct units and possibly fortified.

Two recent discoveries in Germany and Austria respectively may give some hint as to what such *horrea* were like in reality.

In 1949 at Trier,[3] as the result of the bombing of a Benedictine abbey with which the literary authorities had always connected the name 'Orrea', late Roman *horrea* of a distinct type were revealed. Their position outside the original city walls, but within an area encompassed by the later walls, on a low plateau overlooking the Moselle was admirable in that it was easily approached, but safe from the river.

The building (Fig. 65) as a whole measured 70·30 × 53·70 metres. It was divided into two long halls 18·95 metres wide internally separated by a long unroofed courtyard. The whole was bound into one architectural unit by the façade walls. Each of the two long halls was divided internally by two longitudinal rows of piers, so placed that a central nave, 5 metres wide, and two side aisles, 6·15 metres wide, was created in each hall. The building was very substantial, with foundations at least 2·40 metres deep and approximately 1·65 metres wide, and the walls were 95 centimetres thick. The technique of building was typical of a late period and consisted of small unworked lumps of limestone set in mortar with a double course of tiles after every four or six layers.

The walls were strengthened on both sides by pilasters, 3·50 metres apart, with a width of 1·20 metres and a projection of 30 centimetres. Exactly half way between these pilasters, which formed a row of blind arcades on the outer side, were placed slit windows. These windows had

[1] See Chapter VIII (p. 288).   [2] Ammianus Marcellinus XIV. 2. 13.
[3] H. Eiden and H. Mylius, 'Untersuchungen an den spätrömischen Horrea von St. Irminen in Trier', *TrierZ* XVIII (1949), 73 ff.

an inside measurement of 1·65 metres (height) and 1·25 metres (width), but narrowed to a slit on the outside only 1·20 metres high and 43 centimetres wide. On the inside the tops of windows were slightly arched in small sandstone blocks alternated with vertical tiles.

The piers were built of sandstone blocks 80 × 80 centimetres and 30–40 centimetres thick. The flooring was of hard plaster supported by

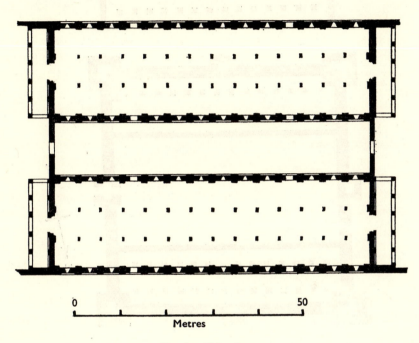

0   50

Metres

Fig. 65   Trier, *horrea*

a lime mortar layer 8 centimetres thick upon a limestone packing 10–15 centimetres thick.

The halls had entrances at each end, perhaps fronted by porticoes, and two smaller doorways equally spaced in each side; and the central yard must have been entered through a gateway in the façade wall. The halls had an upper storey, but there is no evidence for any staircase.

It was claimed by the excavators that it was undoubtedly a store-house and probably for army goods. Its enormous size suggests the military, and the storing of weapons, clothing and equipment may perhaps have been its purpose.

More recently still at Veldidena[1] near Innsbruck has been discovered an exact parallel for the Trier building, but with the added fact that it was fortified. The two halls (Fig. 66) were about 62 metres long ×

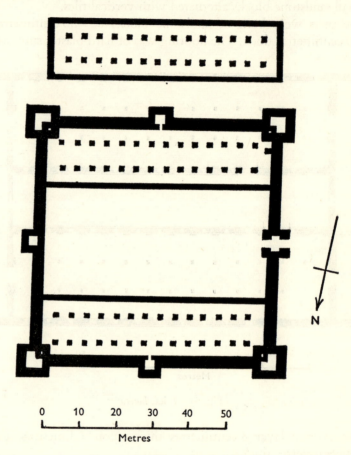

Fig. 66   Veldidena, fortified *horrea*

16 metres wide and separated by a yard some $30\frac{1}{2}$ metres across. The internal arrangements seem to have been exactly the same as those of the Trier example, that is, division into a nave and two aisles by means of two rows of piers in each. However, the whole unit was encompassed by a massive wall, which was built flush against the walls of the

[1] A. Wotschitzky, 'Veldidena: zweiter vorläufiger Bericht über die Ausgrabungen 1954–1957', *ÖJh*, Band xLIV, Beiblatt (1959), 6–70.

halls themselves and which seems to have had four square projecting towers at the four corners of the whole ensemble and three smaller interval towers in the middle of the sides. The fourth side had a more massive gate tower over the entrance to the fort, which opened into the main yard. These fortified *horrea* are dated by coins to the Constantinian period (A.D. 335–61). Apparently they did not afford sufficient storage space, for another single hall of exactly the same dimensions and internal layout was built on the same orientation some 100 yards away. It was without fortification of any kind. The position of the whole ensemble near the frontier, not on it, with good communications and fortifications regarded by the excavators as contemporary, cause it to provide impressive support and illustration of the passage from Ammianus. The internal arrangements of these *horrea*, the division into aisle and naves, need cause no real surprise. For the storage of bulky equipment there was a long tradition, which we can trace back at least as far as Philo's arsenal in the Piraeus and the great building at Eleusis,[1] for such a division into three long units by means of piers. Nor should we forget that in most ordinary rectangular *horrea* the storage may, in fact, have been organised on the same principle—a long central corridor providing access to the laterally stored goods.

There must have been many other fortified *horrea* of this kind in the frontier areas for the system of provisioning implied in the *Codex Theodosianus* to have worked; and one thinks immediately of some of the late Roman *castella* in Gaul. However, a closer examination of those sites reveals no precise parallels for the German examples. At Jublains,[2] although the fort may have been, as Grenier suggests, a fortified post of 'the *fiscus*, the *annona*, and the *cursus publicus*', it was not made up of huge storehouses as at Veldidena.

Perhaps the most important result of the excavations at Veldidena, with their information about the appearance of the fortified *horrea* of the late Empire, is that it must direct attention once more to the small fort-like construction at Brittenburg[3] in Holland.

---

[1] Philo's Arsenal: Durm, *Die Baukunst der Griechen*³, pp. 191 ff.; F. Noack, *Eleusis, die baugeschichtliche Entwicklung des Heiligtums* (Berlin, 1927), pp. 189 ff.

[2] Grenier, *Manuel d'archéologie gallo-romaine* I, p. 450.

[3] J. H. Holwerda, 'Afbeeldingen van de Brittenburg', *Oudheidkundige Mededeelingen* VIII (1927), 1 ff. Franz Oelmann, *Studies presented to David M. Robinson* (ed. Mylonas), I, pp. 451 ff. The latest work on the subject is H. Dijkstra, F. C. J. Ketelaar, *Brittenburg* (Bussum, 1965).

This site, on the sea shore near Katwijk aan Zee immediately to the south of the old Rhine mouth, was revealed in medieval times and attracted such attention that a series of maps and plans of its remarkable foundation walls were made from the early sixteenth to eighteenth centuries. It has since completely disappeared. The site was known by various names, Arx Britannica, burcht te Britten or Brittenburg. In an engraving of 1581 which copied a drawing made by A. Ortellius in 1567/8 the building appears as a four-cornered, square building with sides some 240 *pedes* long, that is, approximately 72 metres. The core of the ensemble was a building strongly constructed in masonry divided down the middle into two rectangular halls of equal size, with the outer walls buttressed on all sides. Around this central building were what seems to be a double system of fortifications, the inner being simply a square of walls while the outer was basically a larger square of walls with great rounded projecting towers—double ones at the corners and a single one in the centre of each side. Two walls, which ran diagonally from the tower in the centre of the side towards the sea, may in fact have belonged to an earlier building. The whole ensemble was considered to be Roman because of the associated finds in the neighbourhood and its similarity to late Roman buildings.

Holwerda, however, has consistently held that Brittenburg was not Roman, but later and belongs in fact to the Carolingian period. He based his belief on three points: (*a*) the Roman finds were made not predominantly at Brittenburg but a kilometre away at Nieuw Vliet or Mallegat in 1571; (*b*) so far as they were dateable they belonged to a middle period of the Empire and are not compatible with the possible late Roman character of the building; (*c*) the positions of other late Roman *castella* on the Rhine were quite different and there are more apt analogies with fortresses of the Middle Ages.

The late Roman date has been defended by A. G. Roos in 1923, Byvanck in 1945 and Franz Oelmann in 1951.[1] Holwerda's assumption that the late Roman *limes* did not pass above Nijmegen has been shown both by archaeological and literary evidence to have been mistaken.

The technique and material of the Carolingian forts were different

---

[1] A. Roos, 'Brittenburg', *Mnemosyne* N.S. II (1923), 327 ff.; A. W. Byvanck, *Nederland in den romeinschen Tijd* II (Leiden, 1945), pp. 420 ff.

and they had no projecting towers. Late Roman fortifications do have such rounded projecting towers and it is even possible to find a Roman parallel with twin towers at the corners.[1]

If, therefore, we may assume the Roman date of the building as proved, we must pass to the further question of what purpose the building served. Oelmann dismissed the possibility of *horrea* on the grounds that the building was too small and a square plan is unusual for *horrea*. He suggested it was a lighthouse which was later fortified.[2] The possible identification as *horrea* has been too lightly dismissed. The size of the buildings is not too small for such a purpose, perhaps some 12 × 25 metres each, and compares well with other examples in German forts. Moreover, we may see in the building two rectangular *horrea* placed side by side and thus evade the objection concerning a square ground plan.

If we are right in detecting some fortified *horrea* here,[3] it may not be out of place to point to the name, Arx Britannica, associated with the building, and recall Ammianus Marcellinus XVIII. 2. 3:

(Julianus Caesar)...civitates multo ante excisas ac vacuas introiret, receptasque communiret, horrea quin etiam extrueret pro incensis, ubi condi possit annona, a Britannis sueta transferri...nam et horrea veloci opere surrexerunt, alimentorumque in isdem satias condita.

The setting of these activities is along the Rhine and the date of them, in the fourth century A.D., is the same as that of the other fortified *horrea*. Perhaps Brittenburg formed part of a chain of such stores.

The importance of these buildings, as has been said, is that for the first time the system of provisioning the garrisons of the frontier in the late Empire, suggested by the *Codex Theodosianus* and supported by meagre

---

[1] Cagnat, *L'armée romaine d'Afrique*, p. 660; Tiaret in North Africa has twin square towers at the corners of its fortifications.

[2] He compared it with the fortification at Richborough; but the great base at the centre of the Richborough fort bears no resemblance in plan to the Brittenburg building and anyway was not a lighthouse. It was originally a great triumphal monument and later stripped to be a watchtower, cf. I. A. Richmond, *Roman Britain* (Harmondsworth, 1955), pp. 147–8. See now the discussion of this monument by D. Strong in *Richborough Report V* (Oxford, 1968), pp. 40 ff.

[3] Since this chapter was written, Dijkstra and Ketelaar, *Brittenburg*, pp. 91 ff., have also supported the idea that the central building at Brittenburg was double *horrea*, later, perhaps in the fourth century A.D., surrounded by fortifications.

literary evidence, is confirmed fully by the archaeological evidence. Their discovery helps to give a more balanced picture of the storage facilities used by the Roman army and to direct our attention away from the *horrea* within the fortresses and forts which have tended to monopolise whatever thought has been given to the problems of the military commissariat in the Empire.

VIII

MILITARY ORGANISATION

The evidence for the organisation of military *horrea* and supplies in the early Empire is relatively slight and often difficult to interpret, while that in the later Empire is much fuller, because of the introduction of a regular tax in kind, the *annona militaris*, for the support of the army. Although the exact date of the introduction of that tax is not known, and will be discussed later, it marks a convenient distinction between the arrangements of the early and late Empire.

EARLY EMPIRE

I

The maintenance of the army under the early Empire was the object of numerous measures, whose burden in fact fell upon the provincials, but no extra tax in kind, such as the *annona militaris* of the late Empire, was levied in general for the support of the army. Hence it is useless to seek for those particular officials and precise arrangements which were characteristic of that tax and are revealed to us by sources such as the *Codex Theodosianus*.

In general, the army was supplied by a series of *ad hoc* measures: special requisitions, foraging expeditions, and above all the system called *frumentum emptum*, grain bought at a fixed price by the State and used for supplementing the *copiae* of the army or the *annona* of Rome itself.[1]

The clearest example of the detailed working of the system of *frumentum emptum* for the army is given by a series of papyri dated A.D. 185-6.[2] They are all concerned with the supply of barley for the *Ala Heracliana* stationed at Koptos and consist of a series of receipts. Three are receipts given by Antonius Justinus, a *duplicarius* dispatched by the prefect of the *ala* to collect the barley due from the villages. In

---

[1] *RE* VII, s.v. *Frumentum*, col. 164 (M. Rostovtseff). Pliny, *Panegyric* 29. Cf. Ogilvie and Richmond, *Tacitus*, 'Agricola' 19 and notes ad loc., for both the system and possible abuses of it.

[2] *P. Ryl.* 85 (A.D. 185), cf. *P. Amh.* 107, 108.

two cases they are addressed to the *strategos* of the nome and in the other to the *basilicogrammateus* who was acting as deputy *strategos*. We may be sure that similar receipts were given to the village elders who supplied the barley, since it is stated each time by Justinus that four copies of his receipts were issued. In each papyrus Justinus acknowledged that he had had measured out to him by the villages concerned that proportion imposed upon them from the 20,000 *artabae* of barley which the Praefect of Egypt had ordered to be *bought up* from a certain year's produce for the requirements of the *ala*. That the barley really was bought from the provincials is shown by the papyrus[1] containing the receipt given to the *strategos* by the village elders, acknowledging that they have received a sum of money from two local officials appointed to collect the money at the government bank for the barley supplied to the *ala*.

Moreover, not only did the government pay the provincials, to some extent at least, for the army supplies, but the soldier too paid for his food. There were regular stoppages from his pay for food, clothing and equipment under the early Empire as the fragments of army accounts show.[2]

2

The evidence concerning the personnel responsible for supplying the troops in this early period is not satisfactory. At first sight we seem to have a mixture of civil and military officials ultimately responsible to a civil authority. Under the general supervision of the secretary *a rationibus* at Rome[3] each province had its governor and his financial assistant, *procurator* or *quaestor*, who were responsible for the payment and feeding of the troops in that province. Most of the details of administration would be carried out by clerks in the *officium rationum*[4] of the province, which must have had close relations with the corresponding *officia* of each legion or auxiliary corps. Van Berchem[5] pours scorn on the idea that there was in the early Empire a central bureau for army supplies, an *officium a copiis* or *cura copiarum exercitus*, which Mommsen and Hirschfeld had assumed. While Van Berchem has shown that Mommsen and Hirschfeld were wrong in thinking that the same central bureau

---

[1] *P. Amh.* 109.
[2] P. A. Brunt, 'Pay and Superannuation in the Roman Army', *PBSR* XVIII (1950), 60 ff.
[3] Statius, *Silvae* III. 3. 98. [4] *CIL* VIII. 3292, III. 1099 = *ILS* 2392.
[5] D. Van Berchem, *L'annone militaire dans l'empire romain au 3ᵉ siècle* (Paris, 1937), p. 142.

was administered in the first century by freedmen and organised in the second century by equestrians (the equestrian appointments were extraordinary ones in time of war), it still remains a fact that the inscriptions of the first-century imperial freedmen described as *a copiis militaribus*[1] were all found in or near Rome itself. The possibility therefore that they formed part of a central bureau for co-ordinating quartermasters' accounts remains strong.

Whether there were in the *officia* of each legion slave *dispensatores* charged with the issuing of supplies, as Van Berchem suggests,[2] seems, however, very doubtful. We only know of such *dispensatores* in a series of undated inscriptions which all come from one fortress, Lambaesis in Africa.[3] Whether there were similar *dispensatores* in all other legionary fortresses is not known. More important, there is no proof that they were concerned with supplies. The fact that in times of war there were *dispensatores rationum copiarum expeditionis*[4] and that in the third century the Greek equivalent of a *dispensator*, an οἰκονόμος, made a monthly payment of corn to an *optio*,[5] do not prove that *dispensatores* were always so employed. The title is non-committal and means anything from 'steward' to 'pay clerk'.

The cost accounting of the soldiers' supplies was done by the *signifer*,[6] who in this period kept the pay accounts of each cohort in which the stoppages of pay for food were entered.

The actual fabric of the *horrea* within the forts at all periods seems to have been the responsibility of the provincial governor, both for the original building and for restoration work.[7] Soldiers with the title *librarii horreorum* are known from the *Digest*,[8] where they are included in a list of *immunes*. That they existed wherever there were *horrea* in forts is likely on general grounds of probability and they will have served presumably much as storemen do in the Army today: responsible for and bound to keep accounts of what was actually in their charge, but working under superior officers and not involved in general

[1] *CIL* VI. 8538–40; *CIL* XIV. 2840 = *ILS* 1571.
[2] Van Berchem, *L'annone militaire*, p. 143.   [3] *CIL* VIII. 3288–91.
[4] *CIL* V. 2155 = *ILS* 1574; *CIL* VI. 8541 = *ILS* 1573.
[5] *P. Oxy.* 735, cf. *CIL* III. 333 = *ILS* 1539.
[6] *PSI* IX. 1063 (A.D. 117), cf. A. von Premerstein, 'Die Buchführung einer ägyptischen Legionsabteilung', *Klio* III (1902–3), 1 ff.
[7] *EE* IX. 1146, cf. *JRS* XXVI (1936), 264; *CIL* VII. 732 for *horrea* in Britain.
[8] *Digest* L. 6. 7.

problems of requisitioning and accounting. Perhaps they were responsible to the *praefectus castrorum*.[1]

We should expect to find *mensores frumenti* associated with these *horrea*, but the only example of a soldier with the precise title *mensor frumenti* attested by an inscription[2] may possibly have acted in that capacity only after his retirement from the army. He is described as *veteranus leg. VIII Aug. stipendiorum XXV mensor frumenti*, whereas his brother on the same stone is *veteranus leg. VIII Aug. imaginifer, stipendiorum XXV*. The placing of *mensor frumenti* after the number of *stipendia* (while his brother's title *imaginifer* is before the number of *stipendia*) may be significant and may indicate that he acted in this capacity only after retirement from the army. The fact that the inscription was found at Aquileia, well known to have had many civil *horrea*,[3] perhaps supports this view and makes it impossible to depend on this evidence. However, soldiers designated *mensor frumenti numer(is)*[4] and *veteranus ex mensore tritici leg. VII Cl.*[5] indicate that, whatever the title, a corn-measuring official perhaps formed part of the organisation of the *horrea* of each fortress or fort.[6]

It has been said earlier that to look in this early period for the officials and arrangements characteristic of the late Roman *annona militaris* would be foolish.

It may not be so foolish, however, to seek for a predecessor, in some sense, to the *primipilares* of the late Empire,[7] in that someone presumably was responsible from the earliest period for ensuring the efficient gathering of supplies for the frontier legions. It has often been assumed that these duties were carried out in the early Empire by either the *frumentarii* or the *evocati*. In fact the evidence is not satisfactory in either case.

The duties of the *frumentarii*[8] in the second and third centuries are not in doubt. In the life of Hadrian it is stated that the Emperor

---

[1] Cf. Vegetius II. 10.　　　　　[2] *CIL* v. 936 = *ILS* 2423 (Vot. trib.).

[3] A. Calderini, *Aquileia Romana* (Milan, 1930), p. cxix.

[4] *CIL* XIII. 7007.　　　　　[5] *ILS* 9091.

[6] *Digest* XLIX. 16. 12. 2 (Macer): officium tribunorum est...frumentationibus commilitonum interesse, frumentum probare, mensorum fraudem coercere.

[7] See pp. 288–9.

[8] In general, *RE* VII, s.v. *Frumentarius*; cf. P. K. Baillie Reynolds, 'The troops quartered in the Castra Peregrinorum', *JRS* XIII (1923), 168 ff.; W. G. Sinnigen, 'The origins of the *Frumentarii*', *MAAR* XXVII (1962), 213 ff.

employed them as secret police.[1] This function and their activities as imperial messengers throughout the empire are attested in many sources for these two centuries. The universal hatred which they incurred led to their abolition under Diocletian, although their job was continued under another name: *agentes in rebus*.[2]

For our purposes there are two linked questions: when were the *frumentarii* created? and why did they have that name? The questions are linked because it makes little sense to suppose that they were *created* under Hadrian as a secret police and given such a name. Moreover, in the Latin papyrus from Geneva[3] giving the military accounts of a legion in Egypt in *Domitian's reign*, one of the soldiers seconded for outside duties *exit cum frum[entariis*. It is possible that their creation goes back to Augustus, although there are no explicitly first-century inscriptions referring to them.

In the first century at least these soldiers must have been associated with corn supplies in some way. It has generally been assumed that the association was particularly with military supplies and that these men formed an elite and trained body for the supplies of the legions.[4] Moreover, the restoration of a mutilated inscription[5]—*Aurelius Lucianus frumentarius [in] legionem II Itali[cam missus ad] frum[en]tarias [res curandas]*—has been used to show that they could retain their original functions into the late second century (for *legio II Italica* was raised by Marcus Aurelius) after their conversion into imperial enquiry agents.

Their later activities as spies and messengers are assumed to have grown naturally from their earlier functions as 'commissaires de vivres' which had necessitated much travelling to and from Rome where they stayed at the *Castra Peregrinorum* from the end of the first century A.D., if not earlier. Although it is clear that the use of the *frumentarii* as messengers and spies must have grown out of the fact that they travelled widely and kept returning to Rome, it is difficult to see why constant travelling to Rome should have been necessary for legionary supply agents in normal times. It seems to me that we should not rule out the possibility that the *frumentarii*, although soldiers, were not necessarily associated with the supplies for the army but with the

[1] SHA, *Hadrian* 11. 4. [2] Aur. Vict., *Caes.* 39. 44.
[3] *P. Geneva Lat.* 1. Recto 11. T. Flavius Celer.
[4] Cagnat, *L'armée romaine d'Afrique*, pp. 320 ff. Baillie Reynolds, 'The troops quartered in the Castra Peregrinorum', pp. 183 ff. Sinnigen, 'The origins of the *Frumentarii*', p. 214, note 10. [5] *CIL* VI. 3340.

ordinary civil supplies for Rome.[1] In the same Latin papyrus from Geneva soldiers were detached for duties in connection with the Egyptian corn supply[2] and it may be that the duties of the *frumentarii* in the first century A.D. necessitated their travelling to and from Rome on the grain ships from the provinces.

A similar document from Moesia Inferior, dated A.D. 105–8, reveals soldiers detached for duties *ad naves frumentarias*.[3] Those ships may have been concerned with military supplies, but an earlier inscription concerning a legate of Moesia, *circa* A.D. 60–7, Ti. Plautius Silvanus Aelianus, in which it is claimed that he *primus ex ea provincia magno tritici modo annonam p(opuli) R(omani) adlevavit*, reveals the possibility of shipments of corn to Rome from that area and under military supervision.[4] That soldiers were regularly employed partly as guards on the grain ships going down the Nile is proved by papyri.[5] It seems unlikely that the *frumentarii* were simply guards: their duties may have been supervisory and may have extended to being military commanders on the grain ships. There is no direct evidence to support such a view (no more than any other), but this one would have the advantage of explaining why these men travelled to and from Rome so much, why special quarters, the *Castra Peregrinorum*, were permanently available for them in Rome, and finally it would make the extension of their duties in the second and third centuries to cover the delivery of messages, the escort of prisoners and the duties of espionage less surprising.

Certainly such evidence as there is hardly supports the idea that they were only legionary commissariat officers. Moreover, on that supposition, we would have a further problem of finding replacements for them after the reign of Hadrian or subtle arguments to show that they could have combined both old and new duties without difficulty.

The evidence concerning the *evocati*[6] is not much more satisfactory.

---

[1] Cf. M. Rostovtseff, 'Frumentum', *RE* VII (1912), col. 181.

[2] *P. Geneva Lat.* I. Recto II. M. Papirius Rufus *exit ad frumentum Neapoli*.

[3] R. O. Fink, 'Hunt's *Pridianum*: British Museum Papyrus 2851', *JRS* XLVIII (1958), 102 ff.; cf. R. Syme, 'The Lower Danube under Trajan', *JRS* XLIX (1959), 26 ff. Particular reference is to col. ii, lines 31–3.

[4] *ILS* 986. The exact date of his legateship in Moesia is disputed but it was certainly under Nero. L. R. Taylor, 'Trebula Suffenas and the Plautii Silvani', *MAAR* XXIV (1956), 29.

[5] *P. Oxy.* 276 (A.D. 77), cf. *P. Oxy.* 522 (second century) and *P. Lond.* 256 Recto (*a*).

[6] *EE* V, pp. 151 ff. (T. Mommsen).

It is true that there seems to be one *evocatus* attached to each legion, that he was closely attached to that legion (unlike the *frumentarii*) and that his duties were generally administrative. However, there is only one inscription[1] which attests a close connection with the com- missariat—*ex evokat., qui se probavit ann. XVII, militavit coh. XI urb. ann. XIII pavit leg. X Gem.* Fiebiger[2] relying on this inscription claimed that the *evocatus* attached to each legion, even when no information as to his duties is given, will have been responsible for its supplies. This is possible, but an *evocatus*[3] at Lambaesis was *curator tabularii castrorum* and we should be wary of simply assuming that the *evocatus* was always responsible for supplies.

So much for the provincial troops. Within the city of Rome itself the Praetorian and Urban Cohorts and the *Vigiles* all acquired the right to draw their supplies from the state storehouses.[4] However, at the beginning of the third century, a time when it is known that the *Vigiles* had this right, two large dedicatory inscriptions were set up to Caracalla by the *Vigiles* in which a man, M. Ulpius Irenaeus, is des- cribed on one as *ho(rrearius)* and on the other as *h(orrearius) c(ohortis)*.[5] The most natural interpretation would be that this is a reference to the *Vigiles'* own storehouses administered by their own men. But what need would they have of such storehouses? The position is further complicated by another dedication made earlier, in A.D. 113, by the *principales* of the fifth cohort of the *Vigiles*, among whom is listed C. Peturcius Pudens, *hor. leg.*[6] The suggested reading is *hor(rearius) leg(ionis?)*. Romanelli[7] has therefore suggested that we should not exclude the possibility that these men may have served as *horrearii* in the state storehouses or other sections of the army and were thus seconded away from their units for these duties. It is difficult to see why *Vigiles* should have been seconded to other units for such duties, and it is certain that in these inscriptions they are listed among other men whose duties were clearly within their own units. It would be very odd to include seconded men on the inscriptions without explanation.

---

1 *CIL* VI. 2893 = *ILS* 2144.   2 *RE* VI, s.v. *evocatus*, col. 1150.
3 *CIL* VIII. 2852. Cf. A. von Domaszewski, *Die Rangordnung des römischen Heeres*[2] (Cologne, 1967), p. 77, note 4.
4 De Ruggiero, *Diz. Epig.* III, s.v. *frumentatio* (G. Cardinali), pp. 261 ff.
5 *CIL* VI. 1057. 2. 87 (A.D. 205); VI. 1058. 2. 4 (A.D. 210) = *ILS* 2157.
6 *CIL* VI. 221 = *ILS* 2160 (A.D. 113); cf. von Domaszewski, *Die Rangordnung des römischen Heeres*[2], p. 14, note 3.
7 Romanelli, p. 980, col. 2.

Moreover, since even in the third century A.D. the right to corn from the state storehouses was dependent on the grant of the *ius quiritium*, which was given to the freedmen *Vigiles* only *after* three years' service,[1] it can be seen that the *Vigiles* would have need of their own *horrea* for the newly enlisted. Thus the presence of men with the title *horrearius* can be explained, although there is still a problem concerning the *hor(rearius) leg-(ionis?)* if that really was the title of Peturcius Pudens.

LATE EMPIRE

I

The most important single change in the provisioning of the army under the Empire was the introduction of the *annona militaris*, a regular tax in kind imposed upon the provinces for the support of the army.[2] Since it was the creation of that tax which encouraged the distinctive organisation of *horrea* and supplies known to us from the *Codex Theodosianus* for at least the fourth century A.D., it is of importance to know *when* that tax was introduced.

Van Berchem in a stimulating study, *L'annone militaire*, has argued that the *annona militaris* was introduced at the beginning of the third century A.D. by Septimius Severus,[3] and this thesis has not to my knowledge been publicly examined and questioned. Brunt[4] has indicated that certain pieces of evidence will not bear the strain which Van Berchem puts upon them, but I believe that in general Van Berchem's conclusion goes beyond what his evidence warrants and that in at least one case the evidence has been completely misinterpreted. There seems to be more plausibility in Rostovtseff's view[5] that certain irregular practices grew up in the third century and that Diocletian transformed what had been essentially emergency measures into a system, whose workings are revealed in the fourth-century *Codex Theodosianus*.

The main objection to Van Berchem's dating is that there is not one piece of explicit evidence for the *annona militaris* as a regular tax in the

[1] *CIL* VI. 220 and notes = *ILS* 2163.

[2] Van Berchem, *L'annone militaire*; Cagnat, *L'armée romaine d'Afrique*, pp. 315 ff.; Romanelli, p. 980.

[3] Van Berchem, *L'annone militaire*, pp. 146 ff.

[4] P. A. Brunt, 'Pay and superannuation in the Roman army', *PBSR* XVIII (1950), 60, note 75. Cf. F. Millar, *A Study of Cassius Dio* (Oxford, 1964), p. 152, note 3.

[5] Rostovtseff, *SEHRE* I, pp. 484, 517; II, p. 712, note 15.

third century. Apart from general arguments about the care shown by Septimius Severus for the troops, Van Berchem uses three main types of argument. (A) Arguments from association: in particular, the argument that, because officials called *actuarii* made their appearance at the beginning of the third century and local senates were introduced in the townships of Egypt at that time, the *annona militaris*, with which they were connected later in the fourth century, was also introduced at that period.[1] (B) Arguments from specific papyri dated to the beginning of the third century A.D., where food seems to be described as issued free to the troops or the word *annona* is mentioned.[2] (C) Arguments from the Antonine Itinerary: it is Van Berchem's ingenious and plausible hypothesis that at least the section of the Itinerary from Rome to Egypt represents the *mansiones* and *stationes* of Caracalla's eastern expedition in A.D. 214–15—the points at which he, his entourage and army could stay and be revictualled. Van Berchem then asks, 'n'est-il pas logique de supposer que les mansiones, bureaux de recettes de l'annone au IVe siècle, l'étaient déjà au début du IIIe?'[3] The supposition seems to me to be not logical and the only real evidence quoted by Van Berchem to have been misinterpreted.

From the appearance of the *actuarii* (or *actarii*) at the beginning of the third century we can deduce no more than that some reform in legionary accounting had taken place. What they did is clear only from their title: they were concerned with the *acta* in which was written daily *totius...legionis ratio sive obsequiorum sive militarium munerum sive pecuniae*.[4] We cannot *assume* that their association with the *annona militaris* revealed by the *Codex Theodosianus* and the famous outburst by Aurelius Victor[5] in the fourth century began as early as this. The fact that at this period they seem to have been recruited from military men and not from civilians,[6] as in the fourth century, may hint at further differences between their activities in the two periods.

Similarly, the introduction of a local senate at Alexandria and at the metropolis of each nome by Septimius Severus on the occasion of his visit to Egypt in A.D. 199–201, although it probably had some tax

---

[1] Van Berchem, *L'annone militaire*, pp. 135 ff. (*actuarii*) and pp. 149 ff. (local senates).
[2] *Ibid.* pp. 146 ff.   [3] *Ibid.* pp. 166 ff., particularly p. 169.
[4] Vegetius II. 19. For the name *vid. Thesaurus Ling. Lat.*, s.v. *actuarius*.
[5] *De Caes.* 33. 13.
[6] *CIL* II. 2663 = *ILS* 2335; *CIL* VIII. 2554 = *ILS* 2445 add., cf. *Cod. Theod.* VII. 4. 24.

purpose, may well, as Wilcken[1] suggested, be no more than an attempt to ensure the more efficient raising of taxes already in existence, rather than to establish new machinery for the raising of a brand new tax, as Van Berchem believes. The fact that these senates were later occupied with the raising of the military *annona*, as well as the other taxes, is no proof that this tax existed at the beginning of the third century.

With regard to the arguments from specific papyri and ostraka, Brunt[2] has pointed out that the ostraka from Dakka in Nubia in the reigns of Severus and Caracalla, which are inscribed with receipts given to an *optio* for corn by soldiers of an equitate cohort, show *not* that there were supplementary payments in kind to troops as early as this, but quite the reverse, that even under Caracalla troops had deductions made from their pay for food, since these issues of supplies were simply advances against pay.

Moreover, papyri and ostraka, which appear for the first time at the beginning of the third century A.D. and which mention payments in kind by provincials for the *annona*, do not in themselves constitute any proof that a regular *annona militaris* was at that time imposed on the provincials. The evidence which Van Berchem cites for payments under that heading in the reigns of Severus and Caracalla in Egypt can all be explained as part of the *extraordinary* taxes imposed upon the province to support the entourage of Severus when he visited the province in A.D. 199 and to support the imperial entourage and armies of Caracalla's eastern expedition in A.D. 214–15. It may also be incorrect to assume for lack of evidence that the government did not pay the provincials at least in part for these extraordinary levies. A Florentine papyrus furnishes important evidence for Severus' visit to Egypt.[3] The Emperor intended to inspect the whole country and preparations were made for his journey, the maintenance of the Emperor, his suite and his soldiers falling upon the provincials as usual. The papyrus is the report of the village scribes to the *strategos* regarding the distribution of the payments of cows, calves, goats, corn, hay and wine. But at the beginning is quoted in full the letter of Arrius Victor,

---

[1] U. Wilcken and L. Mitteis, *Grundzüge und Chrestomathie der Papyruskunde*, I, p. 41 and p. 217.

[2] Brunt, 'Pay and superannuation', p. 60, note 75. U. Wilcken, *Griechische Ostraka aus Aegypten und Nubien* (Leipzig, 1899), 1128–46, receipts for corn given ἄχρι τοῦ ὀψωνίου ἐν προχρ[είᾳ] etc. He also points out that it is doubtful whether Dio 78. 34. 3 refers to the military *annona*, cf. Dio 78. 28. 2.

[3] *PSI* 683, cf. U. Wilcken, *ArchPF* VII (1924), 84 ff.

the *epistrategus* to the *strategoi* of the Arsinoite nome. It asks for a report on the distribution of payments εἰ[ς τὴν] ἀννῶναν τοῖς κ[υ]ρίοις ἡμῶν and in the next paragraph (lines 14 ff.) states that money has been advanced by the treasury to the governor for the cost of the goods.

The suggestion that the word *annona* in such contexts refers to extraordinary and irregular levies and not to a permanent tax is borne out by other more general evidence in the third century. Paul and Ulpian refer to *indictiones temporariae*[1] and Modestinus to *onera annonarum et contributionum temporariarum*.[2]

Van Berchem[3] argues that that part of the Antonine Itinerary which covers the journey from Rome to Egypt was based ultimately on a public edict of Caracalla. This edict published in advance the programme of his journey to the east, giving warning of where he would go, where he was to stay, and where he and his army should be fed. That such edicts were published in elaborate detail in the third century, in order to give warning to the provincials, is known from the reign of Severus Alexander.[4] This suggestion is very plausible and it has been in part borne out by the discovery of an inscription which refers to the arrangements for Caracalla's eastern expedition at Apamea.[5] What then of the remainder of the Antonine Itinerary? Van Berchem's view is that in the third century troop movements regularly gave rise to such edicts and that they were issued even when a *vexillatio* left an army or rejoined its camp, and that the Antonine Itinerary was thus built up over a period of time. It seems, however, more likely that the original creation of the itineraries, other than the one from Rome to Egypt, was similarly brought about by the great expeditions of other Emperors, for example, Septimius Severus' expeditions to Britain and Africa.

Van Berchem, believing that the *annona militaris* had already been established under Severus and that the *mansiones* and *stationes* of the imperial *cursus publicus* were being used already as the regular collecting depots for this tax and for its disbursement to the troops, sees in Caracalla's itinerary an example of the normal working of the system, unusual only in the greater number of troops involved. All the evidence, however, suggests that the arrangements were not based on the normal

---

[1] *Digest* 33. 2. 28.   [2] *Digest* 26. 7. 32. 6.

[3] Van Berchem, *L'annone militaire*, pp. 166 ff.   [4] SHA, *Severus Alexander* 45.

[5] R. Mouterde, 'Une dédicace d'Apamée de Syrie à l'approche de Caracalla et l'*Itinerarium Antonini*', *CRAI* (1952), p. 355 = *IGLS* 1346; but cf. L. Robert, 'Bulletin épigraphique', *REG* LXVII (1954), no. 244.

system, but were extraordinary levies made by the Emperor in connection with his expeditionary forces. In the account of the edict issued by Severus Alexander it is stated *deinde per ordinem mansiones, deinde stativae, deinde ubi annona esset accipienda*. Special arrangements had to be made concerning where the army should be supplied: the ordinary working of a normal system was not assumed. It is true that later in the life of the same Emperor[1] it is said *milites expeditionis tempore sic disposuit ut in mansionibus annonas acciperent, nec portarent cibaria decem et septem, ut solent, dierum nisi in barbarico*, but the implication is that these were special arrangements *expeditionis tempore* and revealed the unusual care shown by Severus Alexander for his troops. Further, if Caracalla was simply using a system already in operation for provisioning troops, Dio Cassius, the *amicus* and councillor of Caracalla, was curiously ignorant of the fact. His record[2] of the provincials' complaints reads oddly if there were a regular *annona militaris* tax in operation throughout the empire already. They complained only and precisely about Caracalla's arrangements.

Finally, Van Berchem puts great emphasis upon the constitution of the *mansio*[3] set up by the governor of Thrace at Pizos in A.D. 202, the year in which Septimius Severus visited that country. Quite apart from the fact that in this case too the arrangements were being made in connection with a visit from the Emperor and his entourage and were therefore not necessarily typical of the normal system, there can be little doubt that Van Berchem has misconstrued the inscription. He lays great stress upon a section of the inscription which refers to παράλημψις and παράδοσις by the ἄρχοντες and τόπαρχοι of the *mansio*, and how their goods are to be held as security ἀπὸ τοῦ χρόνου τῆς παραλήμψεως μέχρι τῆς παραδόσεως. Παράλημψις he claims was the technical term regularly employed for the collection of taxes and particularly the *annona*, while παράδοσις was the term for the distribution to the troops. A careful reading of the inscription shows that παράλημψις and παράδοσις do *not* refer to the collection and distribution of taxes at all, but pick up the verbs παραλαμβάνειν and παραδιδόναι of the previous sentence. There the concern is for the preservation and upkeep of the buildings of the *mansio*.[4] The rule is laid down that there must be a

[1] SHA, *Severus Alexander* 47.   [2] Dio 77. 9. 6.

[3] *IGRR* 766, cf. Dittenberger, *Sylloge*³, 880.

[4] Van Berchem's misinterpretation of this point has also been noticed by L. Robert, 'Inscriptions de Bithynie', *REA* xlii (1940), 307, note 6.

proper 'take-over' of the property by the men in charge and a proper 'transfer' of the property to those who succeed them (μεθ' ἑαυτούς). While the buildings are within their charge, their goods are held as security and they are liable for a fourfold fine in case of loss and damage. Thus the only evidence that the *mansiones* were used at the beginning of the third century to collect the *annona militaris* and distribute it to the troops collapses.

Even though we cannot date the introduction of the *annona militaris* to the reign of Septimius Severus, it seems clear that it was as a result of the extraordinary levies for the great troop movements in the third century, and the development of the *cursus publicus* as a result of the progresses of the Emperors and their armies, that both the idea of a regular tax on the provinces for the support of the army and the machinery for raising it were developed. If it was Diocletian at the end of the century who introduced the *annona militaris*, he was not creating a new tax to be raised by a new means so much as systematising a situation which had developed gradually in the third century.

2

How then was the *annona militaris* organised in the fourth century?[1] The main body of evidence in the *Codex Theodosianus* is grouped in Book 7, Chapter 4 under the heading *De Erogatione Militaris Annonae*. The imperial rescripts there collected were aimed at particular abuses and irregularities and it is only by piecing together incidental references that we are able to build up any picture of the whole.

The main outlines of the organisation seem clear. The *susceptor* (collector of the tax) shall make no issues from the *horrea* for troops without first having received a *pittacium authenticum* (a requisition ticket in the form of a receipt) from the *actuarius* or *actarius* (military accountant).[2] These *pittacia authentica* were to be handed in by the *actuarii* to the *susceptores* either daily or every two days or at the end of thirty days.[3]

Although there is no evidence in the *Codex Theodosianus* itself as to the relationship between these *actuarii* and the *optiones* mentioned with

---

[1] Cf. A. H. M. Jones, *The Later Roman Empire* (Oxford, 1964), I, pp. 456 ff.; II, pp. 626 ff.

[2] *Cod. Theod.* VII. 4. 11 (A.D. 364).

[3] *Cod. Theod.* VII. 4. 11; *Cod. Theod.* VII. 4. 13 (A.D. 365); *Cod. Theod.* VII. 4. 16 (A.D. 370 or 373).

them in three passages,[1] it is very probable, given the general character of the *optio*'s duties,[2] that the *optiones* acted at the level of the *centuriae* and were responsible for the actual distribution of supplies to the troops, once they had been issued by the *susceptores*.[3] The amounts of supplies issued by the *susceptores* were carefully checked in the central office of the province against the *breves* (the account books with the annual requirements of the army) and if it was clear that the *actuarii* and *optiones* had received more than their due, they had to restore twofold the amount.[4]

Thus far there is little difficulty in understanding the system, at least in outline, and the relationships of the various officials one to the other. But there is a further official, *subscribendarius*, mentioned in one passage concerning the military *annona*.[5] The fact that in this passage the *subscribendarius* is coupled with the *optio* and regarded as responsible with him seems to suggest that the *subscribendarius* was in some sense similar to the *actuarius*, with whom the *optio* is usually coupled.[6] Gothofredus, however, in his commentary on the passage, pointed out that, whereas the *actuarii* formed part of individual units and were concerned only with the military accounts of those units, there was only one *subscribendarius* in the *officium* of each of the *Comites* and *Duces*, according to the *Notitia Dignitatum*, in the eastern part of the Empire.[7]

Cagnat[8] therefore cast the *subscribendarius* in the rôle of 'contrôleur du service des vivres au IVe siècle'. He based this suggestion upon Gothofredus' commentary and upon a passage in the *Codex Theodosianus*,[9] where the responsibility for the efficient working of the system of receipts was placed on the *actuarius*, the *susceptor* and the *officium iudicantis, quod non institerit huic iussioni*. To the *subscribendarius*, in Cagnat's view, were submitted all requisition tickets for his stamp of approval and he was thus the administrative head of this service.

There are certain objections to such a view. Although it is clear that the *subscribendarius* was a civil official rather than a military one, it is

---

[1] *Cod. Theod.* VII. 4. I.

[2] Vegetius, *De re milit.* II. 7, cf. von Domaszewski, *Die Rangordnung des römischen Heeres*[2], pp. I ff.

[3] Confirmation of this rôle, at least in Egypt, is given by ostraka.

[4] *Cod. Theod.* VII. 4. 24 (A.D. 398).   [5] *Cod. Theod.* VII. 4. I (A.D. 325).

[6] D–S, s.v. *subscribendarius*.

[7] *Notitia Dignitatum*, ed. Seeck. The comparable equivalent in the west has the title *regerendarius*.

[8] Cagnat, *L'armée romaine d'Afrique*, p. 323.   [9] *Cod. Theod.* VII. 4. 13 (A.D. 364).

very doubtful whether we can attribute such importance to him. First, it is not clear that the *officium* of the provincial governor was held responsible because the man charged with approving the supplies was a member of it, or because such an *officium*, whatever its normal duties, had to see that the Emperor's edicts, of which the passage in question (*Cod. Theod.* VII. 4. 13) was one, were obeyed.

Secondly, and more important, the title *subscribendarius* is a general term, which could be applied to any man with secretarial duties, with perhaps some emphasis on countersigning of orders and receipts. It can be used, like similar titles such as *cornicularius*, almost indiscriminately: if it reveals anything about the rank of the person concerned, it would suggest some lowly occupation. Indeed the only other reference in the *Codex Theodosianus* to *subscribendarii*[1] includes them with *tabularii*, *diurnarii* and other minor officials, and states that provided they have enough wealth and a certain modicum of education they can be joined to a municipal council on completion of their service, *si, cum in officiis essent vilioribus, nulla eos suppliciorum macula turpaverit*. The suggestion, therefore, that in relation to the military supply system they were merely minor clerks associated with the countersigning of orders and receipts for the issue of supplies to the soldiers is very strong indeed.

It is clear that the organisation involved a mixture of civilian officials (*susceptores*, *praepositi pagorum et horreorum* and, in the fourth century, *actuarii*) and purely military men (*optiones* and *tribuni*). The really important figure in the organisation in the fourth century was the *actuarius*. The frequency with which these men are mentioned in the *Codex Theodosianus*[2] and the preoccupation of successive Emperors with malpractice by them reveals their importance and their opportunities for fraud.[3] If further proof were needed both of their importance and their bad character, Aurelius Victor[4] could supply it: *genus hominum, praesertim hac tempestate nequam, venale, callidum, seditiosum, habendi cupidum atque ad patrandas fraudes velandasque quasi ab natura factum, annonae dominans...* They were in the fourth century civil officials and only the fact that they were under the control of the

[1] *Cod. Theod.* VIII. 4. 8 (A.D. 364).
[2] O. Gradenwitz, *Heidelberger Index zum Theodosianus* (Berlin, 1925), s.v. *actuarius*.
[3] For example, *Cod. Theod.* VII. 4. 24 (A.D. 398); VII. 4. 28 (A.D. 406); VIII. 1. 10 (A.D. 365).
[4] *De Caes.* 33. 13.

Magistri Militum and their offices recalled their former military status.[1] Indeed, in A.D. 392 it was expressly ordered that *actuarii* should not be protected by the *privilegium militare*.[2] Constantly the Emperors were concerned to stress the lowly functions and condition of the *actuarii*. They were to be *condicionales*, of ignoble status and therefore subject to torture. They were to perform only their own duties and not to usurp positions of greater dignity.[3] In the time of Valentinian their duties were to last for ten years, after which period, if their administration received a good report from the units they served, they received the title *perfectissimus* and might hope for higher office.[4] It is clear, however, that despite the Emperors, the *actuarii* wielded enormous power, even to the point of being able to stir up revolt among the troops.[5]

Confirmation and illustration of the detail of this organisation are given by papyri of the late Empire found in Egypt.[6] To take just one example: a papyrus from Oxyrhynchus, dated A.D. 295, gives an account of supplies, chiefly of fodder, issued by ἐπιμεληταί of the Oxyrhynchite nome to units designated by the names of their *praepositi*.[7] The issues were actually made to, and the receipts given by, the *optiones* of these units (or in his place a *tesserarius*, a *librarius* or *exceptores*). The list gives (a) the name of the man to whom the supplies were issued, together with his rank, in the dative; (b) the name of the commander of the unit in the formula ὑπὸ—πρεπόσιτον, and if the receipt given was in Latin, there follows (c) the formula ἀκολούθως Ῥωμαϊκῇ αὐτοῦ φρουμαρίᾳ, and then (d) the amount issued. If, however, the receipt given to the ἐπιμεληταί was in Greek, a copy of it is inserted after the phrase τῆς δὲ φρουμαρίας ἐστὶν ἀντίγραφον. These receipts took the following form. The preamble included the name of the recipient together with his rank, in the nominative, the name of the commander of the unit in the formula ὑπὸ—πρεπόσιτον and the name or names of the ἐπιμεληταί Ὀξυρυγχίτου with their title, in the dative; then followed 'I have received from you—. Signed—.' There are slight variations in the phrasing of this. Sometimes

---

[1] *Cod. Theod.* VIII. 1. 15 (A.D. 415).   [2] *Cod. Theod.* XII. 1. 125 (A.D. 392).
[3] *Cod. Theod.* VIII. 1. 5 (A.D. 357).
[4] *Cod. Theod.* VIII. 1. 10 (A.D. 365).   [5] Cf. Ammianus Marcellinus 25. 10. 7.
[6] Van Berchem, *L'annone militaire*, pp. 154 ff.; J. Lesquier, *L'armée romaine d'Égypte d'Auguste à Dioclétien* (Cairo, 1918), chapter VIII; H. I. Bell, V. Martin, E. G. Turner, D. Van Berchem, *The Abbinaeus Archive* (Oxford, 1962), pp. 16 ff.
[7] *P. Oxy.* 43, cf. *P. Oxy.* 735.

the word μόνους is introduced after the amount, sometimes the number of days, for which the amount was intended, is given, sometimes the signature formula is more elaborate: σεσημίωμαι ἐμῇ χειρί.

The parallel with the passages in the *Codex Theodosianus* is remarkably close. Clearly φρουμαρία (φορμαρία, φορμαλεία) is equivalent to the Latin *pittacium* and the ἐπιμεληταί are charged with functions similar to those of the *susceptores*. They were αἱρεθέντες ὑπὸ τῆς κρατίστης βουλῆς, just as the *susceptores* were chosen by the local *ordo* each year to collect the *annona* imposed on each city.[1]

The main implication of the system of provisioning outlined above is that large numbers of troops in the fourth century A.D. were scattered throughout the provinces, split into small units, and that the whole army was not, as in the early Empire, grouped in large units almost exclusively on the frontiers. This system of provisioning, at least in its most *elaborate* form, with its massive bureaucracy and the issuing of supplies to soldiers every two or three days by local civil officials from state storehouses, implies both that the soldiers were stationed near local communities and that they probably had no storehouses of their own. It is clear that, although some of the *horrea* mentioned in these passages of the *Codex Theodosianus* were perhaps 'greniers militaires'[2] in the sense that they were state storehouses reserved almost exclusively for military use, military *horrea* in the sense of those granaries *within* forts and fortresses, known to us so well from excavations, are *not* in question in these passages. This system, therefore, in its most detailed form would be applicable only for local garrison troops within highly organised provinces, such as Egypt, or made possible in other areas by the development of the system of *mansiones*.

3

What of the troops stationed permanently on the frontiers, the *limitanei*? What of the mobile forces, kept in the frontier areas used for waging wars and meeting any barbarian invasion—the *comitatenses*? The *Codex Theodosianus* reveals that in accordance with the general

[1] *P. Tebt.* 403, *C.P. Herm.* 92 and 93; cf. *Cod. Theod.* XII. 1. 8 (A.D. 323), XII. 6. 20 (A.D. 386).

[2] Cagnat, *L'armée romaine d'Afrique*, p. 316, note 2, seems not clear on this distinction and simply divides what he calls military (e.g. *Cod. Theod.* VII. 4. 16 and 32) from what he calls civil *horrea* (e.g. *Cod. Theod.* XII. 6. 16).

principle that transport of supplies over long distances was to be avoided,[1] there was a specific order that frontier troops should have supplies brought by the nearest provincials to the fortress or fort itself.[2] The organisation of these supplies rested with officials called *primipilares* (commissary officers).[3] Despite the military ring to their title, typical of the quasi-military organisation of the administration under the late Empire, they were in fact civilian officials, retired members of the provincial *officium*, particularly associated with provisioning of frontier troops: *qui ad pascendos milites sollemniter ad limitem destinantur.*[4] That they were responsible also for the *comitatenses*, in the East at any rate, appears from the order of Gratian: *a primipilaribus...species horreis erogandae comitatensibus militaribus ex more deferrentur, limitaneis vero pretia darentur.*[5]

The basic pattern in the organisation of frontier supplies was much the same as that for other soldiers. Supplies were organised by non-military officials and delivered straight to the fortresses and forts, or drawn from *horrea* outside them, central collecting places, no doubt, indicated by the *primipilares.* Accounts had to be carefully kept by these officials and supervised by the central authority.[6] But while basically the pattern was the same, the differences must have been no less significant: special commissary officers were used instead of the local *susceptores* and, although this is never expressly stated, supplies must have been organised and issued for much longer periods—the frontier forts had their own granaries calculated to hold up to a year's supplies.[7]

We have seen that none of the ordinances in the *Codex Theodosianus* can be regarded as concerning the *horrea* located within the fortresses and forts. On the other hand the same ordinances reveal that not only the local *susceptores*, but also the *primipilares* in less well-organised areas, had at their disposal *horrea* used for storing military supplies. Where were these? Some of them clearly were located in towns. In the life of Gordian III we learn of the Prefect Timesitheus in the third century that

[1] *Cod. Theod.* XI. 1. 21 and 22 (A.D. 385 and 386), cf. Tac. *Agricola* 19. 3.
[2] *Cod. Theod.* VII. 4. 15 (A.D. 369).
[3] A. Müller, 'Die Primipilares und der pastus primipili', *Philologus*, n.s. XXI (1908), 134 ff.
[4] *Cod. Theod.* VIII. 4. 6 (A.D. 358).   [5] *Cod. Theod.* VIII. 4. 17 (A.D. 389).
[6] *Cod. Theod.* VIII. 4. 6 (A.D. 358), accounts to be kept in office of provincial governor, cf. *P. Oxy.* 1115.
[7] Collingwood and Haverfield, *CW²* XX (1920), 127 ff.; Richmond, *PSAS* LXXIII (1938/9), 129 ff.

cuius viri tanta in re publica dispositio fuit ut nulla esset umquam civitas limitanea potior et quae posset exercitum populi Romani ac principem ferre, quae totius anni in aceto, frumento et larido atque hordeo et paleis condita non haberet, minores vero urbes aliae triginta dierum, aliae quadraginta, nonnullae duum mensium, quae minimum, quindecim dierum.[1]

Others were located in strongly fortified and suitably placed *loca*:

et quoniam inedia gravi afflictabantur, locum petivere Paleas nomine, vergentem in mare, valido muro firmatum, ubi conduntur nunc usque commeatus, distribui militibus omne latus Isauriae defendentibus assueti.[2]

These *loca* must have been great central supply dumps into which officials like the *primipilares* could gather supplies before dividing them between individual forts.

It must have been at points like these that the system of *mansiones*[3] throughout the provinces became part of a system of rear supply bases for the frontiers. Normally the *mansiones* were used by the ordinary *susceptores* for the collection and storage of taxes in kind along the main routes of the Empire, but the fortified fourth-century *horrea* at Veldidena[4] near Innsbruck in Austria, although situated on the main route north from Italy through the Brenner Pass, must have been a suitable base to be used by *primipilares* for frontier supply.[5]

4

In conclusion, the salient fact about the evidence for military *horrea* organisation under the late Empire, despite its fullness, remains that there is no information about the organisation of *horrea* within the fortresses and forts which archaeology has revealed. The tribunes, of course, had a general responsibility for the troops' food,[6] but who actually presided over these *horrea* under the late Empire is never

---

[1] SHA, *Vita Gord. III.* 28. (Possibly a projection of fourth-century conditions back into the third century.)

[2] Ammianus Marcellinus XIV. 2. 13.

[3] See Grenier, *Manuel d'archéologie gallo-romaine* I, p. 437. Cf. *Cod. Theod.* XII. 6. 21 and 19 (A.D. 386 and 383), XI. 1. 21 (A.D. 385).

[4] Wotschitzky, *ÖJh* XLIV (1959), Beiblatt, pp. 6 ff.

[5] The disputed building at Brittenburg in Holland may have served a similar purpose (see p. 267). Compare also the forts at Corbridge and South Shields in Britain; Richmond and Gillam, *AA*[4] XXVIII (1950), 152 ff.; I. A. Richmond, *The Roman Fort at South Shields: A Guide* (South Shields, 1953), p. 2.

[6] *Digest*, XLIX. 16. 12. 2 (Macer).

stated. A quotation from Tarruntenus Paternus (*floruit*, second half of the second century A.D.) in the *Digest*[1] shows that there were soldiers in his time known as *horreorum librarii* and that they ranked as *immunes*. There are no inscriptions to elaborate or confirm this evidence, but it seems not unlikely that soldiers with this or a similar title existed at all periods of the Empire.

POSTSCRIPT

In time of war, at *whatever* period of the Empire, the importance of military *horrea* was of course greatly increased. Among the many inscriptions recording the special commissioners,[2] often equestrians, appointed to look after military supplies in wars and expeditions, whose duties must in fact have covered the problems of storage, there are two which specifically mention the care of *horrea*. A damaged altar inscription from Corbridge in Britain[3] records a [*p*]*raep(ositus) cu*[*ram*] *agens* [*h*]*orr(eorum) tempo*[*r*]*e expeditionis felicissi(mae) Brittanic(ae)*. This was found re-used as building material in the fourth-century reconstruction of the west granary at Corbridge and is assigned to the period of the campaigns of Septimius Severus in Britain. It is worth noting that it was at this period that the fort at South Shields was completely filled with the *horrea* now revealed by excavation. An inscription from Mactar in Africa[4] gives the career of a man, who between holding posts as *praefectus alae* and *tribunus militum* describes himself as *proc(urator) ad solaminia*[5] *et horrea*. His later career seems to have been almost entirely in the Danube frontier area and it is not unlikely that his special procuratorship was connected with an expedition in that area. Presumably these men were particularly responsible for the provision of adequate store dumps along the line of march; and it is interesting to note that what were later to become permanent *horrea*, such as some fourth-century *horrea* at Tupusuctu in Africa,[6] could start life in this way.

[1] *Digest*, L. 6. 7.

[2] A. von Domaszewski, 'Die Annona des Heeres im Kriege', EPITYMBION, *Festschrift H. Swoboda* (1927), p. 17; Van Berchem, *L'annone militaire*, pp. 144 ff.

[3] *EE* IX. 1144, cf. Richmond, *The Roman Fort at South Shields*, p. 2.

[4] *CIL* VIII. 619 = *ILS* 2747.

[5] The meaning of *solaminia* is uncertain, but probably refers to emergency reserve supplies, cf. *CIL* II. 1180 = *ILS* 1403.

[6] *CIL* VIII. 8836 = *ILS* 645.

CONCLUSION

The military and civil organisation of *horrea* have it in common that their development conforms to one pattern. This is the pattern which everyone who studies institutions of any kind under the Empire must encounter, namely, the development from private ownership to public control, from *ad hoc* arrangements to systematisation, from individual enterprise to imperial bureaucracy. Always progress was slow. Practices grew up which were not legalised and codified until much later.

If the arguments put forward in Chapter V are correct,[1] in the civil sphere we have evidence for private ownership and individual enterprise in the first century A.D. gradually being absorbed into imperial control through the greed of individual Emperors. This was to lead ultimately to the bureaucracy of the fourth century revealed in the *Codex Theodosianus*.[2] But it did not come immediately. The renting and hiring of *horrea* by private individuals must have continued, not only in the safe deposit *horrea*, but even in the great State *horrea*.[3] Legal sources show that, although the Emperor might own *horrea*, private contractors could hire them from him[4] and it may be that the small fry in the *Horrea Galbana* and other *horrea* in Rome hired their positions, even in the second century A.D.[5] Ultimately, however, the process was to lead to the crushing State-controlled regimentation revealed in the *Codex Theodosianus* where, as the rescripts show, at the moment of greatest control the whole system was on the point of breaking down.[6]

Similarly in the military sphere the *ad hoc* arrangements of the early Empire gradually gave way to the highly organised *annona militaris*. It would be unwise to assume that that organisation existed before the fourth century A.D., when there is explicit evidence for it, although it was probably based on practices which grew up in the third century A.D. Again, at the moment of maximum control the system was getting out of hand and the *actuarii* became virtually incapable of being controlled.[7] It was the old problem: *Quis custodiet ipsos custodes?*

So far as the structure of the *horrea* is concerned, it is clear that they

---

[1] See Chapter V (p. 164).   [2] See Chapter V (p. 183).
[3] See Chapter VI (p. 194).   [4] See Chapter VI (p. 195).
[5] See Chapter V (p. 176).   [6] See Chapter V (p. 190).
[7] See Chapter VIII (p. 285).

were buildings of imaginative and monumental quality.[1] Their original construction demanded a period of settled conditions, a buoyant economy and plenty of ready money. These conditions were only properly fulfilled in the first two centuries of the Empire, and only in the case either of private families of great wealth or later of the State, that is, the Emperor himself. The evidence suggests that the greatest civil *horrea* were built in the first or second century A.D. if not before; and that in the later, more troubled times they were simply kept in repair as far as was possible.[2] The military *horrea* of course continued to be built during the crises of the late Empire.[3]

It is a well-known fact that periods of war and civil strife leave to posterity their castles and fortresses; periods dominated by the powers of religion leave their abbeys, cathedrals and temples; and periods when a people's energies are concentrated on commerce and industry leave factories, warehouses, docks and such buildings. If these latter have as much creative energy and skill focused on them as, for example, English buildings of this kind had in the years following the industrial revolution, they possess something of the same vigour as the cathedrals themselves.[4]

The first two centuries A.D. were for Rome just such a period of energetic commerce, and one of their most valuable, although neglected, legacies is the Roman *horrea*. To an age such as ours, dominated by functional architecture, material prosperity, creeping bureaucracy, and deep debate over central planning and control, by the government, of economic activities,[5] the study of *horrea* and their organisation is of compelling interest.

[1] See Chapter IV (p. 158).　　　　[2] See Chapter I (p. 85).
[3] See Chapter VII (p. 264).　　　　[4] *Architectural Review* (July 1957).
[5] O. Franks, *Central Planning and Control in War and Peace* (London School of Economics, 1947), *passim*.

SUSPENSURAE

The structural feature of *horrea* used for storing *grain* which has been most commented upon is the raising of the floors off the ground. The method by which this raising was achieved at Ostia was by the construction in each room of a series of longitudinal dwarf walls to a height of some 40 centimetres and then the covering of the intervals between the walls by bipedal bricks 60 centimetres square. The floor was built up of several courses of *bipedales* and a series of air tunnels were thus created underneath. Similar systems were created in the *horrea* in military forts and fortresses. Such *suspensurae* have come to be regarded as a characteristic mark of all Roman granaries of all periods, and yet it is possible, I think, that in this precise form they were a rather late and sophisticated device introduced in the second century A.D.

First it must be made clear what the exact point of this contention is. I am *not* claiming that the Romans had no granaries with raised floors before the second century A.D. Such a claim would easily be disproved by the literary authorities alone, by Pliny, Varro and Columella, etc.[1] Moreover, it seems clear that from neolithic times there was a *common* tradition in Europe for the raising of granaries off the ground, and it is to be detected even in pre-Roman Britain.[2] What I do claim, however, is that in all these cases the granary so raised was of wood or with a wooden floor. It is possible to argue that the Romans did not automatically think of raising a granary floor, unless it was made of wood. Thus the raising of a floor *composed of bipedal bricks* or slabs of stone was, I suspect, a sophisticated method used perhaps not earlier than the second century A.D.

The Ostian evidence, such as it is, is consistent with such a view. Of the three granaries which have *suspensurae*, only the *Horrea Antoniniani*[3] certainly had them from the beginning. The date of the building is believed to be late

---

[1] Columella I. 6. 16; Varro I. 57; Pliny *NH* XVIII. 302.

[2] S. Piggott, 'Timber circles: a re-examination', *AJ* XCVI (1939), 220–1.

[3] Reg. II. Is. II. 7; *Scavi* I, pp. 143 and 204. Cf. Chapter I (p. 42). Meiggs, p. 280, claimed that there were four *horrea* with such *suspensurae* in Ostia. He included, in addition to the three here discussed, the *Horrea di Hortensius* (Reg. V. Is. XII. 1)—a building of Julio-Claudian date. Personal inspection of these *horrea* revealed no such *suspensurae* still visible. Moreover, with the help of Dr M. H. Ballance, formerly Assistant Director of the British School at Rome, and Dr Maria Squarciapino at Ostia, it was confirmed that there was no evidence during the excavations that they had *suspensurae*.

Antonine and probably Commodan (*circa* A.D. 180), although this date is not yet confirmed by brick stamps.

The *Grandi Horrea*[1] were completely rebuilt, probably under Commodus, and this rebuilding was associated by the excavator, G. Calza, with the introduction of raised floors of *bipedales*. The earlier building erected under Claudius had floors of rammed 'cocciopesto' 20 centimetres thick. This must mean some sort of *opus signinum*.

The third *horrea* (Reg. I. Is. VIII. 2), which have[2] raised floors of *bipedales*, were built under Hadrian, a date confirmed by brick stamps. It is just possible, however, that the raised floors may be a later addition. Certainly the brick piers which support the thresholds at the entrances to the rooms are not bonded with the walling, the bricks are different in colour and width, and the mortar joints are much wider. This may represent only a later tampering with the room entrances and not the flooring of the rooms as a whole. At all events, the *suspensurae* (with *bipedales*) of this *horrea* were built certainly not earlier than Hadrian and just possibly later.

To assume from these three examples alone that the *suspensurae* system with *bipedales* was not introduced until the second century A.D. would be absurd.

It is a fact, however, that such other evidence as exists for such *suspensurae* systems supports this conclusion.

The excavation by Calza in 1925,[3] when he laid bare the end of one of the rows of storehouses which surrounded Trajan's harbour, revealed that the original storehouse of *opus mixtum*, brick and reticulate work mixed, had been replaced on the same plan by a storehouse whose walls were faced with brickwork alone. This wholly brick-faced storehouse had its floors raised with *suspensurae*. The very fact that the structure was faced with bricks alone would suggest that the building was not earlier than Antonine in date, if we may judge by building styles at Ostia.

The great *horrea* at Djemila[4] in North Africa which had such *suspensurae* in at least some of its rooms was constructed at the time of Septimius Severus.

Among the military *horrea* of Britain, the earliest granaries with raised floors were entirely of wood.[5] Under Trajan much rebuilding in stone was undertaken, but the evidence yielded, for example, by the rebuilt Welsh auxiliary forts, shows that the floors of the granaries now rebuilt in stone

---

[1] Reg. II. Is. IX. 7; *Scavi* I, p. 118. Calza, 'Gli *horrea* tra il Tevere e il decumano', pp. 371 ff. Cf. Chapter I (p. 50).

[2] *Scavi* I, p. 131; Becatti, '*Horrea Epagathiana et Epaphroditiana*', p. 32; cf. Chapter I (p. 28).

[3] Calza, *NSc* (1925), 58 ff.   [4] Allais, *RAfr* (1933), pp. 259 ff.

[5] Bushe-Fox, *Richborough, Report IV*, pp. 26 and 34; Richmond, *PSAS* LXXIII (1938/9), 129 ff.; cf. Chapter VII (p. 215).

were probably still of wood, for gaps of up to 6 feet occur between the transverse dwarf walls of their *suspensurae*—gaps which could only be spanned by timbers.[1] Only after this period do we find clear examples of the suspended floor composed of tiles or slabs of stone. Moreover it is possible that in the early second century it was not a rigid rule that stone granaries had to have their floors raised, if those floors were of a durable and impermeable material. Thus at forts such as Caerhun, Caersws and Brecon Gaer we find floors of stone or concrete unraised.[2]

It must be stressed that none of the archaeological evidence is conclusive, for it is possible that the *Grandi Horrea* in Ostia and these military *horrea* in Wales did have raised floors, but that the structural evidence for them had disappeared or was missed by the excavators. But the archaeological evidence, as far as it goes, has yet revealed no Roman granary with a floor of stone slabs or bipedal bricks raised by *suspensurae* before the second century A.D.

The conclusion suggested by the archaeological evidence is fully borne out by the literary evidence. The raising of bath-house floors by *suspensurae* was of great interest to authors such as Pliny and Vitruvius,[3] who describe their construction in detail. The idea was something new and to be commented on. Pliny attributed the invention to a man named Sergius Orata *circa* 90 B.C., but Seneca in the *Epistulae Morales*[4] of A.D. 63–5 can refer to the *suspensuras balneorum* as 'devices which have come to light only within our own memory'. Nowhere is it remarked that such *suspensurae* should be, or had been, applied to *horrea*.

On the contrary, the discussions of the construction of *horrea* and *granaria* by the agricultural authors reveal a bewildering variety of opinion. In none of their discussions are *suspensurae* mentioned as such, and there was a strong body of opinion which disapproved of the raising of granary floors and recommended granaries placed on the ground with heavily reinforced walls and floors.

For Cato in 160 B.C.[5] the prime need was to make a concoction from *amurca*, dregs of olives, and smear the whole granary with it.

Varro in 37 B.C.[6] recommended that grain should be stored in *granaria sublimia quae perflentur vento ab exortu ac septentrionum regione*. *Granaria sublimia* are not in fact granaries raised off the ground, but granaries placed on the ground. They are contrasted both with the grain storage pits sunk into the ground, in Cappodocia, Thrace, Spain and Carthage, and the *supra*

---

[1] Nash-Williams, *The Roman Frontier in Wales*, pp. 128 ff.

[2] P. K. Baillie-Reynolds, *Kanovium* (Cardiff, 1938), p. 81 (Caerhun); R. E. M. Wheeler, *Roman Fort near Brecon* (London, 1926), p. 38 (Brecon Gaer).

[3] Pliny, *NH* IX. 168, and *NH* XXVI. 16; Vitruvius V. 10. 2.

[4] Seneca, *Ep. Mor.* XC. 25: *quaedam nostra demum prodisse memoria*.

[5] Cato, *De Agric.* 92.   [6] Varro I. 57.

terram granaria sublimia, which he knows of in Spain and Apulia and which *non solum a lateribus per fenestras, sed etiam subtus a solo ventus re⟨fri⟩gerare possit.* The material of which these raised granaries were made is not mentioned but, as we shall see, it was almost certainly wood. At all events the *recommended* granary is built *on* the ground with walls and floor coated with a stucco of pounded marble and lime, or at least of clay, mixed with grain chaff and *amurca.*

Columella in A.D. 60[1] recommended a division of things to be stored into two categories: wine and oil and such merchandise should be stored on the ground floor, while grain, hay and cattle fodder should be stored upstairs in lofts and only approached by ladders. He does acknowledge, however, that others consider the best storage to be provided by a *horreum* on the ground covered by a vault with the floor treated in a special way. The earthen floor, before it is covered over, should be dug up and soaked with fresh unsalted *amurca* and packed down with rammers like *opus signinum.* After this has dried thoroughly it is to be overlaid with a *pavimenta testacea* in which the lime and sand are to be mixed with oil lees instead of water. This coating again is to be beaten down with great force by rammers and smoothed off. He mentions that in drier climates grain can be stored in pits in the ground, but concludes that in Italy, which is damp, *illam positionem pensilis horrei et hanc curam pavimentorum et parietum probamus.* In short, there are two possibilities, either storage in lofts off the ground, or a *horreum* placed on the ground with its walls and floors elaborately treated.

Pliny, in his *Naturalis Historia,* dedicated to Titus in A.D. 77,[2] succinctly summed up the position which had been reached in his day with regard to the structure of *horrea.* Some recommended that *horrea* should have brick walls, 3 feet thick, which were to be filled from above and have no windows or means for the air to enter, others that they should only have windows facing north-east or north and that they should be constructed without lime, since that was harmful to the grain. On the other hand, there were those who *suspendunt granaria lignea columnis* and preferred that they should be ventilated on all sides even from below. This doctrine was contradicted by others who claimed that grain completely raised off the ground on wooden boards tended to shrink and that if it were covered by tiles it got hot. Again there seem to be two possibilities: either a wooden granary was suspended on stilts or a brick granary was built on the ground.

At no point in any of these discussions is there any reference to *suspensurae* of a type which had to be described in detail for their construction in bath houses. There is not even a veiled reference to them. Moreover, although the existence of wooden *horrea* raised above the ground is admitted, they do not

[1] Columella I. 6. 9 ff.   [2] Pliny, *NH* XVIII. 301 ff.

dominate the discussions. The most important factor which is stressed is the careful treatment of walls and floors of *horrea* set upon the ground. The emphasis laid upon the preparation of floors with a protective layer of marble chips and lime or *opus signinum* mixtures of crushed sherds recalls the concrete floors of the Welsh auxiliary forts and the 'cocciopesto' 20 centimetres thick which Calza found as the original flooring of the *Grandi Horrea*.

To sum up: the idea that the Romans *always* stored their corn on raised floors is entirely a modern assumption not supported by the ancient evidence. So far as that evidence goes, it suggests that there were two schools of thought about grain storage, one preferring raised wooden buildings, the other brick-built granaries, placed on the earth but with floors and walls treated in a special way. This was still the case in the time of Pliny the Elder. It seems a reasonable inference that the raising of stone or tile floors was still to come, and this in fact agrees with the dating of all *suspensurae* of this type, so far discovered, to the second century A.D. In archaeology conclusions may always be refuted by what is dug up tomorrow, but at the moment the onus of proof is on those who would believe that tile *suspensurae* were in use in *horrea* at a date earlier than the second century A.D.

EGYPT

Egypt has furnished by far the greatest amount of evidence for the administration and organisation of *granaries*[1] (as distinct from warehouses in general) in the Roman period. It is difficult therefore not to include some account of this organisation in any study of *horrea*. However, it is well known that Egypt and its arrangements were not typical of the Roman Empire as a whole. No general conclusions for the rest of the Empire can necessarily be drawn from the account that follows.

There is every reason to believe that even in the structure and design of the granaries, Egyptian methods changed hardly at all during the centuries of Pharaonic, Ptolemaic and Roman rule. Essentially there were two types,[2] one with a circular ground plan, the other with a square or rectangular ground plan. The circular buildings were shaped like beehives and were some 5 metres high and 2–3 metres in diameter. The grain was poured in at the top through a trap door by men standing upon ladders, and was extracted when needed at the bottom through a similar trap door. The rectangular version was built on much the same principles with side walls which sloped gradually towards the top, but it had a flat roof. The grain was poured in from the top and taken from the bottom in exactly the same way, but the flat top must have made it easier to supervise how much was being stored. We know of these two types, not only from two literary documents, one from the period of the Hyksos kings, the other a Byzantine mathematical papyrus, but also from representations on the walls of tombs and from excavated examples.[3] Excavation has shown that they could be considerably more elaborate, either doubled or tripled, and have a great permanent ramp leading up to their tops in order to facilitate storage.

Very often it seems that these beehive storehouses were in groups of five or

---

[1] In general see A. Calderini, Θησαυροί, *Studi della Scuola Papirologica* IV, Pt. 3 (1924). J. Schwartz, 'Le Nil et le ravitaillement de Rome', *BInstFrAOr* XLVII (1948), 179 ff.

[2] Wilcken, *Griechische Ostraka aus Aegypten und Nubien* I, pp. 649 ff.

For a list of abbreviated titles of the great collections of papyri, see M. David and B. A. van Groningen, *Papyrological Primer*, 4th ed. (Leyden, 1965), Introduction, pp. 6–11.

[3] A. Eisenlohr, *Ein mathematisches Handbuch der alten Aegypter* (Leipzig, 1877); J. Baillet, 'Papyrus mathématique d'Akhîm', *Mémoires de la Mission Archéologique Française au Caire* IX (1892), 1; T. Whittemore, 'The excavations at El-'Amarnah, Season 1924–5', *JEgA* XII (1926), 9 ff.

six and placed in a walled enclosure.¹ They are pictured like this in tombs and such an arrangement seems to be described in a papyrus of Domitianic date.² Two tenants of a farm belonging to the god Soknopaios sub-let a storehouse belonging to it. This storehouse is described as θησαυρὸν ἐνεργὸν στεγνὸν καὶ τεθυρ[ω]μένον, ἐν ᾧ πύργος καὶ αὐλὴ καὶ ταμῖ[α] πέντε καὶ νουβάσι καὶ σιροῖς καὶ τοῖς λοιποῖς χρηστηρ[ί]οις πᾶσι.—Θησαυρός here seems to mean the whole ensemble, which is described as fit to be used, waterproof(?), and equipped with doors. Within was a πύργος; whether this means a 'tower' is not certain. Liddell and Scott have suggested the meaning 'out-buildings' for its use in this papyrus. There was also an open court, and five ταμιεῖα: these must be the actual storehouses, either round or square. σιροί are well known from many sources³ to have been corn storage pits sunk into the ground. What νουβάσι means is quite unknown.

Whatever the precise details, it is clear that the ordinary granaries, the *thesauo* of the villages and μητροπόλεις cited in so many papyri, bore no resemblance to the Roman *horrea*. It is argued elsewhere⁴ that possibly the great temple magazines of Pharaonic Egypt are part of that architectural tradition in utilitarian building which was widespread in the East and which was perhaps to lead to the typical courtyard *horrea* design in Roman times. But it is certain that Egyptian granaries played no part in that tradition and they remained fixed types uninfluenced by Roman designs when Egypt finally came under Roman rule.

Thesauros, therefore, is the word used for granary in Egypt at all periods. The transliteration ὅρρια appears very rarely and then only from the fourth century A.D. onward. It was used first, it seems, to designate the granaries at Alexandria itself,⁵ and then applied to the granaries of Arsinoe and Babylonia.⁶

Thesauros was the word used to describe the storehouses both of the temples (ἱερῶν) and of the State (διοικήσεως). It is with the latter that we are concerned.

The men placed in charge of these storehouses were the σιτολόγοι.⁷ It is unlikely that in the first century A.D. at least their job was regarded as a liturgy. Some proof of that is given by the fact that at the village of Lysimachis in the Fayûm the man Akusilaos was a *sitologos* from A.D. 11 to 15. A liturgy official would be unlikely to stay in office

¹ A. Erman, H. Ranke, *Aegypten und ägyptisches Leben im Altertum* (Tübingen, 1923), p. 521.
² *P. Lond.* 216, cf. *P. Mich.* v. 226.
³ Not least Pliny, *NH* XVIII. 306.
⁴ Chapter IV (p. 152).
⁵ *P. Flor.* 75. 18 (A.D. 380); *P. Lond.* 1823. 14.
⁶ *P. Lond.* 113. 5 (*b*). 9; *BGU* 838. 25–6 (Arsinoe); *P. Lond.* 1441. 53 (Babylonia).
⁷ Calderini, Θησαυροί, pp. 58 ff.

for more than a year. Later it certainly became a liturgy, in the second century A.D.[1]

It seems clear that there was more than one *sitologos* for each *thesauros*. In the receipts and monthly reports quite often the names of more than one *sitologos* are given; in other cases the existence of other *sitologoi* is covered by the phrase καὶ μέτοχοι. They seem to have been organised in *collegia*.[2]

The job of these *sitologoi* in the Roman as in the Ptolemaic period was the running of the *thesauros*. This involved quite a considerable number of activities. Above all, they were responsible for receiving the payments of grain and other goods into the storehouses. For these payments they issued individual receipts to those paying, of which thousands have survived either on ostraka or papyri.[3] The following form was used in papyrus receipts: Date (that is, of the year)—σιτολόγοι (name with title in nominative or genitive or a mixture of both)—μεμετρήμεθα—day's date—ἀπὸ γενήματος τοῦ × ἔτους—ἐν θησαυρῷ τῆς × κώμης—μέτρῳ × from taxpayer (name in the nominative or εἰς ὄνομα)—for delivery—amount—signature.

They were responsible for the safe keeping of these goods until they surrendered them. This could come about in two ways: either they were authorised by higher authorities to make loans of seed corn to farmers, or they handed them over to ναύκληροι and κυβερνῆται for transport down river to Alexandria. These activities can be seen in the two types of document. First there were the lists of farmers with their names and addresses to whom loans of seed corn had been made and the receipts issued to those who repaid the loan,[4] and secondly the receipts given by the *naukleroi* to the *sitologoi*, acknowledging that so much grain, pure and unadulterated, had been loaded on to their ship from the granaries concerned and that they would transport this to Alexandria.[5]

Besides these documents attesting the activities and responsibilities of the *sitologoi*, there were the lists and summaries of payments and disbursements which the *sitologoi* had to render for the use of the administrative staff of the district to which the granary officials had to account. The periods covered by these summaries vary; some are 5-day accounts, some 11-day, some 15-day, but the most common of all was the monthly account.[6] Ultimately these

---

[1] *P. Lond.* II. 256 (e) and 256 (a). 4; cf. *P. Lond.* III. 1159. 36 ff.; F. Preisigke, *Girowesen im griechischen Aegypten* (Strassburg, 1910). N. Lewis, *Inventory of Compulsory Services in Ptolemaic and Roman Egypt* (Newhaven, 1968), *s.v.* σιτολόγος, gives A.D. 101 (*BGU* 908) as the first clear evidence that the service had become compulsory.

[2] *BGU* 835, *P. Oxy.* 287, 383 and 384.

[3] Wilcken, *Griechische Ostraka* I, 655 ff.

[4] *P. Lond.* II. 254, cf. *P. Ryl.* 72 (verso).

[5] *P. Hib.* 216; *P. Oxy.* 1259, 2125.   [6] Calderini, Θησαυροί, pp. 6–7.

accounts and copies of lists were rendered to the central administration in Alexandria under the ἐπίτροπος τῆς Νέας πόλεως.[1]

An important papyrus from Strassburg contains a copy of a letter from the ἐπίτροπος τῆς Νέας πόλεως in A.D. 194 in which it is stated that a time limit had been laid down within which δέον ἐστὶν καταχωρείζειν τὰ εἰς Ἀλεξάνδρειαν πεμπόμε[να] βιβλία τῶν τε εἰ[σ]πράξεων σιτικῶν τε καὶ ἀργυρικῶν καὶ τῶν ἀπολογισμ[ῶν] καὶ τῶν ἄλλων κατὰ μῆνα ἢ ἀπαιτεῖσθαι ἐπίτιμον τοὺς μὴ ἐνπρ[οθ]έσμως πέμψαντας ('it is necessary to register the "rolls" of the taxes in corn and money and the accounts sent to Alexandria every month, and those who do not send them at the appointed time shall be liable to a fine').

It was also possible for individuals to maintain private deposits at the State granaries. Payments from such accounts were made by the individual issuing an order-to-pay to the *sitologoi* who made the required transfer to the account of the payee, who consequently received a notice of credit. Documents containing orders of this kind have also been preserved.[2]

Given their manifold duties and the extent of their responsibilities, it would be impossible for the *sitologoi* to manage without a considerable staff. The papyri reveal that they had help. The most commonly attested of their staff are the γραμματεῖς to the *sitologoi*.[3] They appear to have been employed at all periods and in all places where there were *thesauroi* of importance. There could be more than one at each place, and their job was to aid the *sitologos* presumably with the mass of paper work involved.

Θησαυροφύλακες[4] are attested at least from the first century B.C. right through until the third century A.D. Their job was that of guarding the store-houses. In a papyrus of the early third century A.D. a liturgy is mentioned τὸ προστῆναι τοῖς δημοσίοις θησαυροῖς καὶ συσφραγίζειν ἅμα τοῖς σιτολόγοις.[5] This job may be the same as that listed in a few other papyri of the third and fourth centuries A.D. which record special officials called ἐπισφραγισταί.[6] These men are sometimes mentioned alone but in one case at least some *naukleroi* give a receipt for wheat which is to be transported to Alexandria to both the *sitologoi* and the ἐπισφραγιστής of the same village.[7]

In addition to these officials there are a very few references to βοηθοὶ σιτολόγων. Because of their rarity it may be that they were relatively un-important people who were co-opted from time to time as *ad hoc* helpers.[8]

---

[1] U. Wilcken, 'Aus der Strassburger Sammlung', *ArchPF* IV (1908), p. 122.

[2] *P. Oxy.* 2588–91.   [3] Calderini, Θησαυροί, pp. 82 ff.

[4] *Ibid.* pp. 87 ff.   [5] *P. Ryl.* II. 90.

[6] Calderini, Θησαυροί, pp. 86 ff.

[7] C. Wessely, *Studien zur Paläographie und Papyruskunde* (Leipzig), XX (1921), No. 32, line 10 (A.D. 231).   [8] Calderini, Θησαυροί, pp. 83 ff.

Perhaps σιτομέτραι (*mensores frumenti*) also formed part of the staff of the storehouses, but officials such as the σιτοπαραλῆμπται, σιταποδέκται, πράκτορες σιτικῶν and δεκάπρωτοι were certainly more concerned with the collecting rather than the storage and protection of grain. However, they seem to have become considerably more important in the late third and fourth centuries A.D. and even to have overshadowed the *sitologoi* at that period.[1]

So much for the organisation and staff of the ordinary storehouses of the villages and the *metropoleis*. What of the higher organisation? The organisation of the movement of the grain from the local granaries to Alexandria was the responsibility of the βασιλικογραμματεύς in co-operation with the στρατηγός who issued a general authorisation (ἐπίσταλμα) for the transport of the grain from the *thesauroi* to the harbours on the canals or to those on the Nile itself.[2] The method of getting the corn to the harbours was by means of donkey train or even camel caravans, and it was then carried in sacks on to the lighters which ferried the goods to the bigger ships in midstream.[3] Once the corn was placed at the harbours it is probable that at least in some areas a fixed system of clearing the granaries one by one was laid down. At least we have the judicial proceedings[4] which took place in April A.D. 208 before the Prefect of Egypt, Subatanius Aquila, where the defendant was the *strategos* of the nome. He was accused by the *prytaneis* of Oxyrhynchus of being responsible for the late delivery of taxes in kind through failure to observe the traditional system of clearing the granaries. This system was described as the clearing of the granaries on the Τῶμις canal first at the time of the inundation, then τὸ κατὰ πάσσαλον τὸ σύνηθες was put into operation, which seems to mean that the villages were cleared from south to north to avoid congestion and aid the transport down river.

Transport of grain down the Nile did of course continue throughout the year, but it was in the months just after the harvest that the bulk of it had to reach

[1] *Ibid.* pp. 85 ff.
[2] In general see W. L. Westermann and C. W. Keyes, *Tax Lists and Transportation Receipts from Theadelphia* (New York, 1932), pp. 98 ff. E. Börner, *Der staatliche Korntransport im griechisch-römischen Aegypten* (Hamburg, 1939). Cf. *P. Lond.* II. 256(*d*). 9–12.
[3] E. G. Turner, *Catalogue of Greek and Latin Papyri and Ostraka in the possession of the University of Aberdeen* (Aberdeen, 1939), 30. *P. Oxy.* 2670 (A.D. 127), cf. O. M. Pearl, 'Varia Papyrologica', *TAPA* LXXI (1940), 372 ff.
[4] *P. Oxy.* XXII. 2341. τὸ κατὰ πάσσαλον τὸ σύνηθες means literally 'the customary system according to peg'. Although the system may have been customary, the phrase was not understood by Aquila himself, who asked its meaning. The answer given was that each area began its collection from the south. πάσσαλος may have been a measuring stick and the system determined the order in which the granaries of the nome were cleared by the height of the flood water shown on the πάσσαλοι of the villages. There appears to be no other reference to help settle the matter.

Alexandria. The harvest in Egypt lasted from about the beginning of April
to the end of May, and although harvest corn could be shipped to Alexandria
until mid-July and even later, the real pressure was in May and June.[1]

The *strategoi* and βασιλικογραμματεῖς were responsible to the governor
and the ἰδιολόγος in general, but in this particular aspect of their work
they were responsible above all to the ἐπίτροπος τῆς Νέας πόλεως.[2] The whole
organisation is well summed up in a shipper's receipt[3] of A.D. 211–12 which
reads: 'Given to the *strategos* of the Oxyrhynchite nome by —, master of
eight boats, ναύκληρος χειρισμοῦ Νέας πόλεως πλοίων, I have received and
had measured out to me the amount ordered by you (*strategos*) and —
βασιλικογραμματεύς of the same nome, from — *sitologoi* of — district, in
accordance with the order of his excellency the *procurator Neaspoleos* (ἐξ
ἀποστόλου τοῦ κρατίστου ἐπιτρόπου τῆς Νέας πόλεως) from public granaries
of the said village at river Tomis, — wheat, produce of year —, which I will
carry to Alexandria and deliver to the officials of the administration safely,
free of all risk and damage by ship. This receipt is valid, there being three
copies of it, of which I have issued two to you the *strategos* and one to the
sitologoi. Date.' The ἐπίτροπος τῆς Νέας πόλεως, whose overall supervision
of the collection, transportation and storage of corn at Alexandria is attested
by several papyri,[4] had the Roman title *procurator Neaspoleos et mausolei
Alexandriae*. Two Latin inscriptions, both of the Antonine period, give the
careers of two men who held this post. Sextus Cornelius Dexter[5] (*circa*
A.D. 138), after the usual triple military posts of an equestrian career (*praefectus cohortis, tribunus legionis, praefectus alae*), became *praefectus* of the Syrian
fleet under Hadrian, and then *procurator Neaspoleos et mausolei*. After this
post he became *iuridicus Alexandreae* and finally *procurator Asiae*. C. Iulius
Celsus[6] (*circa* A.D. 125) had an even more distinguished career. After being a
dilectator in Aquitania he became *procurator XX hereditatum per provincias
Narbonensem et Aquitanicam*, then *proc. Neaspoleos et mausolei Alexandriae*, next
procurator XX hereditatum at Rome itself, then *procurator* of the provinces of
Lugdunum and Aquitanica, and finally *a libellis et censibus*.

In the Strassburg papyrus already referred to,[7] dated A.D. 194, there is a

[1] P. Oxy. 2182 (A.D. 166).   [2] U. Wilcken, *ArchPF* IV (1908), pp. 126 ff.
[3] P. Oxy. 1259.
[4] To the list of references in Calderini, Θησαυροί, p. 57, should be added *PSI* IX. 1053;
P. Hib. II. 215, 216; P. Strassb. 202.
[5] CIL VIII. 8934 (Saldae, Mauretania) = ILS 1400. Cf. H.-G. Pflaum, *Les carrières
procuratoriennes équestres sous le haut-empire Romain* (Paris, 1960), no. 137.
[6] CIL XIII. 1808 (Lugdunum) = ILS 1454. Cf. Pflaum, *Les carrières procuratoriennes
équestres*, no. 106.
[7] U. Wilcken, *ArchPF* IV (1908), p. 126. Cf. CIL VIII. 9371 = ILS 1355. Cf. Pflaum,
Les carrières procuratoriennes équestres, no. 227.

reference by the γραμματεύς of a nome to a letter sent by Sallustius Macrinianus ὁ κράτιστος ἐπίτροπος τῆς Νέας πόλεως περὶ ὀφειλόντ[ων πέμπε]σθαι μηνιαίων λόγων κ[αὶ ἀπολο]γισμῶν. It may well be that this man is the Q. Sallustius Macrinianus known from an inscription from Mauretania as *proc. Augg. utriusque provinciae Mauretaniae.*

The position, therefore, of *procurator Neaspoleos* was, as we might have guessed, a responsible post (with a salary of 100,000 sesterces a year) for worthy equestrians who might hope for the procuratorship of a province after holding it, if nothing more.

What the Νέα πόλις was, although not explicitly explained, is not difficult to guess. The reference must be to a particular part of Alexandria—presumably the new town around the harbour.[1] Here the *procurator* had his office and the whole administration was referred to as the χειρισμός τῆς Νέας πόλεως.

Until recently the earliest reference to this administration was in the fragments of military accounts of either the III (Cyrenaica) or XXII (Deiotariana) Legion belonging to a period A.D. 81–96.[2] Among these fragments are listed a number of soldiers who were seconded for special duties away from their unit. The duty *exit ad frumentum Neapoli* is listed three times. Twice, however, the comparable duty *exit ad frumentum Mercuri* is mentioned. This hinted at the existence of another department and the suspicion was confirmed by the inscription from Capua of a M. Campanius Marcellus[3] who was a *procurator Augustor. ad Mercurium Alexandr.* More recently another inscription[4] has come to light, giving the career of Sex. Attius Suburanus Aemilianus. After being *praefectus alae* he became *adiutor Vibi Crispi leg. Aug. pro pr. in censibus accipiendis Hispaniae Citerioris*, then *adiutor Iuli Ursi praef. annonae, eiusdem in praefect. Aegypti*, and then *proc. Aug. ad Mercurium.* After holding this post in Alexandria he was *proc. Aug. Alpium Cottianarum* (and other assimilated districts) and then *procurator* successively of the provinces of Judaea and Belgica. Moreover, he may be the Suburanus who was made *Praefectus Praetorio* at the beginning of Trajan's reign.

Four other inscriptions discovered in Lepcis Magna have now revealed that a certain M. Iunius Punicus was, in A.D. 201, *procurator centenarius*

[1] T. Mommsen, 'Aegyptische Legionare', *Hermes* xxxv (1900), 445.

[2] *CPL* 106 (Recto 11. 5) (= *P. Geneva Lat.* 1). Cf. A. von Premerstein, 'Die Buchführung einer ägyptischen Legionsabteilung', *Klio* iii (1902–3), p. 15; M. McCrum and A. G. Woodhead, *Select Documents of the Principates of the Flavian Emperors* (Cambridge, 1961), 405. A possible earlier reference to the ἐπίτροπος Νέας πόλεως is in *P. Hib.* 215 (contemporary with Tib. Julius Alexander's prefecture of Egypt).

[3] *CIL* x. 3847 = *ILS* 1398 (after A.D. 161); cf. Pflaum, *Les carrières procuratoriennes équestres*, no. 171.

[4] *AE* (1939), no. 60 (Domitianic). Cf. *PIR*² i, p. 274, no. 1366. Cf. Pflaum, *Les carrières procuratoriennes équestres*, no. 56.

Alexandriae ad Mercurium.[1] In the second and third centuries therefore the post carried a salary of 100,000 sesterces per annum and thus ranked second in the scale of procuratorships, below the *ducenarii* with 200,000 sesterces, but above the *sexagenarii* with only 60,000 sesterces.

In short, the procuratorship *ad Mercurium* in Alexandria is also revealed as a useful post to be held by a rising *eques* who, if he reached it early enough, might hope for provincial procuratorships to follow and even a top post at Rome.

It is almost certain that the title *ad Mercurium* was also descriptive and referred to a certain quarter of Alexandria. But where exactly that quarter was and what the *procurator ad Mercurium* did is not at all clear. There must have been large granaries in the area, if soldiers were detached for special duties *ad frumentum.* Wilcken argued[2] that even in Ptolemaic times a distinction had been drawn between the corn for export from Egypt and that for the feeding of Alexandria itself. Therefore the distinction between the *procurator Neaspoleos* (who seems to have made all the arrangements concerning the *annona*) and the *procurator ad Mercurium* was similarly that between the official in charge of corn export to Rome, and the official in charge of Alexandrian corn. This is possible, but some more recent evidence suggests that the duties of the *procurator ad Mercurium* may have been wider in extent. There is a growing body of evidence to show that the Greek title of the *ad Mercurium* was ἐπίτροπος Ἕρμου.[3] This is confirmed by the reference at different points in one papyrus to the χειρισμὸς τῆς Νέας πόλεως and the Ἕρμους χειρισμός.[4] Unfortunately the references to the ἐπίτροπος Ἕρμου and his department are very fragmentary. However, in a new papyrus[5] from Oxyrhynchus a κράτιστος ἐπίτροπος Ἕρμου, Aelius Sabinus, issued orders in A.D. 253 concerning the alum monopoly. In a fragmentary papyrus of A.D. 136[6] there is a reference to τὴν πρόσοδον τῆς φορολογίας…τὸν τοῦ Ἕρμου χειρισμὸν κατάγεσθαι. If the word φορολογία can be pressed for a technical meaning of 'rent' as opposed to taxation in general, it may be that we have a further association of the *ad Mercurium* department with monopolies. This, however, is very tenuous. In the present state of the evidence

[1] J. Reynolds and J. Ward-Perkins, *Inscriptions of Roman Tripolitania* (Rome: London, 1952), no. 392, 403, 422, 434.
[2] U. Wilcken, 'Zum Germanicus-Papyrus', *Hermes* LXIII (1928), 48 ff.
[3] *P. Osl.* II. 27; cf. *ArchPF* X (1932), pp. 84 ff. (A.D. 244).
[4] *P. Berl. Leihg.* 4, Verso v. 24 (A.D. 165).
[5] *P. Oxy.* 2567, lines 7 ff. It seems now that the ἐπίτροπος νομοῦ of *P. Oxy.* 2116. 10 (to whom accounts of the alum monopoly are sent) might better be read as ἐπίτροπος Ἕρμου. Possibly [Ἐρ]μαϊκὸν ταβουλάριον might also be read instead of the dubious [Ῥω]μαϊκὸν in the same papyrus.
[6] *PSI* VII. 792 (A.D. 136).

we can only say that in the *procurator Neaspoleos* and the *procurator ad Mercurium* we have two parallel departments located in different parts of Alexandria of apparently equal rank, both of which were concerned with the Egyptian corn supply, although the *procurator Neaspoleos* seems to be more exclusively in control of it. The *procurator ad Mercurium*, although he had granaries within his district, may have had other duties;[1] but what those duties were it is difficult to state with precision.

Although the evidence from Egypt is of limited value for arrangements in the remainder of the Empire, it is of the greatest interest in illustrating the general principles on which any granary administration must be based. We may doubt whether the rest of the Empire was so buried in paper and whether there were so many copies of receipts and accounts as in Egypt, but there was probably a tendency for the organisation throughout the whole Empire to develop in this way. The evidence in the late Empire for the organisation of military *horrea*, with its emphasis on requisition tickets, receipts and counter-signing of receipts issued every few days, seems remarkably similar to the Egyptian organisation.

[1] Certain libraries seem to have been located within the Mercury district (*P. Oxy.* 1382, lines 19–20) and it may be the case that under Claudius the learned Ti. Claudius Balbillus held the post, if the restoration [*ad Herm*]*en Alexandreon* (in *AE* (1924), no. 78) is correct. Cf. Pflaum, *Les carrières procuratoriennes équestres*, no. 15.

THE PRIVATE CORN TRADE AND THE FUNCTIONS OF THE *PRAEFECTUS ANNONAE*

Concentration upon the *frumentationes* and the *Princeps'* interest in the corn supply has, I think, distracted attention from the overwhelming part played by private traders. How large was the private corn trade?

Any attempt to answer the question must be based upon statistics already much handled and very liable to error.

How much was the tithe from Sicily in the late Republic and how much other corn was Sicily expected to send? It can be deduced from a celebrated passage of the Verrine orations[1] that the original tithe was some 3,000,000 *modii*, that Verres was ordered to make a purchase of an additional tithe of 3,000,000 *modii* at a payment of 3 sesterces per *modius* (*frumentum emptum*) and in addition to that was to purchase a further 800,000 *modii* a year (*frumentum imperatum*) at the slightly higher price of $3\frac{1}{2}$ sesterces per *modius*.

If 3,000,000 *modii* was a tithe, we can estimate that the total produce of Sicily was expected to be somewhere between 30,000,000 and 40,000,000 *modii* (probably nearer the latter figure once we have allowed for tax collectors' profits and the produce of those cities untaxed).[2] Even at times when the government drew its full 6,800,000 *modii* from Sicily, it must have been the case that it still had a considerable amount for private export.[3] It is also a fact that in times of great crisis the Roman government was able to make extraordinary purchases again and again above the 6,800,000 *modii*. It has been estimated that perhaps as much as 5,000,000 *modii* extra were available for private export to Rome and elsewhere.[4] Thus of some 10 or 11 million *modii* available from Sicily, only 3 million were really *tribute* corn as such.

There is no reason to believe that Sicily was significantly less productive under the Empire. She lost her premier position as a corn-producing province to Egypt and Africa simply because they were even more productive.[5] Just

---

[1] Cicero, *Verrines* II. 3. 163. On this whole topic, see *RE* VII, s.v. *Frumentum* (M. Rostovtseff), col. 129 ff.
[2] Tenney Frank, *ESAR* III, p. 259 (V. Scramuzza).
[3] Cf. Cicero, *De Domo* 11.   [4] Scramuzza, *ESAR* III, p. 263.
[5] *RE* VII, s.v. *Frumentum*, col. 132.

how productive they were is a matter for careful judgment. Aurelius Victor[1] said that in Augustus' day 20 million *modii* came to Rome from Egypt annually. Josephus[2] writing in Nero's reign said that Africa (in the widest terms, including Cyrenaica) fed Rome for eight months of the year and that Egypt sent Rome sufficient corn for four months of the year. Hence Egypt sent 20 million *modii* a year, Africa 40 million *modii* a year. The method whereby these statistics are produced is not above suspicion and the assumption that both Josephus and Aurelius Victor or his source were using the *breviarium totius imperii* left by Augustus[3] is to say the least without proof. The statistics must be handled gingerly and must be interpreted.

To work on the principle of Johnson[4] that these are the figures of the *tribute* in kind of the provinces seems nonsensical.

First, there is a vast discrepancy between a tribute in kind of 20 million *modii* for Egypt under Augustus and 3 million for Sicily in Cicero's day. Yet Sicily had been *the* corn-producing province. We can believe that Egypt was more productive and perhaps more exploited, but can we believe that the amount was seven times more?

Moreover, if the discrepancy between Sicily and Egypt is too great, what can be said of that between Sicily and Africa?

Secondly, if we believe that Africa and Egypt between them produced 60 million *modii* of *tribute* corn, it is difficult to see how there was ever a problem in feeding Rome. The *frumentationes* would take at the most some 15 million *modii*, and even if we suppose that there were twice or three times as many other people to be fed in Rome as well, their needs would have been covered by African and Egyptian *tribute* corn alone, quite apart from the revenue of other provinces, such as Sicily and Sardinia, and the private corn trade. The fluctuations and breakdowns of the corn supply become unbelievable.

Thirdly, Hieronymus[5] in his commentary on Daniel gives the sum of the yearly corn revenues of Ptolemy II Philadelphus (308–246 B.C.) as $1\frac{1}{2}$ million *artabae*, that is, perhaps $6\frac{3}{4}$ million *modii*. If it is granted that Egypt was always rigorously exploited by her rulers, that sum may not be too far wrong for the later corn *tribute* revenue of Egypt. It is certainly much more in line with (although, on whatever calculation, bigger than) the tribute from Sicily.

[1] Victor, *De Caes*. Epit. 1. 6.   [2] Josephus, *Bell. Iud.* II. 383 and 386.
[3] Tac., *Ann.* I. 11. Cf. the cautious remarks by J. E. Packer, 'Housing and Population in Imperial Ostia and Rome', *JRS* LVII (1967), 87.
[4] Tenney Frank, *ESAR* II, p. 481; contrast T. Mommsen, *Römische Geschichte*[5] (Berlin, 1904), V, p. 560. (Eng. trans. 'The Provinces of the Roman Empire' by W. Dickson (1909), II, pp. 239–40.)
[5] *Patrologia Latina* 25, col. 560 (*in Dan.* XI. 5). For the differing size of *artabae* see Wilcken, *Griechische Ostraka* I, p. 412.

Fourthly, it can be deduced from a passage in the life of Septimius Severus[1] that the *total* amount of *tribute* corn coming to Rome in the reign of that Emperor was nearly 28 million *modii*. If we assume that some 7 million *modii* came from Egypt and perhaps double that from Africa, that is 14 million *modii*, this leaves some 7 million *modii* from all other provinces. This makes some sort of sense and seems not unlikely if the figures are regarded as only roughly approximate.

If this is correct, then the conclusion to be drawn is that the figures 20 million *modii* or more from Egypt and 40 million from Africa, if they mean anything, must be regarded as the total exports of corn in a good year from those countries. It is also clear that the proportion of actual *tribute* corn to that available for private export or for further purchase by the government is similar to the proportion in Sicily.

	Tribute corn	Total corn export[2]
Sicily	3 million	10 million+
Egypt	7 million+	20 million+
Africa	14 million+	40 million+

In short, if these figures are even approximately correct, some two-thirds of each country's total corn export was available for extra purchases by the government and for private speculators to buy up and sell on the open market. The reduction of the *tribute* corn to some 28 million *modii*, 15 million of which would be needed for the *frumentationes*, makes it understandable how things might go wrong in a bad year and why the Emperors should be so concerned about private traders.

In Cicero's day[3] if private merchants from Sicily sold their corn elsewhere than in Rome a famine could result.

Augustus[4] was concerned to regulate the corn supply in such a way that the interests of farmers, private grain dealers and populace were all regarded.

Tiberius[5] in A.D. 19 dealt with the high price of grain by ordering it to be sold at less than the market price and himself making up the loss suffered by the grain merchants by paying them a subsidy of 2 sesterces per *modius*.

Claudius,[6] among his other measures to ameliorate the corn supply, held out to the ordinary merchants the certainty of profit by assuming the expense of any loss that they might suffer from storms and offered to the builders of merchant ships certain privileges.

[1] SHA, *Septimius Severus* 8, 23.
[2] *RE* VII, s.v. *Frumentum*, col. 136 (M. Rostovtseff).
[3] Cic., *De Domo* 11.   [4] Suet., *Aug.* 42. 3.
[5] Tac., *Ann.* II. 87.   [6] Suet., *Claud.* 19.

In the first century A.D. the real problem concerning the corn supply was the need to maintain a steady and fairly low price for corn in the open market, when as a matter of fact a large proportion of the corn was brought in by private corn traders and speculators, either large or small. The job of the *Princeps* and his delegate, the *Praefectus Annonae*, was *not* that of running what was more or less a State owned monopoly, but, as the sources precisely state, exercising a *cura*[1] over a free market, attempting to co-ordinate supplies and plan ahead to avoid famines.

The *Praefectus Annonae* was appointed ἐπὶ τοῦ σίτου τῆς τε ἀγορᾶς τῆς λοιπῆς.[2] He was concerned with *orbis terrarum rationes* and with the prevention of fraud and the proper use of weights and measures.[3]

It was to him that application had to be made for permission to export corn to places other than those for which it was earmarked.[4]

But his was not a proper magistracy even: he was precisely the delegate of the Emperor from whose *imperium* his powers were drawn[5] and appeal could always be made to the Emperor from the decision of the *Praefectus*.[6]

He had no power in *criminal* jurisdiction and did not possess the *ius gladii* until the Constantinian period.[7]

He was concerned primarily with the hearing of civil cases particularly concerned with the food market.[8] Complaints and cases, brought even by women, soldiers and slaves, who were otherwise excluded by the *ius ordinarium*, could be brought before him providing that they were *propter utilitatem ad annonam pertinentem*.[9]

Contracts with shippers naturally formed a large part of his business.[10]

The difficulties of the *Praefectus Annonae* are thus clear. He held an irregular magistracy with limited powers to carry out an overall supervision of a largely free market, a post which demanded not only administrative ability but also tact and discretion. Success in the job might pass unnoticed: failure was bound to touch the feelings of the people and the stability of the Emperor.

The job of the *Praefectus Annonae*, although his functions increased, may have become easier as time went by in that the corn supply may have fallen

---

[1] Cf. Tac., *Ann.* III. 54. 6–8: *Hanc curam sustinet princeps...*

[2] Dio 52. 24. 6.

[3] Seneca, *De Brevit. Vitae* 18. 3 and 19. 1. This moral essay was addressed to Pompeius Paulinus in A.D. 49 and he is commonly assumed to have been *Praefectus Annonae* at the time.

[4] Epictetus I. 10. 2 and 9 ff.

[5] *Digest* I. 2. 33 (Pomponius) nam praef. annonae et praef. vigilum non sunt magistratus sed extra ordinem utilitatis causa constituti sunt.

[6] Dio 52. 33. 1. Cf. *Digest* 14. 5. 8 *ad fin.*

[7] See *RE*, s.v. *praefectus*, col. 1267.

[8] *Digest* 14. 5. 8 (Paulus).

[9] *Digest* 48. 2. 13 (Marcianus).

[10] *Digest* 14. 1. 1. 18 (Ulpian).

more and more into the hands of the Emperor himself. It has been pointed out that the great *horrea* of Rome itself fell one by one into the Emperor's private property and the new constructions were dedicated to him. In addition to the means of storage he may have acquired as his personal property most of the sources of supply. The growth of large estates in Italy and the provinces was followed by the rapid concentration of many of them in the hands of the Emperor.[1] It may be an exaggeration that six landlords owned half Africa in the reign of Nero: it is a fact that upon their expropriation by Nero their estates became part of the imperial property.[2] Augustus had already inherited from Agrippa most of the Thracian Chersonese,[3] a rich corn-producing area. Even in Egypt large estates had been created by the Emperors who granted and sold large tracts of land to members of their family and favourites.[4] We can hardly doubt that ultimately these returned, for one reason or another, to the imperial patrimony.

If this is true, then the job of the *Praefectus Annonae* would have been simplified. He would have the administering and organising of his master's own property, acting in short as a steward and using imperial slaves and freedmen to help him.[5]

[1] Rostovtseff, *The Social and Economic History of the Roman Empire*[2], pp. 101 ff.
[2] Pliny, *NH* 18. 35, cf. Frank, *ESAR* IV, 1938, p. 84 (R. M. Haywood).
[3] Dio 54. 29.
[4] Rostovtseff, *SEHRE*, pp. 99 ff. For a list of estates owned by favourites or members of the imperial family see p. 670, n. 45. Cf. the large corn-growing estates of Acte, Nero's mistress, in Sardinia, p. 580, n. 25.
[5] Cf., in general, Franks, *Central Planning and Control in War and Peace*, p. 14. Speaking of the Raw Materials Commission in the Second World War, he says, 'Control of distribution by licence led on to control of acquisition and of stocks by public purchase and ownership.' I imagine a similar transition to have taken place in the duties of the *Praefectus Annonae*.

APPENDIX 4

RELIGIOUS DEDICATIONS
IN *HORREA*

Horrea were particularly exposed to three great dangers—fire, pestilence and robbery. The religious dedications made in them might be expected therefore to be concerned with protection and safe keeping. This expectation is borne out by the evidence.

By far the most common dedication made was that to the *genius* of the building. *Genius*[1] is a word difficult to define, whose precise meaning varied from context to context. Where *genius* is used of a building, whether that building was a theatre, a market or a warehouse, *genius* signified the *deus in cuius tutela hic locus est*.[2] This is brought out clearly in the dedication made at Caesaraugusta in Spain by A. Annius Eucharistus *genio tutelae horreorum*.[3] Similarly in Rome M. Lorinus Fortunatus made a dedication *genio conserva-tori horreorum Galbianorum*.[4] Sometimes the *genius* was associated particularly with the *lares*, as at Ariminum where L. Lepidus Politicus and C. Pupius Blastus made a dedication *genio larum Horrei Pupiani*.[5] At Beneventum the *horrearius* Concordius made his dedication *genio loci* (and *numini Caereris*).[6] Most often, however, the dedications were made simply and without qualifi-cation to the *genius* of the particular *horrea*. Thus at Moguntiacum a *dispen-sator horrei* set up an altar *genio horrei*.[7] At Rome in A.D. 75 the *horrearii* Saturninus and Successus similarly addressed their dedication *genio horreorum*.[8] In some cases the name of the *horrea* was given. L. Volusius Acindynus and his son of the same name dedicated a statue (of Aesculapius) *genio horreor(um) Seian(orum)*, and the freedman Musaeus made his dedication *genio horreorum Leonianorum*.[9] In the shrine in the centre of the *Horrea Agrippiana* a statue of the *genius* of the *horrea* was set up on a base recording that it had been given by three *curatores* of the *collegium* to the other business men associated with the *horrea: s(ua) p(ecunia) d(ono) d(ederunt) negotiantib(us) Genium horreor(um) [A]grippianorum [pro] salut(e)*.[10]

[1] G. Wissowa, *Religion und Kultus der Römer* (Munich, 1902), pp. 154 ff.
[2] W. Henzen, *Acta Fratrum Arvalium* (Berlin, 1874), p. 146.
[3] *CIL* II. 2991 = *ILS* 3667.　　　[4] *CIL* VI. 236 = *ILS* 3668.
[5] *CIL* XI. 357 = *ILS* 3666.　　　[6] *CIL* IX. 1545.
[7] *CIL* XIII. 11802.　　　[8] *CIL* VI. 235 = *ILS* 3663.
[9] *CIL* VI. 238 = *ILS* 3665 (*Horrea Seiana*); *CIL* VI. 237 = *ILS* 3664 (*Horrea Leoniana*).
[10] Wickert, *RM* XL (1925), 213–14; *RM* XLI (1926), 229.

It seems clear that such small shrines and altars could be expected in every warehouse. There is clear evidence for this in the *Horrea Agrippiana* in Rome and it seems equally certain that most of the Ostian *horrea* had, if not a shrine, at least a niche in which a dedicatory statue might be placed. Possibly the *Horrea di Hortensius* had a shrine in its southern range of rooms from an early date before the creation of the late third-century A.D. shrine near the entrance, whose mosaic floor with its inscription gives the building its modern name.[1] In the *Grandi Horrea* in the northern section rebuilt under Severus there was a small shallow *aedicula* created in one of the walls.[2] In the *Horrea Epagathiana et Epaphroditiana* there were two fine niches framed with small ornamental pilasters in brickwork in the central courtyard and two in the entrance corridor.[3] One might expect that statues of the tutelary deities of the building would be placed in these niches, and obvious candidates, apart from the *genius* of the *horrea*, would be Aphrodite and Agathe Tyche (given the names of the two freedmen). Similarly in the smaller Trajanic *horrea* (Reg. III. Is. II. 6) there was a large niche set in the wall facing towards the entrance.[4] In the *Piccolo Mercato* no shrine or niche is discoverable, but set into one of the façade walls between the rooms on the west side of the courtyard there is a tile slab on which is carved a coiled snake.[5] That this had a religious significance and that it was the symbol of the genius of the *horrea* is, I think, certain. Literary authorities attest that the house-snake was the symbol of the *genius*, and wall paintings and small altars at Pompeii prove that the representation of snakes in this capacity of protective symbol of the *genius* was a common device.[6]

There were, however, other tutelary deities who were invoked for the protection of *horrea* either in association with the *genius* of the building or quite independently of it. On the other side of the stone on which he made a dedication *genio conservatori horreorum Galbianorum*, M. Lorinus Fortunatus made a dedication *Fortunae conservatrici* of the building, while Zmaragdus, the imperial slave who was *vilicus* of the same warehouse, invoked the *bona dea Galbilla*.[7] Such a dedication to a particular *bona dea* had nothing to do with the official worship of the Bona Dea at Rome, but was simply another way of referring to the tutelary deity of a place, the *genius loci*.[8]

The popularity of *Silvanus*[9] to whom dedications were made in a wide

[1] See p. 68. [2] See p. 52.
[3] See p. 35 and Pl. 15. [4] See p. 57.
[5] See p. 22.
[6] Cic., *de Div.* I. 36; Pliny, *NH* 29. 72; Pers. I. 113, cf. W. Helbig, *Wandgemälde Campaniens* (Leipzig, 1868), p. 10.
[7] *CIL* VI. 236 = *ILS* 3668 (*Fortunatus*); *CIL* VI. 30855 = *ILS* 1621 (*Zmaragdus*).
[8] Wissowa, *Religion und Kultus*, p. 179.
[9] *Ibid.* pp. 176 ff.

variety of places and contexts also extended to *horrea* and their staff. Two dedications were made to him by *horrearii* in the *Horrea Galbana*, by Anteros, *horrearius chortis III* and by Maior, Diadumenus and the imperial freedman Crescens whom we know to have been working there *circa* A.D. 128.[1] A rather more peculiar dedication was made by some *vilici horreorum* in the Testaccio area to *Iovi Silvano Salutari*.[2]

Two rather unusual dedications may be explained by the nationality or environment of the dedicators. The *horrearius* Heracleon at Myra dedicated in response to a dream a sculptured slab representing Serapis and Pluto,[3] while in Rome itself the Palmyrene family of Tiberius Claudius Felix made a dedication, in the *Horrea Galbana*, *soli sanctissimo*.[4] In the Palmyrene inscription on the altar the gods addressed were specifically stated to be *Malakabelo et diis Palmyrae*.

There can be no doubt, however, that the tutelary deity most often invoked, apart from the *genius* of the building, was Hercules. In A.D. 159 A. Cornelius Aphrodisius restored an *aedicula* in the *Horrea Galbana* and dedicated it *numini domus Aug. sacrum Herculi Salutari*.[5] In the same warehouse in A.D. 128 Maior, Diadumenus and T. Flavius Crescens made a dedication *Herculi domus Augusti sacrum*.[6]

At first sight this close association of the Hercules dedications with the imperial cult might suggest that they were simply the result of the desire to show loyalty to the Emperor and had no independent significance. The identification of the Emperor with Hercules the hero-become-god was something which had started in the first century A.D. and which was particularly fostered by the Antonine Emperors, and reached a peak under Commodus.[7]

However, although this is true and no doubt this aspect of the matter was not lost upon the dedicators, it seems clear that Hercules was a deity favoured by *horrea* officials for his own sake.[8] It was not automatically the case that a dedication in *horrea* to the *numen* of the *domus Augusti* had to be accompanied by some reference to Hercules.[9] On the contrary, a dedication to the *genius*

[1] *CIL* VI. 588 = *ILS* 1624 (Anteros); *CIL* VI. 30813 = 682 = *ILS* 1623 (Maior).
[2] G. Mancini, 'Le recenti scoperte di antichità al Testaccio', *BCom* XXXIX (1911), 258.
[3] Petersen and von Luschan, *Reisen im Südwestlichen Kleinasien* II, p. 41, fig. 31.
[4] *CIL* VI. 710 = *ILS* 4337.   [5] *CIL* VI. 338 = *ILS* 3445.
[6] *CIL* VI. 30901 = *ILS* 1622.
[7] M. Rostovtseff, 'Commodus–Hercules in Britain', *JRS* XIII (1923), 101 ff.
[8] Hercules was particularly associated with trade and merchants, cf. *RE* VIII, col. 587. He is depicted on monuments such as the Arch at Beneventum and the *Porta Argentariorum* in this respect. An important cult centre was in the temple in the Forum Boarium, cf. D. E. Haynes and P. E. Hirst, *Porta Argentariorum* (London, 1939), p. 33.
[9] *CIL* VI. 236 = *ILS* 3668.

of the *horrea* could be joined by a dedication to *Hercules Salutaris*,[1] or a dedication could be made simply to *Hercules* alone.[2] In the latter example the dedication was made by a man who was *cur(ator) collegi Herculis Salutaris chortis primae sagariorum*. It is this aspect of Hercules as *Salutaris* which is particularly stressed in the inscriptions. Stemming ultimately perhaps from the Greek notion of Ἡρακλῆς ἀλεξίκακος, it was Hercules in this rôle who acquired such popularity in the Empire, and it was not least with this aspect of Hercules that the Roman Emperors wished to associate themselves.[3]

The *collegia* of *Hercules salutaris* and the dedications to this god in the *horrea* performed the double purpose of invoking the aid and protection of a tutelary deity associated with trade and paying a compliment to the imperial house at the same time—an arrangement satisfactory to all concerned.

[1] *CIL* VI. 237 = *ILS* 3664. [2] *CIL* VI. 339 = *ILS* 7315.
[3] Wissowa, *Religion und Kultus*, p. 229.

APPENDIX 5

HORREA AS A PLACE NAME

The word *horrea* often came to be associated with areas where there was a concentration of warehouses in Roman times. This association generally grew up under the late Empire and was then continued into medieval and even modern times. Thus for example the Thirteenth Region in Rome, which comprised the Aventine area, came to have the name *horrea* or *orrea* attached to it.[1] Similarly at Trier, the Benedictine abbey which proved to be built on top of two late Roman *horrea* had always had the name *horrea* associated with it. A document of A.D. 895 referred to *Monasterium S. Mariae vocatum Orrea* and the connection was continued in the legend of the mythical founder of the abbey, St Irmina von Oeren, and even in the modern street name Oerenstrasse.[2]

However, quite apart from this association of the word *horrea* with certain areas in late Roman and medieval times, it is a fact that the Romans themselves used the word *horrea* as the name of specific places, towns or forts, in widely differing parts of the Empire. Our knowledge of these comes predominantly from the geographical sources: Ptolemy's *Geography*, the Antonine Itinerary and the later Ravenna Cosmography and Peutinger Table.[3]

Ptolemy flourished, according to ancient tradition, during the principates of Hadrian and Marcus Aurelius. His main source, however, was the Trajanic geographer Marinus, whom he criticised but obviously used extensively. Ptolemy's information is therefore essentially the Flavian or even pre-Flavian information available to Marinus.

The Antonine Itinerary was compiled under Caracalla between A.D. 212 and 216 and revised in the fourth century.

The Ravenna Cosmography was a list of places in the whole Roman world compiled during the seventh century at Ravenna. It has been shown that it derived mainly from a road map of a kind exemplified by the Peutinger Table. The latter is in fact a medieval copy of a map of the late Roman Empire, based upon itineraries.

Two of the seven places known to have borne the place name *Horrea* are recorded in Ptolemy's *Geography*.

[1] Jordan, *Topographie der Stadt Rom im Alterthum* II, p. 317 (A.D. 961: *in regione secunda sub Aventino in loco qui vocatur orrea*).
[2] Eiden and Mylius, *TrierZ* XVIII (1949), 73–4.
[3] I. A. Richmond, ed., *Roman and Native in North Britain* (Edinburgh, 1958), p. 131 and p. 146.

In his description of Albion (Britain), Ptolemy records a Scottish tribe called the *Vennicones* associated with a place name *Orrea*.[1] This is without doubt the Latin *Horrea* which Ptolemy fails to aspirate not only in this reference but also in his reference to *Horrea* (Margi) in Moesia. *Horrea* is placed in the same longitude as the River Tay and its Roman name must identify it as a Roman fort. The source from which either Ptolemy or Marinus ultimately derived the name was probably an early Roman itinerary of Britain. Given its position near the Tay and its function, it would be naturally connected with sea transport, and the Ravenna Cosmography actually lists it as *Poreo Classis*.[2] It was generally accepted until recently that the location should be at or near the Roman site at Carpow, on the southern shore of the Tay estuary near the confluence with the Earn.[3] This would be an admirable position for a sheltered supply base, maintained by sea. It is excellently situated for communication with the auxiliary forts at Strageath and Dealgin Ross on the River Earn, with Fendoch on the River Almond and the great legionary fortress at Inchtuthil on the Tay itself.

Its inclusion in Ptolemy's *Geography* of Albion and its obvious association with the first-century forts listed above both suggested that it was founded early and was an integral and important part of Agricola's arrangements for the permanent control of Fife and south-east Scotland.[4] His use of the fleet in his operations is well known, and the use of it for supply purposes as well would greatly relieve the commissariat problems raised by such extended lines of communication.[5]

Recent excavations at Carpow have, however, revealed up to date only a large forward base of the early third century A.D. It is possible that there may be earlier structures on the site or near it and that these will be revealed by the excavations that still continue there. If no such structures come to light, then we may have to look for the site of *Horrea Classis* elsewhere, perhaps at Bertha further up the Tay.[6]

Its title in the Ravenna Cosmography, *Poreo Classis*, would suggest that it may by this time have become simply an independent fleet base, separately

---

[1] *Ptolemaei Geographia* (C. Müller, ed., 1883), II. 3. 9.

[2] J. Schnetz, ed., *Itineraria Romana* (1939), II, p. 108.

[3] Richmond, *Roman and Native*, p. 143.

[4] Cf. I. A. Richmond, 'Gnaeus Julius Agricola', *JRS* XXXIV (1944), 34 ff.

[5] Richmond, *Roman and Native*, p. 24 (S. Piggott).

[6] R. E. Birley, 'Excavation of the Roman fortress at Carpow, Perthshire, 1961–2', *PSAS* XCVI (1962–3), 184 ff. Excavations continue under Dr J. Wilkes. Ogilvie and Richmond, *Tac. 'Agricola'*, p. 216, still believe in a site at or near Carpow for *Horrea Classis*. See further A. R. Birley, 'Excavations at Carpow', *Studien zu den Militärgrenzen Roms* (6th International Limes Congress) (1967), p. 1.

maintained in advance of the permanent occupation. The truth of the matter will not be known until the site is fully excavated.

There is one other place with the name *Horrea* listed by Ptolemy. In his treatment of Upper Moesia he listed among 'the other towns away from the River Danube' a place called *Orrea*.[1] More precise details about its name and location are given by the later sources. The Antonine Itinerary called it *Horreum Margi* and located it on the road 61 M.P. from *Viminacium* and 57 M.P. from *Naissus*, while the Peutinger Table called it *Horrea Margi* and located it 56 M.P. from *Viminacium* and 57 M.P. from *Naissus*.[2] There is no doubt that the *Margi* of the title refers to the River Margus (the present-day Morava) on which the *Horrea* were situated, and that the site is to be identified with the modern Cuprija in Serbia, on the road between Belgrade and Nish (Naissus).[3]

It is clear that it was an important place at all times, since it is mentioned in all our geographical sources. Moreover there is one certain reference to the place in an inscription of A.D. 224 which may indicate that the town had been made a *municipium* by that date: *M. Aurelius Iustus domo Horrei Margensis m(unicipio?) Moesiae Superioris*.[4]

That the site started life in a more modest way and that it was essentially a military supply base is, I think, certain. Its position on a main road south to Naissus, one of the great communication centres of the whole Balkans area, and on the River Morava which flows northward into the Danube near Viminacium, makes it ideally situated as a supply base for all the Roman military operations in this area in the first century A.D. Later it would be equally well sited as a rear maintenance and supply unit for the Danube *limes* in this area. It is clear that even in the late Empire, despite its growth, it retained a military purpose. In the eastern section of the *Notitia Dignitatum* among the four factories of Illyricum under the command of the *Magister Officiorum* are the *Scutaria Horreomargensis*.[5]

It would be not unnatural that such a military base in the western part of Moesia should have developed into a *municipium* by the early third century A.D. Both Trajan and Hadrian encouraged increasing urbanisation in the area, and there was a tendency for native *vici* and *canabae* (settlements of civilians) to grow up near military forts and fortresses and for these to amalgamate into one settlement which took on the aspect of a real city. To this amalgamation were ultimately granted the rights of a *municipium* or *colonia*.[6]

[1] Ptolemy III. 9. 4.

[2] Ptolemy, *loc. cit.*, *vid.* note *ad loc.*

[3] F. Kanitz, *Römische Studien in Serbien* (Vienna, 1892), p. 68.

[4] *CIL* III. 7591. A possible reference to this place is given in *CIL* VI. 2388, no. 8.

[5] *Not. Dign.* (ed. O. Seeck) (1876), p. 23.

[6] Rostovtseff, *SEHRE*, p. 245.

At Cuprija traces of extensive Roman occupation have been found and the remains of a fine bridge over the River Morava.[1]

These two sites, therefore, one in Britain and one in Moesia, have more in common than the fact that they are both mentioned by Ptolemy and are probably early settlements. They both owed that early settlement to an essentially military purpose. Moreover they were both cleverly sited for the supply and maintenance of a forward frontier area and both, despite the fact that they were on main roads, were placed with an eye to water transport. The importance of that means of transport cannot be stressed too much either in Britain or on the Danube frontier. *Horrea Classis* in Britain perhaps never became as important as the Moesian *Horrea Margi* simply because, with the abandonment of the Vale of Strathmore, it had no chance to develop as a civil as well as a military site. If the opportunity had not been denied, it might well have flourished in an exactly similar way.

These are the two earliest sites we know to have borne the name *horrea*, apart from the reference in Livy to a town in Epirus with that name.[2] If this reference is not anachronistic, it would show that as early as 167 B.C. a town in Epirus had used the designation *horrea* as a name. It has, however, been impossible to identify the site and it presumably lost whatever importance it may have had since there is no reference to it in Ptolemy or any later source.

In Gallia Narbonensis the Antonine Itinerary lists a place *Ad Horrea* which was on the Via Aurelia between Antipolis and Forum Iulii (the modern Fréjus).[3] This was almost certainly the same site which was known to the compiler of the Ravenna Cosmography among the *civitates* of the *Provincia-Septimana* as *Orea*.[4] Its position on the Via Aurelia was settled in 1861 when it was shown that not only was the tiny modern village of La Napoule on the coast near Fréjus, where the rivers Rion and Siagne enter the sea, in exactly the right position, but also that large remnants of Roman *horrea* were known there.[5]

Its position on the coast in a highly civilised and urbanised part of the Roman Empire, and the fact that it would seem not to have been in existence or of importance in the first century (if that can be properly deduced from its absence in Ptolemy) would both suggest that we are dealing here with something different from the sites discussed above. Its foundation and development were for civil rather than military reasons. Its position was excellent for the assembling of the foodstuffs grown on the plateaux of the Rivers Siagne and

---

[1] Kanitz, *Römische Studien*, pp. 68–71.
[2] Livy XLV. 26. 4. 10.   [3] Schnetz, *Itineraria Romana* I, p. 45.
[4] *Ibid*. II, p. 64.
[5] F. Rabou, 'Mémoire sur l'ancienne voie Aurélienne', *RA* III (1861) (1), 114.

Loup, rich in grain, although whether La Napoule was one of the Narbonese ports which exported straight to Rome or whether it acted simply as a *mansio* on the Via Aurelia, where taxes in kind were collected, is difficult to guess. It depends on whether its position on the Via Aurelia or its position on the coast was more important and on whether it had an adequate harbour. It is no argument against La Napoule exporting straight to Rome that it is not listed in the Maritime Itinerary whereas both Antipolis (Antibes) and Forum Iulii (Fréjus) are listed.[1] The Itinerary is describing the coasting voyage along the southern coast of Gaul, and indicating where it is wise to remain close to the coast and where it is possible to sail further out to sea. The reason why *Horrea* (La Napoule) is not mentioned is that it is possible to sail straight from Antipolis to Lerus and Lerinus, islands off shore in the gulf of La Napoule.

In Africa Proconsularis a place named *Horrea Caelia* is referred to three times by the Antonine Itinerary.[2] In the list of towns on the road from Sufetula to Clupea it is called simply *Horrea* (as in the Peutinger Table). On the route from Carthage to Sufetula via Hadrumetum it is called *Horrea Caelia*, while in the third reference it is more fully described as *Horrea Caelia vicus*. It was later the centre of one of the new African bishoprics and at councils in A.D. 258, 411 and 419 a bishop *ab Horreis Caeliae* was present.[3] The site is clearly to be identified with that of the modern Hergla (where remains of warehouses were found) to the south-east of Carthage, on the Tunisian coast near Sousse.[4] It was therefore on the main Roman coastal route in this area, linked to the north with Carthage and to the south with Hadrumetum and the hinterland.[5] Why was it called *Horrea Caelia*? Haywood has suggested that it was the large estates owned by Cicero's friend Caelius Rufus that gave the place its name.[6] This is ingenious and it may well be that the family of the Caelii in this area were responsible for the name, but it is doubtful whether it came about as early as Cicero's time. Ptolemy, who lists most of the coastal towns of this area, does not mention it. Yet it would seem to be of some importance by the early third century A.D. in view of its mentions in the Antonine Itinerary. The Caelian family and their offshoots were important in Africa Proconsularis under the Empire[7] and we know that they even owned brick factories. A tile was found nearby at Hadrumetum

---

[1] For this argument see Rabou, *op. cit.* p. 118.

[2] Schnetz, *Itineraria Romana* I, pp. 7, 8.

[3] See *CIL* VIII, p. 18.

[4] C. Tissot, *Géographie comparée de la province romaine d'Afrique* (Paris, 1884–8), II, pp. 145 ff.

[5] In general see P. Salama, *Les voies romaines de l'Afrique du Nord* (Algiers, 1951).

[6] Frank, *ESAR* IV, p. 22; cf. Cicero, *Pro Caelio* 30 and 72.

[7] See *CIL* VIII, Indices for list of *Caelii*.

bearing the legend *ex figlinis Caelianis*.[1] Thus the origin of the name seems fairly certain even though the date of its introduction is not clear.

Horrea Caelia and *Ad Horrea* in Gallia Narbonensis are exactly comparable in that they had exactly similar sites. Both were located on a coastline between towns rather more important than themselves, and on a main trunk route. The first record of both is similarly in the Antonine Itinerary. Thus it seems certain that *Horrea Caelia* also had a predominantly civil rather than a military purpose, but whether that purpose was to act as a *mansio* and collecting depot or as an exporting centre to Italy is not so clear. Since the district of Byzacena was among the most fertile in Africa, it seems more likely that it acted as an exporting centre.

The place named *Horrea* known to us in Mauretania Caesariensis seems to have been different again from all the places so far discussed. It was known from the Antonine Itinerary to have been on the route from Setif to Saldae on the coast.[2] When two inscriptions (dated to the end of the second century and beginning of the third) were discovered at Ain Zada to the west of Setif, giving the Roman name of the place as *caput saltus horreorum*, it was at first assumed that this was the location of the *Horrea* of the Itinerary.[3] Kiepert soon pointed out that Ain Zada was not in the right position for a place on the route from Setif to Saldae and that Ain Roua in the mountains north of Setif was in precisely the right position.[4] This identification has been universally accepted. *Horrea*, therefore, was on the main road running north from Setif through the mountains to Tupusuctu and on to the fort of Saldae. Presumably the whole area was known as the *saltus horreorum* and Ain Zada was regarded as its headquarters. It seems clear that the *saltus*, whatever their name, were imperial property, since the *coloni* there in A.D. 192 describe themselves as *coloni domini nostri*.[5] Both Setif and Ain Zada are situated on the high central plateau which was rich in cereals, fruit and oil—a situation which combined with excellent communications made Setif a major commercial centre for the whole of this area. *Horrea* at Ain Roua therefore would seem almost certainly to have been created as a *statio* or *mansio* on the route to Saldae, in order to facilitate the transport of the foodstuffs to the coast. Cagnat suggested that it was associated with the provisioning of troops[6] but this seems less likely than that it was concerned with the *annona* for Rome. We should seek supply dumps for the army further south, perhaps at *Cellas* (Kherbet Zerga) nearer the *limes*. It may be that a detachment of troops was

[1] *CIL* VIII. 22632. 13.
[2] Schnetz, *Itineraria Romana* I, p. 4.
[3] *CIL* VIII. 8425 and 8426, p. 722 (= *ILS* 6890).
[4] *CIL* VIII, p. 970, p. 1916 and p. 1919.   [5] *CIL* VIII. 8425.
[6] Cagnat, *L'armée romaine d'Afrique*, p. 316.

set to guard the *Horrea* at Ain Roua. In a very late inscription found at Setif,[1] a certain Valerius Dalmatius, *exarchus* of the *equitum Stablesianorum*, left a gloomy and slightly hysterical epitaph which begins *hic ego infelix receptus Tartara Ditis horrea dira mihi viae vitamque remisi*. The sense is not entirely clear but he may be referring to duty at *horrea* on a road and if this is so, Ain Roua would be the obvious place.

In short, the places known to have borne the name *Horrea* in the Empire can be divided into three groups. The two earliest foundations, *Horrea Classis* (Carpow) and *Horrea Margi* (Cuprija), owed their foundation in the first century to a strictly military purpose. *Horrea* (La Napoule) in Gallia Narbonensis and *Horrea Caelia* (Hergla) in Africa Proconsularis were probably founded later and are known not from Ptolemy but from the Antonine Itinerary. Although they both have positions on important main roads, it may well be that their positions on the coast were even more important and that they acted as export centres. *Horrea* (Ain Roua) in Mauretania Caesariensis owed its creation and its whole importance probably to its position on a main road. That road was from the fertile area in the hinterland near Setif to the coast, and *Horrea* (Ain Roua) acted as a link between the stores of Setif and those of Tupusuctu and the port of Saldae.

---

[1] *AE* (1916), no. 7. For the *equites Stablesianorum* see Cagnat, *L'armée romaine d'Afrique*, p. 729. The meaning of *exarchus* is not clear, perhaps a commander of six men. It is curious that almost all usages in this sense seem to be connected with Dalmatia in some way, see *Thes. Ling. Lat.*, s.v. *exarchus*.

HORREA IN THE CURIOSUM AND NOTITIA

We have two documents from the late Empire, cataloguing in some detail the buildings in each of the regions of Rome. They are the *Curiosum* (inventory) *Urbis Regionum XIV* and the *Notitia* (catalogue) *Regionum XIV*. Both appear to be editions of a description of Rome written in the reign of Constantine and it is now thought that the *Notitia* dates from A.D. 354 and the *Curiosum* from A.D. 375.[1]

In each region of Rome the major buildings are listed separately first, and then the numbers of different types of buildings, such as *insulae, domi, balnea*, are given. At the end a *breviarium*, or summary, lists the numbers of such buildings for the whole city. In each region the number of *horrea* is given, and the total figure of 290 *horrea* is listed for the whole city at the end.

Is it possible by studying the figures closely to build up some sort of picture of the distribution of *horrea* in Rome, at least in the late Empire?

Such a study has its difficulties not least because numbers in ancient texts often become corrupted. Something has gone awry with the number of *horrea* because although both *Curiosum* and *Notitia* agree that the total number of *horrea* in the city was 290, the addition of the individual figures for each region brings the total not to 290 but 335. At least one of the individual figures is likely to be wrong. The number of *horrea* given for Region x, the Palatine area, is 48, which seems much too high. The number of *horrea* in ten of the other regions varied between 16 and 27, and even in Region xiii, the Aventine area, where the greatest concentration of *horrea* in Rome was situated, the number given is only 35. Because of this discrepancy Jordan[2] has suggested emending 48 to 18 as the number of *horrea* in the Palatine area, thereby bringing it into line with the number of *horrea* in Regions iii, iv, vi and viii. Even so that does not bring the total of the individual regional figures to 290. It is impossible to emend any of the figures with confidence or accuracy because of the lack of other evidence needed.

If we ignore the freak figure of 48 for the Palatine area, we find that, as one might expect, the Aventine area (Region xiii) with 35 *horrea* has the greatest number of storehouses. It was the docks area of Rome, so this is not

---

[1] A. Nordh, *Libellus de Regionibus Urbis Romae* (Gleerup, 1949). Jordan, *Topographie der Stadt Rom* ii, pp. 541 ff. D. Dudley, *Urbs Roma* (London, 1967).

[2] Jordan, *Topographie der Stadt Rom*, p. 68.

surprising. What is at first sight surprising is that, with only 2,487 *insulae*, Region XIII has the fewest *insulae* in the city, only half as many *insulae* as lay across the river in Region XIV. That region, *Trans Tiberim*, had 4,405 *insulae*. But the Aventine area had quite a high number of aristocratic houses, 130 in all. It seems therefore that the low-lying flat area near the river was almost wholly taken up with commercial structures, while on the Aventine slopes itself well-to-do families had their houses and there was therefore relatively little space for the blocks of flats characteristic of lower-class dwellings. Almost certainly the *horrea* in this area were, during the Empire, great State-owned commercial structures rather than safe-deposits, which were more frequently to be found in other regions away from the river.

Region XII, *Piscina Publica*, which lay immediately to the east of the Aventine area, had 27 *horrea* in it, a large number perhaps connected with the commercial activities which spread from Region XIII, away from the river. It is certainly characterised again by a small number of *insulae*, 2,487, and a surprising number of individual houses, 113 in fact.

The other region in which there were 27 *horrea*, Region II, *Caelimontium*, and the two regions, in each of which there were 25 *horrea*, Region IX, *Circus Flaminius*, and Region VII, *Via Lata*, perhaps owe their *horrea* to other causes.

In all three cases we are dealing with areas of dense population, away from the actual monumental centre of the city and yet not too far away. Some of the *horrea*, particularly in Region IX, which comprised largely the Campus Martius, may have been directly connected with trade, but most, I suspect, were safe deposits in which any person could store anything. Region II, the area of the Caelian Hill with 3,600 *insulae* and 127 houses, and a large number of barracks including the *Castra Peregrinorum*, was densely populated and contained a mixture of both high and low life. Region IX, with the great public buildings in the Campus Martius which were largely the work of the Empire, had room for fewer *insulae*, 2,777, but there were more stately houses, 170, in the area. Region VII, to the north of the area of the Imperial *fora* and east of the Campus Martius, contrasted with the latter area in having 3,805 *insulae* densely packed, and only 120 individual houses. In these areas and in the densely populated Region XIV, across the Tiber, and Region V on the Esquiline (with 4,405 *insulae* and 3,850 *insulae*, and with 180 *domi* and 150 *domi* respectively) the need for plentiful storehouses was obvious and they were provided. Region XIV and Region V have 22 *horrea* each.

The areas in which there were fewer than 20 *horrea* tend to be either out-lying areas of the city given over perhaps mainly to use as cemeteries or parkland, *or* the heart of the city itself where there must literally have been too little room. Thus we find that in Region I, *Porta Capena*, which was largely a district of tombs between the *Porta Capena* and the *Porta Latina*, there were only 16 *horrea*. The same number existed in Region XI, the narrow region adjoining Region I which stretched through the *Circus Maximus* down to the river and the Forum Boarium. It was a region tightly packed with public structures and with a relatively low number of both *insulae*, 2,500, and *domi*, 88.

Areas with only 18 *horrea* include Region VIII, *Forum Romanum*, Region IV, *Templum Pacis*, the crowded district of the Subura, and Region III, *Isis and Serapis*, and Region VI, *Alta Semita*, both dominated by great baths and by parklands.

It seems therefore that although the numbers of *horrea* given in the *Curiosum* and *Notitia* must be treated with a certain caution, and although mere numbers do not indicate the varying size and importance of individual buildings, some conclusions can be drawn from the figures in the late regionary catalogues. *Horrea*, whether connected directly with trade or simply used as safe deposits, were distributed throughout the city of Rome. There was no region in which there were fewer than 16 *horrea*. The differing density of distribution makes sense when the character of the individual regions and their needs are looked at in relation to the numbers of *horrea*. Finally, this evidence, no less than all the other evidence, indicates the important rôle played by *horrea* in the life of Rome. After all, the regionary catalogues show that while there were 290 *horrea*, there were only 254 *pistrina*: Rome in the late Empire had more storehouses than bakeries.

BIBLIOGRAPHY

A special bibliography for the British and German military *horrea* follows the list of Articles, on p. 336.

REFERENCE BOOKS

Dictionnaire des Antiquités (Daremberg et Saglio).
Dictionnaire d'Archéologie Chrétienne et de Liturgie (Cabrol et Leclercq).
Dizionario Epigrafico di Antichità Romane (de Ruggiero).
Real-Encyclopädie der classischen Altertumswissenschaft (Pauly–Wissowa).
Thesaurus Linguae Latinae.

BOOKS

Alzon, C. *Problèmes relatifs à la location des entrepôts en Droit romain* (Paris, 1965).

Avi-Yonah, M. and others. *Masada, Survey and Excavations, 1955–6* (Reprint of *Israel Exploration Journal*, vol. 7, no. 1) (Jerusalem, 1957).

Baillie-Reynolds, P. K. *The Vigiles of Imperial Rome* (London, 1926).

Bartoccini, R. *Il porto romano di Leptis Magna* (Rome, 1960).

Bell, H. I., Martin, V., Turner, E. G. and Berchem, D. Van. *The Abbinaeus Archive* (Oxford, 1962).

Benndorf, O. and Niemann, G. *Reisen im Südwestlichen Kleinasien* I (Vienna, 1884).

Berchem, D. Van. *L'annone militaire dans l'empire romain au 3e siècle* (Paris, 1937).

Birley, E. *Research on Hadrian's Wall* (Kendal, 1961).

Blake, M. *Ancient Roman Construction in Italy to Augustus* (Washington, 1947).

Roman Construction in Italy from Tiberius through the Flavians (Washington, 1959).

Bloch, H. *I bolli laterizi e la storia edilizia romana* (Rome, 1938).

The Roman Brick Stamps not Published in CIL XV. 1 (Harvard Studies in Classical Philology (1947), pp. 1–128), referred to simply as 'Bloch, Supplement'.

Boak, A. and Peterson, E. *Karanis, topographical and architectural report of excavations during the seasons 1924–1928* (Michigan, 1931).

Boëthius, A. *The Golden House of Nero* (Michigan, 1960).

Börner, E. *Der staatliche Korntransport im griechisch-römischen Aegypten* (Hamburg, 1939).

Brünnow, R. and Domaszewski, A. von. *Die Provincia Arabia* (Strassburg, 1904–9).

Bruns, C. *Fontes Iuris Romani Antiqui* (7th ed., O. Gradenwitz) (Tübingen, 1909).

Buckland, W. *A Text-Book of Roman Law*, 3rd ed. (Cambridge, 1963).

Bushe-Fox, J. P. *Richborough, Report IV* (Oxford, 1949).

Byvanck, A. W. *Nederland in den romeinschen Tijd* II (Leiden, 1945).

Caffarelli, E. and Caputo, G. *The Buried City: excavations at Leptis Magna* (London, 1966).

Cagnat, R. *L'armée romaine d'Afrique* (Paris, 1913).

Calderini, A. Θησαυροί, *Studi della Scuola Papirologica* IV, Part 3 (Milan, 1924). *Aquileia Romana* (Milan, 1930).

Calza, G., Becatti, G., Gismondi, I. and others. *Scavi di Ostia* I, *Topografia generale* (Rome, 1953); II, *I mitrei* (Rome, 1954).

Calza, R. and Nash, E. *Ostia* (Florence, 1960).

Carettoni, G., Colini, A., Cozza, L. and Gatti, G. *La pianta marmorea di Roma antica*, 2 vols. (Rome, 1955. Reprinted 1961).

Cichorius, C. *Die Reliefs der Traianssäule* (Berlin, 1896–1900).

Cunliffe, B. *Richborough, Report V* (Oxford, 1968).

David, M. and Groningen, B. A. Van. *Papyrological Primer*, 4th ed. (Leyden, 1965).

Degrassi, A. *I fasti consolari dell'impero romano* (Rome, 1952).

Dijkstra, H. and Ketelaar, F. C. J. *Brittenburg* (Bussum, 1965).

Domaszewski, A. von. *Die Rangordnung des römischen Heeres*, 2nd ed. (by B. Dobson) (Cologne, 1967).

Dubois, C. *Pouzzoles antique* (Paris, 1907).

Dudley, D. *Urbs Roma* (London, 1967).

Durm, J. *Die Baukunst der Römer* (Stuttgart, 1905). *Die Baukunst der Griechen* (Leipzig, 1910).

Eisenlohr, A. *Ein mathematisches Handbuch der alten Aegypter* (Leipzig, 1877).

Erman, A. and Ranke, H. *Aegypten und ägyptisches Leben im Altertum* (Tübingen, 1923).

Frank, Tenney (ed.). *An Economic Survey of Ancient Rome*, 5 vols. (Baltimore, 1933–40).

Frankfort, H. *The Art and Architecture of the Ancient Orient* (Harmondsworth, 1954).

Franks, O. *Central Planning and Control in War and Peace* (London School of Economics, 1947).

Frazer, J. G. *Pausanias' Description of Greece*, 6 vols. (London, 1898).

Frutaz, A. P. *Le piante di Roma*, 3 vols. (Rome, 1962).

Girard, P. *Textes de Droit romain*, 6th ed. (Paris, 1937).

Gradenwitz, O. *Heidelberger Index zum Theodosianus* (Berlin, 1925).

Grenier, A. *Manuel d'archéologie gallo-romaine*, 4 vols. (Paris, 1931–60).

Gualandi, G. *Legislazione imperiale e giurisprudenza II* (Milan, 1963).

Haynes, D. E. and Hirst, P. E. *Porta Argentariorum* (Suppl. Paper, British School at Rome) (London, 1939).

Helbig, W. *Wandgemälde Campaniens* (Leipzig, 1868).

Henzen, W. *Acta Fratrum Arvalium* (Berlin, 1874).

Hölscher, U. *The Excavation of Medinet Habu* (Chicago, 1934).

Hülsen, Ch. *Forum und Palatin* (Munich, 1926).

Jones, A. H. M. *The Later Roman Empire, A.D. 284–602*, 3 vols. (Oxford, 1964).

Jordan, H. *Forma Urbis Romae Regionum XIIII* (Berlin, 1874).
Topographie der Stadt Rom im Alterthum, 2 vols. (Berlin, 1871–1907).

Kanitz, F. *Römische Studien in Serbien* (Vienna, 1892).

La Blanchère, M. de. *Terracine, essai d'histoire locale* (Paris, 1884).

Lanciani, R. *Ancient Rome in the Light of Recent Discoveries* (London, 1888).
Forma Urbis Romae (Milan, 1893–1901).
Pagan and Christian Rome (London, 1895).
The Ruins and Excavations of Ancient Rome (London, 1897).
The Destruction of Ancient Rome (New York, 1899).

Le Gall, J. *Le Tibre, fleuve de Rome, dans l'antiquité* (Paris, 1953).

Lesquier, J. *L'armée romaine d'Égypte d'Auguste à Dioclétien* (Cairo, 1918).

Lewis, N. *Inventory of Compulsory Services in Ptolemaic and Roman Egypt* (Newhaven and Toronto, 1968).

Loane, H. J. *Industry and Commerce of the City of Rome, 50 B.C.–200 A.D.* (Baltimore, 1938).

Lugli, G. *I monumenti antichi di Roma e suburbio*, 3 vols. (Rome, 1931–8).
Roma antica, il centro monumentale (Rome, 1946).
La tecnica edilizia romana, 2 vols. (Rome, 1957).

Lugli, G. and Filibeck, G. *Il Porto di Roma imperiale e l'agro Portuense* (Rome, 1935; not available in England).

McCrum, M. and Woodhead, A. G. *Select Documents of the Principates of the Flavian Emperors* (Cambridge, 1961).

MacDonald, W. L. *The Architecture of the Roman Empire* (Newhaven and London, 1965).

Mau, A. (trans. F. Kelsey) *Pompeii, its Life and Art* (New York, 1899).

Meiggs, R. *Roman Ostia* (Oxford, 1960).

Millar, F. *A Study of Cassius Dio* (Oxford, 1964).

Mitteis, L. and Wilcken, U. *Grundzüge und Chrestomathie der Papyruskunde*, 2 vols. in 4 pts. (Leipzig, 1912).

Mommsen, T. *Chronica Minora* I (1892).

Römische Geschichte v, *Die Provinzen* (Berlin, 1904).

Monumenti inediti pubbl. dall'Instituto di corrispondenza archeologica, 12 vols. (Rome and Paris, 1829–51).

Nash, E. *Pictorial Dictionary of Ancient Rome*, 2 vols. (London, 1961, 1962).

Nash-Williams, V. *The Roman Frontier in Wales* (Cardiff, 1954).

Nicholas, J. K. B. *An Introduction to Roman Law* (Oxford, 1962).

Noack, F. *Eleusis, die baugeschichtliche Entwicklung des Heiligtums* (Berlin, 1927).

Nordh, A. *Libellus de Regionibus Urbis Romae* (Gleerup, 1949).

Ogilvie, R. M. and Richmond, I. A. *Tacitus, 'Agricola'* (Oxford, 1967).

Parrot, A. *Mission archéologique de Mari* II, *Le Palais, Architecture* (Paris, 1958).

Paschetto, L. *Ostia, colonia romana; storia e monumenti* (Rome, 1912).

Pendlebury, J. *A Handbook to the Palace of Minos, Knossos* (new ed., London, 1954).

The City of Akhenaten (London, 1951).

Pernier, L. *Il palazzo minoico di Festos* (Rome, 1935–51).

Petersen, E. *Die Marcus-Säule auf Piazza Colonna in Rom* (Munich, 1896).

Petersen, E. and Luschan, F. von. *Reisen im Südwestlichen Kleinasien* II (Vienna, 1889).

Petrikovits, H. von. *Das römische Rheinland, Archäologische Forschungen seit 1945* (Cologne, 1960).

Pflaum, H.-G. *Les carrières procuratoriennes équestres sous le haut-empire romain* (Paris, 1960).

Platner, S. B. and Ashby, T. *A Topographical Dictionary of Ancient Rome* (London, 1929).

Preisigke, F. *Girowesen im griechischen Aegypten* (Strassburg, 1910).

Quibell, J. E. *The Ramesseum* (London, 1898).

Reynolds, J. and Ward-Perkins, J. *Inscriptions of Roman Tripolitania* (Rome: London, 1952).

Riccobono, S. *Fontes Iuris Romani Anteiustiniani* (Florence, 1941).

Richmond, I. A. *The City Wall of Imperial Rome* (Oxford, 1930).

The Roman Fort at South Shields: A guide (South Shields, 1953).

Roman Britain (Pelican History of England I) (Harmondsworth, 1955).

(ed.) *Roman and Native in North Britain* (Edinburgh, 1958).

Hod Hill II (London, 1968).

Robinson, D. M. *Excavations at Olynthus*, Pt. XII, *Domestic and Public Architecture* (Baltimore, 1946).

Rostovtseff, M. *Dura Europos and its Art* (Oxford, 1938).

The Social and Economic History of the Hellenistic World, 3 vols. (Oxford, 1941).

The Social and Economic History of the Roman Empire, 2nd ed. (by P. M. Fraser), 2 vols. (Oxford, 1957).

Rostovtseff, M., Brown, F. E. and Welles, C. B. *Excavations at Dura Europos, 7th and 8th Seasons* (New Haven, 1939).

Excavations at Dura Europos, 9th Season (New Haven, 1944).

Rougé, J. *Recherches sur l'organisation du commerce maritime en Méditerranée sous l'empire romain* (Paris, 1966).

Ruggini, L. *Economia e società nell' 'Italia Annonaria' dal IV al VI secolo d.C.* (Milan, 1961).

Salama, P. *Les voies romaines de l'Afrique du Nord* (Algiers, 1951).

Schaal, H. *Ostia, Der Welthafen Roms* (Bremen, 1957).

Schnetz, J. (ed.). *Itineraria Romana* (Leipzig, 1939).

Schulten, A. *Numantia, Die Ergebnisse der Ausgrabungen 1905–1912* III, *Die Lager des Scipio* (Munich, 1927); IV, *Die Lager bei Renieblas* (Munich, 1929).

Schulz, F. *Classical Roman Law* (Oxford, 1951).

Smith, G. E. Kidder. *Italy Builds* (London, 1955).

Smith, W. S. *The Art and Architecture of Ancient Egypt* (Harmondsworth, 1958).

Syme, R. *The Roman Revolution* (Oxford, 1939).

Szalay, A. von and Böhringer, E. *Altertümer von Pergamon* X, *Die hellenistischen Arsenale* (Berlin, 1937).

Tissot, C. *Géographie comparée de la province romaine d'Afrique*, 2 vols. (Paris, 1884–8).

Turner, E. G. *Catalogue of Greek and Latin Papyri and Ostraka in the possession of the University of Aberdeen* (Aberdeen, 1939).

Valentini, R. and Zucchetti, G. *Codice topografico della città di Roma*, 4 vols. (Rome, 1940–53).

Vats, M. S. *Excavations at Harappā* (Delhi, 1940).

Waltzing, J. P. *Étude historique sur les corporations professionnelles chez les romains*, 4 vols. (Louvain, 1895–1900).

Ward, J. *Romano-British Buildings and Earthworks* (London, 1911).

Webster, G. *The Roman Imperial Army* (London, 1969).

Westermann, W. L. and Keyes, C. W. (ed.). *Tax Lists and Transportation Receipts from Theadelphia* (New York, 1932).

Wetzel, F. and Weissbach, F. H. *Das Hauptheiligtum des Marduk in Babylon, Esagila und Etemenanki* (Leipzig, 1938).

Wheeler, R. E. M. *The Indus Civilization*[3] (Cambridge, 1968).

Civilization of the Indus Valley and Beyond (London, 1966).

Wilcken, U. *Griechische Ostraka aus Aegypten und Nubien*, 2 vols. (Leipzig, 1899).

Wilcken, U. and Mitteis, L. *Grundzüge und Chrestomathie der Papyruskunde*, 2 vols. (Leipzig, 1912).
Wissowa, G. *Religion und Kultus der Römer* (Munich, 1902).
Wycherley, R. E. *How the Greeks Built Cities* (London, 1949).
Yadin, Y. *Masada: Herod's Fortress and the Zealots' Last Stand* (London, 1966).

ARTICLES

Albertini, E. 'Table de mesures de Djemila', *CRAI* (1920), 315.
'Une inscription de Djemila', *CRAI* (1924), 253.
Allais, Y. 'Les greniers publics de Djemila', *RAfr* (1933), 259.
Aubin, H. 'Der Rheinhandel in römischer Zeit', *BonnJb* cxxx (1925), 1.
Baillet, J. 'Papyrus mathématique d'Akhîm', *Mémoires de la Mission Archéologique Française au Caire* ix (1892), 1.
Baillie-Reynolds, P. K. 'The troops quartered in the Castra Peregrinorum', *JRS* xiii (1923), 168.
Barosso, M. 'Le costruzioni sottostanti la Basilica Massenziana e la Velia', *Atti del V Congresso Naz. di Studi Romani* ii (1940), 58.
Bartoli, A. 'Gli *horrea Agrippiana* e la *diaconia* di San Teodoro', *MonAnt* xxvii (1921), col. 373.
Becatti, G. '*Horrea Epagathiana et Epaphroditiana* e *horrea* adiacenti a nord', *NSc* xviii (1940), 32.
Benoit, F. 'Le sanctuaire d'Auguste et les cryptoportiques d'Arles', *RA* xxxix (1952), 31.
'Observations sur les cryptoportiques d'Arles', *RStLig* xxiii (1957), 107.
Berucci, M. 'L'architettura degli *Horrea Agrippiana*', *Palladio*, n.s. iv (1954), 145.
Birley, A. R. 'Excavations at Carpow', *Studien zu den Militärgrenzen Roms* (6th International Limes Congress) (1967), 1.
Birley, E. 'Excavations at Corstopitum 1906–1958', *AA*⁴ xxxvii (1959), 12.
Birley, E., Richmond, I. A. and Stanfield, J. 'Excavations at Chesterholm-Vindolanda, Third Report', *AA*⁴ xiii (1936), 225.
Birley, R. E. 'Excavation of the Roman fortress at Carpow, Perthshire, 1961–2', *PSAS* xcvi (1962–3), 184.
Blair, P. H. 'Housesteads Milecastle', *AA*⁴ xi (1934), 108.
Bloch, H. 'I bolli laterizi: il "quartier des docks" in Ostia', *BCom* lxv (1937), 87.
'Ostia: iscrizioni rinvenute tra il 1930 e il 1939', *NSc* (1953), 297.
Boëthius, A. 'Roman architecture from its classicistic to its late Imperial phase', *Göteborgs Högskolas Årsskrift* xlvii (1941), 8.

Brunt, P. A. 'Pay and superannuation in the Roman army', *PBSR* XVIII (1950), 60.

Calza, G. 'Ostia—Scavo presso l'edificio delle Pistrine', *NSc* (1914), 246.

'Gli *horrea* tra il Tevere e il decumano, nel centro di Ostia antica', *NSc* (1921), 360.

'Ostia — Esplorazione dell'isolato a ovest del Campidoglio di Ostia', *NSc* (1923), 178.

'Le origini Latine dell'abitazione moderna II', *Architettura e Arti Decorative* I, no. 2 (1923), 54.

'Ricognizioni topografiche nel Porto di Traiano', *NSc* (1925), 58.

Cannata, C. A. 'Su alcuni problemi relativi alla *locatio horrei* nel diritto Romano classico', *SDHI* XXX (1964), 235.

Caranache, V. 'L'édifice à mosaïque découverte devant le port de Tomis', *Studii Clasice* III (1961), 227.

Carcopino, J. 'Ostiensia', *Mélanges* XXX (1910), 421.

Casson, L. 'The Isis and her voyage', *TAPA* LXXXI (1950), 51.

'The size of ancient merchant ships', *Studi in onore di Calderini e Paribeni* I (1956), 231.

'Harbour and river boats of ancient Rome', *JRS* LV (1965), 31.

Charles-Picard, G. 'Pouzzoles et le paysage portuaire', *Latomus* XVIII (1959), 23.

'Civitas Mactaritana', *Karthago* VIII (1957), 136.

Collingwood, R. and Haverfield, F. 'The provisioning of Roman forts', CW^2 XX (1920), 127.

Cook, J. M. 'Archaeology in Greece, 1952', *JHS* LXXIII (1953), 120.

Cressedi, G. 'Sterri al Lungotevere Testaccio', *NSc* X (1956), 19.

Cunliffe, B. 'Excavations at Fishbourne, 1962', *Antiquaries Journal* XLIII (1963), 1.

'Fishbourne 1961-4', *Antiquity* XXXIX (1965), 178.

Deman, E. Van. 'The Neronian *Sacra Via*', *AJA* XXVII (1923), 400.

'The *Sacra Via* of Nero', *MAAR* V (1925), 115.

Domaszewski, A. von. 'Die annona des Heeres im Kriege', *EPITYMBION, Festschrift H. Swoboda* (1927), 17.

Eiden, H. and Mylius, H. 'Untersuchungen an den spätrömischen Horrea von St. Irminen in Trier', *TrierZ* XVIII (1949), 73.

Fink, R. 'Hunt's *Pridianum*: British Museum Papyrus 2851', *JRS* XLVIII (1958), 102.

Florescu, R. 'Les phases de construction du castrum Drobeta (Turnu Severin)', *Studien zu den Militärgrenzen Roms* (Cologne, 1967), 144.

Gatti, G. 'Frammento d'iscrizione contenente la *lex horreorum*', *BCom* XIII (1885), 110.

'Alcune osservazioni sugli orrei Galbani', *RM* I (1886), 72.

'Frammento di una nuova *lex horreorum*', *BCom* XXXIX (1911), 120.

'"Saepta Iulia" e "Porticus Aemilia" nella "Forma Severiana"', *BCom* LXII (1934), 123.

Groller, M. von. 'Die Grabungen in Carnuntum: die Lagergebäude', *Der Römische Limes in Österreich*, Heft X, 35.

Guéraud, O. 'Sachet ayant contenu un échantillon d'orge', *AnnEg* XXXIII (1933), 62.

'Un vase ayant contenu un échantillon de blé (DEIGMA)', *JJurP* IV (1950), 107.

Haverfield, F. 'Corbridge excavations, 1910', *PSAL*, 2nd series, XXIII (1911), 478.

Henzen, W. 'Di una iscrizione rinvenuta presso il Monte Testaccio', *BCom* XIII (1885), 51.

'Iscrizione relativa alle *Horrea Galbana*', *RM* I (1886), 42.

Holt, J. and Nix, J. S. 'Safe in store', *Farmer and Stockbreeder* (9 May 1961), 103.

Holwerda, J. H. 'Afbeeldingen van de Brittenburg', *Oudheidkundige Mededeelingen* VIII (1927), 1.

Hülsen, Ch. 'Di una pittura antica ritrovata sull'Esquilino nel 1668', *RM* XI (1896), 213 and 225.

'Ausgrabungen auf dem Forum Romanum', *RM* XVII (1902), 95.

Jardé, A. 'Le Magasin des Colonnes de Délos', *BCH* XXIX (1905), 21.

Koenen, C. 'Beschreibung von Novaesium', *BonnJb* CXI/CXII (1904), 186.

Kraus, T. and Röder, J. 'Mons Claudianus', *MDInstKairo* XVIII (1962), 89.

Lanciani, R. 'Ricerche topografiche sulla città di Porto', *Ann.Inst.* XL (1868), 144 and 178.

'Di un frammento della pianta marmorea Severiana rappresentante il clivo della Vittoria ed il vico Tusco', *BCom* XIII (1885), 157.

'I magazzini delle droghe orientali (*Horrea Piperataria*)', *BCom* XXVIII (1900), 8.

Lugli, G. 'Aedes Caesarum in Palatio et templum Divi Augusti', *BCom* LXIX (1941), 56.

Mancini, G. 'Le recenti scoperte di antichità al Testaccio', *BCom* XXXIX (1911), 258.

Minoprio, A. 'A restoration of the Basilica of Constantine, Rome', *PBSR* XII (1932), 23.

Mommsen, T. 'Aegyptische Legionare', *Hermes* XXXV (1900), 445.

Moosbrugger-Leu, R. 'Grabungen 1959 Areal Oelhafen', *Jahresbericht Pro Vindon.* (1959/60), 16.

Mouterde, R. 'Une dédicace d'Apamée de Syrie à l'approche de Caracalla et l'*Itinerarium Antonini*', *CRAI* (1952), 355.

Müller, A. 'Die Primipilares und der pastus primipili', *Philologus*, n.s. XXI (1908), 134.

Nix, J. S. 'Drying and storing grain, the economic aspects', Report no. 44. Issued by the School of Agriculture, Cambridge (1956).

Oelmann, F. 'Zum Problem der Brittenburg bei Katwijk', *Studies Presented to David M. Robinson* (1951, ed. G. Mylonas), I, p. 451.

Packer, J. E. 'Housing and Population in Imperial Ostia and Rome', *JRS* LVII (1967), 87.

Pearl, O. M. 'Varia Papyrologica', *TAPA* LXXI (1940), 372.

Piggott, S. 'Timber circles: a re-examination', *AJ* XCVI (1939), 220.

Poinssot, M. 'Inscriptions de Suo et de Maxula', *CRAI* (1936), 285.

Premerstein, A. von. 'Die Buchführung einer ägyptischen Legionsabteilung', *Klio* III (1902–3), 1.

Promis, C. 'Le antichità di Aosta', *Memorie della R. Accademia di Scienze di Torino*, Sez. II, vol. XXI (1862).

Rabou, F. 'Mémoire sur l'ancienne voie Aurélienne', *RA* III (1861) (1), 112.

Richards, J. M. (ed.). 'The Functional Tradition', *Architectural Review* (July 1957), 8.

Richmond, I. A. 'The Agricolan fort at Fendoch', *PSAS* LXXIII (1938–9), 129.
'Gnaeus Julius Agricola', *JRS* XXXIV (1944), 34.
'The Agricolan legionary fortress at Inchtuthil', *Limes-Studien* (3rd International Limes Congress) (Basel, 1959).

Richmond, I. A. and Child, F. A. 'Gateways of forts on Hadrian's Wall', *AA*[4] XX (1942), 140.

Richmond, I. A. and Gillam, J. P. 'Excavations on the Roman site at Corbridge 1946–1949', *AA*[4] XXVIII (1950), 152.

Robert, L. 'Inscriptions de Bithynie', *REA* XLII (1940) (Mélanges Radet), 307.

Romanelli, P. 'Horrea', *Diz. Epig.* VII (1922).

Roos, A. 'Brittenburg', *Mnemosyne* LI (1923), 327.

Rostovtseff, M. 'Commodus–Hercules in Britain', *JRS* XIII (1923), 101.

Schneider-Graziosi, G. 'La identificazione topografica delle *Horrea Germaniciana et Agrippiana* dell'ottava regione Augustea', *BCom* XXXIX (1911), 158.
'*Genius horreorum Agrippianorum*', *BCom* XLII (1914), 25.

Schwartz, J. 'Le Nil et le ravitaillement de Rome', *BInstFrAOr* XLVII (1948), 179.

Scialoja, V. 'Di una *lex horreorum* recentemente scoperta', *Studi giuridici* I (1933), 288.

Simpson, F. G., Richmond, I. A. and others. 'Milecastles on Hadrian's Wall explored in 1935-6', *AA*[4] XIII (1936), 270.

'The Roman fort on Hadrian's Wall at Benwell', *AA*[4] XIX (1941), 18.

Sinnigen, W. G. 'The origins of the *Frumentarii*', *MAAR* XXVII (1962), 213.

Sjöqvist, E. 'Gli avanzi antichi sotto la chiesa di S. Maria in Via Lata', *Opuscula Archaeologica* IV (1946), 48.

Staccioli, R. 'I criptoportici forensi di Aosta e di Arles', *RAL* IX (1954), 645.

'Gli edifici sotterranei di Bavai', *ACl* VI (1954), 284.

'Gli edifici sotterranei dell'agora di Smirne e ancora sui criptoportici forensi', *Latomus* XVI (1957), 275.

'Ancora sui criptoportici', *AntCl* XXVII (1958), 390.

'Le "taberne" a Roma attraverso la *"forma urbis"*', *RAL* XIV (1959), 56.

'Tipi di *horrea* nella documentazione della *Forma Urbis*', *Hommages à Albert Grenier* (Collection *Latomus* vol. LVIII), III (1962), 1430.

Syme, R. 'The Lower Danube under Trajan', *JRS* XLIX (1959), 26.

Taylor, L. R. 'Trebula Suffenas and the Plautii Silvani', *MAAR* XXIV (1956), 29.

Testaguzza, O. 'The Port of Rome', *Archaeology* XVII (1964), 173.

Thomas, J. A. C. '*Custodia* and *Horrea*', *RIntDroitsAnt*[3] VI (1959), 371.

'Return to *Horrea*', *RIntDroitsAnt*[3] XIII (1966), 353.

Vaglieri, De. 'Monumenti repubblicani di Ostia', *BCom* XXXIX (1911), 228.

Wahle, O. 'Die Proviantmagazine der Saalburg', *Die Saalburg, Mitteilungen der Vereinigung der Saalburg-Freunde* II, Nr. 2 (1920), 10 April, p. 29.

Wallinga, H. T. 'Nautika I: The units of capacity for ancient ships', *Mnemosyne* XVII (1964), 1.

Whittemore, T. 'The excavations at El-'Amarnah, Season 1924/5', *JEgA* XII (1926), 9 and 10.

Wickert, L. 'Nota epigraphica', *RM* XL (1925), 213.

'Nachtrag zu *RM* XL, p. 213', *RM* XLI (1926), 229.

Wilcken, U. 'Zum Germanicus-Papyrus', *Hermes* LXIII (1928), 48.

Wilkes, J. 'Early fourth-century rebuilding in Hadrian's Wall forts', *Britain and Rome* (ed. M. Jarrett) (1966), p. 126.

Wilson, F. H. 'Studies in the social and economic history of Ostia', Part I, *PBSR* XIII (1935), 51; Part II, *PBSR* XIV (1936), 157.

Wotschitzky, A. 'Veldidena: zweiter vorläufiger Bericht über die Ausgrabungen 1954-1957', *ÖJh* XLIV (1959), Beiblatt, 6.

Wubbe, F. 'Zur Haftung des *Horrearius*', *ZSavignyStift* LXXVI (1959), 508.

Zilliacus, H. 'Neue Ptolemäertexte zum Korntransport und Saatdarlehen', *Aegyptus* XIX (1939), 62.

BIBLIOGRAPHY FOR BRITISH AND GERMAN
MILITARY *HORREA*

Britain

Ambleside   R. G. Collingwood, *CW*² xv (1915), 24.

Baginton   B. Hobley, *JRS* LVIII (1968), 188.

Balmuildy   S. N. Miller, *Roman Fort at Balmuildy* (Glasgow, 1922), p. 26.

Bar Hill   G. Macdonald, *Roman Forts on the Bar Hill* (Glasgow, 1906), p. 40.

Beckfoot   J. K. St Joseph, *JRS* XLI (1951), 56 and pl. IV. 2.

Benwell   F. G. Simpson and I. A. Richmond, *AA*⁴ XIX (1941), 17.

Birdoswald   I. A. Richmond, *CW*² XXXI (1931), 122.

Birrens   D. Christison, *PSAS* XXX (1895–6), 112; E. Birley, *PSAS* LXXII (1937–8), 280.

Brecon Gaer   R. E. M. Wheeler, *Roman Fort near Brecon* (London, 1926), p. 38.

Cadder   J. Clarke, *Roman Fort at Cadder* (Glasgow, 1933), p. 41.

Caerhun   P. K. Baillie-Reynolds, *Kanovium* (Cardiff, 1938), p. 81.

Caernarvon   R. E. M. Wheeler, *Arch.Cambr.* LXXVII (1922), 302.

Camelon   M. Buchanan, *PSAS* XXXV (1900), 365.

Cappuck   G. H. Stevenson and S. N. Miller, *PSAS* XLVI (1912), 458.

Castell Collen   H. Evelyn-White, *Arch.Cambr.* XIV (1914), 19.

Castlecary   M. Buchanan, *PSAS* XXXVII (1903), 308.

Castleshaw   J. Petch, *Trans. Lancs & Ches. A.S.* LXXI (1961), 163.

Chester   D. F. Petch and F. H. Thompson, *Journal of the Chester Arch. Soc.* XLVI (1959), 33.

Chesters   J. C. Bruce, *Handbook to the Roman Wall*, 9th ed. (by R. G. Collingwood) (1933), p. 81.

Corbridge   I. A. Richmond and J. P. Gillam, *AA*⁴ XXVIII (1950), 152.

Drumburgh   F. Haverfield, *CW*¹ XVI (1900), 86.

Fendoch   I. A. Richmond and J. McIntyre, *PSAS* LXXIII (1938–9), 129.

Gellygaer   J. Ward, *Roman Fort at Gellygaer* (London, 1903), p. 50 and pp. 60–4; cf. G. Simpson, *Arch.Cambr.* CXII (1963), 53.

Haltonchesters   J. P. Gillam, *Durham University Gazette* (Dec. 1961), 6; cf. *JRS* LI (1961), 164.

Haltwhistle Burn   J. Gibson and F. G. Simpson, *AA*³ v (1909), 250.

Hardknott   R. G. Collingwood, *CW*² XXVIII (1928), 329, but see D. Charlesworth, *CW*² LXIII (1963), 148.

High Rochester   J. C. Bruce, *AA*² I (1857), 76.

Housesteads   R. Bosanquet, *AA*² XXV (1904), 235.

Inchtuthil   *JRS* LI (1961), 158, fig. 9.

Longthorpe   S. Frere, *JRS* LVIII (1968), 189.

Lyne   D. Christison, *PSAS* xxxv (1901), 180.

Mumrills   G. Macdonald and A. Curle, *PSAS* LXIII (1929), 431.

Newstead   J. Curle, *A Roman Frontier Post and its People* (Glasgow, 1911), p. 58; cf. I. A. Richmond, *PSAS* LXXXIV (1949–50), 19.

Old Church, Brampton   F. G. Simpson and I. A. Richmond, *CW²* xxxvi (1936), 174.

Old Kilpatrick   S. N. Miller, *Roman Fort at Old Kilpatrick* (Glasgow, 1928), p. 21.

Pen Llystyn   Grace Simpson, *Britons and the Roman Army: a study of Wales and the Southern Pennines in 1st–3rd Centuries* (London, 1964).

Pennydarren   F. James, *Arch.Cambr.* VI (1906), 193–208.

Ribchester   J. Hopkinson, *Roman Fort at Ribchester* (3rd ed. by D. Atkinson) (Manchester, 1928), p. 14.

Rough Castle   *PSAS* xxxix (1905), 474.

Rudchester   P. Brewis, *AA⁴* I (1925), 99.

South Shields   I. A. Richmond, *AA⁴* XI (1934), 92; I. A. Richmond, *The Roman Fort at South Shields: a Guide* (South Shields, 1953).

Stanwix   F. G. Simpson and I. A. Richmond, *JRS* xxxi (1941), 130.

Templeborough,   T. May, *The Roman Forts of Templeborough* (Rotherham, 1922), p. 39.

Wall   J. Gould, *Trans. Lich. & Staffs Arch. & Hist. Soc.* v (1963–4), 7.

Germany

Arnsburg   *ORL*, Lief. XVII, Nr. 16, p. 7.

Benningen   *ORL*, Lief. XVII, Nr. 58, p. 6.

Bonn   H. von Petrikovits, *Das römische Rheinland*, Archäologische Forschungen seit 1945 (Cologne, 1960), p. 46.

Gnotzheim   *ORL*, Lief. XXIX, Nr. 70, p. 10.

Haltern   *Mitteilungen der Altertums-Kommission für Westfalen* IV (1905), 73; VII (1922), 5; *Römisch-Germanisches Korrespondenzblatt* VI (1913), 26.

Hüfingen   *ORL*, Lief. LV, Nr. 62 a, p. 20.

Kapersburg   *ORL*, Lief. XXVII, Nr. 12, p. 13.

Niederbieber   *ORL*, Lief. LV, Nr. 1 a, p. 25.

Nijmegen   H. Brunsting, *Numaga* XII (1965), 69.

Novaesium (Neuss)   C. Koenen, *BonnJb* CXI–CXII (1904–5), 186 ff.

Okarben   *ORL*, Lief. XVI, Nr. 25 a, p. 8.

Pfünz   *ORL*, Lief. XIV, Nr. 73, p. 7.

Rödgen   H. Schönberger, *Saalburg Jahrbuch* XXI (1963–4), 95 ff.

Ruffenhofen   *ORL*, Lief. IV, Nr. 68, p. 4.

Saalburg   *ORL*, Lief. LVI, Nr. 11, p. 34.

Theilenhofen   *ORL*, Lief. XXIV, Nr. 71 a, p. 9.

Urspring   *ORL*, Lief. xxiv, Nr. 66 *a*, p. 20.

Vindonissa   Chr. Simonett, *Zeitschr. für Schweiz. Archäol. und Kunstgesch.* 1 (1939), 106 ff.

Weissenburg   *ORL*, Lief. xxvi, Nr. 72, p. 14.

Wiesbaden   *ORL*, Lief. xxxi, Nr. 31, p. 31.

Plans of some of the legionary fortresses and auxiliary forts discussed in Chapter VII are conveniently collected in G. Webster, *The Roman Imperial Army* (London, 1969).

For Germany, see now the important article by H. Schönberger, 'The Roman Frontier in Germany: An Archaeological Survey', *JRS* lix (1969), 144–97.

GENERAL INDEX

Numbers in italics indicate references of particular importance.

INDEX OF CLASSICAL AUTHORS

INDEX OF INSCRIPTIONS

INDEX OF PAPYRI

INDEX OF GREEK WORDS

348

INDEX OF GREEK WORDS